Logic a ... :

...ings

Logic and Philosophy for Linguists:
A Book of Readings

Edited by

J. M. E. MORAVCSIK

Stanford University

MOUTON PUBLISHERS
THE HAGUE – PARIS

HUMANITIES PRESS
ATLANTIC HIGHLANDS N. J.

American edition published by Humanities Press Inc. - Atlantic Highlands, N. J.

Library of Congress Cataloging in Publication Data

Main entry under title:

Logic and philosophy for linguists.

Bibliography: p.
1. Languages – Philosophy – Addresses, essays, lectures. 2. Logic – Addresses, essays, lectures. 3. Semantics (Philosophy) – Addresses, essays, lectures. 4. Linguistics – Methodology – Addresses, essays, lectures. I. Moravcsik, J. M. E.
P39.L59 1975 401 75-23015
ISBN 0 391 00399 2

Printed in The Netherlands by Mouton & Co., The Hague

Contents

_____

Introduction

———————————————————————

WHY SHOULD LINGUISTS STUDY LOGIC AND PHILOSOPHY?

HOW TO USE THIS BOOK

The study of language — like language itself — is a many-splendored thing. Being an all-pervasive phenomenon, language became the object of study for several disciplines. Anthropology, linguistics, philosophy, psychology, and certain parts of physics and medicine are all concerned with some aspect of language. In this respect, the study of language parallels the study of material bodies. There is no single science dealing with material bodies. Geometry, chemistry, physics, and other sciences deal with a variety of aspects of material things.

To study a certain set of phenomena rigorously means to concentrate on certain aspects of those phenomena. Thus science involves abstraction in two ways; on the one hand we abstract when we decide which aspects of a set of phenomena we will study, and on the other hand in the study of such aspects we will posit theoretical constructs — entities that are not observable, but the existence of which seems required in order to explain the observable.

These general observations apply to the study of language in the same way in which they apply to the study of anything else. It follows from this that linguists will study only certain aspects of the use of language. To make this anthology relevant to the concerns of linguists, it will be shown, briefly, why the study of what logicians and philosophers said about language helps the linguist in pursuing the work that serves his interest.

Logic deals with the rules of justified inference. Deductive logic deals with those inferences that exhibit the task of drawing out of a set of premisses sentences whose meaning, in a sense, is already contained in the premisses. In this way, the study of the rules of deductive logic, as they apply to natural languages, is tied in with questions of meaning, and since legitimate inferences depend on the structural composition of sentences, also with questions of grammar. This in itself is a non-trivial claim. It is interesting to speculate on what it would be like to have a system of communication in which questions of sentence-formation and meaning would be totally distinct from and unrelated to the application of the rules of deductive inference.

On the assumption, then, that rules of reasoning are intimately tied to rules of meaning and syntax, there is strong motivation for linguists to become familiar with some of the results of logic, and some of the technical devices that have proved themselves to be so useful in the study of deductive inferences.

The preoccupation of philosophers with language goes back at least to Socrates. To sum up the situation briefly, one of the strong recurrent themes in the history of Western philosophy has been the claim that a careful study of the general features of human languages will help to comprehend the nature of human understanding. Thus philosophers have made repeated attempts to answer such questions as: what is meaning? what is truth? what are the essential features of human languages? Needless to say, answers to these questions are of great interest to linguists who — like other scientists — have some concern with the theoretical foundations of their discipline.

The branch of logic that is strongly represented in this volume is often called FORMAL SEMANTICS. This discipline takes as its data some of the purely cognitive aspects of language use, i.e. the facts that we use language to refer to things, to describe them, to assert truths and falsehoods, and to reason about things. Formal semantics attempts to present a rigorous theory which represents these aspects of linguistic competence.

The work on formal semantics that is represented in this book can be described on three levels. First, there are papers introducing the reader to theories of reference, satisfaction, and truth, applicable to simple indicative sentences without modals, complements, and names for properties of properties, such as 'colour', or 'excellence'. These papers also help to explain how we can determine the descriptive and inferential content of complex sentences by starting with the analysis of their simple constituents. On the second level, there are papers that extend formal semantics to cover the analysis of sentences involving modals such as 'necessarily, or 'possibly', and sentences with complements such as 'John believes that ...' or 'Mary hopes that ...'. Thirdly, there are papers that extend the analysis to cover sentences containing reference to tenses as well as to places that are specified relative to the speaker and intended audience.

In emphasizing the central role of the notions of reference, predication, and truth, formal semantics represents meaning, and semantic rules, as involving essentially relations between language and reality. It is admitted that there are other aspects of meaning as well. There is the issue of MOOD, a variety of communicative aspects of language use (such as the facts that we use language to perform certain acts, e.g. of promising, warning, etc.), and there is the aspect of meaning best described as association; but it is assumed that the analysis of these presupposes the analysis performed by formal semantics while the dependency does not hold in the opposite direction. This is a controversial assumption, and the section on alternative conceptions of meaning includes some writings that deny this thesis.

When one compares the conception of semantics embodied in these papers on formal semantics with the conceptions familiar from the recent linguistic literature (componential analysis, semantic markers as in the system of Fodor and Katz, etc.) the crucial difference lies in the emphasis of the former on the relation between language and reality and the preoccupation of the latter with rules relating parts of language to other parts of language. Thus linguists concern themselves with questions of synonymy, paraphrase, and disambiguation. The position taken by most people working in formal semantics is that the adequate solution of such issues presupposes a theory of reference, satisfaction, and truth. To borrow a felicitous phrase from D. F. Pears — who employed it in a different context — we can put semantics on a firm footing only when we find and explicate the "way out of the maze of words", i.e. the points at which language is related by the competent speaker-hearer to reality. Formal semantics attempts to present a theory about these points, and linguists should be at least familiar with such theories before deciding on the extent of their relevance and utility for their own research.

What are presented as alternative conceptions of meaning either attempt a different representation of cognitive content, or else suggest that the priority of such content may not be a useful assumption in an adequate analysis of all of the uses of human languages.

The structure that determines the inference-potential and conditions of truth for sentences has been called at times THE LOGICAL FORM of a sentence. There are serious disagreements on the question of whether sentences of natural languages have one unique logical form, or whether to posit a logical form for a sentence is like formulating an empirical hypothesis — in the sense that the latter activity goes naturally with the assumption that a variety of hypotheses may explain the same set of phenomena equally well. Thus one of the questions that philosophers ask is whether a sentence must have just one logical form. Another is the question of the extent to which syntactic rules in natural languages admit of semantic justification. That is to say, we must examine the logical form, or logical forms, of a sentence, and see what the relation of that structure is to what is syntactically the fundamental structure of a sentence. The issue of the relation between logical form and syntactic deep structure is one of the most important questions facing linguists today. The first section of this book helps to understand what logical form really is, and the third section contains some philosophical considerations on why the two structures should or should not be independent. Both of these questions are discussed in the papers contained in the third part of this book. A related question emerging from the papers in this section is: to what extent, if any, can one assume that the rules, and the primitive entities in terms of which the rules are specified, have psychological reality?

Finally, it is useful for linguists to become aware of the debates that have taken place in recent philosophy concerning the desirable methodology for the science of linguistics. Some of the crucial issues that come up in this connection are: what is the proper range of phenomena that should be regarded as evidence for or against hypotheses in linguistics? What is the proper explanatory power of linguistic hypotheses? What are useful theoretical constructs to be employed within linguistics? In connection with the last question perhaps the most important controversies take place with regard to some of the new technical terms introduced by Chomsky, such as innate knowledge, internalization of rules, tacit knowledge of rules, creativity, etc. Several of these terms have a long history in philosophy; others are new in every way. The proper context for these discussions is the comparison of linguistics to other sciences. E.g. is the notion of competence in linguistics analogous to the notion of idealization in the other sciences? Are the theoretical constructs proposed by recent linguists such as Chomsky related to empirical evidence analogously to the indirect relations between theoretical entities and empirical evidence that one finds in the modern natural sciences?

Finally, a question that underlies much of the discussion in parts II, III, and IV, is: what are the limitations of the range of phenomena that linguistics should be concerned with? As was pointed out in the beginning of this brief introduction, every science has to limit itself to studying certain aspects of a set of events. How are we to delimit the relevant aspect for linguistics? A careful perusal of the several papers contained in this volume will give — indirectly — a variety of different answers to this question. Needless to say, this issue is currently a much debated topic among linguists. Thus in this context too, an issue within a specific discipline, i.e. linguistics, can benefit from the kind of conceptual analysis that is one of the main tasks of philosophy.

As this brief introduction shows, the sections are arranged in natural order. One cannot discuss relations between syntax and semantics, syntactic deep structure and logical form before one has a thorough grasp of what rigorous semantics is really like, and what specific proposals have been made concerning logical form.

It is advisable to read the papers in the first section in the order in which they are presented. Frege's classic paper lays out the main issues of semantics, and the main subjects of analysis: singular term, general term, sentence. The subsequent papers deal with the development of formal semantics at various stages. Montague's paper shows how formal semantics can be applied to a fragment of English, and Reichenbach's selection shows the problems we face when trying to account for tenses and adverbial constructions. The last two papers lead us to some of the pioneer-work done today on formal semantics. This section should be studied either by those who already had some introduction to symbolic logic (such as selections from the introductory books by Mates, Quine, or Suppes — see bibliography), and some elementary familiarity with modal logic (such as can be acquired from some of the early chapters of Hughes and Cresswell — see bibliography), or by those without any background in logic, for whom selections from the textbooks mentioned are assigned as the instructor sees fit, in conjunction with the assignments from this anthology.

The alternative approaches outlined in part II all assume general familiarity with the main outlines of formal semantics. For those wishing to look at alternatives in greater depths, it is advisable to look in detail at Wittgenstein's *Philosophical Investigations*, and J. L. Austin's *How To Do Things With Words.*

The most profitable way of reading parts III and IV is that of keeping the main outlines of transformational grammar and Chomsky's comments on methodology in one's mind. For that is the kind of linguistic theory that the authors of these sections are concerned with; both with regard to its methodology, and with regards to its relationship to semantical considerations. Presumably a general introductory course to transformational grammar would be a sufficient background for these sections, provided that such a course paid attention to some of the recent methodological reflexions of linguists as well.

In the past seven years philosophers have turned in increasing numbers to the careful study of recent developments in linguistics. Recently, this attention has been reciprocated by linguists. Such cooperation and mutual interest is obviously desirable, if the claims made in the beginning of this introduction are correct. But it is very important that in the attempt to master a related field, the practitioner should get a thorough grounding in the fundamentals, including those basic techniques and formal devices the understanding of which is absolutely essential for a deep grasp of the significance of the field and specific results within it. It is hoped that this volume will make a modest contribution toward enabling students of linguistics to achieve proper understanding of formal semantics and the related work in the philosophy of language.

Stanford, 1972   **J. M. E. Moravcsik**

Part I

MEANING AND FORMAL SEMANTICS

- -

G. Frege

ON SENSE AND REFERENCE

[25] Equality[1] gives rise to challenging questions which are not altogether easy to answer. Is it a relation? A relation between objects, or between names or signs of objects? In my *Begriffsschrift*[2] I assumed the latter. The reasons which seem to favour this are the following: $a = a$ and $a = b$ are obviously statements of differing cognitive value; $a = a$ holds *a priori* and, according to Kant, is to be labelled analytic, while statements of the form $a = b$ often contain very valuable extensions of our knowledge and cannot always be established *a priori*. The discovery that the rising sun is not new every morning, but always the same, was one of the most fertile astronomical discoveries. Even to-day the identification of a small planet or a comet is not always a [26] matter of course. Now if we were to regard equality as a relation between that which the names 'a' and 'b' designate, it would seem that $a = b$ could not differ from $a = a$ (i.e. provided $a = b$ is true). A relation would thereby be expressed of a thing to itself, and indeed one in which each thing stands to itself but to no other thing. What is intended to be said by $a = b$ seems to be that the signs or names 'a' and 'b' designate the same thing, so that those signs themselves would be under discussion; a relation between them would be asserted. But this relation would hold between the names or signs only in so far

Reprinted from: G. Frege, *Philosophical Writings* ed. and transl. by P. Geach and M. Black (New York, Philosophical Library, 1952), 56-78. First published in *Zeitschrift für Philosophie und philosophische Kritik* 100 (1892), 25-50.
[1] I use this word strictly and understand '$a = b$' to have the sense of 'a is the same as b' or 'a and b coincide'.
[2] [The reference is to Frege's *Begriffsschrift, eine der arithmetischen nachgebildete Formelsprache des reinen Denkens* (Halle, 1879). Ed.]

as they named or designated something. It would be mediated by the connexion of each of the two signs with the same designated thing. But this is arbitrary. Nobody can be forbidden to use any arbitrarily producible event or object as a sign for something. In that case the sentence $a = b$ would no longer refer to the subject matter, but only to its mode of designation; we would express no proper knowledge by its means. But in many cases this is just what we want to do. If the sign 'a' is distinguished from the sign 'b' only as object (here, by means of its shape), not as sign (i.e. not by the manner in which it designates something), the cognitive value of $a = a$ becomes essentially equal to that of $a = b$, provided $a = b$ is true. A difference can arise only if the difference between the signs corresponds to a difference in the mode of presentation of that which is designated. Let a, b, c be the lines connecting the vertices of a triangle with the midpoints of the opposite sides. The point of intersection of a and b is then the same as the point of intersection of b and c. So we have different designations for the same point, and these names ('point of intersection of a and b', 'point of intersection of b and c') likewise indicate the mode of presentation; and hence the statement contains actual knowledge.

It is natural, now, to think of there being connected with a sign (name, combination of words, letter), besides that to which the sign refers, which may be called the reference of the sign, also what I should like to call the SENSE of the sign, wherein the mode of presentation is contained. In our example, accordingly, the [27] reference of the expressions 'the point of intersection of a and b' and 'the point of intersection of b and c' would be the same, but not their senses. The reference of 'evening star' would be the same as that of 'morning star', but not the sense.

It is clear from the context that by 'sign' and 'name' I have here understood any designation representing a proper name, which thus has as its reference a definite object (this word taken in the widest range), but not a concept or a relation, which shall be discussed further in another article.[3] The designation of a single object can also consist of several words or other signs. For brevity, let every such designation be called a proper name.

The sense of a proper name is grasped by everybody who is sufficiently familiar with the language or totality of designations to which it belongs;[4]

[3] [See his "Über Begriff und Gegenstand", *Vierteljahrsschrift für wissenschaftliche Philosophie* XVI (1892), 192-205. Ed.]

[4] In the case of an actual proper name such as 'Aristotle' opinions as to the sense may differ. It might, for instance, be taken to be the following: the pupil of Plato and teacher of Alexander the Great. Anybody who does this will attach another sense to the sentence 'Aristotle was born in Stagira' than will a man who takes as the sense of the name: the teacher of Alexander the Great who was born in Stagira. So long as the

but this serves to illuminate only a single aspect of the reference, supposing it to have one. Comprehensive knowledge of the reference would require us to be able to say immediately whether any given sense belongs to it. To such knowledge we never attain.

The regular connexion between a sign, its sense, and its reference is of such a kind that to the sign there corresponds a definite sense and to that in turn a definite reference, while to a given reference (an object) there does not belong only a single sign. The same sense has different expressions in different languages or even in the same language. To be sure, exceptions to this regular behaviour occur. To every expression belonging to a complete totality of signs, there should certainly correspond [28] a definite sense; but natural languages often do not satisfy this condition, and one must be content if the same word has the same sense in the same context. It may perhaps be granted that every grammatically well-formed expression representing a proper name always has a sense. But this is not to say that to the sense there also corresponds a reference. The words 'the celestial body most distant from the Earth' have a sense, but it is very doubtful if they also have a reference. The expression 'the least rapidly convergent series' has a sense; but it is known to have no reference, since for every given convergent series, another convergent, but less rapidly convergent, series can be found. In grasping a sense, one is not certainly assured of a reference.

If words are used in the ordinary way, what one intends to speak of is their reference. It can also happen, however, that one wishes to talk about the words themselves or their sense. This happens, for instance, when the words of another are quoted. One's own words then first designate words of the other speaker, and only the latter have their usual reference. We then have signs of signs. In writing, the words are in this case enclosed in quotation marks. Accordingly, a word standing between quotation marks must not be taken as having its ordinary reference.

In order to speak of the sense of an expression 'A' one may simply use the phrase 'the sense of the expression "A"'. In reported speech one talks about the sense, e.g., of another person's remarks. It is quite clear that in this way of speaking words do not have their customary reference but designate what is usually their sense. In order to have a short expression, we will say: In reported speech, words are used INDIRECTLY or have their INDIRECT reference. We distinguish accordingly the CUSTOMARY from the INDIRECT reference of word; and its CUSTOMARY sense from its INDIRECT sense. The indirect reference of a word is ac-

---

reference remains the same, such variations of sense may be tolerated, although they are to be avoided in the theoretical structure of a demonstrative science and ought not to occur in a perfect language.

cordingly its customary sense. Such exceptions must always be borne in
mind if the mode of connexion between sign, sense, and reference in
particular cases is to be correctly understood.

[29] The reference and sense of a sign are to be distinguished from the
associated idea. If the reference of a sign is an object perceivable by the
senses, my idea of it is an internal image,[5] arising from memories of sense
impressions which I have had and acts, both internal and external, which
I have performed. Such an idea is often saturated with feeling; the clarity
of its separate parts varies and oscillates. The same sense is not always
connected, even in the same man, with the same idea. The idea is subjective: one man's idea is not that of another. There result, as a matter
of course, a variety of differences in the ideas associated with the same
sense. A painter, a horseman, and a zoologist will probably connect
different ideas with the name 'Bucephalus'. This constitutes an essential
distinction between the idea and the sign's sense, which may be the
common property of many and therefore is not a part of a mode of the
individual mind. For one can hardly deny that mankind has a common
store of thoughts which is transmitted from one generation to another.[6]

In the light of this, one need have no scruples in speaking simply of
THE sense, whereas in the case of an idea one must, strictly speaking,
add to whom it belongs and at what time. It might perhaps be said:
Just as one man connects this idea, and another that idea, with the same
word, so also one man can associate this sense and another that sense.
But there still remains a difference in the mode of connexion. They are
not prevented from grasping the same sense; but they cannot have the
same [30] idea. *Si duo idem faciunt, non est idem.* If two persons picture
the same thing, each still has his own idea. It is indeed sometimes possible to establish differences in the ideas, or even in the sensations, of
different men; but an exact comparison is not possible, because we cannot
have both ideas together in the same consciousness.

The reference of a proper name is the object itself which we designate
by its means; the idea, which we have in that case, is wholly subjective;
in between lies the sense, which is indeed no longer subjective like the
idea, but is yet not the object itself. The following analogy will perhaps
clarify these relationships. Somebody observes the Moon through a
telescope. I compare the Moon itself to the reference; it is the object of
the observation, mediated by the real image projected by the object

---

[5] We can include with ideas the direct experiences in which sense-impressions and
acts themselves take the place of the traces which they have left in the mind. The
distinction is unimportant for our purpose, especially since memories of sense-impressions and acts always help to complete the perceptual image. One can also understand
direct experience as including any object, in so far as it is sensibly perceptible or spatial.
[6] Hence it is inadvisable to use the word 'idea' to designate something so basically
different.

glass in the interior of the telescope, and by the retinal image of the observer. The former I compare to the sense, the latter is like the idea or experience. The optical image in the telescope is indeed one-sided and dependent upon the standpoint of observation; but it is still objective, inasmuch as it can be used by several observers. At any rate it could be arranged for several to use it simultaneously. But each one would have his own retinal image. On account of the diverse shapes of the observers' eyes, even a geometrical congruence could hardly be achieved, and an actual coincidence would be out of the question. This analogy might be developed still further, by assuming A's retinal image made visible to B; or A might also see his own retinal image in a mirror. In this way we might perhaps show how an idea can itself be taken as an object, but as such is not for the observer what it directly is for the person having the idea. But to pursue this would take us too far afield.

We can now recognize three levels of difference between words, expressions, or whole sentences. The difference may concern at most the ideas, or the sense but not the reference, or, finally, the reference as well. With respect to the first level, it is to be [31] noted that, on account of the uncertain connexion of ideas with words, a difference may hold for one person, which another does not find. The difference between a translation and the original text should properly not overstep the first level. To the possible differences here belong also the colouring and shading which poetic eloquence seeks to give to the sense. Such colouring and shading are not objective, and must be evoked by each hearer or reader according to the hints of the poet or the speaker. Without some affinity in human ideas art would certainly be impossible; but it can never be exactly determined how far the intentions of the poet are realized.

In what follows there will be no further discussion of ideas and experiences; they have been mentioned here only to ensure that the idea aroused in the hearer by a word shall not be confused with its sense or its reference.

To make short and exact expressions possible, let the following phraseology be established: A proper name (word, sign, sign combination, expression) EXPRESSES its sense, STANDS FOR or DESIGNATES its reference. By means of a sign we express its sense and designate its reference.

Idealists or sceptics will perhaps long since have objected: 'You talk, without further ado, of the Moon as an object; but how do you know that the name 'the Moon' has any reference? How do you know that anything whatsoever has a reference?' I reply that when we say 'the Moon', we do not intend to speak of our idea of the Moon, nor are we satisfied with the sense alone, but we presuppose a reference. To assume that in the sentence 'The Moon is smaller than the Earth' the idea of the

Moon is in question, would be flatly to misunderstand the sense. If this is what the speaker wanted, he would use the phrase 'my idea of the Moon'. Now we can of course be mistaken in the presupposition, and such mistakes have indeed occurred. But the question whether the presupposition is perhaps always mistaken [32] need not be answered here; in order to justify mention of the reference of a sign it is enough, at first, to point out our intention in speaking or thinking. (We must then add the reservation: provided such reference exists.)

So far we have considered the sense and reference only of such expressions, words, or signs as we have called proper names. We now inquire concerning the sense and reference for an entire declarative sentence. Such a sentence contains a thought.[7] Is this thought, now, to be regarded as its sense or its reference? Let us assume for the time being that the sentence has reference. If we now replace one word of the sentence by another having the same reference, but a different sense, this can have no bearing upon the reference of the sentence. Yet we can see that in such a case the thought changes; since, e.g. the thought in the sentence 'The morning star is a body illuminated by the Sun' differs from that in the sentence 'The evening star is a body illuminated by the Sun'. Anybody who did not know that the evening star is the morning star might hold the one thought to be true, the other false. The thought, accordingly, cannot be the reference of the sentence, but must rather be considered as the sense. What is the position now with regard to the reference? Have we a right even to inquire about it? Is it possible that a sentence as a whole has only a sense, but no reference? At any rate, one might expect that such sentences occur, just as there are parts of sentences having sense but no reference. And sentences which contain proper names without reference will be of this kind. The sentence 'Odysseus was set ashore at Ithaca while sound asleep' obviously has a sense. But since it is doubtful whether the name 'Odysseus', occurring therein, has reference, it is also doubtful whether the whole sentence has one. Yet it is certain, nevertheless, that anyone who seriously took the sentence to be true or false would ascribe to the name 'Odysseus' a reference, not merely [33] a sense; for it is of the reference of the name that the predicate is affirmed or denied. Whoever does not admit the name has reference can neither apply nor withhold the predicate. But in that case it would be superfluous to advance to the reference of the name; one could be satisfied with the sense, if one wanted to go no further than the thought. If it were a question only of the sense of the sentence, the thought, it would be unnecessary to bother with the reference of a part of the sentence; only the sense, not the reference, of the part is relevant to the

---

[7] By a thought I understand not the subjective performance of thinking but its objective content, which is capable of being the common property of several thinkers.

sense of the whole sentence. The thought remains the same whether 'Odysseus' has reference or not. The fact that we concern ourselves at all about the reference of a part of the sentence indicates that we generally recognize and expect a reference for the sentence itself. The thought loses value for us as soon as we recognize that the reference of one of its parts is missing. We are therefore justified in not being satisfied with the sense of a sentence, and in inquiring also as to its reference. But now why do we want every proper name to have not only a sense, but also a reference? Why is the thought not enough for us? Because, and to the extent that, we are concerned with its truth value. This is not always the case. In hearing an epic poem, for instance, apart from the euphony of the language we are interested only in the sense of the sentences and the images and feelings thereby aroused. The question of truth would cause us to abandon aesthetic delight for an attitude of scientific investigation. Hence it is a matter of no concern to us whether the name 'Odysseus', for instance, has reference, so long as we accept the poem as a work of art.[8] It is the striving for truth that drives us always to advance from the sense to the reference.

We have seen that the reference of a sentence may always be sought, whenever the reference of its components is involved; and that this is the case when and only when we are inquiring after the truth value.

[34] We are therefore driven into accepting the TRUTH VALUE of a sentence as constituting its reference. By the truth value of a sentence I understand the circumstance that it is true or false. There are no further truth values. For brevity I call the one the True, the other the False. Every declarative sentence concerned with the reference of its words is therefore to be regarded as a proper name, and its reference, if it has one, is either the True or the False. These two objects are recognized, if only implicitly, by everybody who judges something to be true — and so even by a sceptic. The designation of the truth values as objects may appear to be an arbitrary fancy or perhaps a mere play upon words, from which no profound consequences could be drawn. What I mean by an object can be more exactly discussed only in connexion with concept and relation. I will reserve this for another article.[9] But so much should already be clear, that in every judgment,[10] no matter how trivial, the step from the level of thoughts to the level of reference (the objective) has already been taken.

[8] It would be desirable to have a special term for signs having only sense. If we name them, say, representations, the words of the actors on the stage would be representations; indeed the actor himself would be a representation.
[9] [See his "Über Begriff und Gegenstand", *Vierteljahrsschrift für wissenschaftliche Philosophie* XVI (1892), 192-205. Ed.]
[10] A judgment, for me is not the mere comprehension of a thought, but the admission of its truth.

One might be tempted to regard the relation of the thought to the True not as that of sense to reference, but rather as that of subject to predicate. One can, indeed, say: 'The thought, that 5 is a prime number, is true.' But closer examination shows that nothing more has been said than in the simple sentence '5 is a prime number'. The truth claim arises in each case from the form of the declarative sentence, and when the latter lacks its usual force, e.g. in the mouth of an actor upon the stage, even the sentence 'The thought that 5 is a prime number is true' contains only a thought, and indeed the same thought as the simple '5 is a prime number'. It follows that the relation of the thought to the True may not be compared with that of subject to predicate. [35] Subject and predicate (understood in the logical sense) are indeed elements of thought; they stand on the same level for knowledge. By combining subject and predicate, one reaches only a thought, never passes from sense to reference, never from a thought to its truth value. One moves at the same level but never advances from one level to the next. A truth value cannot be a part of a thought, any more than, say, the Sun can, for it is not a sense but an object.

If our supposition that the reference of a sentence is its truth value is correct, the latter must remain unchanged when a part of the sentence is replaced by an expression having the same reference. And this is in fact the case. Leibniz gives the definition: *Eadem sunt, quae sibi mutuo substitui possunt, salva veritate.* What else but the truth value could be found, that belongs quite generally to every sentence if the reference of its components is relevant, and remains unchanged by substitutions of the kind in question?

If now the truth value of a sentence is its reference, then on the one hand all true sentences have the same reference and so, on the other hand, do all false sentences. From this we see that in the reference of the sentence all that is specific is obliterated. We can never be concerned only with the reference of a sentence; but again the mere thought alone yields no knowledge, but only the thought together with its reference, i.e. its truth value. Judgments can be regarded as advances from a thought to a truth value. Naturally this cannot be a definition. Judgment is something quite peculiar and incomparable. One might also say that judgments are distinctions of parts within truth values. Such distinction occurs by a return to the thought. To every sense belonging to a truth value there would correspond its own manner of analysis. However, I have here used the word 'part' in a special sense. I have in fact transferred the relation between the parts and the whole of the sentence to its reference, by calling the reference of a word part of the reference of the sentence, if the [36] word itself is a part of the sentence. This way of speaking can certainly be attacked, because the whole reference and one part of it do not suffice to determine the remainder, and because the word 'part' is already used in another sense of bodies. A special term would need to be invented.

The supposition that the truth value of a sentence is its reference shall now be put to further test. We have found that the truth value of a sentence remains unchanged when an expression is replaced by another having the same reference: but we have not yet considered the case in which the expression to be replaced is itself a sentence. Now if our view is correct, the truth value of a sentence containing another as part must remain unchanged when the part is replaced by another sentence having the same truth value. Exceptions are to be expected when the whole sentence or its part is direct or indirect quotation; for in such cases, as we have seen, the words do not have their customary reference. In direct quotation, a sentence designates another sentence, and in indirect quotation a thought.

We are thus led to consider subordinate sentences or clauses. These occur as parts of a sentence complex, which is, from the logical standpoint, likewise a sentence — a main sentence. But here we meet the question whether it is also true of the subordinate sentence that its reference is a truth value. Of indirect quotation we already know the opposite. Grammarians view subordinate clauses as representatives of parts of sentences and divide them accordingly into noun clauses, adjective clauses, adverbial clauses. This might generate the supposition that the reference of a subordinate clause was not a truth value but rather of the same kind as the reference of a noun or adjective or adverb — in short, of a part of a sentence, whose sense was not a thought but only a part of a thought. Only a more thorough investigation can clarify the issue. In so doing, we shall not follow the grammatical categories strictly, but rather group together what is logically of the same kind. Let us first search for cases in which the sense of the subordinate clause, as we have just supposed, is not an independent thought.

[37] The case of an abstract[11] noun clause, introduced by 'that', includes the case of indirect quotation, in which we have seen the words to have their indirect reference coinciding with what is customarily their sense. In this case, then, the subordinate clause has for its reference a thought, not a truth value; as sense not a thought, but the sense of the words 'the thought, that ...', which is only a part of the thought in the entire complex sentence. This happens after 'say', 'hear', 'be of the opinion', 'be convinced', 'conclude', and similar words.[12] There is a

---

[11] [A literal translation of Frege's 'abstracten Nennsätzen' whose meaning eludes me. Ed.]

[12] In 'A lied in saying he had seen B', the subordinate clause designates a thought which is said (1) to have been asserted by A (2) while A was convinced of its falsity.

different, and indeed somewhat complicated, situation after words like 'perceive', 'know', 'fancy', which are to be considered later.

That in the cases of the first kind the reference of the subordinate clause is in fact the thought can also be recognized by seeing that it is indifferent to the truth of the whole whether the subordinate clause is true or false. Let us compare, for instance, the two sentences 'Copernicus believed that the planetary orbits are circles' and 'Copernicus believed that the apparent motion of the sun is produced by the real motion of the Earth'. One subordinate clause can be substituted for the other without harm to the truth. The main clause and the subordinate clause together have as their sense only a single thought, and the truth of the whole includes neither the truth nor the untruth of the subordinate clause. In such cases it is not permissible to replace one expression in the subordinate clause by another having the same customary reference, but only by one having the same indirect reference, i.e. the same customary sense. If somebody were to conclude: The reference of a sentence is not its truth value, for in that case it could always be replaced by another sentence of the same truth value; he would prove too much; one might just as well claim that the reference of 'morning star' is not Venus, since one may not always say 'Venus' in place of 'morning star'. One has the right to conclude only that the reference of a sentence is not ALWAYS its truth value, and that 'morning star' does not always [38] stand for the planet Venus, viz. when the word has its indirect reference. An exception of such a kind occurs in the subordinate clause just considered which has a thought as its reference.

If one says 'It seems that ...' one means 'It seems to me that ...' or 'I think that ...' We therefore have the same case again. The situation is similar in the case of expressions such as 'to be pleased', 'to regret', 'to approve', 'to blame', 'to hope', 'to fear'. If, toward the end of the battle of Waterloo,[13] Wellington was glad that the Prussians were coming, the basis for his joy was a conviction. Had he been deceived, he would have been no less pleased so long as his illusion lasted; and before he became so convinced he could not have been pleased that the Prussians were coming — even though in fact they might have been already approaching.

Just as a conviction or a belief is the ground of a feeling, it can, as in inference, also be the ground of a conviction. In the sentence: 'Columbus inferred from the roundness of the Earth that he could reach India by travelling towards the west', we have as the reference of the parts two thoughts, that the Earth is round, and that Columbus by travelling to the west could reach India. All that is relevant here is that Columbus was convinced of both, and that the one conviction was a ground for the

---

[13] [Frege uses the Prussian name for the battle — 'Belle Alliance'. Ed.]

other. Whether the Earth is really round, and whether Columbus could really reach India by travelling to the west, are immaterial to the truth of our sentence; but it is not immaterial whether we replace 'the Earth' by 'the planet which is accompanied by a moon whose diameter is greater than the fourth part of its own'. Here also we have the indirect reference of the words.

Adverbial final clauses beginning 'in order that' also belong here; for obviously the purpose is a thought; therefore: indirect reference for the words, subjunctive mood.

A subordinate clause with 'that' after 'command', 'ask', 'forbid', would appear in direct speech as an imperative. Such a clause has no reference but only a sense. A command, a request, are indeed not thoughts, yet they stand on the same level as thoughts. Hence in subordinate clauses depending upon [39] 'command', 'ask', etc., words have their indirect reference. The reference of such a clause is therefore not a truth value but a command, a request, and so forth.

The case is similar for the dependent question in phrases such as 'doubt whether', 'not to know what'. It is easy to see that here also the words are to be taken to have their indirect reference. Dependent clauses expressing questions and beginning with 'who', 'what', 'where', 'when', 'how', 'by what means', etc., seem at times to approximate very closely to adverbial clauses in which words have their customary references. These cases are distinguished linguistically [in German] by the mood of the verb. With the subjunctive, we have a dependent question and indirect reference of the words, so that a proper name cannot in general be replaced by another name of the same object.

In the cases so far considered the words of the subordinate clause had their indirect reference, and this made it clear that the reference of the subordinate clause itself was indirect, i.e. not a truth value but a thought, a command, a request, a question. The subordinate clause could be regarded as a noun, indeed one could say: as a proper name of that thought, that command, etc., which it represented in the context of the sentence structure.

We now come to other subordinate clauses, in which the words do have their customary reference without however a thought occurring as sense and a truth value as reference. How this is possible is best made clear by examples.

Whoever discovered the elliptic form of the planetary orbits died in misery.

If the sense of the subordinate clause were here a thought, it would have to be possible to express it also in a separate sentence. But this does not work, because the grammatical subject 'whoever' has no independent sense and only mediates the relation with the consequent clause 'died in misery'. For this reason the sense of the subordinate clause is not a complete thought, and its reference is Kepler, not a truth value. One might object that the sense of the whole does contain a thought as part, viz. that there was somebody who first discovered the elliptic form of the planetary orbits; for whoever takes the whole to be true cannot [40] deny this part. This is undoubtedly so; but only because otherwise the dependent clause 'whoever discovered the elliptic form of the planetary orbits' would have no reference. If anything is asserted there is always an obvious presupposition that the simple or compound proper names used have reference. If one therefore asserts 'Kepler died in misery', there is a presupposition that the name 'Kepler' designates something; but it does not follow that the sense of the sentence 'Kepler died in misery' contains the thought that the name 'Kepler' designates something. If this were the case the negation would have to run not

Kepler did not die in misery

but

Kepler did not die in misery, or the name 'Kepler' has no reference.

That the name 'Kepler' designates something is just as much a presupposition for the assertion

Kepler died in misery

as for the contrary assertion. Now languages have the fault of containing expressions which fail to designate an object (although their grammatical form seems to qualify them for the purpose) because the truth of some sentences is a prerequisite. Thus it depends on the truth of the sentence:

There was someone who discovered the elliptic form of the planetary orbits

whether the subordinate clause

Whoever discovered the elliptic form of the planetary orbits

really designates an object or only seems to do so while having in fact no reference. And thus it may appear as if our subordinate clause contained as a part of its sense the thought that there was somebody who discovered the elliptic form of the planetary orbits. If this were right the negation would run:

Either whoever discovered the elliptic form of the planetary orbits did not die in misery or there was nobody who discovered the elliptic form of the planetary orbits.

[41] This arises from an imperfection of language, from which even the symbolic language of mathematical analysis is not altogether free; even there combinations of symbols can occur that seem to stand for something but have (at least so far) no reference, e.g. divergent infinite series. This can be avoided, e.g., by means of the special stipulation that divergent infinite series shall stand for the number 0. A logically perfect language (*Begriffsschrift*) should satisfy the conditions, that every expression grammatically well constructed as a proper name out of signs already introduced shall in fact designate an object, and that no new sign shall be introduced as a proper name without being secured a reference. The logic books contain warnings against logical mistakes arising from the ambiguity of expressions. I regard as no less pertinent a warning against apparent proper names having no reference. The history of mathematics supplies errors which have arisen in this way. This lends itself to demagogic abuse as easily as ambiguity — perhaps more easily. 'The will of the people' can serve as an example; for it is easy to establish that there is at any rate no generally accepted reference for this expression. It is therefore by no means unimportant to eliminate the source of these mistakes, at least in science, once and for all. Then such objections as the one discussed above would become impossible, because it could never depend upon the truth of a thought whether a proper name had a reference.

With the consideration of these noun clauses may be coupled that of types of adjective and adverbial clauses which are logically in close relation to them.

Adjective clauses also serve to construct compound proper names, though, unlike noun clauses, they are not sufficient by themselves for this purpose. These adjective clauses are to be regarded as equivalent to adjectives. Instead of 'the square root of 4 which is smaller than 0', one can also say 'the negative square root of 4'. We have here the case of a compound proper name constructed from the expression for a concept with the help of the singular definite article. This is at any rate permissible if the [42] concept applies to one and only one single object.[14]

Expressions for concepts can be so constructed that marks of a concept are given by adjective clauses as, in our example, by the clause 'which is smaller than 0'. It is evident that such an adjective clause cannot have a thought as sense or a truth value as reference, any more than the noun clause could. Its sense, which can also be expressed in many cases by a single adjective, is only a part of a thought. Here, as in the case of the

---

[14] In accordance with what was said above, an expression of the kind in question must actually always be assured of reference, by means of a special stipulation, e.g. by the convention that 0 shall count as its reference, when the concept applies to no object or to more than one.

noun clause, there is no independent subject and therefore no possibility of reproducing the sense of the subordinate clause in an independent sentence.

Places, instants, stretches of time, are, logically considered, objects; hence the linguistic designation of a definite place, a definite instant, or a stretch of time is to be regarded as a proper name. Now adverbial clauses of place and time can be used for the construction of such a proper name in a manner similar to that which we have seen in the case of noun and adjective clauses. In the same way, expressions for concepts bringing in places, etc., can be constructed. It is to be noted here also that the sense of these subordinate clauses cannot be reproduced in an independent sentence, since an essential component, viz. the determination of place or time, is missing and is only indicated by a relative pronoun or a conjunction.[15]

In conditional clauses, also, there may usually be recognized to [43] occur an indefinite indicator, having a similar correlate in the dependent clause. (We have already seen this occur in noun, adjective, and adverbial clauses.) In so far as each indicator refers to the other, both clauses together form a connected whole, which as a rule expresses only a single thought. In the sentence

If a number is less than 1 and greater than 0, its square is less than 1 and greater than 0

the component in question is 'a number' in the conditional clause and 'its' in the dependent clause. It is by means of this very indefiniteness that the sense acquires the generality expected of a law. It is this which is responsible for the fact that the antecedent clause alone has no complete thought as its sense and in combination with the consequent

---

[15] In the case of these sentences, various interpretations are easily possible. The sense of the sentence, 'After Schleswig-Holstein was separated from Denmark, Prussia and Austria quarrelled' can also be rendered in the form 'After the separation of Schleswig-Holstein from Denmark, Prussia and Austria quarrelled'. In this version, it is surely sufficiently clear that the sense is not to be taken as having as a part the thought that Schleswig-Holstein was once separated from Denmark, but that this is the necessary presupposition in order for the expression 'after the separation of Schleswig-Holstein from Denmark' to have any reference at all. To be sure, our sentence can also be interpreted as saying that Schleswig-Holstein was once separated from Denmark. We then have a case which is to be considered later. In order to understand the difference more clearly, let us project ourselves into the mind of a Chinese who, having little knowledge of European history, believes it to be false that Schleswig-Holstein was ever separated from Denmark. He will take our sentence, in the first version, to be neither true nor false but will deny it to have any reference, on the ground of absence of reference for its subordinate clause. This clause would only apparently determine a time. If he interpreted our sentence in the second way, however, he would find a thought expressed in it which he would take to be false, beside a part which would be without reference for him.

clause expresses one and only one thought, whose parts are no longer thoughts. It is, in general, incorrect to say that in the hypothetical judgment two judgments are put in reciprocal relationship. If this or something similar is said, the word 'judgment' is used in the same sense as I have connected with the word 'thought', so that I would use the formulation: 'A hypothetical thought establishes a reciprocal relationship between two thoughts.' This could be true only if an indefinite indicator is absent,[16] but in such a case there would also be no generality.

If an instant of time is to be indefinitely indicated in both conditional and dependent clauses, this is often achieved merely by using the present tense of the verb, which in such a case however does not indicate the temporal present. This grammatical form is then the indefinite indicator in the main and [44] subordinate clauses. An example of this is: 'When the Sun is in the tropic of Cancer, the longest day in the northern hemisphere occurs'. Here, also, it is impossible to express the sense of the subordinate clause in a full sentence, because this sense is not a complete thought. If we say: 'The Sun is in the tropic of Cancer', this would refer to our present time and thereby change the sense. Just as little is the sense of the main clause a thought; only the whole, composed of main and subordinate clauses, has such a sense. It may be added that several common components in the antecedent and consequent clauses may be indefinitely indicated.

It is clear that noun clauses with 'who' or 'what' and adverbial clauses with 'where', 'when', 'wherever', 'whenever' are often to be interpreted as having the sense of conditional clauses, e.g. 'who touches pitch, defiles himself'.

Adjective clauses can also take the place of conditional clauses. Thus the sense of the sentence previously used can be given in the form 'The square of a number which is less than 1 and greater than 0 is less than 1 and greater than 0'.

The situation is quite different if the common component of the two clauses is designated by a proper name. In the sentence:

Napoleon, who recognized the danger to his right flank, himself led his guards against the enemy position

two thoughts are expressed:

1. Napoleon recognized the danger to his right flank.
2. Napoleon himself led his guards against the enemy position.

When and where this happened is to be fixed by the context, but is nevertheless to be taken as definitely determined thereby. If the entire

---

[16] At times an explicit linguistic indication is missing and must be read off from the entire context.

sentence is uttered as an assertion, we thereby simultaneously assert both component sentences. If one of the parts is false, the whole is false. Here we have the case that the subordinate clause by itself has a complete thought as sense (if we complete it by indication of place and time). The reference of the subordinate clause is accordingly a truth value. We can therefore expect that it may be replaced, without harm to the truth value of the whole, by a sentence having the same truth [45] value. This is indeed the case; but it is to be noticed that for purely grammatical reasons, its subject must be 'Napoleon', for only then can it be brought into the form of an adjective clause belonging to 'Napoleon'. But if the demand that it be expressed in this form be waived, and the connexion be shown by 'and', this restriction disappears.

Subsidiary clauses beginning with 'although' also express complete thoughts. This conjunction actually has no sense and does not change the sense of the clause but only illuminates it in a peculiar fashion.[17] We could indeed replace the conditional clause without harm to the truth of the whole by another of the same truth value; but the light in which the clause is placed by the conjunction might then easily appear unsuitable, as if a song with a sad subject were to be sung in a lively fashion.

In the last cases the truth of the whole included the truth of the component clauses. The case is different if a conditional clause expresses a complete thought by containing, in place of an indefinite indicator, a proper name or something which is to be regarded as equivalent. In the sentence

If the Sun has already risen, the sky is very cloudy

the time is the present, that is to say, definite. And the place is also to be thought of as definite. Here it can be said that a relation between the truth values of conditional and dependent clauses has been asserted, viz. such that the case does not occur in which the antecedent stands for the True and the consequent for the False. Accordingly, our sentence is true if the Sun has not yet risen, whether the sky is very cloudy or not, and also if the Sun has risen and the sky is very cloudy. Since only truth values are here in question, each component clause can be replaced by another of the same truth value without changing the truth value of the whole. To be sure, the light in which the subject then appears would usually be unsuitable; the thought [46] might easily seem distorted; but this has nothing to do with its truth value. One must always take care not to clash with the subsidiary thoughts, which are however not explicitly expressed and therefore should not be reckoned in the sense. Hence, also, no account need be taken of their truth values.[18]

---

[17]   Similarly in the case of 'but', 'yet'.
[18]   The thought of our sentence might also be expressed thus: 'Either the Sun has not

The simple cases have now been discussed. Let us review what we have learned.

The subordinate clause usually has for its sense not a thought, but only a part of one, and consequently no truth value as reference. The reason for this is either that the words in the subordinate clause have indirect reference, so that the reference, not the sense, of the subordinate clause is a thought; or else that, on account of the presence of an indefinite indicator, the subordinate clause is incomplete and expresses a thought only when combined with the main clause. It may happen, however, that the sense of the subsidiary clause is a complete thought, in which case it can be replaced by another of the same truth value without harm to the truth of the whole — provided there are no grammatical obstacles.

An examination of all the subordinate clauses which one may encounter will soon provide some which do not fit well into these categories. The reason, so far as I can see, is that these subordinate clauses have no such simple sense. Almost always, it seems, we connect with the main thoughts expressed by us subsidiary thoughts which, although not expressed, are associated with our words, in accordance with psychological laws, by the hearer. And since the subsidiary thought appears to be connected with our words of its own accord, almost like the main thought itself, we want it also to be expressed. The sense of the sentence is thereby enriched, and it may well happen that we have more simple thoughts than clauses. In many cases the sentence must be understood in this way, in others it may be doubtful whether the subsidiary thought belongs to the sense of the sentence or only [47] accompanies it.[19] One might perhaps find that the sentence

> Napoleon, who recognized the danger to his right flank, himself led his guards against the enemy position

expresses not only the two thoughts shown above, but also the thought that the knowledge of the danger was the reason why he led the guards against the enemy position. One may in fact doubt whether this thought is merely slightly suggested or really expressed. Let the question be considered whether our sentence be false if Napoleon's decision had already been made before he recognized the danger. If our sentence could be true in spite of this, the subsidiary thought should not be understood as part of the sense. One would probably decide in favour of this. The alternative would make for a quite complicated situation: We would have more simple thoughts than clauses. If the sentence

---

risen yet or the sky is very cloudy' — which shows how this kind of sentence connexion is to be understood.

[19] This may be important for the question whether an assertion is a lie, or an oath a perjury.

Napoleon recognized the danger to his right flank

were now to be replaced by another having the same truth value, e.g.

Napoleon was already more than 45 years old

not only would our first thought be changed, but also our third one. Hence the truth value of the latter might change — viz. if his age was not the reason for the decision to lead the guards against the enemy. This shows why clauses of equal truth value cannot always be substituted for one another in such cases. The clause expresses more through its connexion with another than it does in isolation.

Let us now consider cases where this regularly happens. In the sentence:

Bebel mistakenly supposes that the return of Alsace-Lorraine would appease France's desire for revenge

two thoughts are expressed, which are not however shown by means of antecedent and consequent clauses, viz.:

(1) Bebel believes that the return of Alsace-Lorraine would appease France's desire for revenge
[48] (2) the return of Alsace-Lorraine would not appease France's desire for revenge.

In the expression of the first thought, the words of the subordinate clause have their indirect reference, while the same words have their customary reference in the expression of the second thought. This shows that the subordinate clause in our original complex sentence is to be taken twice over, with different reference, standing once for a thought, once for a truth value. Since the truth value is not the whole reference of the subordinate clause, we cannot simply replace the latter by another of equal truth value. Similar considerations apply to expressions such as 'know', 'discover', 'it is known that'.

By means of a subordinate causal clause and the associated main clause we express several thoughts, which however do not correspond separately to the original clauses. In the sentence: 'Because ice is less dense than water, it floats on water' we have

(1) Ice is less dense than water;
(2) If anything is less dense than water, it floats on water;
(3) Ice floats on water.

The third thought, however, need not be explicitly introduced, since it is contained in the remaining two. On the other hand, neither the first and third nor the second and third combined would furnish the sense of our sentence. It can now be seen that our subordinate clause because ice is less dense than water

expresses our first thought, as well as a part of our second. This is how it comes to pass that our subsidiary clause cannot be simply replaced by another of equal truth value; for this would alter our second thought and thereby might well alter its truth value.

The situation is similar in the sentence

If iron were less dense than water, it would float on water.

[49] Here we have the two thoughts that iron is not less dense than water, and that something floats on water if it is less dense than water. The subsidiary clause again expresses one thought and a part of the other.

If we interpret the sentence already considered

After Schleswig-Holstein was separated from Denmark, Prussia and Austria quarrelled

in such a way that it expresses the thought that Schleswig-Holstein was once separated from Denmark, we have first this thought, and secondly the thought that at a time, more closely determined by the subordinate clause, Prussia and Austria quarreled. Here also the subordinate clause expresses not only one thought but also a part of another. Therefore it may not in general be replaced by another of the same truth value.

It is hard to exhaust all the possibilities given by language; but I hope to have brought to light at least the essential reasons why a subordinate clause may not always be replaced by another of equal truth value without harm to the truth of the whole sentence structure. These reasons arise:

(1) when the subordinate clause does not stand for a truth value, inasmuch as it expresses only a part of a thought;

(2) when the subordinate clause does stand for a truth value but is not restricted to so doing, inasmuch as its sense includes one thought and part of another.

The first case arises:

(a) in indirect reference of words

(b) if a part of the sentence is only an indefinite indicator instead of a proper name.

In the second case, the subsidiary clause may have to be taken twice over, viz. once in its customary reference, and the other time in indirect reference; or the sense of a part of the subordinate clause may likewise be a component of another thought, which, taken together with the thought directly expressed by the subordinate clause, makes up the sense of the whole sentence.

It follows with sufficient probability from the foregoing that the cases where a subordinate clause is not replaceable by another of the same value it cannot be brought in disproof of our view [50] that a truth value is the reference of a sentence having a thought as its sense.

Let us return to our starting point.

When we found '$a = a$' and '$a = b$' to have different cognitive values, the explanation is that for the purpose of knowledge, the sense of the sentence, viz., the thought expressed by it, is no less relevant than its reference, i.e. its truth value. If now $a = b$, then indeed the reference of 'b' is the same as that of 'a', and hence the truth value of '$a = b$' is the same as that of '$a = a$'. In spite of this, the sense of 'b' may differ from that of 'a', and thereby the sense expressed in '$a = b$' differs from that of '$a = a$'. In that case the two sentences do not have the same cognitive value. If we understand by 'judgment' the advance from the thought to its truth value, as in the above paper, we can also say that the judgments are different.

R. Carnap

MEANING AND SYNONYMY IN NATURAL LANGUAGES

1. MEANING ANALYSIS IN PRAGMATICS AND SEMANTICS

The analysis of meanings of expressions occurs in two fundamentally different forms. The first belongs to PRAGMATICS, that is, the empirical investigation of historically given NATURAL LANGUAGES. This kind of analysis has long been carried out by linguists and philosophers, especially analytic philosophers. The second form was developed only recently in the field of symbolic logic; this form belongs to SEMANTICS (here understood in the sense of pure semantics, while descriptive semantics may be regarded as part of pragmatics), that is, the study of constructed LANGUAGE SYSTEMS given by their rules.

The theory of the relations between a language — either a natural language or a language system — and what language is about may be divided into two parts which I call the theory of extension and the theory of intension, respectively.[1] The first deals with concepts like denoting, naming, extension, truth, and related ones. (For example, the word 'blau' in German, and likewise the predicate 'B' in a symbolic language system if a rule assigns to it the same meaning, denote any object that is blue; its extension is the class of all blue objects; 'der Mond' is a name of the moon; the sentence 'der Mond ist blau' is true if and only if the moon is

Reprinted from: R. Carnap, *Meaning and Necessity* (Chicago, Phoenix, 1956), 233-47.

[1] This distinction is closely related to that between radical concepts and L-concepts which I made in *Introduction to Semantics* (Cambridge, Mass., 1942). The contrast between extension and intension is the basis of the semantical method which I developed in *Meaning and Necessity*. Quine calls the two theories "theory of reference" and "theory of meaning", respectively.

blue.) The theory of intension deals with concepts like intension, synonymy, analyticity, and related ones; for our present discussion let us call them INTENSION CONCEPTS. (I use 'intension' as a technical term for the meaning of an expression or, more specifically, for its designative meaning component; see below. For example, the intension of 'blau' in German is the property of being blue; two predicates are synonymous if and only if they have the same intension; a sentence is analytic if it is true by virtue of the intensions of the expressions occurring in it.)

From a systematic point of view, the description of a language may well begin with the theory of intension and then build the theory of extension on its basis. By learning the theory of intension of a language, say German, we learn the intensions of the words and phrases and finally of the sentences. Thus the theory of intension of a given language L enables us to UNDERSTAND the sentences of L. On the other hand, we can apply the concepts of the theory of extension of L only if we have, in addition to the knowledge of the theory of intension of L, also sufficient empirical knowledge of the relevant facts. For example, in order to ascertain whether a German word denotes a given object, one must first understand the word, that is, know what is its intension, in other words, know the general condition which an object must fulfil in order to be denoted by this word; and secondly he must investigate the object in question in order to see whether it fulfils the condition or not. On the other hand, if a linguist makes an empirical investigation of a language not previously described, he finds out first that certain objects are denoted by a given word, and later he determines the intension of the word.

Nobody doubts that the pragmatical investigation of natural languages is of greatest importance for an understanding both of the behavior of individuals and of the character and development of whole cultures. On the other hand, I believe with the majority of logicians today that for the special purpose of the development of logic the construction and semantical investigation of language systems is more important. But also for the logician a study of pragmatics may be useful. If he wishes to find out an efficient form for a language system to be used, say, in a branch of empirical science, he might find fruitful suggestions by a study of the natural development of the language of scientists and even of the everyday language. Many of the concepts used today in pure semantics were indeed suggested by corresponding pragmatical concepts which had been used for natural languages by philosophers or linguists, though usually without exact definitions. Those semantical concepts were, in a sense, intended as explicata for the corresponding pragmatical concepts.

In the case of the semantical intension concepts there is an additional motivation for studying the corresponding pragmatical concepts. The reason is that some of the objections raised against these semantical concepts concern, not so much any particular proposed explication, but the question of the very existence of the alleged explicanda. Especially Quine's criticism does not concern the formal correctness of the definitions in pure semantics; rather, he doubts whether there are any clear and fruitful corresponding pragmatical concepts which could serve as explicanda. That is the reason why he demands that these pragmatical concepts be shown to be scientifically legitimate by stating empirical, behavioristic criteria for them. If I understand him correctly, he believes that, without this pragmatical substructure, the semantical intension concepts, even if formally correct, are arbitrary and without purpose. I do not think that a semantical concept, in order to be fruitful, must necessarily possess a prior pragmatical counterpart. It is theoretically possible to demonstrate its fruitfulness through its application in the further development of language systems. But this is a slow process. If for a given semantical concept there is already a familiar, though somewhat vague, corresponding pragmatical concept and if we are able to clarify the latter by describing an operational procedure for its application, then this may indeed be a simpler way for refuting the objections and furnish a practical justification at once for both concepts.

The purpose of this paper is to clarify the nature of the pragmatical concept of intension in natural languages and to outline a behavioristic, operational procedure for it. This will give a practical vindication for the semantical intension concepts; ways for defining them, especially analyticity, I have shown in a previous paper (Carnap, 1952). By way of introduction I shall first (in §2) discuss briefly the pragmatical concepts of denotation and extension; it seems to be generally agreed that they are scientifically legitimate.

2. THE DETERMINATION OF EXTENSIONS

We take as example the German language. We imagine that a linguist who does not know anything about this language sets out to study it by observing the linguistic behavior of German-speaking people. More specifically, he studies the German language as used by a given person Karl at a given time. For simplicity, we restrict the discussion in this paper mainly to predicates applicable to observable things, like 'blau' and 'Hund'. It is generally agreed that, on the basis of spontaneous or elicited utterances of a person, the linguist can ascertain whether or not the person is willing to apply a given predicate to a given thing, in other words, whether the predicate denotes the given thing for the person. By collecting results of this kind, the linguist can determine first, the extension of the predicate 'Hund' within a given region for Karl, that is, the class of the

things to which Karl is willing to apply the predicate, second, the extension of the contradictory, that is, the class of those things for which Karl
denies the application of 'Hund', and, third, the intermediate class of those
things for which Karl is not willing either to affirm or to deny the predicate. The size of the third class indicates the degree of vagueness of the
predicate 'Hund', if we disregard for simplicity the effect of Karl's ignorance about relevant facts. For certain predicates, e.g., 'Mensch', this
third class is relatively very small; the degree of their extensional vagueness is low. On the basis of the determination of the three classes for the
predicate 'Hund' within the investigated region, the linguist may make a
hypothesis concerning the responses of Karl to things outside of that
region, and maybe even a hypothesis concerning the total extension in the
universe. The latter hypothesis cannot, of course, be completely verified,
but every single instance of it can in principle be tested. On the other
hand, it is also generally agreed that this determination of extension involves uncertainty and possible error. But since this holds for all concepts
of empirical science, nobody regards this fact as a sufficient reason for
rejecting the concepts of the theory of extension. The sources of uncertainty
are chiefly the following: first, the linguist's acceptance of the result that a
given thing is denoted by 'Hund' for Karl may be erroneous, e.g., due to a
misunderstanding or a factual error of Karl's; and, second, the generalization to things which he has not tested suffers, of course, from the uncertainty of all inductive inference.

3. THE DETERMINATION OF INTENSIONS

The purpose of this paper is to defend the thesis that the analysis of
intension for a natural language is a scientific procedure, methodologically
just as sound as the analysis of extension. To many linguists and philosophers this thesis will appear as a truism. However, some contemporary
philosophers, especially Quine,[2] and White (1950), believe that the
pragmatical intension concepts are foggy, mysterious, and not really
understandable, and that so far no explications for them have been given.
They believe further that, if an explication for one of these concepts is
found, it will at best be in the form of a concept of degree. They acknowledge the good scientific status of the pragmatical concepts of the theory of
extension. They emphasize that their objection against the intension concepts is based on a point of principle and not on the generally recognized
facts of the technical difficulty of linguistic investigations, the inductive
uncertainty, and the vagueness of the words of ordinary language. I shall

[2]   W. V. Quine (1953); for his criticism of intension concepts see especially Essays II
(Quine 1951), III, and VII.

therefore leave aside in my discussion these difficulties, especially the two mentioned at the end of the last section. Thus the question is this: GRANTED THAT THE LINGUIST CAN DETERMINE THE EXTENSION OF A GIVEN PREDICATE, HOW CAN HE GO BEYOND THIS AND DETERMINE ALSO ITS INTENSION?

The technical term 'intension', which I use here instead of the ambiguous word 'meaning', is meant to apply only to the cognitive or designative meaning component. I shall not try to define this component. It was mentioned earlier that determination of truth presupposes knowledge of meaning (in addition to knowledge of facts); now, cognitive meaning may be roughly characterized as that meaning component which is relevant for the determination of truth. The non-cognitive meaning components, although irrelevant for questions of truth and logic, may still be very important for the psychological effect of a sentence on a listener, e.g. by emphasis, emotional associations, motivational effects.

It must certainly be admitted that the pragmatical determination of intensions involves a new step and therefore a new methodological problem. Let us assume that two linguists, investigating the language of Karl, have reached complete agreement in the determination of the extension of a given predicate in a given region. This means that they agree for every thing in this region, whether or not the predicate in question denotes it for Karl. As long as only these results are given, no matter how large the region is — you may take it, fictitiously, as the whole world, if you like — it is still possible for the linguists to ascribe to the predicate different intensions. For there are more than one and possibly infinitely many properties whose extension within the given region is just the extension determined for the predicate.

Here we come to the core of the controversy. It concerns the nature of a linguist's assignment of one of these properties to the predicate as its intension. This assignment may be made explicit by an entry in the German-English dictionary, conjoining the German predicate with an English phrase. The linguist declares hereby the German predicate to be synonymous with the English phrase. THE INTENSIONALIST THESIS in pragmatics, which I am defending, says that the assignment of an intension is an empirical hypothesis which, like any other hypothesis in linguistics, can be tested by observations of language behavior. On the other hand, THE EXTENSIONALIST THESIS asserts that the assignment of an intension, on the basis of the previously determined extension, is not a question of fact but merely a matter of choice. The thesis holds that the linguist is free to choose any of those properties which fit to the given extension; he may be guided in his choice by a consideration of simplicity, but there is no question of right or wrong. Quine seems to maintain this thesis; he says: "The finished lexicon is a case evidently of *ex pede*

Herculem. But there is a difference. In projecting Hercules from the foot we risk error but we may derive comfort from the fact that there is something to be wrong about. In the case of the lexicon, pending some definition of synonymy, we have no stating of the problem; we have nothing for the lexicographer to be right or wrong about" (1953:63).

I shall now plead for the intensionalist thesis. Suppose, for example, that one linguist, after an investigation of Karl's speaking behavior, writes into his dictionary the following:

(1)   *Pferd,* horse,

while another linguist writes:

(2)   *Pferd,* horse or unicorn.

Since there are no unicorns, the two intensions ascribed to the word 'Pferd' by the two linguists, although different, have the same extension. If the extensionalist thesis were right, there would be no way for empirically deciding between (1) and (2). Since the extension is the same, no response by Karl, affirmative or negative, with respect to any actual thing can make a difference between (1) and (2). But what else is there to investigate for the linguist beyond Karl's responses concerning the application of the predicate to all the cases that can be found? The answer is, he must take into account not only the actual cases, but also possible cases.[3] The most direct way of doing this would be for the linguist to use, in the German questions directed to Karl, modal expressions 'corresponding to "possible case" or the like. To be sure, these expressions are usually rather ambiguous; but this difficulty can be overcome by giving suitable explanations and examples. I do not think that there is any objection of principle against the use of modal terms. On the other hand, I think that their use is not necessary. The linguist could simply describe for Karl cases, which he knows to be possible, and leave it open whether there is anything satisfying those descriptions or not. He may, for example, describe a unicorn (in German) by something corresponding to the English formulation: "a thing similar to a horse, but having only one horn in the middle of the forehead". Or he may point toward a thing and then describe the intended modification in words, e.g.: "a thing like this one but having one horn in the middle of the forehead". Or, finally, he might just point to a picture representing a unicorn. Then he asks Karl whether he is willing to apply

[3]   Some philosophers have indeed defined the intension of a predicate (or a concept closely related to it) as the class of the possible objects falling under it. For example, C. I. Lewis defines: "The comprehension of a term is the classification of all consistently thinkable things to which the term would correctly apply." I prefer to apply modalities like possibility not to object but only to intensions, especially to propositions or to properties (kinds). (Compare *Meaning and Necessity,* 66f.) To speak of a possible case means to speak of a kind of objects which is possibly non-empty.

the word 'Pferd' to a thing of this kind. An affirmative or a negative answer will constitute a confirming instance for (2) or (1) respectively. This shows that (1) and (2) are different empirical hypotheses.

All LOGICALLY POSSIBLE cases come into consideration for the determination of intensions. This includes also those cases that are causally impossible, i.e., excluded by the laws of nature holding in our universe, and certainly those that are excluded by laws which Karl believes to hold. Thus, if Karl believes that all P are Q by a law of nature, the linguist will still induce him to consider things that are P but not Q, and ask him whether or not he would apply to them the predicate under investigation (e.g., 'Pferd').

The inadequacy of the extensionalist thesis is also shown by the following example. Consider, on the one hand, these customary entries in German-English dictionaries:

(3)   *Einhorn*, unicorn. *Kobold*, goblin,

and, on the other hand, the following unusual entries:

(4)   *Einhorn*, goblin. *Kobold*, unicorn.

Now the two German words (and likewise the two English words) have the same extension, viz., the null class. Therefore, if the extensionalist thesis were correct, there would be no essential, empirically testable difference between (3) and (4). The extensionalist is compelled to say that the fact that (3) is generally accepted and (4) generally rejected is merely due to a tradition created by the lexicographers, and that there are no facts of German language behavior which could be regarded as evidence in favor of (3) as against (4). I wonder whether any linguist would be willing to accept (4). Or, to avoid the possibly misguiding influence of the lexicographers' tradition, let us put the question this way: would a man on the street, who has learned both languages by practical use without lessons or dictionaries, accept as correct a translation made according to (4)?

In general terms, the determination of the intension of a predicate may start from some instances denoted by the predicate. The essential task is then to find out what variations of a given specimen in various respects (e.g. size, shape, color) are admitted within the range of the predicate. The intension of a predicate may be defined as its range, which comprehends those possible kinds of objects for which the predicate holds. In this investigation of intension, the linguist finds a new kind of vagueness, which may be called INTENSIONAL VAGUENESS. As mentioned above, the extensional vagueness of the word 'Mensch' is very small, at least in the accessible region. First, the intermediate zone among animals now living on earth is practically empty. Second, if the ancestors of man are considered, it is probably found that Karl cannot easily draw a line; thus there is an intermediate zone, but it is relatively small. However, when the linguist proceeds to the determination of the INTENSION of the word 'Mensch', the situation is quite different. He has to test Karl's responses to descriptions of strange kinds of animals, say intermediate between man and dog, man and lion, man and hawk, etc. It may be that the linguist and Karl know that these kinds of animals have never lived on earth; they do not know whether or not these kinds will ever occur on earth or on any other planet in any galaxy. At any rate, this knowledge or ignorance is irrelevant for the determination of intension. But Karl's ignorance has the psychological effect that he has seldom if ever thought of these kinds (unless he happens to be a student of mythology or a science-fiction fan) and therefore never felt an urge to make up his mind to which of them to apply the predicate 'Mensch'. Consequently, the linguist finds in Karl's responses a large intermediate zone for this predicate, in other words, a high intensional vagueness. The fact that Karl has not made such decisions means that the intension of the word 'Mensch' for him is not quite clear even to himself, that he does not completely understand his own word. This lack of clarity does not bother him much because it holds only for aspects which have very little practical importance for him.

The extensionalist will perhaps reject as impracticable the described procedure for determining intensions because, he might say, the man on the street is unwilling to say anything about nonexistent objects. If Karl happens to be over-realistic in this way, the linguist could still resort to a lie, reporting, say, his alleged observations of unicorns. But this is by no means necessary. The tests concerning intensions are independent of questions of existence. The man on the street is very well able to understand and to answer questions about assumed situations, where it is left open whether anything of the kind described will ever actually occur or not, and even about nonexisting situations. This is shown in ordinary conversations about alternative plans of action, about the truth of reports, about dreams, legends, and fairy tales.

Although I have given here only a rough indication of the empirical procedure for determining intensions, I believe that it is sufficient to make clear that it would be possible to write along the lines indicated a manual for determining intensions or, more exactly, for testing hypotheses concerning intensions. The kinds of rules in such a manual would not be essentially different from those customarily given for procedures in psychology, linguistics, and anthropology. Therefore the rules could be understood and carried out by any scientist (provided he is not infected by philosophical prejudices).[4]

---

[4]   After writing the present paper I have become acquainted with a very interesting new book by Arne Naess (1953). This book describes in detail various procedures for testing hypotheses concerning the synonymity of expressions with the help of ques-

4. INTENSIONS IN THE LANGUAGE OF SCIENCE

The discussions in this paper concern in general a simple, pre-scientific language, and the predicates considered designate observable properties of material bodies. Let us now briefly take a look at the LANGUAGE OF SCIENCE. It is today still mainly a natural language (except for its mathematical part), with only a few explicitly made conventions for some special words or symbols. It is a variant of the pre-scientific language, caused by special professional needs. The degree of precision is here in general considerably higher (i.e. the degree of vagueness is lower) than in the every day language, and this degree is continually increasing. It is important to note that this increase holds not only for extensional but also for intensional precision; that is to say that not only the extensional intermediate zones (i.e. those of actual occurrences) but also the intensional ones (i.e. those of possible occurrences) are shrinking. In consequence of this development, also the intension concepts become applicable with increasing clarity. In the oldest books on chemistry, for example, there were a great number of statements describing the properties of a given substance, say water or sulphuric acid, including its reactions with other substances. There was no clear indication as to which of these numerous properties were to be taken as essential or definitory for the substance. Therefore, at least on the basis of the book alone, we cannot determine which of the statements made in the book were analytic and which synthetic for its author. The situation was similar with books on zoology, even at a much later time; we find a lot of statements, e.g. on the lion, without a clear separation of the definitory properties. But in chemistry there was an early development from the state described to states of greater and greater intensional precision. On the basis of the theory of chemical elements, slowly with increasing explicitness certain properties were selected as essential. For a compound, the molecular formula (e.g. 'H_2O') was taken as definitory, and later the molecular structure

---

tionnaires, and gives examples of statistical results found with these questionnaires. The practical difficulties and sources of possible errors are carefully investigated. The procedures concern the responses of the test persons, not to observed objects as in the present paper, but to pairs of sentences within specified contexts. Therefore the questions are formulated in the metalanguage, e.g. "Do the two given sentences in the given context express the same assertion to you?" Although there may be different opinions concerning some features of the various procedures, it seems to me that the book marks an important progress in the methodology of empirical meaning analysis for natural languages. Some of the questions used refer also to possible kinds of cases, e.g. "Can you imagine circumstances (conditions, situations) in which you would accept the one sentence and reject the other, or vice versa?" (p. 368). The book, both in its methodological discussions and in its reports on experiences with the questionnaires, seems to me to provide abundant evidence in support of the intensionalist thesis (in the sense explained in §3 above).

diagram. For the elementary substances, first certain experimental properties were more and more clearly selected as definitory, for example the atomic weight, later the position in Mendeleev's system. Still later, with a differentiation of the various isotopes, the nuclear composition was regarded as definitory, say characterized by the number of protons (atomic number) and the number of neutrons.

We can at the present time observe the advantages already obtained by the explicit conventions which have been made, though only to a very limited extent, in the language of empirical science, and the very great advantages effected by the moderate measure of formalization in the language of mathematics. Let us suppose — as I indeed believe, but that is outside of our present discussion — that this trend toward explicit rules will continue. Then the practical question arises whether rules of extension are sufficient or whether it would be advisable to lay down also rules of intension. In my view, it follows from the previous discussion that rules of intension are required, because otherwise intensional vagueness would remain, and this would prevent clear mutual understanding and effective communication.

5. THE GENERAL CONCEPT OF THE INTENSION OF A PREDICATE

We have seen that there is an empirical procedure for testing, by observations of linguistic behavior, a hypothesis concerning the intension of a predicate, say 'Pferd', for a speaker, say Karl. Since a procedure of this kind is applicable to any hypothesis of intension, the general concept of the intension of any predicate in any language for any person at any time has a clear, empirically testable sense. This general concept of intension may be characterized roughly as follows, leaving subtleties aside: the intension of a predicate 'Q' for a speaker X is the general condition which an object y must fulfil in order for X to be willing to ascribe the predicate 'Q' to y. (We omit, for simplicity, the reference to a time t.) Let us try to make this general characterization more explicit. That X is able to use a language L means that X has a certain system of interconnected dispositions for certain linguistic responses. That a predicate 'Q' in a language L has the property F as its intension for X, means that among the dispositions of X constituting the language L there is the disposition of ascribing the predicate 'Q' to any object y if and only if y has the property F. (F is here always assumed to be an observable property, i.e., either directly observable or explicitly definable in terms of directly observable properties.) (The given formulation is oversimplified, neglecting vagueness. In order to take vagueness into account, a pair of intensions F_1, F_2 must be stated: X has the disposition of ascribing affirmatively the predicate 'Q' to an object y if and only if y has F_1; and the disposition of denying 'Q' for y if and only if y has F_2. Thus, if y has neither F_1 nor F_2, X will give neither an affirmative nor a negative response; the property of having neither F_1 nor F_2 constitutes the zone of vagueness, which may possibly be empty.)

The concept of intension has here been characterized only for thing-predicates. The characterization for expressions of other types, including sentences, can be given in an analogous way. The other concepts of the theory of intension can then be defined in the usual way; we shall state only those for 'synonymous' and 'analytic' in a simple form without claim to exactness.

Two expressions are SYNONYMOUS in the language L for X at time t if they have the same intension in L for X at t.

A sentence is ANALYTIC in L for X at t if its intension (or range or truth-condition) in L for X at t comprehends all possible cases.

A language L was characterized above as a system of certain dispositions for the use of expressions. I shall now make some remarks on the METHODOLOGY OF DISPOSITIONAL CONCEPTS. This will help to a clearer understanding of the nature of linguistic concepts in general and of the concept of intension in particular. Let D be the disposition of X to react to a condition C by the characteristic response R. There are in principle, although not always in practice, two ways for ascertaining whether a given thing or person X has the disposition D (at a given time t). The first method may be called BEHAVIORISTIC (in a very wide sense); it consists in producing the condition C and then determining whether or not the response R occurs. The second way may be called the METHOD OF STRUCTURE ANALYSIS. It consists in investigating the state of X (at t) in sufficient detail such that it is possible to derive from the obtained description of the state with the help of relevant general laws (say of physics, physiology, etc.) the responses which X would make to any specified circumstances in the environment. Then it will be possible to predict, in particular, whether, under the condition C, X would make the response R or not; if so, X has the disposition D, otherwise not. For example, let X be an automobile and D be the ability for a specified acceleration on a horizontal road at a speed of 10 miles per hour. The hypothesis that the automobile has this ability D may be tested by either of the following two procedures. The behavioristic method consists in driving the car and observing its performance under the specified conditions. The second method consists in studying the internal structure of the car, especially the motor, and calculating with the help of physical laws the acceleration which would result under the specified conditions. With respect to a psychological disposition and, in particular, a linguistic disposition of a person X, there is first the familiar behavioristic method and second, at least theoretically, the method of a micro-physiological investigation of the body of X, especially the central nervous system. At the present state of physiological knowledge of the human organism and especially the central nervous system, the second method is, of course, not practicable.

6. THE CONCEPT OF INTENSION FOR A ROBOT

In order to make the method of structure analysis applicable, let us now consider the pragmatical investigation of the language of a robot rather than that of a human being. In this case we may assume that we possess much more detailed knowledge of the internal structure. The logical nature of the pragmatical concepts remains just the same. Suppose that we have a sufficiently detailed blueprint according to which the robot X was constructed and that X has abilities of observation and of use of language. Let us assume that X has three input organs A, B, and C, and an output organ. A and B are used alternatively, never simultaneously. A is an organ of visual observation of objects presented. B can receive a general description of a kind of object (a predicate expression) in the language L of X, which may consist of written marks or of holes punched in a card. C receives a predicate. These inputs constitute the question whether the object presented at A or any object satisfying the description presented at B is denoted in L for X by the predicate presented at C. The output organ may then supply one of three responses of X, for affirmation, denial, or abstention; the latter response would be given, e.g., if the observation of the object at A or the description at B is not sufficient to determine a definite answer. Just as the linguist investigating Karl begins with pointing to objects, but later, after having determined the interpretation of some words, asks questions formulated by these words, the investigator of X's language L begins with presenting objects at A, but later, on the basis of tentative results concerning the intensions of some signs of L, proceeds to present predicate expressions at B which use only those interpreted signs and not the predicate presented at C.

Instead of using this behavioristic method, the investigator may here use the method of structure analysis. On the basis of the given blueprint of X, he may be able to calculate the responses which X would make to various possible inputs. In particular, he may be able to derive from the given blueprint, with the help of those laws of physics which determine the functioning of the organs of X, the following result with respect to a given predicate 'Q' of the language L of X and specified properties F_1 and F_2 (observable for X): If the predicate 'Q' is presented at C, then X gives an affirmative response if and only if an object having the property F_1 is presented at A and a negative response if and only if an object with F_2 is presented at A. This result indicates that the boundary of the intension of 'Q'

is somewhere between the boundary of F_1 and that of F_2. For some predicates the zone of indeterminateness between F_1 and F_2 may be fairly small and hence this preliminary determination of the intension fairly precise. This might be the case, for example, for color predicates if the investigator has a sufficient number of color specimens.

After this preliminary determination of the intensions of some predicates constituting a restricted vocabulary V by calculations concerning input A, the investigator will proceed to make calculations concerning descriptions containing the predicates of V to be presented at B. He may be able to derive from the blueprint the following result: If the predicate 'P' is presented at C, and any description D in terms of the vocabulary V is presented at B, X gives an affirmative response if and only if D (as interpreted by the preliminary results) logically implies G_1, and a negative response if and only if D logically implies G_2. This result indicates that the boundary of the intension of 'P' is between the boundary of G_1 and that of G_2. In this way more precise determinations for a more comprehensive part of L and finally for the whole of L may be obtained. (Here again we assume that the predicates of L designate observable properties of things.)

It is clear that the method of structure analysis, if applicable, is more powerful than the behavioristic method, because it can supply a general answer and, under favorable circumstances, even a complete answer to the question of the intension of a given predicate.

Note that the procedure described for input A can include empty kinds of objects and the procedure for input B even causally impossible kinds. Thus, for example, though we cannot present a unicorn at A, we can nevertheless calculate which response X would make if a unicorn were presented at A. This calculation is obviously in no way affected by any zoological fact concerning the existence or nonexistence of unicorns. The situation is different for a kind of objects excluded by a law of physics, especially, a law needed in the calculations about the robot. Take the law l_1: "Any iron body at 60° F is solid". The investigator needs this law in his calculation of the functioning of X, in order to ascertain that some iron cogwheels do not melt. If now he were to take as a premise for his derivation the statement "A liquid iron body having the temperature of 60° F is presented at A", then, since the law l_1 belongs also to his premises, he would obtain a contradiction; hence every statement concerning X's response would be derivable, and thus the method would break down. But even for this case the method still works with respect to B. He may take as premise "The description 'liquid iron body with the temperature of 60° F' (that is, the translation of this into L) is presented at B". Then no contradiction arises either in the derivation made by the investigator or in that made by X. THE DERIVATION CARRIED OUT BY THE INVESTIGATOR contains the premise just mentioned, which does not refer to an iron body but to a description, say a card punched in a certain way; thus there is no contradiction, although the law l_1 occurs also as a premise. On the other hand, in THE DERIVATION MADE BY THE ROBOT X, the card presented at B supplies, as it were, a premise of the form "y is a liquid iron body at 60° F"; but here the law l_1 does not occur as a premise, and thus no contradiction occurs. X makes merely logical deductions from the one premise stated and, if the predicate 'R' is presented at C, tries to come either to the conclusion "y is R" or "y is not R". Suppose the investigator's calculation leads to the result that X would derive the conclusion "y is R" and hence that X would give an affirmative response. This result would show that the (causally impossible) kind of liquid iron bodies at 60° F is included in the range of the intension of 'R' for X.

I have tried to show in this paper that in a pragmatical investigation of a natural language there is not only, as generally agreed, an empirical method for ascertaining which objects are denoted by a given predicate and thus for determining the extension of the predicate, but also a method for testing a hypothesis concerning its intension (designative meaning).[5] The intension of a predicate for a speaker X is, roughly speaking, the general condition which an object must fulfil for X to be willing to apply the predicate to it. For the determination of intension, not only actually given cases must be taken into consideration, but also possible cases, i.e., kinds of objects which can be described without self-contradiction, irrespective of the question whether there are any objects of the kinds described. The intension of a predicate can be determined for a robot just as well as for a human speaker, and even more completely if the internal structure of the robot is sufficiently known to predict how it will function under various conditions. On the basis of the concept of intension, other pragmatical concepts with respect to natural languages can be defined, synonymy, analyticity, and the like. The existence of scientifically sound pragmatical concepts of this kind provides a practical motivation and justification for the introduction of corresponding concepts in pure semantics with respect to constructed language systems.

---

[5] Y. Bar-Hillel in a recent paper (1954) defends the concept of meaning against those contemporary linguists who wish to ban it from linguistics. He explains this tendency by the fact that in the first quarter of this century the concept of meaning was indeed in a bad methodological state; the usual explanations of the concept involved psychologistic connotations, which were correctly criticized by Bloomfield and others. Bar-Hillel points out that the semantical theory of meaning developed recently by logicians is free of these drawbacks. He appeals to the linguists to construct in an analogous way the theory of meaning needed in their empirical investigations. The present paper indicates the possibility of such a construction. The fact that the concept of intension can be applied even to a robot shows that it does not have the psychologistic character of the traditional concept of meaning.

BIBLIOGRAPHY

Bar-Hillel, Y.
  1954 "Logical Syntax and Semantics", *Language* 30, 230-237.
Carnap, R.
  1942 *Introduction to Semantics* (Cambridge, Mass.).
  1952 "Meaning Postulates", *Phil. Studies* 3, 65-73.
Naess, A.
  1953 *Interpretation and Preciseness* (Oslo).
Quine, W. V. O.
  1951 "Two Dogmas of Empiricism", *Philos. Review* 60, 20-43.
  1953 *From a Logical Point of View* (Cambridge, Mass.).
White, M. G.
  1950 "The Analytic and the Synthetic", in S. Hook, ed., *John Dewey* (New York).

Robert Rogers

A SURVEY OF FORMAL SEMANTICS

My purpose in this paper is to present an account of certain of the principal results that have been obtained in the field of formal semantics. These results will be stated in what from the logician's point of view is an informal way; that is, in stating them there will be little or no use of a precisely formalized language (though we shall of course speak about such languages). These results will, however, be stated as precisely as is possible within a non-formalized language. Taken together, my statements of these results will constitute what I believe to be a representative survey of what has been accomplished within the field of formal semantics.

The paper will be divided into the following four parts: First, an introductory section in which I give a definition of the term 'formal semantics', together with a statement of certain of the leading concepts and distinctions within formal semantics. Second, I shall give statements of two different basic concepts in terms of which much of semantical theory can be developed, and show how the concept of truth can be defined in terms of each of these concepts. These will be the concept of satisfaction, as developed by Alfred Tarski, and the concept of multiple denotation, as recently developed by Richard Martin. Third, I shall present two further concepts in terms of which the so-called L-CONCEPTS, viz., analyticity and its related concepts, can be defined. These will be the concept of a state-description, as developed by Rudolf Carnap, and the concept of an interpretation, as developed by John G. Kemeny.

Fourth, and finally, I shall present what certain writers have taken to be the significance of formal semantics for problems of ontology.

Reprinted from: *Synthese* 15 (1963), 17-56.

I

As the term 'formal semantics' is understood by those writers I am directing my attention to in this paper, it is the name of a certain kind of systematic inquiry into the problems of meaning and interpretation. More specifically, it is concerned with the problems of meaning in the sense of COGNITIVE, or DECLARATIVE meaning, as contrasted with such other types of meaning as emotive or exhortative meaning. Roughly speaking, a SEMANTICAL THEORY is a theory that provides us with a set of concepts by means of which we can give an account of the meaning of statements, or whole bodies of statements, and of the terms appearing within them. Now a FORMALIZED SEMANTICAL THEORY is one that proceeds with respect to a formalized language. Within such a theory, the semantical problems and concepts being dealt with are relativized to some well-defined language, called the OBJECT-LANGUAGE. A distinction is made between this language and the language in which the semantical analyses are being carried out, this latter language being called the META-LANGUAGE with respect to that given object-language. The object-language is always an example of what is called a FORMALIZED LANGUAGE, while the meta-language may or may not itself be a formalized language.

Before I give an account of the nature of formalized languages, let me state why it is that formal semantics has come to use such languages. Principally, it is because of the clarity and precision that are made possible once one relativizes the problems of semantics to such languages. There is about them, and results based upon the use of them, a kind of definiteness which it is impossible to obtain when one is working with an ordinary language. And because, though formalized, such languages have much in common with ordinary languages, and can be made successively to approximate such languages in power of expression, semantic analyses carried out with respect to formalized languages are of interest not only to students of such languages, but also to those who are especially interested in the semantics of ordinary, unformalized languages.

There is in addition a technical type of consideration which argues strongly for the use of formalized languages. This concerns the so-called SEMANTICAL PARADOXES. There are a number of such paradoxes known, each of which seems to lead to the impossible conclusion that a contradiction is true. These paradoxes seem to be forced upon us once we decide to carry out semantical investigations within an ordinary language. By carefully setting up a distinction between a formalized object-language and its meta-language, however, we can avoid the known paradoxes. Let me briefly state one such paradox, a version of the well-known paradox of the liar.

Consider the following sentence:

The sentence on page 50, line 2, is not true.

Clearly this sentence is true if and only if the sentence on page 50, line 2, is not true. But the sentence on page 50, line 2, is just this sentence itself. Thus we conclude that the sentence in question is true if and only if it is not true; that is, that it is both true and not true, both true and false. But this is a contradiction. Yet it seems that every step in the above argument is an admissible step within the logic of the ordinary English language. Until that language is more precisely specified than it has been heretofore, the conclusion seems inescapable that anyone who wishes to develop semantical theory within it is committed to this type of contradiction. As we shall illustrate later, however, the semantical paradoxes known to date can be successfully avoided if one has recourse to properly developed formalized languages.

Let us now give an account of what a formalized language is. In order to do this, we make use of the distinction between an OBJECT-LANGUAGE and a META-LANGUAGE. The language being formalized, and thus being TALKED ABOUT, is called the OBJECT-LANGUAGE; the language within which we formalize this language, that is, the language we *use* for this purpose, is called the META-LANGUAGE. Let us call the object-language '*L*', and the meta-language '*M*'. In order to formalize *L*, within *M* we first lay down rules which determine the SYNTAX of *L*; and then rules which determine the SEMANTICS of *L*, and thus provide an interpretation of *L*. As the first of our syntactical rules, we give a full specification of the PRIMITIVE SIGNS of *L*, that is, its alphabet and punctuation signs. Such a rule provides first for those signs that are to be used as punctuation signs and logical connectives; e.g. parentheses, a comma, a sign to play the role of negation, and a sign to play the role of material implication. This rule also specifies which signs are to be used as subject matter variables and constants. Then a FORMATION RULE is introduced, for the purpose of defining which combinations of these primitive signs of *L* are accepted as well-formed formulas of *L*. Usually this rule is in the form of a recursive definition. When it takes this form, first the most elementary or atomic types of wffs (we use 'wff' as an abbreviation of 'well-formed formula') are given a general characterization, and then the various means by which the more complex types of wffs are built up out of simpler wffs are enumerated. Next, definitions of bound and free occurrences of variables are given, and those wffs of *L* (if any) which contain no free occurrences of variables are identified as the SENTENCES of *L*. Finally, among one's list of rules determining the syntax of *L* one may include a characterization of certain of the wffs of *L* as AXIOMS, and then specify RULES OF INFERENCE by means of which one may legitimately infer certain wffs from others. And one may also include rules which permit us to abbreviate certain wffs in certain ways.

If we add no more rules than these syntactical rules, our language *L* is not yet really a language at all, but merely what is called a 'calculus', or an uninterpreted system. In order that *L* be truly a LANGUAGE, we shall have to provide an interpretation for *L*. This we do by laying down certain SEMANTICAL RULES for *L* in our meta-language *M*. There are various ways of doing this, and I shall examine a number of them later, in our next section. Still, each of these ways presupposes that our meta-language *M* has a number of certain well-defined features, and I specify these now. Within *M* we are to give an interpretation of *L*. To do this, within *M* we must first be able to talk about any and all expressions of *L*. We must therefore have within *M* a way of forming NAMES for any and all expressions of *L*. The usual means of accomplishing this end is to include within *M* specific names for each of the primitive symbols of *L*, together with an operation sign for concatenation. By putting the concatenation sign between any two signs of *M* which stand for given expressions *a* and *b* of *L*, we form an expression in *M* which stands for the result in *L* of putting the two expressions *a* and *b* together. For example, let '*P*' and '*x*' be two primitive symbols of *L*; let '*pee*' and '*ex*' be their respective names in *M*; and let '⌢' be the sign in *M* for concatenation. Then '*pee*⌢*ex*' is an expression in *M* which names the expression '*Px*' of *L*. With such means as I have just described at our disposal, we are able in *M* to refer to, or speak about, all of the expressions within *L*, since all such expressions are formed by concatenating together a finite number of the primitive symbols of *L*.

Second, if we are to interpret the expressions of *L*, we must not only be able to speak about them, but must also be able to speak about whatever they are speaking about. That is, we must be able to say within *M* whatever can be said within *L*; that is, *M* must contain a translation of each of the meaningful expressions of *L*. And, as a final requirement for giving an interpretation of *L*, we must have within *M* some way of relating the expressions of *L* to whatever they are about. This we do by making use of some SPECIFICALLY SEMANTICAL TERM or TERMS. It is principally at this point that there is considerable room for choice as to how the semantics of *L* is to be given. There are a number of specifically semantical concepts which are known to be adequate to the job. I shall examine some of these in my next section, and show how each of them suffices for the purpose of interpreting an object-language *L*. And I shall show how each of them permits us to give an analysis of the semantical concept of truth. Once we have an analysis of this concept, we are in a position to give an interpretation to each of the sentences of *L*. For with respect to each of the sentences *S* of *L*, we can form within *M* the following sentence: "_____ is true in L if and only if ...", where in the position marked '_____' we put the name of S, and in the position marked '...' we put the translation of S into the language M. Such a sentence will constitute an interpretation of S within M, for it tells us within M the conditions under which S is true. And it provides this interpretation without using any vaguely-defined terms, such as the term 'meaning'; in place of such terms, only the precisely-defined and (supposedly) contradiction-free term 'true in L' is used. Thus it is easy to see why one of the most important tasks of all in interpreting a formalized language L is the task of defining within its meta-language the concept of truth in L.

II

There are essentially two different ways in which one can introduce semantical terms into a meta-language. First, one may introduce such terms by DEFINING them all in terms of the specifically non-semantical terms already available in one's meta-language M. These latter terms fall into three distinct groups: (1) the LOGICAL VOCABULARY of M, including the logical constants (e.g., 'not', 'or', 'all', etc.), and variables; (2) the SYNTACTICAL VOCABULARY, including names of each of the primitive symbols of the object-language L, a sign for concatenation, and syntactical variables ranging over the expressions of L; and finally (3) the TRANSLATION VOCABULARY, which must permit us to translate into M all the meaningful expressions of L. This means of introducing semantical terms into a meta-language by way of definition was first developed by Tarski, and is probably the most frequently used method for introducing such terms within formal semantics. A strong argument in favor of it is that by defining all one's semantical terms exclusively in terms of non-semantical terms, one has a kind of guarantee that the paradoxes associated with the use of semantical terms will not appear in one's meta-language — supposing, of course, that these paradoxes are not already present in some form in the non-semantical part of that language.

A second way in which one might introduce semantical terms into M is one in which we do not define all such terms in the manner discussed above, but introduce certain of them as UNDEFINED TERMS of M, and then lay down axioms governing these terms. We then define the remainder of our semantical terms by means of these primitive terms. Such a procedure is comparable to Peano's treatment of arithmetical terms in his axiomatization of arithmetic, whereas the former procedure is comparable to the manner in which Frege and Russell introduce arithmetical terms into logic; viz. by means of definitional analyses which reduce such terms to terms of logic. Tarski is the originator of this second method also, and has suggested the possibility of introducing the term 'true' itself into a meta-language in this manner.

1. I now take up two different bases for semantics. The first of them, by Tarski, illustrates the former of the above two methods of introducing semantical terms, viz. by definition; the second, by Richard Martin, is of the latter type.

Tarski takes as his basic semantical concept the concept of SATIS-FACTION.[1] The relation of satisfaction is one between objects, or sequences of objects, and wffs; objects, or sequences of objects, are said to SATISFY wffs. For example, consider the wff 'x is a city'. This wff is satisfied by anything that is a city, and by nothing else; for example, by New York City, but not by John Jones. Not all wffs are of one free variable, as this one is, however; wffs may contain any finite number of free variables, and in the extreme case of sentences, no such variables at all. Tarski formulates a definition of satisfaction which will cover all cases. In order to achieve this generality, he defines the relation of satisfaction so that it holds not between objects and wffs, or between ordered n-tuples of objects and wffs, but between INFINITE SEQUENCES OF OBJECTS and such formulas. His definition presupposes an enumeration of the variables of L. As examples illustrating his definition, we may say that any infinite sequence that has New York City as its first term satisfies the wff 'x_1 is a city', where 'x_1' is the first individual variable of L; and any infinite sequence that has Boston, Mass., as its first term, and Savannah, Ga., as its second, satisfies the wff 'x_1 is to the north of x_2', where 'x_1' and 'x_2' are the first and second individual variables of L, respectively.

In order to state Tarski's definition of the satisfaction relation, we need to give a fairly definite statement of the object language L with respect to which we are defining this relation. I choose for this purpose an example of a SIMPLE, APPLIED, FUNCTIONAL CALCULUS OF FIRST ORDER; that is, a language having all of its variables of one type, taken to range over some non-empty domain of individuals, and having predicate constants but no predicate variables. Let us take the primitive sentential connectives of our language L to be the sign '$-$', for negation, and the sign '$\vee$', for disjunction; and let us take the universal quantifier as the sole undefined quantifier. Let us take the individual variables of L to be defined by the following infinite series: 'x_1', 'x_2', 'x_3',...; one variable for each positive integer n, the variable with the subscript n counting as the n-th variable.

[1] See Alfred Tarski, "The Concept of Truth in Formalized Languages", and "The Establishment of Scientific Semantics" both in his *Logic, Semantics, Metamathematics* (Oxford, 1956), 152-278 and 401-08; also "The Semantic Conception of Truth and the Foundations of Semantics", *Philosophy and Phenomenological Research* 4 (1944), 341-76.

For purposes of simplicity, let us suppose that there are but three predicate constants: 'P''', a one-place constant; 'P'''', a three-place constant; and 'P''''', a four-place constant. And for further simplicity, let us suppose that L contains no individual constants. As examples of wffs of L, we have the following: '$P'x_1$', '$P''x_2x_3x_4$', '$P'''x_1x_1x_2x_3$', '$-(x_1)\,P'x_1$'. The last of these wffs is a sentence.

In order to give a recursive definition of 'satisfies in L', for this particular L, we consider first the simplest type of wffs, viz., the so-called ATOMIC wffs; and then each of the various ways in which one may build up complex wffs from simpler ones. It is in the first part of this definition, in our consideration of the atomic wffs of L, that we give an interpretation to each of the primitive predicate constants of L; for it is here that we specify just what the conditions are under which given sequences of objects satisfy the atomic wffs in which these constants appear. In particular, we shall take the predicate constant 'P''' to stand for the property (of an instantaneous event) of occurring within the twentieth century; the constant 'P'''' to stand for the temporal relation of occurring later than one event and earlier than another; and 'P''''' to stand for the relation of two events being equidistant in time with two other events. We take the variables of L to range over instantaneous events.

In my statement of the definition of 'satisfies in L', I shall not use the precise, but cumbersome (until considerably abbreviated), syntactical notation wherein we employ names of each of the primitive symbols of L, together with a sign for concatenation. Rather, I use a more convenient version of the quasi-quotes notation, wherein wherever within a context of quasi-quotes we wish to refer to one of the primitive symbols of L we use that symbol itself rather than its name, with the concatenation sign being implicit. Let us use 'J', 'K' and 'N' as syntactical variables ranging over wffs of L. Then '$\ulcorner(K \vee N)\urcorner$', for example, is understood to be a name of the expression in L which results from writing first the left-hand parenthesis, then the wff K, then the disjunction sign '$\vee$', then the wff N, and finally the right-hand parenthesis; while '$\ulcorner P'x_n\urcorner$', for example, is understood to be a name of the expression in L which results from writing first the predicate-constant 'P''' of L, then 'x' with a subscript n, for some positive integer n. In referring to expressions of L, I use the quasi-quotes notation only when there appears within that notation at least one occurrence of an expression which is not an expression of L; otherwise, I use the usual quotes notation, as in '"x"', for example.

I now state the definition of 'satisfies (in L)', with respect to our given L, using 'f' and 'g' as variables ranging over infinite sequences of events:

f IS A SEQUENCE SATISFYING K in L if and only if f is a sequence of instantaneous events, K is a wff of L, and one of the following conditions holds:

(1) K is $\ulcorner P'x_n \urcorner$, for some positive integer n, and the n-th term of the sequence f is an event occurring within the twentieth century; (2) K is $\ulcorner P''x_m x_n x_o \urcorner$, for some positive integers m, n, and o, and the n-th term of the sequence f temporally precedes the o-th term of f, and temporally succeeds the m-th term; (3) K is $\ulcorner P'''x_m x_n x_o x_p \urcorner$, for some positive integers m, n, o, and p, and the temporal distance between the m-th and the n-th terms of f is equal to the temporal distance between the o-th and the p-th terms of f; (4) there is a wff J, such that K is $\ulcorner -J \urcorner$, and f does not satisfy J; (5) there are wffs J and N, such that K is $\ulcorner (J \vee N) \urcorner$, and either f satisfies J or f satisfies N; (6) there is a positive integer n and a wff J, such that K is $\ulcorner (x_n)J \urcorner$, and every infinite sequence of events which differs from f in at most the n-th term satisfies J.

The first three of the conditions in this definition give an interpretation of the primitive predicate constants of L. Thus, condition (1) interprets the predicate constant 'P'' so that the wff $\ulcorner P'x_n \urcorner$ means that x_n is an event occurring within the twentieth century. Condition (2) interprets the predicate constant 'P''' so that the wff $\ulcorner P''x_m x_n x_o \urcorner$ means that event x_n temporally precedes event x_o and succeeds event x_m. And condition (3) interprets 'P'''' so that the wff $\ulcorner P'''x_m x_n x_o x_p \urcorner$ means that the temporal distance between events x_m and x_n is equal to the temporal distance between events x_o and x_p. The fourth and fifth conditions give an interpretation of the two signs ' $-$ ' and ' $\vee$ ' of L, as being the signs for logical negation and disjunction, respectively. And the sixth condition gives an interpretation of the sign $\ulcorner (x_n) \urcorner$, as being the sign for universal quantification on the variable $\ulcorner x_n \urcorner$, for any positive integer n; for if J is satisfied by all sequences differing from f in at most the n-th place (and thus by the sequence f, also), whatever J asserts of x_n must hold true of all events, since any one event appears in the n-th place of some sequence.

Now that we have a definition of 'satisfies in L' at hand, we are in a position to define 'true in L', for the sentences of L. The definition that Tarski offers of this term is the following explicit one:

K IS A TRUE SENTENCE OF L if and only if K is a sentence of L, and K is satisfied by every infinite sequence of objects of L.[2]

Let us examine the plausibility of this definition. In the first place, a sentence is defined as a wff with no free variables. Thus whether a given sequence satisfies a given sentence is in no way dependent upon what the terms of that sequence are. If any sequence satisfies a given sentence, all sequences do; and, conversely, if one sequence does not satisfy a given sentence, no sequences do. Thus every sentence is satisfied either by all sequences or by none. Consideration of a specific example will illustrate the decision to identify the true sentences with those that are satisfied by all sequences, and the false sentences with those that are satisfied by none.

[2]   A. Tarski, *Logic, Semantics, Metamathematics*, 195.

Consider the following sentence of L: '$-(x_1)P'x_1$'. Let f be an arbitrary sequence of instantaneous temporal events. By condition (4) of the definition of 'satisfies', f satisfies this sentence if and only if f does not satisfy '$(x_1)P'x_1$'. And, by condition (6), f does not satisfy '$(x_1)P'x_1$' if and only if there is some sequence g differing from f in at most the first place which does not satisfy '$P'x_1$'. Now by condition (1), to say that g does not satisfy '$P'x_1$' is to say that the first term of g is an event not occurring within the twentieth century. Thus we conclude that our given sentence '$-(x_1)P'x_1$' is satisfied by any arbitrary infinite sequence of events if and only if not every event lies within the twentieth century. But if we take this condition to be what our given sentence asserts, we conclude that for our sentence to be true it must be satisfied by any arbitrary infinite sequence, that is, by all infinite sequences.

The above definition of 'true in L' permits us to infer within M that '$-(x_1)P'x_1$' is true in L if and only if not every event lies within the twentieth century. That is, it permits us to infer the following statement: '_____ is true in L if and only if ...', where the position marked '_____' is occupied by the sentence-name '"$-(x_1)P'x_1$"', and the position marked '...' is occupied by the translation in M of the sentence that is named by this sentence-name, viz., by the sentence "Not every event lies within the twentieth century". This result holds in general. For every sentence K of L, Tarski's definition of 'true in L' implies the following statement: '_____ is true in L if and only if ...', where the position marked '_____' is occupied by an expression which names K, and the position marked '...' is occupied by a translation of K into M. In addition, we have the result that whatever is true in L is a sentence of L. It is precisely these two results that the so-called CRITERION OF ADEQUACY requires of any definition of any term designating the concept of truth in L. A definition of any such terms is regarded as an ADEQUATE DEFINITION OF TRUTH IN L if and only if it meets this criterion.[3] It follows that all adequate definitions of 'true in L', for any given L, are equivalent to one another: any sentence which is true in L according to one of these definitions will be true according to all. Thus, for example, on any adequate definition of 'true in L' for the particular L I have been considering, the sentence '$-(x_1)P'x_1$' is true in L if and only if not every event lies within the twentieth century. And because any adequate semantic definition of truth has the properties mentioned in the criterion of adequacy, Tarski contends that all such definitions "do justice to the intuitions which adhere to the CLASSICAL ARISTOTELIAN CONCEPTION OF TRUTH";[4] viz., to say of what is that it is

[3] A. Tarski, *Logic, Semantics, Metamathematics*, 187-88.
[4] A. Tarski, "The Semantic Conception of Truth and the Foundations of Semantics", *Philosophy and Phenomenological Research* 4 (1944), 342.

not, or of what is not that it is, is false; while to say of what is that it is, or of what is not that it is not, is true.

Notice that the criterion of adequacy is not itself a DEFINITION of truth. Nor can we regard the infinitely many sentences which follow from any adequate definition of 'true in L' as together constituting a definition of truth in L; for a definition of truth must itself be a (finitely-long) sentence. Indeed, a definition of truth is a kind of "finite product" of these infinitely many sentences, accomplishing in FINITELY many words what they accomplish only in INFINITELY many words.

It is easy to see that from Tarski's definition of truth, and thus from any adequate definition of truth, the following two very important properties of truth follow: every sentence of L is such that either it or its negation is true in L, and no sentence of L is such that both it and its negation are true in L.

Having defined the concept of truth with respect to L, we are now in a position to define a number of other useful semantical concepts with respect to L. Thus, for example, a sentence of L is FALSE IN L if and only if it is not true in L; one sentence of L *materially implies in L* another if and only if either the first is false in L or the second is true in L; two sentences are MATERIALLY EQUIVALENT IN L if and only if either both are true in L or both are false in L; and so on.

Let us now see just how it is that the semantical definition of truth in L permits us to avoid the paradox of the liar, which I earlier stated in terms of an unrestricted concept of truth. Here of course we have no such concept, but only one that is relativized to a particular language. And further, here we are requiring that any expression designating the concept of truth with respect to a given language appear not within that language itself, but within its meta-language. Thus the crucial sentence in my earlier statement of the paradox now takes the following form:

The sentence on page 50, line 2, is not true in L, where this sentence — let us call it 'A' — appears not within L, but within L's meta-language, M (supposing that within M we can make reference to page 50, line 2). There can, of course, be no question of A's being either true in L or false in L, for A is not even a sentence of L; at most A can be either true, or false, or both, within M. Now for A to be a meaningful sentence within M, the variable implicit within the descriptive phrase 'The sentence on page 50, line 2', must be a variable ranging over wffs of L (for 'true in L' is defined only with respect to such variables). Thus, the sense of the descriptive phrase appearing within A, together with the criterion of adequacy for 'true in M', assures us that on any adequate definition of 'true in M', A is true in M only if there is a sentence of L on page 50, line 2, which is not a true sentence of L. But as there is no sentence of L at all at this position, we conclude that A is not a true sentence of M.

Thus A is not both true and false in M, but is merely false in M. Thus we see that the distinctions bound up with the semantic definition of truth permit us to escape from the paradox of the liar when stated in the form I have been considering.

2. In order to define the truth-concept for a given language L, Tarski must speak, within its meta-language M, of infinite sequences of the kinds of entities that are discussed within L. This forces him to use as a meta-language M a language which employs variables of higher type than any of the variables appearing within L (supposing that we are restricting ourselves to meta-languages based on the logical theory of types). An alternative approach to semantics, which I shall not examine here in detail, is one that Carnap has examined extensively.[5] Here Carnap takes as basic the semantical concept of DESIGNATION. He interprets the individual and predicate constants of L by specifying just which individuals and properties and relations are designated by those constants. And he argues that we may even go further and take whole sentences of L to be designatory expressions, designating propositions. Within this method of semantical analysis, we speak not of infinite sequences of entities discussed within L, but of the individuals, properties, relations and propositions designated by the designatory expressions of L. This approach, too, forces us to adopt as a meta-language for L one that employs variables of a higher type than that of any of the variables of L; viz., variables ranging over properties, relations, and propositions.

Now it is known that any meta-language in which we can define the concept of truth for a given object-language L must be ESSENTIALLY RICHER than L, roughly in the sense that although M contains an interpretation of L, it is impossible to give an interpretation of M within L.[6] If this requirement were not satisfied, we could introduce the paradox of the liar into L, by first defining 'true in L' within M, and then interpreting M within L, thereby obtaining a definition of 'true in L' within L itself. The requirement of essential richness is met by both Tarski and Carnap by using as a meta-language for L one that employs variables of higher type than any of the variables of L. Indeed, it is precisely because they have such variables at their disposal that they are able to introduce all of their semantical terms by way of definition. From a 'nominalistic' point of view, however, one might be interested in the question whether it is possible to develop a semantical approach that does not force one to use in one's meta-language variables of higher type than those of the object-language being investigated. One might wish to avoid the infinite sequences,

[5] Rudolf Carnap, *Introduction to Semantics*, Part B. (Harvard University Press, Cambridge, Mass., 1948).
[6] See Alfred Tarski, *Logic, Semantics, Metamathematics*, 247-54.

classes of classes, positive integers and so on that one is committed to if one does semantics in the manner of Tarski; and one might wish to avoid making reference to the properties and propositions that one is committed to by certain of the methods of Carnap. As a matter of fact, such nominalistic requirements can be satisfied. It is possible to construct a satisfactory approach to semantics, up to the point of defining truth at any rate, which does not require that our meta-language contain variables of higher type than the variables of the object-language, and makes no reference to either infinite sequences or to properties and propositions (supposing, of course, that no such entities are referred to within the language being investigated itself). Within such an approach the requirement that the meta-language M be essentially richer than L is met, not by introducing into M variables of higher type than any of the variables of L, but by introducing into M one or more undefined semantical constants. I shall now examine one example of such an approach; viz. that of Richard Martin.

Martin takes as his semantical primitive the term 'Den', standing for a concept of MULTIPLE DENOTATION.[7] (Strictly speaking, of course, the term 'Den', like the term 'satisfies', has to be understood as relativized to some language L.) This primitive term is offered as satisfactory for the semantics of any first-order language: that is, any language all of whose variables range over some one class of entities, called the INDIVIDUALS of that language. The term 'Den' is not introduced into the meta-language by way of definition, but is introduced as an undefined term, with axioms being laid down governing its meaning. The one-place predicate constants of L are the only expressions of L that are said to denote, and they are said to denote not classes, or properties, but severally each of the individuals to which they apply. Thus, for example, the one-place predicate constant 'dog' is here said to denote not the class of dogs, or the property of being a dog, but each dog: Rover, Fido, etc. As Martin points out, the concept of multiple denotation is one that was used by Hobbes.

Martin's concept of denotation is meant to be used in connection with a first-order language which employs abstracts. Abstracts are expressions that are obtained by prefacing any wff with one or more instances of an abstraction operator. (For purposes of simplicity, I shall suppose in the following discussion that the languages we are dealing with contain only one-place abstracts.) An abstraction operator binds within any wff to which it is applied all free occurrences of whatever variable appears within the operator. If there are no remaining free variables within the abstract, the abstract functions as a one-place predicate constant. Thus, for example, if we apply the abstraction operator '$\ni$' to the wff 'x is a man' so as to bind the variable 'x', we obtain the abstract '$x \ni x$ is a man', which

[7] Richard Martin, *Truth and Denotation* (Chicago, 1958).

will function as a one-place predicate constant, denoting severally each man. All such one-place abstracts of L involving no free variables, together with the primitive one-place predicate constants of L, are taken as the DENOTING EXPRESSIONS of L. It is to be noted in particular that the two-or-more-place primitive predicate constants of L are NOT spoken of as denoting anything.

Two types of axioms are laid down in M governing the sign 'Den'.[8] First, there is a restrictive axiom, to the effect that the only expressions of L which denote are the ONE-PLACE PREDICATE CONSTANTS of L; that is, the one-place primitive predicate constants, together with the one-place abstracts with no free variables. Second, rather than a single axiom, an AXIOM-SCHEMA is laid down, providing for an infinite number of axioms, one in connection with each one-place predicate constant of L. It is these axioms which interpret the predicate constants of L. Roughly speaking, this axiom-schema in effect assures us that the one-place predicate constants of L denote just those entities that satisfy the conditions associated with those constants. Its formulation is as follows, where we let K be any wff of L involving free occurrences of just the variable 'x', and let B be the translation of K into the meta-language M (I use 'a' as a syntactical variable ranging over expressions of L):

(x) (a Den x if and only if ...x...), where either (1) in place of 'a' we put the abstract-name '$\ulcorner x \ni K \urcorner$', and in place of '...$x$...' we put the translation B, or (2) in place of 'a' we put the name of any one-place primitive predicate constant of L, and in place of '...x...' we put the translation of that primitive predicate constant into M, with the variable 'x' in its argument-place.

If we take as L the simple language used earlier in connection with my discussion of the concept of satisfaction (understanding that language now to contain abstracts), this axiom-schema takes the following form (using 'K' and 'B' as before):

(x_1) (a Den x_1 if and only if ...x_1...), where either (1) in place of 'a' we put '$\ulcorner x_1 \ni K \urcorner$' and in place of '...$x_1$...' we put B, or (2) in place of 'a' we put '"P'"' and in place of '...x_1...' we put 'x_1 is an instantaneous event lying within the twentieth century'.

As examples of the infinitely many axioms provided for by this schema, by (2) we have '(x_1) ('P'' Den x_1 if and only if x_1 is an instantaneous event lying within the twentieth century)'; and by (1) we have '(x_1) ('$x \ni (Ex_2) (Ex_3) P'' x_2 x_1 x_3$' Den x_1 if and only if there is an event x_2 which precedes x_1 and an event x_3 which succeeds x_1)". Thus we see that this axiom-schema in condition (2) gives the interpretation of the one-place primitive predicate constants of L, and in condition (1) provides for the interpretation of the one-place abstracts of L, and thereby of the two-or-

8 Richard Martin, *Truth and Denotation*, 108-10.

more-place primitive predicate constants of L (since all such constants appear within some one-place abstract, as in my above second example of an axiom on 'Den').

Once we have the concept of denotation, we are in a position to define a number of other interesting semantical concepts. Thus, with Martin, we may say that an expression a of L COMPREHENDS an expression b of L if and only if a and b are both predicate constants of L, and a denotes everything that b does; a NULL predicate constant is one that denotes nothing; a UNIVERSAL predicate constant is one that denotes everything; a predicate constant a is the SEMANTICAL SUM of two predicate constants b and c if and only if a denotes x, if and only if either b denotes x or c denotes x; and so on.[9]

Martin presents a number of ways in which we may define an adequate truth-concept for any first-order language on the basis of the concept of multiple denotation.[10] I present here one of the simplest of these definitions, one that makes use of the logical notion of the prenex normal form of a formula. It is a well-known theorem in logic that corresponding to any given formula K in a first-order language L, there is at least one formula J of L which is logically equivalent to K, and has all of its quantifiers appearing at the beginning of the formula, with the scopes of these quantifiers each extending to the end of the formula. Such a formula J is said to be in PRENEX NORMAL FORM. Indeed, for any K, there is always a formula J, logically equivalent to K, which is in prenex normal form, and has a universal quantifier as its initial quantifier. Any sentence which is of this special form, i.e., any sentence which is in prenex normal form and has a universal quantifier as its initial quantifier, Martin calls an ATOMIC UNIVERSAL SENTENCE. For every sentence K of L, there will be an atomic universal sentence which is logically equivalent to K. Let us speak of the abstract which is formed from an atomic universal sentence by replacing the initial quantifier of that sentence by the abstraction operator involving the same variable as appears in that initial quantifier, as the ASSOCIATED ABSTRACT of that atomic universal sentence. Thus, for example, the associated abstract of the atomic universal sentence '$(x_1)P'x_1$' is the expression '$x_1 \ni P'x_1$'.

Now it is clear that in order for an atomic universal sentence to be true, it is necessary and sufficient that its associated abstract be universal; that is that its associated abstract denote everything in the domain of discourse. Further, every sentence is logically equivalent to some atomic universal sentence. We may, then, define the truth concept for all sentences of any first-order L as follows:

K IS TRUE IN L if and only if K is a sentence of L, and there is an atomic

[9]   Richard Martin, *Truth and Denotation*, 104-08.
[10]   Richard Martin, *Truth and Denotation*, 115-19.

universal sentence J of L which is logically equivalent to K, such that the associated abstract of J is universal.

Martin is able to show that this definition of truth is adequate, in the sense of the criterion of adequacy, and that it implies that every sentence of L is such that either it or its negation is true in L, and no sentence is such that both it and its negation are true in L.[11] Further, he is able to show how, with the concept of denotation, one can define truth for the very powerful languages of the Zermelo set theory and the simple theory of types.[12]

When we introduce all semantical terms into our meta-language M by way of definition, we have a kind of guarantee that M is consistent if its translational and syntactical parts are consistent. When we introduce one or more semantical terms as undefined primitives, as Martin does, however, a special RELATIVE-CONSISTENCY proof is called for, showing that M is consistent, and thus that by introducing our undefined semantical primitives into M we have not thereby introduced any semantical paradoxes into M that were not already present in M in some form. The need for such a proof was first pointed out by Tarski, who suggested the possibility of introducing a sign for truth into the meta-language as an undefined term, and then laying down as axioms governing this sign all those infinitely many formulas described in the statement of the criterion of adequacy; viz., (1) all sentences of the form '_____ is true in L if and only if ...', where the position '_____' is occupied by the name of some sentence of L, and the position '...' is occupied by the translation of this sentence into M, together with (2) a sentence to the effect that the term 'true in L' applies only to sentences of L[13] Tarski showed that if the translational and syntactical parts of M are consistent BEFORE such additions are made, M will also be consistent AFTER they are made. And, in a similar manner, Martin shows that the result of adding 'Den', together with its infinitely many axioms, to a meta-language M will be consistent if M is consistent before these additions.

III

I turn now to the semantic analysis of an especially important type of concepts, viz., the so-called L-CONCEPTS. These concepts include as principal examples the concept of L-truth, or analyticity; L-falsity, or self-contradiction; and L-implication, or logical implication. Each of these concepts has, of course, played an important role in much of modern philosophy. The concept of analyticity, for example, makes one of its

[11]   Richard Martin, *Truth and Denotation*, 119-22.
[12]   Richard Martin, *Truth and Denotation*, Chapter VI.
[13]   Alfred Tarski, *Logic, Semantics, Metamathematics*, 255-63.

earliest appearances in a fairly clear form in the writings of Leibniz, in the form of a distinction between necessary and contingent truths; necessary truths being described as those that hold in all possible worlds, and contingent truths being described as those that hold in the actual world, but not in all possible worlds. The various semantic analyses of the concept of analytic truth may indeed be taken to be attempts to define in a precise way Leibniz's notion of a truth's holding in all possible worlds.

In order to give an analysis of the L-concepts, we shall need some semantical concept which permits us to make reference to all the 'possible worlds' with respect to a given language L. By a POSSIBLE WORLD with respect to a given language we mean, roughly, a complete state of affairs concerning the individuals within the domain of that language, in so far as that state of affairs can be described by means of the expressions appearing within that language. In this section I shall examine two basic semantical concepts which permit us to speak of all possible worlds. First I shall present Carnap's semantical theory of STATE-DESCRIPTIONS, and show how the concept of a state-description permits us to give an analysis of the L-concepts.[14] Second, I shall present a formulation of a semantical theory in terms of the basic concept of an INTERPRETATION, as recently developed by John G. Kemeny.

1. The concept of a state-description is one that is meant to be used for the semantic analysis of a language L only when that language possesses, for every individual within the intended domain of discourse, an individual constant designating that individual. Now as the term 'language' is usually understood by logicians, no language contains more than a denumerable infinity of signs, and thus no more than a denumerable infinity of individual constants. The method of state-descriptions must be confined, then, to the semantic analysis of those languages that have no more than a denumerable infinity of individuals within their intended domains of discourse. In particular, this method could not be used for the semantic analysis of a first-order language which included among the values of its individual variables the real numbers.

Let us suppose that we have a simple applied language L of first-order, with a finite number of predicate constants, there being at most a denumerable infinity of individuals in the domain of the variables, with L containing an individual constant for each individual in its domain. And let the signs for negation, disjunction and universal quantification be the primitive logical constants of L. We first define an ATOMIC SENTENCE of L as an expression consisting of an n-place predicate constant of L followed by n individual constants, not necessarily all distinct. We then define a

---

[14] See Rudolf Carnap, *Introduction to Semantics*, Part C; and *Logical Foundations of Probability* (Chicago, 1950), 70-89.

STATE-DESCRIPTION of L as a class of sentences of L which contains for every atomic sentence of L either that atomic sentence or its negation (not both), and no other sentences.

As an example of a state-description, let us suppose that L contains just two individual constants, and two one-place predicate constants. Let these be 'a', 'b', 'P' and 'Q', respectively. Then the class consisting of the sentences 'Pa', 'Pb', 'Qa' and 'Qb' constitutes one state-description with respect to L. For this particular L, there are sixteen state-descriptions in all.

I now show how to introduce into a meta-language the basic semantical concept of a sentence's holding in a given state-description, by means of the following recursive definition:

K HOLDS IN THE STATE-DESCRIPTION S OF L if and only if K is a sentence of L, S is a state-description of L, and one of the following conditions is satisfied: (1) K is an atomic sentence, and K is an element of S; (2) K is the negation of a sentence J of L, and J does not hold in S; (3) K is a disjunction of two sentences, one of which holds in S; (4) K is a universal quantification of the wff J of L, and J holds in S for every value of the free variable appearing in J.

To say, then, that a given sentence holds in a given state-description is to say, roughly, that that sentence would be true if that state-description were true, that is, if all the sentences appearing within that state-description were true. Now every sentence either holds or does not hold in a given state-description. Thus the truth of any one state-description of L uniquely determines the truth or falsity of every sentence of L. It is in this sense that we may say, provisionally at any rate, that every state-description of L determines a possible world with respect to L.

Certain sentences of L can readily be seen to hold in ALL the state-descriptions of L. By condition (2) of the definition of a sentence's holding in a state-description, for any arbitrary sentence K of L, and any arbitrary state-description S of L, either K or $\ulcorner -K \urcorner$ holds in S. Thus, by condition (3), the disjunction $\ulcorner K \vee -K \urcorner$ holds in S. In general, all the sentences of L which are logical theorems of L, in the sense of being theorems either within the propositional calculus or quantification theory, will hold in all state-descriptions of L.

Now at first Carnap proposed to identify analyticity in a given language with the property of holding in all the state-descriptions of that language.[15] But then it was noticed that certain state-descriptions may not correspond to possible worlds; that is, once a definite interpretation is given to each of the individual and predicate constants of L, it may be logically impossible that certain state-descriptions be true, in the sense

15 Rudolf Carnap, *Introduction to Semantics*, 134-38.

that all of the sentences appearing within them be true. An example readily shows how this is possible. Suppose that L contains 'P' and 'Q' as one-place predicate constants, and 'a' as an individual constant. Suppose further that we intend to interpret L so that the sign 'P' is taken to name the property of being perfectly spherical in shape, and the sign 'Q' is taken to name the property of being perfectly cubical in shape. Now one or more state-descriptions of L (indeed, one quarter of them) will contain both the atomic sentence 'Pa' and the atomic sentence 'Qa'. But, on the interpretation intended, no such state-descriptions could possibly be true, since no matter what 'a' is taken to denote, that object a cannot be both perfectly spherical and perfectly cubical in shape. Thus no such state-descriptions represent any possible world with respect to L under the intended interpretation of L.

A number of ways of handling this difficulty have been proposed. I shall consider here that method which makes use of so-called MEANING POSTULATES.[16] According to this method, whenever we interpret the individual and predicate constants of L in such a way that certain of these constants become logically dependent upon others, the logical dependencies of those constants upon one another are to be indicated by laying down certain postulates, the so-called MEANING POSTULATES. Thus, for example, if L contains 'P' and 'Q' as one-place predicate constants, and we intend to interpret these constants as designating respectively the property of being perfectly spherical in shape and the property of being perfectly cubical in shape, then we must lay down the following meaning postulate: '$(x)(-Px \lor -Qx)$'. Under the intended interpretation, this postulate says that whatever is perfectly spherical in shape is not also perfectly cubical in shape. Now the only state-descriptions of this particular L which represent possible worlds are those in which this particular meaning postulate holds. No such state-descriptions contain both 'Pa' and 'Qa'. In general, for any language L, the only state-descriptions with respect to that language which represent possible states are those in which all the meaning postulates forced upon us by the intended interpretation of L hold.

We are now in a position to define the L-concepts. Let us agree to include among the meaning postulates of L all axioms and definitions of L. A sentence of L is then said to be L-TRUE IN L, or ANALYTIC IN L, if and only if that sentence holds in all those state-descriptions of L in which the meaning postulates of L hold. Similarly, a sentence of L is L-FALSE IN L if and only if its negation holds in all such state-descriptions; and one sentence J is said to L-IMPLY, or logically entail, another sentence K if and

---

[16] See Rudolf Carnap, "Meaning Postulates", *Philosophical Studies* 3 (1952), 65-73. Carnap here ascribes the method of meaning postulates to John G. Kemeny.

only if the material implication from J to K holds in all such state-descriptions. A sentence which is either L-true or L-false is L-DETER-MINATE; otherwise, FACTUAL.

We may speak of a state-description in which the meaning postulates hold as an ADMISSIBLE state-description; and of the RANGE of a sentence as the class of all admissible state-descriptions in which that sentence holds. Employing the concept of range, we may then define an L-true sentence as one whose range is the class of all admissible state-descriptions; an L-false sentence as one whose range is the null class of admissible state-descriptions; and similarly for the remaining L-concepts. The concept of range is, then, a basic one for the theory of the L-concepts, and Carnap also takes it as basic in his construction of a theory of probability.

Notice that in order to define the L-concepts with respect to a given language L it is not necessary that we first give an interpretation of L. If we wish in addition to interpret L, we may now do this, among other ways, with the help of the defined concept of THE TRUE STATE-DESCRIPTION with respect to L. First, we must state what we take to be the domain of the individual variables of L. Then we must interpret the individual and predicate constants of L. This we may do by making use of any one of the semantical methods discussed in the preceding section, for example. That is, we may interpret these constants by laying down designation rules for them, or by laying down denotation rules, or by making use of the concept of satisfaction. Next we need to define the concept of a true atomic sentence. Once again, this may be done as before. We now define THE TRUE STATE-DESCRIPTION with respect to L as that state-description which contains all the true atomic sentences of L, together with the negations of all the remaining atomic sentences of L. Finally, we define a sentence as being true in L if and only if it holds in the true state-description with respect to L. Thus we see that in order to define the L-concepts with respect to a language L, it suffices to have in the meta-language of L the concept of a sentence's holding in a given state-description; while in order to give in addition an interpretation to L, we need to add to the meta-language of L some such semantical concept as was considered in the preceding section.

2. It should be noticed that Carnap's concept of a state-description, together with the concept of holding in a state-description, are syntactical concepts, and are not semantical in the strict sense of the term 'semanti-cal'. That is, they make reference only to the expressions of L, and not to the entities discussed when using L. Thus, on Carnap's analysis the L-concepts turn out to be syntactical concepts. Specifically semantical concepts enter only when the individual and predicate constants are interpreted, as by designation rules, for example. On the analysis we are now

to consider, by Kemeny, the L-concepts are defined as genuinely semantical concepts.

The concept of a MODEL is a fundamental one within that part of mathematics known as meta-mathematics, that is, the theory of mathematical languages. It is of course not necessary to confine its use to the study of mathematical languages alone; it may be used in the study of languages in general. When so used, the concept of a model becomes one of the fundamental concepts of semantics.

Kemeny makes use of four important concepts in his construction of a semantical system.[17] These are the concepts of a VALUE-ASSIGNMENT, a SEMI-MODEL, a MODEL, and an INTERPRETATION. He defines and illustrates these concepts with respect to a very general type of language, employing type symbols. We shall not follow him in this respect, but shall present an adaptation of his concepts to a simple, applied functional calculus of first order, in which there are no abstracts.

A VALUE-ASSIGNMENT is simply an assignment of individuals from the domain of L to each of the individual variables of L; each variable is assigned one individual, and it is not required that distinct variables be assigned distinct individuals. Since any one value assignment covers all the variables of L, each of the value-assignments of L assigns to each of the free variables of any expression of L some one individual. There are, of course, as many distinct value-assignments as there are distinct ways of assigning values to the individual variables of L, two value-assignments being regarded as distinct if and only if at least one individual variable has one individual assigned to it by one of these value-assignments and a different individual assigned to it by the other.

Kemeny defines a SEMI-MODEL with respect to L as (1) an assignment of a domain of individuals to the individual variables of L, together with (2) an assignment of an interpretation within this domain to each of the individual and predicate constants of L. To each of the individual constants of L, if any, a semi-model assigns an individual within the assigned domain. To each of the one-place predicate constants of L, a semi-model assigns a class of individuals from the assigned domain. Thus, for example, a semi-model might assign the class of dogs as the domain of L; it might then assign the particular dog Fido to the individual constant 'a', and the class of Dalmatians to the one-place predicate constant 'D'. In general, a semi-model of L assigns to each n-place predicate constant of L a class of n-tuples of individuals from the domain assigned to L by that semi-model. And there are as many semi-models of L as there are distinct ways of assigning domains to L and then interpreting the individual and predicate constants of L within those domains.

---

[17] John G. Kemeny, "A New Approach to Semantics", *The Journal of Symbolic Logic* 21 (1956), 1-27 and 149-61.

In contrast with the method of state-descriptions, it is not here required that the domain of individuals assigned to L be at most denumerable. The method of state-descriptions has to impose this requirement in order to be able to characterize each of the possible worlds; if there were a non-denumerable number of entities in the domain of L, no state-description could completely characterize any one of the possible worlds with respect to that domain. As was pointed out earlier, this is because in that case there would not be a sufficient number, viz., a non-denumerable number, of atomic sentences or negations of atomic sentences to give such a characterization as a state-description is supposed to give. But on the method we are now considering, a possible world with respect to a given language is not characterized by a syntactical entity, such as a class of atomic sentences and negations of atomic sentences, but by a genuinely semantical entity, viz., that part of a semi-model in which we make definite assignments to each of the individual and predicate constants of L. Such an assignment of values to these constants of L does the work of a state-description. That is, it determines (with respect to a given semi-model), whether a given n-place predicate constant applies to a given n-tuple or not. (As we shall see later, an n-place predicate constant applies to a given n-tuple of individuals if and only if that n-tuple is an element of the class of n-tuples assigned to that predicate constant.) The assignment of a class of n-tuples of individuals to a constant, however, does not itself involve the names of those individuals; rather, it involves just those individuals themselves. And in order to MAKE, or GIVE, the assignment of a class of n-tuples of individuals to a constant, we need not actually name any of the individuals in that class; the class may be given by mentioning its defining property, as when we refer to a certain class as the class of real numbers, for example. The method of models does not, then, as does the method of state-descriptions, presuppose that we have a name for each of the individuals within the domain of L. As a consequence, L may indeed possess a non-denumerable domain.

We need now the concept of a wff's holding in a given semi-model with respect to a given value-assignment. Kemeny defines this concept by recursion, as follows:

K HOLDS IN THE SEMI-MODEL M OF THE LANGUAGE L WITH RESPECT TO THE VALUE-ASSIGNMENT V if and only if K is a wff of L, M is a semi-model of L, V is a value-assignment to the individual variables of L, defined over the domain assigned to L by M, and one of the following conditions is satisfied: (1) K is an n-place atomic wff, and the n-tuple of individuals assigned to the argument expressions of K by the semi-model M and the value-assignment V is an element of the class of n-tuples assigned to the predicate constant of K by the semi-model M; (2) there is a wff J, such that K is $\ulcorner -J \urcorner$, and J does not hold in M with respect to V; (3) there are wffs J and N, such that K is $\ulcorner(J \vee N)\urcorner$, and either J or N holds in M with respect to V; (4) there is an individual variable $\ulcorner a_n \urcorner$ and a wff J, such that K is $\ulcorner(a_n)J\urcorner$, and J holds in M with respect to every value-assignment which is defined over the domain which M assigns to L, and which differs from V in at most its assignment to $\ulcorner a_n \urcorner$.

The intuitive meaning of the above definition is that a wff K holds in a semi-model M with respect to a value-assignment V if and only if that wff would be true if one were to interpret the individual variables and individual and predicate constants within it in accordance with the interpretation put upon them by M and V. The definition very closely resembles that of the earlier definition of the concept of satisfaction. It is, indeed, a generalization of that definition. In the concept of a wff's being satisfied by an infinite sequence, we fix the meaning of the individual and predicate constants of L, and vary the assignments to the individual variables of L by varying the infinite sequences of individuals. In the concept of a wff's holding in (or being satisfied by) a semi-model with respect to a value-assignment, on the other hand, we vary not only the assignments to the individual variables of L, by means of the different value-assignments, but also the meaning of the individual and predicate constants of L, by means of the different semi-models of L. The restricted concept of satisfaction suffices for the definition of truth and its related concepts, with their reference being only to the actual world; while the more general concept (or some equivalent substitute) of holding in a semi-model with respect to a value assignment is needed in order to define the L-concepts, their reference being to all possible worlds.

Kemeny next defines a wff as VALID in a given semi-model if and only if that wff holds in that semi-model with respect to every value-assignment; and CONTRAVALID in a given semi-model if and only if it holds in that semi-model with respect to no value-assignment. Now a sentence is a wff having no free variables. Thus every sentence is either valid or contravalid in any given semi-model. We may say, informally, that a sentence's being valid in a given semi-model amounts to its being true when understood in accordance with that semi-model.

Next, we define a MODEL of a language L as a semi-model of L in which the meaning postulates of L are valid (we again use the term "meaning postulate" in the broad sense, so as to include all axioms and definitions of L among the meaning postulates of L). This definition corresponds to our earlier restriction of attention to those state-descriptions of L in which the meaning postulates of L hold.

Notice now the plausibility of defining an analytic sentence of L as a sentence which is valid in all the models of L. A model of a language L defines a possible world with respect to that language. Thus, for example, suppose that in one model of L we include the dog Rover within the class of individuals assigned to the predicate constant 'Br', which we intend to interpret as standing for the class of brown things within the domain of L; while in another model of L we include the dog Rover within the class of things assigned to the predicate constant 'Bl', which we intend to interpret as standing for the class of black things within the domain of L. Then the first model represents a possible world in which Rover is brown; while the second model represents a possible world in which Rover is black. There is no possibility, however, that any model assign Rover both to the class of things that are brown (all over) and to the class of things that are black (all over); for no such model would satisfy the meaning postulates.

Now Kemeny writes that at first he intended to take the concept of a model as the basic concept of semantics. But he then noticed that certain results of logic make this impossible; viz., the so-called INCOMPLETENESS THEOREMS of Kurt Gödel. These theorems concern deductive systems, where by a DEDUCTIVE SYSTEM I mean any system which contains an underlying logic together with certain additional constants, and axioms governing these additional constants. Gödel's theorems show that whenever we are dealing with a sufficiently strong deductive system (viz., any system strong enough to contain elementary number theory), that system will be incomplete. Without at this point attempting to give a perfectly general definition of 'complete', we may illustrate the meaning of Gödel's incompleteness theorems as follows: Consider a formalization of elementary number theory within a second-order functional calculus. Since we may bind predicate variables within the second-order calculus, our formulation of number theory will contain SENTENCES of number theory; that is, it will contain wffs of number theory which contain no free variables. Now Gödel's incompleteness theorems assure us that within our formulation of number theory there will be (infinitely many) pairs of sentences, which are such that in each pair one sentence is the negation of the other, and yet neither sentence is provable within our system. Nor will any addition to our axioms and rules of inference — short of making our system contradictory — so strengthen our system as to permit us to derive one sentence from each such pair of sentences. Our system will be irremediably incomplete.

The significance for semantics of the above result is as follows: Once we give our formulation of number theory its usual interpretation, each of the sentences within that formulation becomes either true or false. Certain of the true sentences within this formulation L, however, will not be provable within L. Now it is known, from further results of logic, that the reason that these sentences are not provable in L is because they are not valid in all of the models of L.[18] Thus, if we were to define an

---

[18]   John Kemeny, "A New Approach to Semantics", Theorem 27. See Leon Henkin,

analytic sentence of L as any sentence of L which is valid in all of the models of L, these true but unprovable sentences would not be analytic in our particular L. As they are surely not contradictory, we would have to describe them as synthetic. But such a result would be intuitively unacceptable. Any particular true but unprovable sentence of L will be provable — and thus analytic — in the system L', where L' is obtained from L merely by adding that particular sentence as a further axiom. Thus, if we were to speak of the true but unprovable sentences within our particular formulation of number theory as synthetic, the boundary between the analytic and the synthetic would become perfectly arbitrary. But when we call a wff ANALYTIC, we mean to say, roughly, that its truth is determined by considerations of meaning alone, as contrasted with factual considerations. Thus the distinction between the analytic and the synthetic is NOT arbitrary, once our sentences are interpreted. Surely, then, if we are to count the provable sentences within some axiomatic approach to number theory as analytic, we must count the true but unprovable sentences as analytic also; for their truth is as much determined by considerations of meaning as is the truth of the provable sentences. Let us suppose that on independent grounds we have decided to regard all the true sentences of number theory — or, indeed, of mathematics in general — as analytic, and the false sentences as contradictory. The conclusion which we must then infer from Gödel's incompleteness theorems is that if we are to obtain a semantic definition of 'analytic' which will permit us to record this decision within our language, we shall have to define an analytic wff of any language in some other way than as one which is valid in each of the models of that language.

Let us call those models of any incomplete deductive system in which certain of the analytically true but unprovable sentences of that system are not valid, INCOMPLETENESS MODELS (the term is mine, not Kemeny's). These models clearly interpret incomplete systems in ways they were not meant to be interpreted. It would be desirable if we could eliminate all such models. But they are a consequence of any incomplete system; every incomplete system admits of incompleteness models. Because we are unable in an incomplete system to lay down a set of meaning postulates which captures all the formal relations which hold between our individual and predicate constants once these constants are given their intended interpretations, any set of meaning postulates we DO lay down will admit of models within which certain of these formal relations are denied. Only if we could complete our formal system, could we exclude all such models.

Now what Kemeny proposes in the view of those results is that the

"Completeness in the Theory of Types", *The Journal of Symbolic Logic* 15 (1950), 81-91. See also Alonzo Church, *An Introduction to Mathematical Logic*, Vol. I (Princeton, 1956), 307-15.

question whether a wff is valid in an incompleteness model be regarded as irrelevant to the question whether that wff is analytic or not. He proposes to define analyticity within a language not in terms of the set of ALL models of that language, but in terms of a certain sub-set of the set of all of its models, which we might informally call the set of INTENDED models of that language. The problem we now have to take up is the problem of how to define this set.

Before attempting to define the set of intended models of a language, Kemeny points out that a language may contain constants such that every model we regard as an intended model makes the same assignment to these constants. That is, within the set of intended models the interpretations of these constants are fixed. Kemeny calls all such constants, LOGICAL CONSTANTS. (The signs which play the role of *and*, *or* and *all* are special cases of logical constants.) As an example, suppose that our language contains an axiomatic approach to elementary number theory. Then no model will count as an intended model of that language unless it assigns the non-negative integers as a domain to the number variables, and then assigns the number zero to the numeral '0', the number one to the numeral '1', and so on. Now if the intended models all make the same assignments to the number-theoretical constants of our language, then every number-theoretical statement within our language will either be valid in all intended models, or contravalid in all intended models. By identifying analyticity with validity in all intended models, and self-contradiction with contravalidity in all intended models, we obtain the desired result that each of our number-theoretical statements is either analytic or self-contradictory. And of course the situation is precisely similar for any other branch of mathematics, or any branch of knowledge at all. If we require that all intended models make the same assignments to the individual and predicate constants used in our formulation of any area of knowledge, then all the statements within our formulation of that area will be either analytic or self-contradictory. Thus, whether we lay down this requirement for the constants appearing within our formulation of any area of knowledge will depend upon whether we wish to admit any of our statements within that area to be neither analytic nor self-contradictory. Within a formulation of a branch of empirical science, of course, the requirement would not be laid down. That is, here different assignments to the individual and predicate constants would be admitted within the class of intended models. Obviously, in our formulation of any language it is of the utmost importance that we give a complete list of its logical constants; i.e. those constants which receive a fixed interpretation within the classes of intended models.

We may now define the class of intended models, or as Kemeny calls them, the class of INTERPRETATIONS. We first choose a certain model of *L* as that model which assigns those meanings to the individual and predicate constants of L which we intend to regard as their 'official' meanings; that is, those meanings we assign to these constants when we use L for purposes of communication. Let us call this model 'M^*', and let us call the domain it assigns to L, 'R'. Then by an INTERPRETATION of L we mean any model of L which (1) assigns R as a domain to L, and (2) differs from M^* at most only in assignments to those constants of L which are not logical constants of L. M^* is itself, of course, an interpretation; indeed, what we might call the 'official' interpretation of L. Kemeny is able to show, however, that no incompleteness model is an interpretation.

The above definition of the term 'interpretation' may present the appearance of being circular. It is easy to see, however, that it is not circular in any bad sense. When defining a language L, we present a list of constants, which we intend as the logical constants of L. The interpretations of L are then well-defined in terms of this list, together with the domain of the particular model we have chosen as our M^*.

Consider now the class of all models of L, except those models (in the case of incomplete systems) which are incompleteness models of L. Kemeny is able to show that a wff is valid in all interpretation if and only if it is valid in all of these models. The L-concepts may therefore be given satisfactory definitions in terms of the class of interpretations. Kemeny thus proposes the following definitions of these concepts, defining them for wffs in general, rather than for sentences alone: K IS ANALYTICALLY TRUE (L-TRUE) IN L if and only if K is a wff of L which is valid in all of the interpretations of L; and K IS SELF-CONTRADICTORY (L-FALSE) IN L if and only if K is a wff of L which is contravalid in all interpretations of L. A wff is SYNTHETIC if and only if it is neither analytically true nor self-contradictory. One sentence (logically) IMPLIES a second if and only if the second is valid in all those interpretations in which the first is valid; and two sentences are (logically) EQUIVALENT if and only if they are valid in the same interpretations. And a language L is said to be COMPLETE if and only if all its analytically true wffs are provable in L.

(The method of state-descriptions apparently does not require that for the purpose of defining the L-concepts we first define a restricted class of state-descriptions, corresponding to the restricted class of models called 'interpretations'. This is because state-descriptions themselves do not assign domains to L, as do models. On the method of state-descriptions, the assignment of a domain to L is made independently, and the state-descriptions of L can then be understood as defining possible states within that domain. Thus the problem of unintended domains does not arise.)

In order to define truth and its related concepts for a given language L, we need an interpretation of the individual and predicate constants of L. Such an interpretation is already at hand. The model M^* was understood

to be just that model which assigns to these constants those interpretations we intend to regard as their 'official' interpretations. The definition
of 'true in L', for wffs of L, is thus as follows: a wff of L is TRUE IN L if and
only if that wff is valid in M^*; and a wff is FALSE IN L if and only if that wff
is contravalid in M^*. These definitions readily yield the desired results
that every sentence of L is either true or false in L, and no sentence is
both. Also, of course, we have the results that whatever is analytically
true is true, and whatever is self-contradictory is false. And Kemeny is
able to show that this definition of 'true in L' is adequate in the sense of
the criterion of adequacy.

IV

I now turn to a number of distinct but interrelated topics, which center
in the problem of ontological commitment.

I have earlier remarked that in order to know what a given (declarative)
sentence means, it is necessary and sufficient that we be able to state,
within some language we admittedly understand, the conditions under
which that sentence is true. Now being able to state these conditions
implies being able to determine just what entities that sentence explicitly
assumes to exist. Thus we conclude that in order to understand a given
(declarative) sentence, one must be able to determine just what the
ONTOLOGICAL COMMITMENTS of that sentence are. For the purposes of
semantic analysis, then, it is of the greatest importance that we possess
some criterion by means of which we can determine just what entities a
given sentence or theory is explicitly committing us to when we assert that
sentence or theory.

W. V. O. Quine has proposed a criterion for determining the ontological commitments of any given body of discourse.[19] Quine first argues that
the mere using of a name or descriptive phrase does not commit one to
the view that there is some entity which is designated by that name or
descriptive phrase.[20] He points out that Russell in his theory of descriptions has shown how to eliminate singular descriptive phrases, that is,
phrases of the form 'the so-in-so', from sentences. By means of Russell's
method, we can replace any sentence containing a singular descriptive
phrase by another sentence equivalent to it in which no descriptive phrases
appear. For example, by Russell's method the sentence 'The Bishop of

---

[19]   See W. V. O. Quine, "Designation and Existence", *Journal of Philosophy* 36 (1939),
701-09; "On What There Is", *Review of Metaphysics* 2 (1948), 21-38; "Logic and
the Reification of Universals" in *From a Logical Point of View* (Cambridge, Mass.,
1953), 102-29.
[20]   W. V. O. Quine, *Review of Metaphysics* 2 (1948), 25 ff.

Milan in wealthy', is transformed into the sentence 'There is something x which is a bishop of Milan; everything which is a bishop of Milan is identical with that thing x; and that thing x is wealthy'. Consider now the case where a sentence contains a descriptive phrase which we would suppose designates nothing; e.g. the sentence 'There is no such person as the author of *Principia Mathematica*'. One might suppose that the descriptive phrase appearing in this sentence must after all designate SOMETHING, in order for the sentence to be meaningful. With the help of Russell's analysis, however, we can see how such a sentence can be meaningful, and even true, though the descriptive phrase appearing within it designates nothing. On that analysis, our sentence is seen to be equivalent to the sentence 'There is no person who is an author of *Principia Mathematica*, and is identical with every person x who is an author of *Principia Mathematica*'. By examining this latter sentence, which contains no descriptive phrases, we can readily see how the sentence of which it is an analysis can be both meaningful and true, though the descriptive phrase it contains designates nothing. We cannot, then, in general, determine the ontological commitments of any body of discourse by supposing that among these commitments must be included entities designated by the various descriptive phrases appearing in that body of discourse.

Nor, in determining the ontological commitments of a body of discourse, can we in general proceed on the supposition that each of the proper names appearing therein designates something. It is possible for a sentence to be meaningful, and even true, even though that sentence contains proper names which really name nothing. That this is possible may be regarded as but one illustration among many of the fact that being meaningful is one thing, while being a name of something is another. Furthermore, one may, as Quine shows, treat proper names as abbreviations of descriptive phrases, and then eliminate them *via* Russell's analysis. In determining the ontological commitments of any body of discourse, then, we are not entitled to suppose in general either that the descriptive phrases, or that the proper names, appearing therein designate anything whatsoever. They may, or they may not.

Where then are we to look in order to determine what entities we are explicitly committed to whenever we assert a given sentence or theory? In answer to this question, Quine proposes the following CRITERION OF ONTOLOGICAL COMMITMENT: 'An entity is assumed by a theory if and only if it must be counted among the values of the variables in order that the statements affirmed in the theory be true'.[21] The variables that we use, either explicitly or implicitly, play the role of pronouns, and by their

---

[21] W. V. O. Quine, *From a Logical Point of View*, 103.

means we express the logical notions of ALL and SOME. It is to them that we are to look when determining ontological commitment, according to Quine, rather than to proper names and descriptive phrases. Thus, for example, when we assert the sentence, 'There are five books on the table', we explicitly commit ourselves to the existence of whatever entities must lie within the range of the existential quantifiers implicit within this statement in order for the statement to be true; viz. five books. We do not, however, explicitly commit ourselves to the existence of some entity designated by the term 'five'. Not even when we assert such a sentence as 'Five is less than six' do we so commit ourselves. However, we would explicitly commit ourselves to such an entity were we to assert the sentence 'There is a prime number lying between four and six', for example. For here the number five must be included within the range of the existential quantifier appearing within this statement if the statement is to be true. Quantification over numbers is, of course, the usual practice in mathematics. Now it seems that numbers must be thought of as abstract entities. Quine's conclusion is that 'Classical mathematics ... is up to its neck in commitments to an ontology of abstract entities'.[22]

The distinction between NOMINALISTIC and REALISTIC languages is one that Quine is able to draw with the help of his criterion, supposing that we are already able to distinguish the concrete and the abstract.[23] Abstract terms may appear in either type language, but may appear as substituents for variables only in realistic languages. Realistic languages contain variables ranging over abstract entities, while nominalistic languages do not. If the nominalist uses variables which seemingly range over abstract entities of any sort, he must either find some way of eliminating them in favor of a more primitive notation in which they do not appear, or renounce nominalism in favor of realism. Here realism, understood as a thesis in the philosophy of science, is defined by Quine as maintaining that a complete expression of all scientific knowledge requires that we use a realistic language, while nominalism is understood as insisting that for this purpose a nominalistic-type language suffices.

It is, of course, one thing to determine what a given language says that there is; and quite another thing to determine what there is. Quine's criterion of ontological commitment is clearly directed primarily towards the first of these two questions. The importance of his, or any, criterion of ontological commitment for the problem of ontology, understood as the problem of what types of entities exist, is indirect, but nonetheless important. In order to significantly raise the question as to what types of entities exist, one will have to do so within a language with respect to

²² W. V. O. Quine, *Review of Metaphysics* 2 (1948), 32.
²³ W. V. O. Quine, *Journal of Philosophy* 36 (1939), 708.

which the problem of commitment can be settled. Until we are able to determine what kinds of entities we are explicitly committing ourselves to when we speak, we are in no position to raise ontological problems at all. As Alonzo Church has put it, the relation of the question of ontological commitment to the question of ontology is that of "a necessary-preliminary issue concerning the logic of the matter".[24]

A further respect in which a criterion of ontological commitment bears indirectly on the problem of ontology is as follows. Suppose that employing such a criterion one came to the conclusion that it was possible, at least in principle, to state all of scientific and mathematical knowledge in a nominalistic language; and that, further, it was in principle possible to develop satisfactory theories of the nature of knowledge, morals, art and other areas of philosophy, in a nominalistic language. Presumably, one could not infer, as a logical consequence of such a conclusion, that abstract entities did not exist; but one could, it seems, infer that there was no good reason to believe that they did (supposing, of course, that one was treating the question as to whether they did or did not exist as an objective-type problem, admitting of only one correct answer; and thus not as a problem to be settled by adopting some convention or other). Suppose, however, that one were to conclude that for the purpose of developing some area of knowledge or other, a realistic-type language was needed. Once again, presumably it would not follow, as a logical consequence of this conclusion, that there really were abstract entities. One might, however, care to infer that one now had good reasons for believing that there were. In either case, then, it seems that a criterion of ontological commitment would bear at least indirectly on the problem of ontology itself.

Are there any areas of knowledge in which we are committed to the existence of abstract entities of any sort? I have mentioned that classical mathematics seems to be such an area; at least until a nominalistic interpretation of mathematics is given, the possibility of which seems very doubtful. More germane to the general topic of this paper is the question whether the area of semantics itself is one in which we are committed to abstract entities. We know that the meta-language of a given object-language must be stronger than the object-language itself. Thus, if a given object-language presupposes abstract entities, so must its semantical meta-language. Let us, then, consider the question whether a semantical meta-language must presuppose abstract entities even when its object-language does not. And let us pass over the question whether syntax itself — a part of semantics — is committed to abstract entities.[25] Our

[24] Alonzo Church, "Ontological Commitment", *Journal of Philosophy* 55 (1958), 1008.
[25] See Nelson Goodman and W. V. O. Quine, "Steps Towards a Constructive Nominalism", *Journal of Symbolic Logic* 12 (1947), 105-22, and Richard Martin, *Truth*

question is whether the specifically semantical part of a satisfactory semantical meta-language need commit us to abstract entities.

On Tarski's approach to semantics, *via* the concept of satisfaction, abstract entities are presupposed. Classes, sequences and positive integers all make their appearance. All the abstract entities that Tarski needs may be defined in terms of classes, but classes he must have; and classes, as distinct from heaps, are abstract entities. The method of models, as developed by Kemeny, is ontologically comparable to the method of satisfaction: it, too, requires no other abstract entities than those that can be defined in terms of classes, the commitment to classes themselves, however, being evident. Certain of Carnap's various approaches to semantics presuppose not only such entities as can be defined in terms of classes, but entities which apparently cannot; viz. properties and propositions. Forming an interesting contrast to these writers, on the other hand, Richard Martin, as we have seen, has succeeded in showing how to develop semantics up to the point of defining truth without introducing any abstract entities not already presupposed by the object-language itself. To what extent Martin's particular approach can be extended so as to provide satisfactory answers to such problems as the problems of analyticity, strict synonymity, belief contexts and contrary-to-fact conditionals, remains to be seen.[26]

One who has repeatedly insisted on the importance of keeping one's ontological commitments to a minimum is Quine. Quine has been ready to admit the propriety in semantics of appealing to classes, as we do, for example, when we assign as extensions to general terms the classes of those entities to which these terms apply.[27] He has insisted many times, however, that no good purpose is served in semantics by introducing such abstract entities as are often spoken of as MEANINGS; in particular, properties as meaning of general terms, and propositions as meanings of statements.[28] As Quine sees it, in order to explain how an expression is meaningful, it is unnecessary to introduce an entity which that expression is said to have as its meaning. And not only is it redundant and pointless to do so, but many of the very entities which are customarily introduced as meanings (in particular, properties and propositions) are most peculiar,

and Denotation, Chapters XI and XII. See also R. M. Martin and J. H. Woodger, "Toward an Inscriptional Semantics", *The Journal of Symbolic Logic* 16 (1951), 193-203.

[26] See Richard Martin, *The Notion of Analytic Truth* (University of Pennsylvania Press, Philadelphia, 1959).

[27] W. V. O. Quine, "Semantics and Abstract Objects", *Proceedings of the American Academy of Arts and Sciences* 80 (1951), 94-95.

[28] See W. V. O. Quine, "Semantics and Abstract Objects", 91-94; also W. V. O. Quine, "Two Dogmas of Empiricism", *Philosophical Review* 60 (1951), 22.

due to the fact that, unlike classes, generally-accepted identity-conditions for them are not yet known. In considering an argument for meanings by a hypothetical person McX, Quine writes as follows:

I feel no reluctance toward refusing to admit meanings, for I do not thereby deny that words and statements are meaningful. McX and I may agree to the letter in our classification of linguistic forms into the meaningful and the meaningless, even though McX construes meaningfulness as the having (in some sense of 'having') of some abstract entity which he calls a meaning, whereas I do not. I remain free to maintain that the fact that a given linguistic utterance is meaningful (or *significant* as I prefer to say so as not to invite hypotasis of meanings as entities) is an ultimate and irreducible matter of fact; or, I may undertake to analyse it in terms directly of what people do in the presence of the linguistic utterance in question and other utterances similar to it ... The problem of explaining these adjectives 'significant' and 'synonymous' with some degree of clarity and rigor — preferably, as I see it, in terms of behavior — is as difficult as it is important. But the explanatory value of special and irreducible intermediary entities called meanings is surely illusory.[29]

Recently, however, Quine has come to look more favorably upon the introduction of such entities as properties and propositions into semantic analysis. Among the problems of semantics, in one of the more inclusive senses of the term 'semantics', is included the problem of providing correct analyses of propositional attitudes, such as knowing and believing, and of what Quine calls 'attributary attitudes', such as hunting and fearing. One of the principal problems in connection with the analysis of these attitudes is that of identifying their objects — supposing that they have objects. Certain philosophers have argued that their objects might be taken to be linguistic entities, such as predicates and sentences. Other philosophers have rejected analyses in terms of linguistic entities as too artificial, however, and Quine presently agrees with them. Still, he is apparently at present ready to concede that the attributary and propositional attitudes are relational in nature, and thus demand objects of some sort. If one is to assign objects at all, the natural choices seem to be attributes as objects of such attitudes as hunting and fearing, and propositions as objects of such attitudes as believing and wishing. Quine writes:

Lion-hunting it not, like lion-catching, a transaction between men and individual lions; for it requires no lions. We analyse lion-catching, rabbit-catching etc. as having a catching relation in common and varying only in the individuals caught; but what of lion-hunting, rabbit-hunting, etc.? If any common relation is to be recognized here, the varying objects of the relation must evidently be taken not as individuals but as kinds. Yet not kinds in the sense of classes, for then unicorn-hunting would cease to differ from griffin-hunting. Kinds rather in the sense of attributes.

[29] W. V. O. Quine, *Review of Metaphysics* 2 (1948), 30-31.

Some further supposed abstract objects that are like attributes with respect to the identity problem, are the *propositions* — in the sense of entities that somehow correspond to sentences as attributes correspond to predicates. Now if attributes clamor for recognition as objects of the attributary attitudes, so do propositions as objects of the propositional attitudes: believing, wishing, and the rest.[30]

Not that Quine feels that the identity problem has been solved for such abstract entities as properties and propositions: he does not. Nevertheless, he is now ready to admit them into semantic analysis as a curious kind of 'half-entity'. He writes: 'We might keep attributes and propositions after all, but just not try to cope with the problem of their individuation .... Why not just accept them thus, as twilight half-entities to which the identity concept is not to apply?'[31] Abstract entities, then, have recently come to gain favor even with one of their most determined critics.

Among contemporary semanticists, Alonzo Church probably argues most strongly for the need for abstract entities in semantics. Defining the task which any reasonably complete semantical theory must set itself, Church writes as follows:

Let us take it as our purpose to provide an abstract theory of the actual use of language for human communication — not a factual or historical report of what has been observed to take place, but a norm to which we may regard everyday linguistic behavior as an imprecise approximation, in the same way that e.g. elementary (applied) geometry is a norm to which we may regard as imprecise approximations the practical activity of the land-surveyor in laying out a plot of ground, or of the construction foreman as seeing that building plans are followed. We must demand of such a theory that it have a place for all observably informative kinds of communication — including such notoriously troublesome cases as belief statements, modal statements, conditions contrary to fact — or at least that it provide a (theoretically) workable substitute for them. And solutions must be available for puzzles about meaning which may arise, such as the so-called 'paradox of analysis'.[32]

The theory which Church takes to be most satisfactory for accomplishing these objectives, and which, he writes, 'seems to recommend itself above others for its relative simplicity, naturalness and explanatory power',[33] is a modification of Frege's semantic theory, which was based on the concepts of sense and denotation. Quine's scruples as regards

[30]   W. V. O. Quine, "Semantics and Abstract Objects", *Proceedings and Addresses of the American Philosophical Association* 31 (1957-1958), 19.
[31]   W. V. O. Quine, "Semantics and Abstract Objects", 20.
[32]   Alonzo Church, "The Need for Abstract Entities in Semantic Analysis", *Proceedings of the American Academy of Arts and Sciences* 80 (1951), 100-01.
[33]   Alonzo Church, "The Need for Abstract Entities in Semantic Analysis".

meanings are on this proposed theory laid aside; meanings are embraced whole-heartedly. Briefly, this modification of Frege's theory, which is due to Church, has as its principal features the following:[34] Every name in the language being investigated is regarded as having both a DENOTATION and a SENSE; a name is said to denote its DENOTATION, and to EXPRESS its sense. The term 'name' is taken in a broad sense, so as to include under it not only individual constants, but also predicates and sentences. Proper names are taken to denote individuals; predicate expressions are taken to denote the classes of *n*-tuples of individuals to which they apply; and sentences are said to denote their own truth-values, viz., truth or false-hood. Sense of names are said to be CONCEPTS of the denotations of these names. Thus, the sense of an individual constant is an INDIVIDUAL-CONCEPT; the sense of a one-place predicate constant is a CLASS-CONCEPT, which is taken to be a property; and the sense of a sentence is a TRUTH-VALUE-CONCEPT, taken to be a PROPOSITION.

There is, further, a second type of meaningful expression under this theory, viz. the class of FORMS. A name is defined as a meaningful expres-sion without free variables; any expression which differs from a name only in possessing free variables at certain of the places where that name possesses constants, is said to be a FORM. Now every variable possesses not only a range, but also a *sense-range*, which is the class of the senses of the admissible substituents for that variable. A form is then said to have not only a VALUE for every admissible assignment to its free variables, but also a SENSE-VALUE corresponding to each of its values. Thus, while a name has a unique denotation and a unique sense, corresponding to each form there is on the one hand a whole class of values, and on the other hand a whole class of sense-values. We may say, then, that both names and forms are assigned two types of meaning, in parallel fashion.

In order to handle NON-EXTENSIONAL, or OBLIQUE, contexts, — e.g. con-texts of the form 'believes that ...', 'thinks that ...' — further distinc-tions are introduced.[35] Church agrees with Frege that if a name is used in both ordinary and oblique contexts, it does not have the same denotation in the latter contexts as it does in the former; in oblique contexts, the denotation of a name is taken to be its usual sense. Thus, for example, in the sentence 'John believes that the world is round', the denotation of the expression 'the world is round' is not the truth-value of that expression, but its usual sense; viz. the proposition that the world is round. However, Church regards it as a desideratum — in a formalized system, at least — that every name have but one denotation and one sense. Thus, he proposes that rather than follow Frege, and use a given name both in ordinary and oblique contexts, a second name be chosen to be used in the case of the

[34] Alonzo Church, "The Need for Abstract Entities in Semantic Analysis", 101-04.
[35] A. Church, "A Review of Quine", *The Journal of Symbolic Logic* 8 (1943), 45-47.

oblique contexts. That second name will have as its denotation the sense of the first name. This second name will itself have a sense; this sense will have a name; and so on. When applied to the analysis of oblique contexts, Church's semantical approach thus becomes exceedingly complex.

Senses, that is, concepts, are of course abstract in nature. Further, as Church thinks of them, they are as independent of language as are denotations. Church writes:

A concept in this sense is not to be thought of as associated with any particular language or system of notation, since names in different languages may express the same sense (or concept). We suppose that a concept may in some sense exist even if there is no language in actual use that contains a name expressing this concept. And we even wish to admit a non-denumerable infinity of concepts — thus more concepts than there can be names to express in any one actual language.[36]

That this theory involves a considerable commitment to abstract entities is evident. It is Church's opinion, however, that the extent to which a theory is committed to such entities is but one of the criteria by which its worth is to be judged. Others include workability and generality. Taking all these considerations together, Church contends that his theory, though surely open to possible correction or modification, is worth investigation. Complex though it is, 'the problems which give rise to the proposal are difficult and a simpler theory is not known to be possible'.[37]

University of Colorado, Boulder, Colorado, U.S.A.

---

[36] A. Church, "A Formulation of the Logic of Sense and Denotation", *Structure, Meaning and Method*, ed. by P. Henle, (Liberal Arts Press, 1951), 11.
[37] A. Church, *Proceedings of the American Academy of Arts and Sciences* 80 (1951), 104.

W. V. O. Quine

TRUTH

TRUTH AND SATISFACTION

Logicians and grammarians are alike in habitually talking about sentences. But we saw the difference. The logician talks of sentences only as a means of achieving generality along a dimension that he cannot sweep out by quantifying over objects. The truth predicate then preserves his contact with the world, where his heart is.

Between logicians and grammarians there is a yet closer bond than the shared concern with sentences. Take in particular the artificial grammar of Chapter 2, which was made for logic. The relevance of such a grammar to logic is that logic explores the truth conditions of sentences in the light of how the sentences are grammatically constructed. Logic chases truth up the tree of grammar.

In particular the logic of truth functions chases truth up through two constructions, negation and conjunction, determining the truth values of the compounds from those of the constituents. Implicitly all truth functions get this treatment, thanks to iteration.

If logic traces truth conditions through the grammatical constructions, and the truth functions are among these constructions, truth-function logic is assured. And conversely, if logic is to be centrally concerned with tracing truth conditions through the grammatical constructions, an artificial grammar designed by logicians is bound to assign the truth functions a fundamental place among its constructions. The grammar that we

Reprinted from: W. V. O. Quine, *Philosophy of Logic* (Englewood, Prentice-Hall, 1970), 35-46 (= Chapter 3).

logicians are tendentiously calling standard is a grammar designed with no other thought than to facilitate the tracing of truth conditions. And a very good thought this is.

We chose a standard grammar in which the simple sentences are got by predication, and all further sentences are generated from these by negation, conjunction, and existential quantification. Predication, in this grammar, consists always in adjoining predicates to variables and not to names. So all the simple sentences are OPEN sentences, like 'x walks' and '$x>y$'; they have free variables. Consequently they are neither true nor false; they are only satisfied by certain things, or pairs of things, or triples, etc. The open sentence 'x walks' is satisfied by each walker and nothing else. The open sentence '$x>y$' is satisfied by each descending pair of numbers and no other pairs.

Already at the bottom of the tree, thus, logic's pursuit of truth conditions encounters a complication. The relevant logical trait of negation is not just that negation makes true closed sentences out of false ones and vice versa. We must add that the negation of an open sentence with one variable is satisfied by just the things that that sentence was not satisfied by; also that the negation of an open sentence with two variables is satisfied by just the pairs that that sentence was not satisfied by; and so on.

I have taken to speaking of pairs. The pairs wanted are ORDERED pairs; that is, we must distinguish the pairs $\langle x, y \rangle$ and $\langle y, x \rangle$ so long as $x \neq y$. For we have to say that the pair $\langle 3, 5 \rangle$ satisfies '$x<y$' while $\langle 5, 3 \rangle$ does not. The law of ordered pairs is that if $\langle x, y \rangle = \langle z, w \rangle$ then $x = z$ and $y = w$. Beyond that the properties of the ordered pair are of no concern. If one wants to decide just what objects the ordered pairs are to be, one can decide it quite arbitrarily as long as the above law is fulfilled. One well-known way belongs to the elementary theory of finite classes, finite sets. To form the pair $\langle x, y \rangle$ we begin by forming the set $\{x, y\}$ whose members are x and y, and the set $\{x\}$ whose sole member is x. Then we explain $\langle x, y \rangle$ as the set $\{\{x\}, \{x, y\}\}$ whose members are the sets $\{x\}$ and $\{x, y\}$. This version of $\langle x, y \rangle$ is very artificial, but no matter. It is simple, and one easily shows that it fulfills the law of ordered pairs.

In thus construing ordered pairs we do not assume that within the standard language under discussion — the OBJECT LANGUAGE — the values of the variables include sets, nor that they include ordered pairs in any sense. The use I propose to make of ordered pairs proceeds wholly within the METALANGUAGE — the ordinary unformalized language in which I describe and discuss the object language. When I say that the pair $\langle 3, 5 \rangle$ satisfies the sentence '$x<y$', I am assuming for the time being that the sentence '$x<y$' belongs to the object language and that

the domain of objects of the object language includes the numbers 3 and 5; but I do not need to assume that this domain include their pair $\langle 3, 5 \rangle$. The pair belongs to the apparatus of my study of the object language, and this is enough.

Satisfaction of open sentences with three free variables calls for ordered triples, $\langle x, y, z \rangle$; and so on up. These triples, quadruples, and so on, are subject to the law that is the obvious extension of the law of pairs. Any definition of triples, quadruples, and the rest is acceptable so long as it fulfills this law. One easy way (though not the handiest for detailed work) is to iterate the pair. The triple $\langle x, y, z \rangle$ can be taken as the pair $\langle \langle x, y \rangle, z \rangle$, the quadruple $\langle x, y, z, x' \rangle$ can then be taken as the pair $\langle \langle x, y, z \rangle, x' \rangle$, and so on. This series of the pair, the triple, the quadruple, and so on, can do also with a head: the SINGLE $\langle x \rangle$, identifiable with x itself.

SATISFACTION BY SEQUENCES

Let us refer to singles, pairs, triples, and so on, collectively as SEQUENCES. This term will enable us to speak of the satisfaction of sentences in a briefer and more general way, by sparing us the need of considering each different number of variables separately. We may speak of a sequence as satisfying a sentence if the sentence comes out true when we take the first thing of the sequence as the value of the variable 'x' in the sentence, and the second thing of the sequence as the value of the variable 'y' in the sentence, and so on, ticking the variables off in alphabetical order: 'x', 'y', 'z', 'x'', etc.

Thus take the open sentence 'x conquered y'. (Strictly speaking, not to complicate our logical grammar with tense, we should think of the predicate 'conquered' as meaning, tenselessly, 'conquereth at some time'.) This open sentence is satisfied by the pair $\langle$Caesar, Gaul$\rangle$; for 'x' and 'y' are the first and second variables of the alphabet, and Caesar and Gaul are the first and second things in the pair, and Caesar conquered Gaul.

This formulation allows the length of the sequence to exceed the number of variables in the sentence. The things in the sequence corresponding to missing variables simply have no effect. For instance, the sentence 'x conquered y' is satisfied by the sequence $\langle$Caesar, Gaul, $a\rangle$ for any a; it is only the first two places of the sequence that are relevant to 'x conquered y'.

It goes naturally with this convention, moreover, to speak of any sentence simply as TRUE when it is true for all values of its free variables and thus satisfied by all sequences. Thus '$x = x$' counts as true. This convention will save us some tedious clauses in subsequent pages. And let us call a sentence FALSE when false for all values.

A technical question arises when a sequence is too short to reach all the variables of a sentence. The most convenient ruling is this: when a sequence has fewer than i places, define its ith element as identical with its last element — as if this were repeated over and over.[1] Thus the sentence '$x \leq y$' is satisfied by the sequence $\langle 1 \rangle$, which is to say simply 1; for, it is satisfied by $\langle 1,1 \rangle$. In addition, in view of the second paragraph back, it is satisfied by $\langle 1,1, y \rangle$ for every choice of y.

The austerity of our standard grammar, which bans even names and functors, is a convenience insofar as we are concerned not to use a language but to talk about it. In use, names and functors are convenient. So austerity will prevail only in the object language, whose sentences 'x walks', '$x < y$', 'x conquered y', etc., I am talking about. In speaking of these austere sentences, and of what sequences satisfy them, I freely use our own conveniently less austere everyday language; hence names like 'Caesar' and 'Gaul', and compound singular terms like '$\langle$Caesar, Gaul$\rangle$'.

Still the sentences even of the object language do not all have free variables. The simple sentences do; closed simple sentences like 'Caesar conquered Gaul' are not available. But there are complex closed sentences, such as '$(\exists x)\ (\exists y)\ (x$ conquered $y)$'. So it is proper to ask, still, what sequences might be said to satisfy a closed sentence; and the answer is easy. Just as all but the first and second things in a sequence are irrelevant to 'x conquered y', so all the things in a sequence are irrelevant to a sentence devoid of free variables. Thus a closed sentence is satisfied by every sequence or none according simply as it is true or false.

This last remark applies indeed to open sentences as well as closed ones, thanks to the convention that we adopted a half page back. Every sequence satisfies every true sentence and no false one. The definition of TRUTH in terms of satisfaction is easy indeed: SATISFACTION BY ALL SEQUENCES. Satisfaction is the concept that the work goes into.

This work, to which we now turn, is due to Tarski except for minor details. It will be facilitated by our new apparatus of sequences and our accompanying conventions. Turning back now to the truth functions, we can say once for all that a sequence satisfies the negation of a given sentence if and only if it does not satisfy the given sentence. Similarly a sequence satisfies a conjunction if and only if it satisfies each of the sentences. We can say these things without regard to how long the sequences are and without regard to how many free variables the sentences have, if indeed any.

There is something artificial and arbitrary, one feels, about the appeal to alphabetical order of variables. A seemingly gratuitous difference is

[1] Here I am indebted to George Boolos and James A. Thomas.

thereby created between the open sentences 'x conquered y' and 'y conquered z'; ⟨Caesar, Gaul⟩ satisfies the one and not the other. Would we perhaps do better to appeal not to alphabetical order but to order of first appearance in the sentence? This way, ⟨Caesar, Gaul⟩ would satisfy 'x conquered y' and 'y conquered z' indifferently.

Conjunction holds the answer to this question. On our alphabetical approach, ⟨Caesar, Gaul, Brutus⟩ satisfies both 'x conquered y' and 'z killed x' and also therefore their conjunction 'x conquered y· z killed x'; all is thus in order. On the other approach, ⟨Caesar, Gaul⟩ would satisfy 'x conquered y'; ⟨Brutus, Caesar⟩ would satisfy 'z killed x'; and only a rather complicated rule of conjunction could lead us from these data to the desired conclusion, that ⟨Caesar, Gaul, Brutus⟩ satisfies 'x conquered y· z killed x'. It is alphabetical order, thus, that helps us pair up the variables across conjunctions. The difference between 'x conquered y' and 'y conquered z' is after all not gratuitous, when you think how differently they fare in conjunction with some further clause such as 'z killed x'.

We arrived at a compact statement of the satisfaction conditions of negations and conjunctions, relative to their constituents. The negation is satisfied by just the sequences that its constituent is not satisfied by, and the conjunction is satisfied by just the sequences that its constituents are both satisfied by. Now what of the remaining construction, existential quantification? An existential quantification consists of some sentence preceded by an existential quantifier whose variable is, say, the ith variable of the alphabet. This quantification, then, is satisfied by a given sequence if and only if the constituent sentence is satisfied by some sequence that matches this one except perhaps in its ith place.

For example, take '$(\exists y)$ (x conquered y)'. This is satisfied by a given sequence if and only if 'x conquered y' is satisfied by a sequence that matches the given one except perhaps in second place. Thus '$(\exists y)$ (x conquered y)' is true, as desired, of every sequence whose first thing is Caesar; we get this result because 'x conquered y' is satisfied by every sequence whose first and second things are Caesar and Gaul.

Note how our recent device for overlong sequences figures here. '$(\exists y)$ (x conquered y)' is satisfied by Caesar, that is, ⟨Caesar⟩, and by every prolongation of ⟨Caesar⟩; and 'x conquered y' is satisfied by every prolongation of ⟨Caesar, Gaul⟩.

TARSKI'S DEFINITION OF TRUTH

A reasonable way of explaining an expression is by saying what conditions make its various contexts true. Hence one is perhaps tempted to see the above satisfaction conditions as explaining negation, conjunction, and existential quantification. However, this view is untenable; it involves a vicious circle. The given satisfaction conditions for negation, conjunction, and quantification presuppose an understanding of the very signs they would explain, or of others to the same effect. A negation is explained as satisfied by a sequence when the constituent sentence is NOT satisfied by it; a conjunction is satisfied by a sequence when the one constituent sentence AND the other are satisfied by it; and an existential quantification is satisfied by a sequence when the constituent sentence is satisfied by SOME suitably similar sequence. If we are prepared to avail ourselves thus of 'not', 'and', and 'some' in the course of explaining negation, conjunction, and existential quantification, why not proceed more directly and just offer these words as direct translations?

Tarski, to whom the three satisfaction conditions are due, saw their purpose the other way around; not as explaining negation, conjunction, and quantification, which would be untenable, but as contributing to a definition of satisfaction itself and so, derivatively, of truth. To begin with, let us go back down and define satisfaction for the simple sentences, or predications. Here we shall have a definition corresponding to each predicate of the object language, as follows.

The sentence consisting of 'walks', accompanied by the alphabetically ith variable, is satisfied by a sequence if and only if the ith thing in the sequence walks.

The sentence consisting of 'conquered', flanked by the alphabetically ith and jth variables, is satisfied by a sequence if and only if the ith thing in the sequence conquered the jth.

Similarly for each further predicate, supposing them finite in number and listed. In this way, one is told what it means to say of any predication in the object language that it is satisfied by a given sequence of things. One is told this only insofar, of course, as one already understands the predicates themselves; for note how 'walks' and 'conquered' got reused in the explanatory parts of the above two paragraphs.

Sentences may be graded in point of complexity. Predications have complexity 0; negations and existential quantifications of sentences of complexity n have complexity $n+1$; and conjunctions have complexity $n+1$ if one of the constituents has complexity n and the other has n or less. What one was last told, then, was what it means for a sequence to satisfy a sentence of complexity 0. But then the satisfaction conditions for negation, conjunction, and existential quantification tell one what it means for a sequence to satisfy a sentence of next higher complexity, once one knows what it means for a sequence to satisfy a sentence of given complexity. So, step by step, one finds out what it means for a sequence to satisfy a sentence of any preassigned complexity. Complexity n, for each n, takes n such steps.

This plan affords a definition of satisfaction, for all sentences of the object language, which is RECURSIVE or INDUCTIVE. Starting with simple cases and building up, it sets forth, case by case, the circumstances in which to say that a sequence satisfies a sentence. Let us review this inductive definition schematically. Let us call the *i*th variable of the alphabet var(*i*). Let the *i*th thing in any sequence x be x_i. Then, if we think of '*A*' as one of the one-place predicates of the object language, the inductive definition of satisfaction begins thus:

(1) For all i and x: x satisfies '*A*' followed by var(*i*) if and only if Ax_i.

There is such a clause for each one-place predicate in the lexicon. Similarly for each two-place predicate, '*B*' say:

(2) For all i, j, and x: x satisfies '*B*' followed by var(*i*) and var(*j*) if and only if Bx_ix_j.

After making such a provision for each predicate in the lexicon, the recursive definition concludes as follows.

(3) For all sequences x and sentences y: x satisfies the negation of y if and only if x does not satisfy y.

(4) For all sequences x and sentences y and y': x satisfies the conjunction of y and y' if and only if x satisfies y and x satisfies y'.

(5) For all x, y, and i: x satisfies the existential quantification of y with respect to var(*i*) if and only if y is satisfied by some sequence x' such that $x_j = x_j'$ for all $j \neq i$.

Taken altogether, the inductive definition tells us what it is for a sequence to satisfy a sentence of the object language. Incidentally it affords a definition also of truth, since, as lately noted, this just means being satisfied by all sequences.

Definitions come in two grades. At its best, definition enables us to eliminate and dispense with the defined expression. Some definitions accomplish this by specifying a substitute expression outright. An example is the definition of '5' as '4 + 1', or of the universal quantifier '(x)' as '$\sim(\exists x)\sim$'. Some definitions accomplish it rather by showing how to paraphrase all contexts of the defined expression. An example is definition of the particle 'or' of alternation by systematically explaining all its immediate context, '*p* or *q*' in form, as '$\sim(\sim p \cdot \sim q)$'. This definition offers no direct substitute for the particle 'or' itself, but still it serves to eliminate that particle wherever it might appear. Definition of either sort is called DIRECT definition, and constitutes the higher grade.

Definition in the lower grade, on the other hand, does not eliminate. Still it completely fixes the use of the defined expression. Our inductive definition of satisfaction is of this kind. It SETTLES JUST WHAT SEQUENCES SATISFY EACH SENTENCE, but it does not show how to eliminate 'x satisfies y' with variable x and y.

With help of some heavy equipment from set theory, we can raise the one grade of definition to the other. We can define 'satisfies' directly and eliminably, granted set-theoretic resources. The reasoning is as follows.

We may think of a RELATION as a set of ordered pairs. The satisfaction relation is the set of all pairs $\langle x, y \rangle$ such that x satisfies y. Now the inductive definition (1)-(5) does settle just what pairs $\langle x, y \rangle$ belong to the satisfaction relation; for, note the sentence lately italicized. If, bringing in a variable 'z', we modify (1)-(5) to the extent of writing 'bears the relation z to' instead of 'satisfies', then the stipulations (1)-(5) thus modified compel z to be the satisfaction relation. If we abbreviate (1)-(5), thus modified, as 'SRz', then 'SRz' says in effect 'z is the satisfaction relation'. But now we have a direct definition of 'x satisfies y' after all. We can write 'x bears z to y' as '$\langle x, y \rangle \in z$' and then put '$x$ satisfies y' thus:

(6) $(\exists z)(\text{SR}z \cdot \langle x, y \rangle \in z)$.

PARADOX IN THE OBJECT LANGUAGE

We have arrived at a direct definition, (6), of satisfaction. In formulating it we have not limited ourselves to the means available within the object language with which this relation of satisfaction has to do. Let us next consider the possibility of reconstructing this definition within the object language itself. If we reckon the predicate '$\in$' of set theory to the lexicon of the object language, then all of (6) except the heavy clause 'SRz' goes over into the object language without a hitch. Even the complex term '$\langle x, y \rangle$' resolves out, through contextual definitions that I shall not pause over. In the end (6) expands into just '$\in$', variables, truth functions, quantification, AND 'SRz'. The requisite steps are evident from various logic and set-theory texts.

What now of 'SRz'? Its needs are just the needs of (1)-(5), minus 'satisfies' (which gave way everywhere to '$\in z$'). Scanning (1)-(5), we see that we shall need not only to use but to talk ABOUT various simple and complex expressions: predicates, variables, negations, conjunctions, quantifiers; also that we shall need to talk of sequences and numbers, and to specify variables numerically, and to specify positions in sequences numerically. Now the talk of sequences and of numbers can be got down to set theory — ultimately to '∈', variables, truth functions, and quantifiers again. Similarly for identity, used in (5). As for the talk of expressions, it can be got down to these same elements plus a modest lexicon of special predicates for spelling. One of these is a three-place predicate 'C' of concatenation: '$Cxyz$' means that x, y, and z are strings of signs and that x consists of y followed by z. The others are one-place predicates each of which identifies a single sign; thus 'Ax' might mean that x is the accent, 'Lx' might mean that x is the left-hand parenthesis, and so on. Passing over a mass of detail that is available elsewhere[2] to the interested reader, I shall simply report that 'SRz' reduces to this modest lexicon of predicates — '∈', 'C', 'A', 'L', and the rest — together with variables, truth functions, and quantification.

As a point of curiosity, I might remark that by an artifice of Gödel's we can even reduce this lexicon of predicates to '∈' alone. The artifice consists in letting positive integers go proxy for signs and strings of signs. Thus suppose, to make it easy, that our alphabet of signs runs to nine or fewer. We can arbitrarily identify these with the numbers from 1 to 9, and then identify each string of signs with the number expressed by the corresponding string of digits. By this indirection we can accomplish all the work of the spelling predicates 'C', 'A', 'L', etc., in arithmetical terms; and the arithmetic boils down in turn to '∈', variables, truth functions, and quantification.

With or without this last refinement, we can see 'SRz' into the object language with its standard grammar and a specifiable lexicon of predicates. And so, through (6), 'x satisfies y' gets translated into the object language.

This news sounds cheerful, but we shall soon find cause to fret over it. Consider Grelling's paradox, commonly known as the heterological paradox. It can be phrased as having to do with open sentences in a single variable. All sorts of things can satisfy these sentences. Sentences satisfy some of them. Some of them satisfy themselves. The open sentence 'x is short' is a short sentence and thus satisfies itself. The open sentence 'x satisfies some sentences' satisfies some sentences and thus satisfies itself. Also many open sentences fail to satisfy themselves. Examples: 'x is long'; 'x is German'; 'nothing satisfies x'. Now try the open sentence 'x does not satisfy itself'. Clearly if it satisfies itself it does not, and vice versa.

This shows that 'x does not satisfy itself' must not get into the object language. For the object language already had, in its spelling predicates, the machinery by which to specify any of its own strings of signs as objects for its variables to refer to. If one of these strings of signs were

---

[2] For example, in my *Mathematical Logic*, last chapter. But note that the ideas in the present section and the preceding two are Tarski's except for detail.

'x does not satisfy itself', or rather the full expansion thereof into the basic notation, then, by taking that very string of signs as the object to be referred to by 'x', we would get the contradiction.

But we just previously concluded that 'x satisfies y' is translatable into the object language, as a straightforward open sentence. But then '$\sim(x$ satisfies $x)$', or 'x does not satisfy itself', is translatable equally. Apparently then we are caught in contradiction.

RESOLUTION IN SET THEORY

Its resolution lies in set theory. The inductive definition represented by (1)-(5) was all right, and can be translated wholly into the object language except of course for the new term that is being inductively defined — the verb 'satisfies'. Accordingly 'SRz', which we get from (1)-(5) by dropping that verb and supplying 'z', is fully translatable into the object language. Moreover, 'SRz' does indeed require of z that its member pairs be precisely the pairs $\langle x, y \rangle$ such that x satisfies y. So far so good. But IS THERE a set z meeting this requirement? If so, (6) serves its purpose of defining 'x satisfies y'; if not, (6) is simply false for all x and y. And the answer is indeed negative, by *reductio ad absurdum*; there is no such set z, or we would be back in Grelling's contradiction.

The general question what sets there are has been long and notoriously unsettled. An open sentence is said to determine a set if the sentence is true of all and only the members of the set. It is common sense to consider that we have specified the set when we have given the sentence; hence that every open sentence determines a set. But the paradoxes of set theory, notably Russell's, teach us otherwise; the sentence '$\sim(x \in x)$' determines no set. If there were such a set, it would have to be a member of itself if and only if not a member of itself.

So the set theorist has to try to settle which open sentences still to regard as determining sets. Different choices give different set theories, some stronger than others. When we accorded '$\in$' to the lexicon of our object language, we left open the question how strong a set theory was to go with it. But of this we can now be sure: it cannot, consistently with the rest of the object language, be a set theory containing a set z such that SRz.

Tarski's work thus forges a new link between the so-called semantical paradoxes, of which Grelling's is the prime example, and the set-theoretic paradoxes, of which Russell's is the prime example. At any rate we have been forced by Grelling's paradox to repudiate a supposed set z. But it should be noted that this repudiation is a weaker paradox than Russell's in this respect: the z that it repudiates was not a set that was purportedly determined by any open sentence expressible in the object language. It purported indeed to be the set of all pairs $\langle x, y \rangle$ such that x satisfies y, and so it purported indeed to be determined by the open sentence 'x satisfies y'. But this is not a sentence of the object language. As Grelling's paradox has taught us, it is untranslatable foreign language.

We can still accept 'x satisfies y' as a sentence of the meta-language, and at that level we can even accept it as determining a set z. On these terms, (6) is acceptable still as defining 'x satisfies y'; but as defining it in the metalanguage for the object language. The metalanguage can tolerate a stronger set theory than the object language can; it can tolerate a set z such that SRz.

It should be mentioned that the resistance of a language to its satisfaction predicate is not absolute. A language can contain its own satisfaction predicate and truth predicate with impunity if, unlike what we have considered, it is weak in auxiliary devices that would be needed in reaping the contradiction.[3]

[3] There is an example in John R. Myhill, "A complete theory of natural rational, and real numbers", *Journal of Symbolic Logic* 15 (1950), 185-96.

Richard Montague

ENGLISH AS A FORMAL LANGUAGE

1. INTRODUCTION[1]

I reject the contention that an important theoretical difference exists between formal and natural languages. On the other hand, I do not regard as successful the formal treatments of natural languages attempted by certain contemporary linguists. Like Donald Davidson[2] I regard the construction of a theory of truth — or rather, of the more general notion of truth under an arbitrary interpretation — as the basic goal of serious syntax and semantics; and the developments emanating from the Massachusetts Institute of Technology offer little promise towards that end.

In the present paper I shall accordingly present a precise treatment, culminating in a theory of truth, a formal language that I believe may be reasonably regarded as a fragment of ordinary English. I have restricted myself to a very limited fragment, partly because there are portions of English I do not yet know how to treat, but also for the sake of simplicity

Reprinted from: Bruno Visentini, et al., *Linguaggi nella societa e nella tecnica* (Milan, 1970), 189-223.
[1] Some of the ideas in the present paper were adumbrated in seminar lectures in Amsterdam in January and February of 1966 and in Los Angeles in March of 1968. An earlier version of the present paper was delivered at the University of British Columbia in July of 1968. Much of the work reported here was supported by U.S. National Science Foundation Grant GP-7706. I should like to express my appreciation, for valuable criticism and suggestions, to Professors Yehoshua Bar-Hillel, David Lewis, Terence Parsons, Barbara Hall Partee, Dana Scott, and J. F. Staal, Messrs. Donald Berkey, John Cooley, and Perry Smith, and especially my student Dr. J. A. W. Kamp, without whose suggestions the present paper would not have been possible.
[2] In Davidson (1970).

and the clear exposition of certain basic features. It is already known how to extend the treatment rather widely in various directions, and some of the extensions will be sketched in Part II of this paper;[3] the present fragment is, however, sufficiently comprehensive to illuminate the following features of English: its apparatus of quantification, the function of the definite article, the nature of ambiguity, and the role of adjectives and adverbs. The fragment may also hold some interest for those not concerned with natural languages; it provides an example of a fairly rich formal language — capable of accommodating modal operators, indirect contexts, and the definite article — not requiring for its interpretation a distinction between sense and denotation.

The treatment given here will be found to resemble the usual syntax and model theory (or semantics) of the predicate calculus,[4] but leans rather heavily on the intuitive aspects of certain recent developments in intensional logic.[5] In my semantic categories will be found echoes of the SYNTACTIC categories of Ajdukiewicz (1960) and in my syntactic rules traces of the observations in Chapters III and IV of Quine (1960). My treatment of quantification bears some resemblance to the rather differently motivated treatment in Bohnert and Backer (1967) — a work that certainly antedates mine, but with which I did not become acquainted until after completing the present development. An important aspect of the present treatment — the semantics of adjectives and adverbs[6] — is due independently to J. A. W. Kamp and Terence Parsons. neither of whom has yet published his work in this domain.

2. BASIC SYNTACTIC CATEGORIES

The basic, or unanalyzed, expressions of our formal language fall into the following nine categories, $B_0, ..., B_8$.

B_0 (or the set of BASIC NAME PHRASES) consists of all proper nouns of English, together with the symbols $v_0, ..., v_n, ...$, which are known as (individual) VARIABLES.[7]

---

[3] [Part II is not reprinted here. Ed.]
[4] The model theory of the predicate calculus is of course due to Alfred Tarski; see for instance Tarski (1936, 1952, and 1954).
[5] In particular, those of Montague (1970).
[6] It is Donald Davidson who, in Davidson (1967a, b) has emphasized that adverbs appear to present special problems.
[7] Thus v_n is to be THE nth VARIABLE (of the object language). Strictly speaking, then, the expressions 'v_0', 'v_1', and the like are not variables but metalinguistic names of object language variables. (We need not specify the exact form of the latter, but it would certainly be possible to do so; for instance, v_n might be identified with the result of appending n primes to the letter 'x'.)

B_1 (or the set of BASIC FORMULAS) $= \{\ulcorner\text{it rains}\urcorner\}$.[8]

B_2 (or the set of BASIC ONE-PLACE VERB PHRASES) $= \{\ulcorner\text{walks}\urcorner\}$.

B_3 (or the set of BASIC TWO-PLACE VERB PHRASES) $= \{\ulcorner\text{walks}\urcorner, \ulcorner\text{loves}\urcorner, \ulcorner\text{cuts}\urcorner, \ulcorner\text{is}\urcorner\}$.

B_4 (or the set of BASIC COMMON NOUN PHRASES) consists of all common nouns of English (as listed, say, in some standard dictionary), together with the phrase $\ulcorner\text{brother of } v_0\urcorner$.

B_5 (or the set of BASIC ADFORMULA PHRASES) $= \{\ulcorner\text{not}\urcorner, \ulcorner\text{necessarily}\urcorner, \ulcorner v_0 \text{ believes that}\urcorner\}$.

B_6 (or the set of BASIC AD-ONE-VERB PHRASES) $= \{\ulcorner\text{rapidly}\urcorner, \ulcorner\text{in } v_0\urcorner, \ulcorner\text{with } v_0\urcorner, \ulcorner\text{through } v_0\urcorner, \ulcorner\text{between } v_0 \text{ and } v_1\urcorner\}$.

B_7 (or the set of BASIC AD-TWO-VERB PHRASES) $= B_6$.

B_8 (or the set of BASIC ADJECTIVE PHRASES) consists of all 'ordinary' descriptive adjectives of English (that is to say, with the exception of such 'indexical' adjectives as $\ulcorner\text{former}\urcorner$, such 'quantificational' adjectives as $\ulcorner\text{every}\urcorner$, $\ulcorner\text{most}\urcorner$, and $\ulcorner\text{three}\urcorner$, and adjectives of certain other exceptional varieties), together with the phrases $\ulcorner\text{bigger than } v_0\urcorner$, $\ulcorner\text{in } v_0\urcorner$, and $\ulcorner\text{between } v_0 \text{ and } v_1\urcorner$.

A few remarks are in order. We speak here of BASIC name phrases, BASIC formulas, and the like. This is because we shall later extend the categories $B_0, B_1, \ldots$ to sets $C_0, C_1, \ldots$, which will be regarded as the full categories of name phrases, of formulas, and so on.

Roughly speaking, basic one-place and two-place verb phrases (apart from $\ulcorner\text{is}\urcorner$), are what one usually calls INTRANSITIVE and TRANSITIVE VERBS respectively. There are examples in English of three-place verb phrases, like $\ulcorner\text{gives}\urcorner$, and possibly of verb phrases having a still greater number of places; but for simplicity we ignore these in our fragment. (In connection with a more highly inflected language such as Latin, the maximum number of places of verbs could perhaps be fixed more easily and naturally, as the number of CASES in the language that have uses associated with verbs; we thus exclude the vocative.) Notice that $\ulcorner\text{walks}\urcorner$ is both in-

---

[8] By $\{a\}$ I understand the unit set of a, by $\{a, \beta\}$ the set having the objects a and β as its only members, and so on. Corners (or quasi-quotes) are used in the manner of Quine [1]. Roughly speaking, the convention is this. If $\Gamma_0, \ldots, \Gamma_n$ are designatory expressions of the metalanguage (in particular, names of English expressions or variables referring to English expressions; we shall employ lower-case Greek letters as variables of this sort), then the expression

$$\ulcorner\Gamma_0, \ldots, \Gamma_n\urcorner$$

is to designate the concatenation of the expression to which $\Gamma_0, \ldots, \Gamma_n$ refers. If, however, any of $\Gamma_0, \ldots, \Gamma_n$ are not designatory expressions of the metalanguage but rather individual words of the object language, we first replace such words by their quotation names. For instance, if λ is an expression of English, then $\ulcorner\text{walks } \lambda\urcorner = \ulcorner\text{'walks' } \lambda\urcorner =$ the result of writing 'walks' followed by λ; $\ulcorner\text{walks}\urcorner = \ulcorner\text{'walks'}\urcorner = \text{'walks'}$; and $\ulcorner\text{it rains}\urcorner = \ulcorner\text{'it' 'rains'}\urcorner =$ the result of writing 'it' followed by 'rains' $=$ 'it rains'.

transitive (as in ⌜John walks rapidly⌝) and transitive (as in ⌜John walks a dog⌝). ⌜Cuts⌝ and ⌜loves⌝ also have intransitive uses, but for simplicity we ignore them.

Traditional grammar groups together modifiers of formulas, of verbs of various numbers of places, of adjectives, and of adverbs, and calls them all adverbs. It will be important, however, to distinguish these various sorts of modifiers. Accordingly, we shall speak of ADFORMULAS and ADVERBS, the latter in the narrow sense of modifiers of verbs, and sub-divided into AD-ONE-VERBS and AD-TWO-VERBS according as the verbs modified are of one or two places; and we could in an extension of the present fragment, speak of adadjectives, adad-one-verbs, adad-two-verbs, adadadjectives, adadad-one-verbs, and adadad-two-verbs as well. (The word ⌜very⌝ would for instance belong to all of these categories.) It may seem artificial, in view of the coincidence of the categories B_6 and B_7, to introduce them both; and it is perhaps not really necessary to do so in the present context. (It has, however, been suggested that ⌜and conversely⌝ appears to qualify as an ad-two-verb that is not an ad-one-verb.) Still, it is certainly possible to imagine languages in which it would be highly desirable on semantic grounds to countenance two coextensive syntactic categories.

3. SEMANTIC CATEGORIES

In the following we think of A as the set of possible individuals to which our object language refers and I as the set of possible worlds. We consider now the possible denotations of English expressions relative to A and I; these will fall into nine categories $U_{0,A,I}, ..., U_{8,A,I}$, corresponding to the syntactic categories $B_0, ..., B_8$. (I shall, however, generally suppress the subscripts 'A' and 'I', and write simply 'U_0', ..., 'U_8'.)

Fundamental categories

U_0 (or the universe of possible denotations of name phrases, relative to A and I) $= A$.

U_1 (or the universe of possible denotations of formulas) $= 2^I$.

(Here we use two common set-theoretical notations. The number 2 is identified with the set $\{0, 1\}$; and if X, Y are any sets, X^Y is to be the set of functions with domain Y and range included in X. Further, we identify 0 and 1 with the respective truth values falsehood and truth; thus U_1 becomes the set of all functions from possible worlds to truth values, that is, the set of all PROPOSITIONS [relative to I].)

Derived categories

All other semantic categories to be considered will have the form $V_0^{V_1 \times \cdots \times V_n}$, where $n \geq 1$ and $V_0, \ldots, V_n$ are themselves semantic categories. (By $V_1 \times \ldots \times V_n$ is understood the Cartesian product of the sets $V_1, \ldots, V_n$, that is, the set of ordered n-tuples of which the respective constituents are members of $V_1, \ldots, V_n$; thus $V_0^{V_1 \times \cdots \times V_n}$ is the set of n-place functions with arguments drawn from $V_1, \ldots, V_n$ respectively and with values in V_0.) Not every such combination generated by the fundamental categories is exemplified in English, and still fewer are exemplified in the fragment we treat here. In particular, we consider the following seven additional categories.

U_2 (or the universe of possible denotations of one-place verb phrases) $=$ $U_1^{U_0}$.

(The members of U_2 are thus what we might regard as PROPERTIES of individuals, or, as we shall sometimes say, one-place PREDICATES of individuals.[9])

U_3 (or the universe of possible denotations of two-place verb phrases) $=$ $U_1^{U_0 \times U_0}$.

(The members of U_3 are thus two-place RELATIONS-IN-INTENSION, or PREDICATES, of individuals.)

U_4 (or the universe of possible denotations of common noun phrases) $=$ $U_1^{U_0} (= U_2)$.
U_5 (or the universe of possible denotations of adformula phrases) $= U_1^{U_1}$.
U_6 (or the universe of possible denotations of ad-one-verb phrases) $=$ $U_2^{U_2}$.
U_7 (or the universe of possible denotations of ad-two-verb phrases) $=$ $U_3^{U_3}$.
U_8 (or the universe of possible denotations of adjective phrases) $= U_4^{U_4}$.

4. MODELS

A MODEL is an ordered 11-tuple $\langle A, I, G_0, \ldots, G_8 \rangle$ such that (1) A is a set containing at least two elements,[10] (2) I is a nonempty set, and (3) $G_0, \ldots, G_8$ are functions assigning appropriate denotation functions to the member of $B_0, \ldots, B_8$ respectively.

[9] The present notion of a property, as well as those of a relation-in-intension and a proposition, are essentially those of Kripke (1963).
[10] This assumption is for convenience only. We could manage with assuming simply that A is nonempty, but the stronger assumption somewhat simplifies a few definitions given below and explicitly noted.

I shall of course spell out clause (3) in exact terms. The idea is this. We have supplemented the 'usual' basic expressions of English by expressions containing free variables. Such an expression will not in general denote anything in an absolute sense, but only WITH RESPECT TO a given infinite sequence of individuals. This sequence will provide the values of all variables, and in such a way that the nth constituent of the sequence will be regarded as the value of v_n. Thus a model should assign to a basic expression not a denotation but a DENOTATION FUNCTION, that is, a function that maps each infinite sequence of individuals onto a possible denotation of the expression. The exact clauses corresponding to (3) are accordingly the following. (As above, A and I are regarded as the sets of possible individuals and possible worlds respectively. Recall also that in set-theoretical usage ω is the set of natural numbers; hence A^ω is the set of infinite sequences of members of A.)

(3a) $G_0, ..., G_8$ are functions with the respective domains $B_0, ..., B_8$.

(3b) $G_0(a) \in U_0{}^{A\omega}$ whenever $a \in B_0$; ...; $G_8(a) \in U_8{}^{A\omega}$ whenever $a \in B_8$.

(3c) If H is any one of $G_0, ..., G_8$, a is in the domain of H, x and y are in A_ω, and $x_n = y_n$ for all n such that v_n occurs in a, then $H(a)(x) = H(a)(y)$. (Thus although each denotation function, regarded as a function on individuals, is infinitary, its value will always be determined by the arguments occupying a certain finite set of argument places — and indeed, just those places that correspond to variables of the corresponding expression.)

The remaining clauses require that certain definite denotation functions be assigned to certain basic expressions, in particular, variables, ⌜is⌝, ⌜not⌝, ⌜entity⌝, and ⌜necessarily⌝, which are thus treated as logically determinate.

(3d) $G_0(v_n)$ is that function f in $A^{A\omega}$ such that, for all $x \in A^\omega, f(x) = x_n$.

(3e) G_3 (⌜is⌝) is that function f in $((2^I)^{A \times A})^{A\omega}$ such that, for all $x \in A^\omega$, all $t, u \in A$, and all $i \in I, f(x)(t, u)(i) = 1$ if and only if $t = u$.

(3f) G_4 (⌜entity⌝) is that function f in $((2^I)^A)^{A\omega}$ such that, for all $x \in A^\omega$, all $t \in A$, and all $i \in I$, $f(x)(t)(i) = 1$. (Thus with respect to every infinite sequence ⌜entity⌝ denotes the universal property of individuals.)

(3g) G_5 (⌜not⌝) is that function f in $((2^I)^{2^I})^{A\omega}$ such that for all $x \in A^\omega$, all $p \in 2^I$, and all $i \in I, f(x)(p)(i) = 1$ if and only if $p(i) = 0$.

(3h) G_5 (⌜necessarily⌝) is that function f in $((2^I)^{2^I})^{A\omega}$ such that for all $x \in A^\omega$, all $p \in 2^I$, and all $i \in I$, $f(x)(p)(i) = 1$ if and only if $p(j) = 1$ for all $j \in I$. (We thus employ STANDARD, or UNIVERSAL, or LEIBNIZIAN necessity, amounting to truth in all possible worlds.)

It is because the categories of basic expressions overlap that we must have separate functions $G_0, \ldots, G_8$, rather than a single function assigning denotation functions to all basic expressions.

5. SYNTACTIC CATEGORIES

In this section we shall extend the basic syntactic categories $B_0, B_1, \ldots, B_8$ to the full syntactic categories C_0 (or the set of name phrases), C_1 (or the set of formulas), ..., C_8 (or the set of adjective phrases). These sets will be 'introduced', in a sense that will be made precise below, by the following SYNTACTICAL (or GRAMMATICAL) *rules*, S1-S17; let it only be said that $C_0, \ldots, C_8$ will be defined in such a way as to make S1-S17 true. (I use '&' as an abbreviation of 'and' and '$\rightarrow$' as an abbreviation 'if ... then').

Rule of basic expressions:

S1. $B_0 \subseteq C_0, \ldots, B_8 \subseteq C_8$.

Rules corresponding to functional application:

S2. $\delta \in C_2$ & $a \in C_0$ & $\langle \delta, a, \varphi \rangle \in R_2 \rightarrow \varphi \in C_1$,

where R_2 is that three-place relation among expressions such that if δ, a, φ are any expressions, then δ, a, φ stand in the relation R_2 — that is, $\langle \delta, a, \varphi \rangle \in R_2$ — if and only if $\varphi = \ulcorner a\delta \urcorner$. (According to S2, if δ is a one-place verb phrase and a a name phrase, and $\varphi = \ulcorner a\,\delta \urcorner$, then φ is a formula. For example, if $\delta = \ulcorner \text{walks} \urcorner$ and $a = \ulcorner \text{John} \urcorner$, then $\ulcorner \text{John walks} \urcorner$ is a formula in view of S2.)

S3. $\delta \in C_3$ & $a, \beta, \in C_0$ & $\langle \delta, a, \beta, \varphi \rangle \in R_3 \rightarrow \varphi \in C_1$,

where $\langle \delta, a, \beta, \varphi \rangle \in R_3$ if and only if there exist a (possibly empty) expression μ and an expression $\gamma \in B_3$ such that $\delta = \ulcorner \gamma\,\mu \urcorner$ and $\varphi = \ulcorner a\,\gamma\,\beta\,\mu \urcorner$. (For example, if $\delta = \ulcorner \text{cuts} \urcorner$ and a, β are the respective variables v_0, v_1, then δ, a, β 'bear the relation R_3 to $\ulcorner v_0$ cuts $v_1 \urcorner$' — that is to say, $\langle \delta, a, \beta, \ulcorner v_0 \text{cuts } v_1 \urcorner \rangle \in R_3$ — and hence $\ulcorner v_0$ cuts $v_1 \urcorner$ is a formula. Also, if $\delta = \ulcorner \text{cuts rapidly} \urcorner$, then δ, v_0, v_1 bear the relation R_3 to $\ulcorner v_0$ cuts v_1 rapidly $\urcorner$. As far as the present fragment is concerned, we could replace the 'syntactical relations' R_2-R_{17} by TOTAL FUNCTIONS, that is relations for which the last argument (the VALUE) is uniquely determined by the preceding arguments, and which are TOTAL in the sense that a value will exist for any choice of expressions[11] as occupants of the preced-

---

[11] I have used the word 'expression' without indicating its precise meaning. For our present purposes an expression (of the object language) could be understood as a

ing argument places. The former condition, of functionality, is indeed satisfied by the syntactical relations we consider, but would naturally and conveniently be violated in connection with languages having a more flexible word order than English, or indeed in connection with richer fragments of English that admit synonymous sets of expressions of various sorts. Most of our syntactical relations — for instance, R_3 — fail, on the other hand, to be total; but this feature is a pure convenience and could be eliminated at the expense of complicating their definitions.)

S4. $\delta \in C_5$ & $\varphi \in C_1$ & $\langle \delta, \varphi, \psi \rangle \in R_4 \to \psi \in C_1$,

where $\langle \delta, \varphi, \psi \rangle \in R_4$ if and only if either (i) $\delta \neq \ulcorner \text{not} \urcorner$ and $\ulcorner \delta \varphi \urcorner = \psi$, or (ii) $\delta = \ulcorner \text{not} \urcorner$, φ does not end with $\ulcorner \text{not} \urcorner$, and $\ulcorner \varphi \, \delta \urcorner = \psi$. (For instance, if $\varphi = \ulcorner \text{John loves Jane} \urcorner$, then $\ulcorner \text{necessarily John loves Jane} \urcorner$ and $\ulcorner \text{John loves Jane not} \urcorner$ are formulas according to S4. As the second example indicates, our fragment involves an archaic style of negation. The more modern form (for example, $\ulcorner \text{John does not love Jane} \urcorner$) involves certain complications that will be discussed later. The clause 'φ does not end with $\ulcorner \text{not} \urcorner$' in the characterization of R_4 is included in order to avoid double negations, but for simplicity is stronger than necessary for this purpose; it also prevents the formation of such combinations as $\ulcorner \text{John loves a woman such that that woman loves John not not} \urcorner$.)

S5. $\delta \in C_6$ & $\mu \in C_2$ & $\langle \delta, \mu, \nu \rangle \in R_5 \to \nu \in C_2$,

where $\langle \delta, \mu, \nu \rangle \in R_5$ if and only if $\nu = \ulcorner \mu \, \delta \urcorner$. (Thus the result of appending an ad-one-verb to a one-play verb phrase is a one-place verb phrase. For instance, the one-place verb phrase $\ulcorner \text{walks rapidly} \urcorner$ is 'obtained' by S5 from the one-place verb phrase $\ulcorner \text{walks} \urcorner$.)

S6. $\delta \in C_7$ & $\mu \in C_3$ & $\langle \delta, \mu, \nu \rangle \in R_6 \to \nu \in C_3$,

where $\langle \delta, \mu, \nu \rangle \in R_6$ if and only if $\ulcorner \mu \, \delta \urcorner = \nu$. (For instance, $\ulcorner \text{cuts with } v_0 \urcorner$ is obtained by S6 from $\ulcorner \text{cuts} \urcorner$.)

S7. $\delta \in C_8$ & $\zeta \in C_4$ & $\langle \delta, \zeta, \eta \rangle \in R_7 \to \eta \in C_4$,

where $\langle \delta, \zeta, \eta \rangle \in R_7$ if and only if either δ is one word long and $\eta = \ulcorner \delta \, \zeta \urcorner$, or δ is not one word long and $\eta = \ulcorner \zeta \, \delta \urcorner$. (For instance, the common noun phrases $\ulcorner \text{big house} \urcorner$ and $\ulcorner \text{house between } v_0 \text{ and } v_1 \urcorner$ are obtained by S7 from the common noun phrase $\ulcorner \text{house} \urcorner$.)

---

finite and possibly empty concatenation of various words — in particular, the words (including variables) that make up basic expressions, together with the words $\ulcorner \text{every} \urcorner$, $\ulcorner \text{that} \urcorner$, $\ulcorner \text{a} \urcorner$, $\ulcorner \text{an} \urcorner$, and $\ulcorner \text{the} \urcorner$. A fairly obvious enlargement of the basic constituents of expressions would be necessary for the extensions of our present fragment that are proposed later.

Rules of substitution and quantification for formulas:

S8. $\varphi \in C_1$ & a, $\beta \in C_0$ & $\langle \varphi, a, \beta, \psi \rangle \in R_8 \to \psi \in C_1$,

where $\langle \varphi, a, \beta, \psi \rangle \in R_8$ if and only if a is a variable and ψ is obtained from φ by replacing all occurrences of a by β. (For instance, the formulas ⌜John walks through v_1⌝ and ⌜John walks through Amsterdam⌝ are obtained by S8 from the formula ⌜John walks through v_0⌝.)

S9. $\varphi \in C_1$ & $a \in C_0$ & $\zeta \in C_4$ & $\langle \varphi, a, \zeta, \psi \rangle \in R_9 \to \psi \in C_1$,

where $\langle \varphi, a, \zeta, \psi \rangle \in R_9$ if and only if a is a variable and ψ is obtained from φ by replacing the first occurrence of a by ⌜every ζ⌝ and all other occurrences of a by ⌜that η⌝, where η is the member of B_4 that occurs first in ζ. (For instance, the formulas ⌜every tall man in Amsterdam loves a woman such that that woman loves that man⌝ is obtained by S9 from the formula ⌜v_0 loves a woman such that that woman loves v_0⌝. It would be a little more natural to say ⌜every tall man in Amsterdam loves a woman such that that woman loves HIM⌝. Thus the phrase ⌜that η⌝, where η is a basic common noun phrase, plays the role of a pronoun, but is a little more flexible and avoids the complications associated with gender and case. As another example of S9, notice that ⌜every man loves that man⌝ can be obtained from ⌜v_0 loves v_0⌝; here it would be much more natural to say ⌜every man loves HIMSELF⌝. It would be quite possible to give rules providing for such locutions, but I decline to do so because of the rather uninteresting complications that would be involved).[12]

[12] There may, however, be some interest in the following tentative observation, which would be relevant to the formulation of such rules. If the first occurrence of a variable a in a formula φ is as the "subject" of a basic verb phrase, and ζ is a common noun phrase, then it appears that we may construct a "universal generalization" of φ (restricted to ζ) by replacing the first occurrence of a by ⌜every ζ⌝ and each other occurrence of a by a reflexive pronoun (⌜himself⌝, ⌜herself⌝, or ⌜itself⌝, depending on ζ) or an ordinary ⌜pronoun⌝ (⌜he, him⌝, ⌜she⌝, ⌜her⌝, ⌜it⌝, depending on considerations of gender and case), according as the occurrence of a in question does or does not stand as an argument of the same occurrence of a basic verb phrase as the first occurrence of a. Thus from ⌜v_0 loves v_0⌝, ⌜v_0 loves a woman such that that woman loves v_0⌝, and ⌜v_0 loves a woman such that v_0 knows that woman⌝ we may obtain ⌜every man loves himself⌝, ⌜every man loves a woman such that that woman loves him⌝, and ⌜every man loves a woman such that he knows that woman⌝ respectively; but from the second we may not obtain ⌜every man loves a woman such that that woman loves himself⌝. Also, the present rule will not allow us to obtain ⌜every man loves him⌝ from ⌜v_0 loves v_0⌝. This is as it should be; for although ⌜every man loves him⌝ is grammatically correct, it is not a universal generalization of ⌜v_0 loves v_0⌝.

The present rule, if, as appears somewhat doubtful, it is indeed accurate, would give us a way of distinguishing between those verb phrases that ought to be taken as basic and those that ought to be regarded as generated by simpler components. For instance, ⌜gives ... to⌝ could only be basic, because ⌜every man gives v_1 to himself⌝, and not ⌜every man gives v_1 to him⌝, is a universal generalization of ⌜v_0 gives v_1 to v_0⌝; the same comment would apply to ⌜sends ... to⌝. On the other hand, ⌜takes ... with⌝ would

S10. $\varphi \in C_1$ & $a \in C_0$ & $\zeta \in C_4$ & $\langle \varphi, a, \zeta, \psi \rangle \in R_{10} \rightarrow \psi \in C_1$,

where $\langle \varphi, a, \zeta, \psi \rangle \in R_{10}$ if and only if a is a variable and ψ is obtained from φ by replacing the first occurrence of a by $\ulcorner a\ \zeta \urcorner$ (or $\ulcorner an\ \zeta \urcorner$, according as ζ begins with a consonant or not) and all other occurrences of a by $\ulcorner that\ \eta \urcorner$, where η is the member of B_4 that occurs first in ζ. (For instance, the formulas $\ulcorner a$ woman in Amsterdam loves a man such that that man loves that woman$\urcorner$ and $\ulcorner$John is a man$\urcorner$ are obtained by S10 from the formulas $\ulcorner v_0$ loves a man such that that man loves $v_0 \urcorner$ and $\ulcorner$John is $v_1 \urcorner$ respectively.)

S11. $\varphi \in C_1$ & $a \in C_0$ & $\zeta \in C_4$ & $\langle \varphi, a, \zeta, \psi \rangle \in R_{11} \rightarrow \psi \in C_1$,

where $\langle \varphi, a, \zeta, \psi \rangle \in R_{11}$ if and only if a is a variable and ψ is obtained from φ by replacing the first occurrence of a by $\ulcorner the\ \zeta \urcorner$ and all other occurrences of a by $\ulcorner that\ \eta \urcorner$, where η is the member of B_4 that occurs first in ζ. (For instance, $\ulcorner the$ woman in Amsterdam loves a man such that that man loves that woman$\urcorner$ is obtained by S11 from $\ulcorner v_0$ loves a man such that that man loves $v_0 \urcorner$.)

Rules of substitution and quantification for common noun phrases:

S12. $\zeta \in C_4$ & $a, \beta, \in C_0$ & $\langle \zeta, a, \beta, \eta \rangle \in R_{12} \rightarrow \eta \in C_4$,

where $R_{12} = R_8$. (For instance, the common noun phrase $\ulcorner$brother of John$\urcorner$ is obtained by S12 from the common noun phrase $\ulcorner$brother of $v_0 \urcorner$.)

S13. $\zeta, \eta \in C_4$ & $a \in C_0$ & $\langle \eta, a, \zeta, \theta \rangle \in R_{13} \rightarrow \theta \in C_4$,

where $R_{13} = R_9$. (For instance, $\ulcorner$man such that that man loves every woman$\urcorner$ is obtained by S13 from $\ulcorner$man such that that man loves $v_1 \urcorner$.)

S14. $\zeta, \eta \in C_4$ & $a \in C_0$ & $\langle \eta, a, \zeta, \theta \rangle \in R_{14} \rightarrow \theta \in C_4$,

where $R_{14} = R_{10}$. (For instance, $\ulcorner$man such that that man loves a woman$\urcorner$ is obtained by S14 from $\ulcorner$man such that that man loves $v_1 \urcorner$.)

---

not be basic, because $\ulcorner v_0$ takes v_1 with $v_0 \urcorner$ has $\ulcorner$every man takes v_1 with him$\urcorner$ and not $\ulcorner$every man takes v_1 with himself$\urcorner$ as a universal generalization. In some cases, as with $\ulcorner v_0$ keeps v_1 near $v_0 \urcorner$, one feels that a correct universal generalization can be obtained in either way — that is, with the use of either a reflexive or an ordinary pronoun; this may be taken either as reflecting indecision as to whether $\ulcorner$keeps ... near$\urcorner$ is to be basic or as indicating that $\ulcorner v_0$ keeps v_1 near $v_0 \urcorner$ may be generated in two ways — either from a basic verb phrase $\ulcorner$keeps ... near$\urcorner$, or from $\ulcorner$keeps$\urcorner$ together with an adverbial phrase $\ulcorner$near $v_0 \urcorner$.

By way of clarification I should mention that in the tentative rule considered above we should understand 'argument' in such a way that v_0 qualifies as an argument of $\ulcorner$gives ... to$\urcorner$ in $\ulcorner v_0$ gives a book to $v_0 \urcorner$, $\ulcorner v_0$ gives the book to $v_0 \urcorner$, and $\ulcorner v_0$ gives every book to $v_0 \urcorner$ as well as in $\ulcorner v_0$ gives v_1 to $v_0 \urcorner$.

We have spoken about universal generalizations, which are introduced by S9; but completely parallel remarks could be made about the operations involved in S10, S11, S13-S16 below.

S15. ζ, $\eta \in C_4$ & $a \in C_0$ & $\langle \eta, a, \zeta, \theta \rangle \in R_{15} \rightarrow \theta \in C_4$,

where $R_{15} = R_{11}$. (For instance, $\ulcorner$man such that that man loves the woman in Amsterdam$\urcorner$ is obtained by S15 from $\ulcorner$man such that that man loves $v_1\urcorner$.)

Rule of relative clauses:

S16. $\zeta \in C_4$ & $\varphi \in C_1$ & $a \in C_0$ & $\langle \zeta, \varphi, a, \eta \rangle \in R_{16} \rightarrow \eta \in C_4$,

where $\langle \zeta, \varphi, a, \eta \rangle \in R_{16}$ if and only if a is a variable and $\eta = \ulcorner \zeta$ such that $\psi \urcorner$, where ψ comes from φ by replacing all occurrences of a by $\ulcorner$that $\theta \urcorner$ where θ is the member of B_4 that occurs first in ζ. (For instance, if $\zeta = \ulcorner$tall woman in Amsterdam$\urcorner$, $\varphi = \ulcorner v_0$ loves every man such that that man loves $v_0\urcorner$, and $a = v_0$, we obtain by S16 the common noun phrase $\ulcorner$tall woman in Amsterdam such that that woman loves every man such that that man loves that woman$\urcorner$. The latter could be more idiomatically formulated as $\ulcorner$tall woman in Amsterdam such that that woman loves every man such that that man loves HER$\urcorner$ — which, as intimated earlier, will be avoided because of the minor complications of gender and case it would introduce — or as $\ulcorner$tall woman in Amsterdam that loves every man such that that man loves that woman$\urcorner$, or, applying the same principle of formulation to the inner relative clause, as $\ulcorner$tall woman in Amsterdam that loves every man that loves that woman$\urcorner$. This usage too would involve complications that I should prefer here to avoid.)[13]

Rule of predicate adjectives:

S17. $a \in C_0$ & $\delta \in C_8$ & $\langle a, \delta, \varphi \rangle \in R_{17} \rightarrow \varphi \in C_1$,

[13] Let me indicate, briefly and rather vaguely, how to account for the last style of relative clause. It would perhaps be best to retain S16, because it is applicable to any formula φ whatever, and to add a rule of less generality having roughly the following content: if ζ is a common noun phrase, φ is a formula, a is a variable occurring in φ, and the first occurrence of a in φ is as an argument of the main occurrence of a verb phrase in φ, then ζ $\ulcorner$that $\delta \urcorner$ is a common noun phrase, where δ comes from φ by deleting the first occurrence of a and replacing all other occurrences of a by $\ulcorner$that $\theta \urcorner$, where θ is the basic common noun phrase that occurs first in ζ. By this rule we could obtain the last example in the text, as well as the common noun phrase $\ulcorner$woman that John loves$\urcorner$. The fourth hypothesis of the rule is required to avoid such ungrammatical combinations as $\ulcorner$room that John walks through$\urcorner$ (traditionally a borderline case of grammaticality), $\ulcorner$man that a brother of is tall$\urcorner$, $\ulcorner$city that Amsterdam is between and Paris,$\urcorner$ and $\ulcorner$man that a woman that loves is tall$\urcorner$. The complications connected with the present rule all derive from its fourth hypothesis, and have to do with precisely characterizing the notions of an ARGUMENT and a MAIN OCCURRENCE OF A VERB PHRASE; for an analogous situation see the discussion below of modern negation and the MAIN OCCURRENCE OF A VERB.

I should perhaps mention that S16 leads to such "vacuous" common noun phrases as $\ulcorner$woman such that John loves Mary$\urcorner$. It would be easy enough to exclude them, simply by adding 'a occurs in φ' to the characterization of R_{16}; but there seems to be no particular point in doing so.

where $\langle a, \delta, \varphi \rangle \in R_{17}$ if and only if $\varphi = \ulcorner a$ is $\delta \urcorner$. (For example, we obtain by S17 the formulas $\ulcorner$John is big$\urcorner$ and $\ulcorner$John is in $v_0\urcorner$.)

Having stated the syntactical rules, we now address ourselves to their precise rôle. The following theorem, due in large part to Mr. Perry Smith, has a simple proof that will not be given here.

Theorem. There is exactly one 'minimal sequence' of sets satisfying S1–S17 — that is, exactly one sequence $\langle C_0, ..., C_8 \rangle$ such that S1–S17 hold for $C_0, ..., C_8$ and such that, for every sequence $\langle D_0, ..., D_8 \rangle$, if S1–S17 hold for $D_0, ..., D_8$ (taken in place of $C_0, ..., C_8$ respectively), then $C_0 \subseteq D_0, ..., C_8 \subseteq D_8$.

We are now in a position to define in an exact way the full syntactic categories $C_0, ..., C_8$: C_0 (or the set of NAME PHRASES), ..., C_8 (or the set of ADJECTIVE PHRASES) are respectively the $0^{th}, ..., 8^{th}$ constituents of the minimal sequence satisfying S1–S17. (Thus the precise formal rôle of S1–S17 is simply to occur as a part of the present definition, as well as of the Theorem above.)

We can also characterize exactly the set of sentences of our fragment: φ is a SENTENCE if and only if $\varphi \in C_1$ and no variable occurs in φ.

6. SEMANTIC OPERATIONS

Corresponding to the syntactic rules S2, ..., S17 (and to given sets A and I) we introduce semantic operations $F_{2,A,I}, ..., F_{17,A,I}$ with the following intuitive significance: if the expression μ is 'obtained' by the nth syntactic rule from the expressions $\delta_0, ..., \delta_k$ — that is to say, if $\langle \delta_0, ..., \delta_k, \mu \rangle \in R_n$ — and if $g_0, ..., g_k$ are possible denotation functions of $\delta_0, ..., \delta_k$ respectively, then $F_{n,A,I}(g_0, ..., g_k)$ is to be the corresponding denotation function of μ. (The possibility of introducing such an operation $F_{n,A,I}$ imposes a SEMANTIC RESTRICTION on the relation R_n: though, as observed above, R_n is not required to be a function (or 'uni-valued'), its values for a given sequence of initial arguments must all have the same intended denotation.)

The operations $F_{n,A,I}$ will of course have various numbers of arguments, depending on the numbers of arguments of the corresponding relations R_n. We may as well assume, however, that the domain of definition for each argument place of each $F_{n,A,I}$ is always the same, and indeed is the set of all possible denotation functions corresponding to A and I, that is, the union of the sets $U_{0,A,I}{}^{A\omega}, ..., U_{8,A,I}{}^{A\omega}$. We may therefore completely characterize $F_{2,A,I}, ..., F_{17,A,I}$ by specifying their values for arbitrary sequences of arguments; as usual we shall suppress the subscripts 'A' and 'I', and write simply 'F_2', ..., 'F_{17}'.

$F_2(d, a) =$ that function p with domain A^ω such that, for all $x \in A^\omega$, $p(x) = d(x)(a(x))$.

(The right side makes SOME [conventionally determined] sense no matter what d, a are. We shall of course be interested only in the case in which d, a are denotation functions 'of the right sort' — that is, in this instance, are in $U_2{}^{A\omega}$, $U_0{}^{A\omega}$ respectively; and in this case the right side makes INTUITIVE sense. Similar remarks will apply to the characterizations of $F_3, \ldots, F_{17}$.)

$F_3(d, a, b) =$ that function p with domain A^ω such that, for all $x \in A^\omega$, $p(x) = d(x)(a(x), b(x))$.
$F_4(d, p) = F_2(d, p)$.
$F_5(d, m) = F_2(d, m)$.
$F_6(d, m) = F_2(d, m)$.
$F_7(d, z) = F_2(d, z)$.

(Thus we see why syntactical rules S2–S7 were grouped together as corresponding to 'functional application'.)

$F_8(p, a, b) =$ that function $q \in U_1{}^{A\omega}$ such that, for all $x \in A^\omega$, $q(x) = p(x^n{}_{b(x)})$, where n is the index of the variable represented by a (that is, the unique natural number n such that, for all $y \in A^\omega$, $a(y) = y_n$), and $x^n{}_t$ is in general the sequence exactly like x except that the nth constituent is t.

(It is for the sake of this rather intuitive characterization of F_8 [as well as of F_9–F_{16} below] that A was required to contain at least two elements. With the weaker assumption that A simply be nonempty, the following somewhat less transparent characterization of F_8 gives the correct result: $F_8(p, a, b) =$ the unique function $q \in U_1{}^{A\omega}$ such that, for all $x \in A^\omega$ and all $n \in \omega$, if $a(y) = y_n$ for all $y \in A^\omega$, then $q(x) = p(x^n{}_{b(x)})$. Similar alternative characterizations would be possible in the cases of F_9–F_{16} as well.)

$F_9(p, a, z) =$ that function $q \in U_1{}^{A\omega}$ such that, for all $x \in A^\omega$ and all $i \in I$, $q(x)(i) = 1$ if and only if $p(x^n{}_t)(i) = 1$ whenever t is a member of A for which $z(x)(t)(i) = 1$, where n is as above (in the characterization of F_8).
$F_{10}(p, a, z) =$ that function $q \in U_1{}^{A\omega}$ such that, for all $x \in A^\omega$ and all $i \in I$, $q(x)(i) = 1$ if and only if $p(x^n{}_t)(i) = 1$ for some $t \in A$ such that $z(x)(t)(i) = 1$, where n is as above.
$F_{11}(p, a, z) =$ that function $q \in U_1{}^{A\omega}$ such that, for all $x \in A^\omega$ and all $i \in I$, $q(x)(i) = 1$ if and only if there exists $t \in A$ such that $\{t\}$ is the set of objects $u \in A$ for which $z(x)(u)(i) = 1$, and $f(x^n{}_t)(i) = 1$, where n is as above.

$F_{12}(z, a, b) =$ that function $e \in U_4^{A\omega}$ such that, for all $x \in A^\omega$, $e(x) = z(x^n_{b(x)})$, where n is as above.

$F_{13}(e, a, z) =$ that function $h \in U_4^{A\omega}$ such that, for all $x \in A^\omega$, all $u \in A$, and all $i \in I$, $h(x)(u)(i) = 1$ if and only if $e(x^n_t)(u)$ $(i) = 1$ whenever t is a member of A for which $z(x)(t)(i) = 1$, where n is as above.

$F_{14}(e, a, z) =$ that function $h \in U_4^{A\omega}$ such that, for all $x \in A^\omega$, all $u \in A$, and all $i \in I$, $h(x)(u)(i) = 1$ if and only if $e(x^n_t)(u)(i)$ $= 1$ for some $t \in A$ such that $z(x)(t)(i) = 1$, where n is as above.

$F_{15}(e, a, z) =$ that function $h \in U_4^{A\omega}$ such that for all $x \in A^\omega$, all $u \in A$, and all $i \in I$, $h(x)(u)(i) = 1$ if and only if there exists $t \in A$ such that $\{t\}$ is the set of objects $v \in A$ for which $z(x)$ $(v)(i) = 1$, and $e(x^n_t)(u)(i) = 1$, where n is as above.

$F_{16}(z, p, a) =$ that function $e \in U_4^{A\omega}$ such that, for all $x \in A^\omega$, all $t \in A$, and all $i \in I$, $e(x)(t)(i) = 1$ if and only if $z(x)(t)(i) = 1$ and $p(x^n_t)(i) = 1$, where n is as above.

$F_{17}(a, d) =$ that function $p \in U_1^{A\omega}$ such that, for all $x \in A_\omega$ and all $i \in I$, $p(x)(i) = 1$ if and only if $d(x)(z(x))(a(x))(i) = 1$, where z is that function in $U_4^{A\omega}$ such that, for all $x \in A^\omega$, all $t \in A$, and all $i \in I$, $z(x)(t)(i) = 1$.

7. ANALYSES AND DENOTATIONS

Models, as we have seen, assign denotations (or, strictly speaking, denotation functions) to basic expressions only. Using the semantic operations, we shall wish to assign denotations to arbitrary DENOTING EXPRESSIONS (that is, arbitrary members of the union of $C_0, ..., C_8$). This task is complicated by the fact that we have no unique readability theorem for English, or even the present fragment. Many denoting expressions are syntactically ambiguous, in the sense that they can be built up in several essentially different ways on the basis of the syntactic rules. We may, however construct TREES to represent the various possible analyses of a denoting expression, in a manner indicated by the following example.

Let φ be the formula ⌐a woman loves every man⌐. Then φ has two essentially different analyses, and we may represent them by the following two trees. (There are other analyses, but each of them will differ only trivially — indeed, only in a choice of variables — from one of the following two.) In these trees each nonbasic expression is accompanied by the number of the syntactic rule among S2–S17 BY which it is obtained, and we place beneath it the expressions FROM which it is obtained, in the order in which they appear as arguments of the syntactical relation in question (among R2–R17). Each BASIC expression is accompanied by the index of its intended syntactic category.

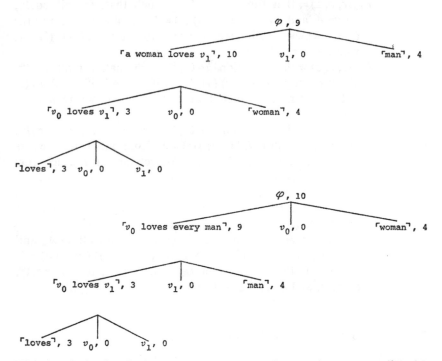

We may indeed call these trees ANALYSES of φ, and corresponding to each of them (as well as to a given model) we may assign a denotation function to φ. In particular, let ζ be a model, let $\zeta = \langle A, I, G_0, ..., G_8 \rangle$,y and let f, g be the two analyses given above, in the order in which the are displayed. Then, 'reading' the tree f and using the semantic operation $F_2, ..., F_{17}$, we may 'compute' the denotation function of φ that corresponds to f and ζ as $F_9(F_{10}(F_3(G_3(\ulcorner \text{loves} \urcorner), G_0(v_0), G_0(v_1)), G_0(v_0), G_4(\ulcorner \text{woman} \urcorner)), G_0(v_1), G_4(\ulcorner \text{man} \urcorner))$. Similarly, the denotation function of φ corresponding to the analysis g and the model ζ is $F_{10}(F_9(F_3(G_3(\ulcorner \text{loves} \urcorner), G_0(v_0), G_0(v_1)), G_0(v_1), G_4(\ulcorner \text{man} \urcorner)), G_0(v_0), G_4(\ulcorner \text{woman} \urcorner))$.

Although the notions of an analysis and of the denotation function corresponding to an analysis are probably already clear, I shall put down for reference the exact definitions. (The impatient reader may skip these safely.) We understand SEQUENCES in such a way that they may have any ordinal, finite or transfinite, as their length. By Λ is understood the empty sequence, by $\langle x \rangle$ the 1-place sequence of which the only constituent is the object x, and by $s\hat{\ }t$ the concatenation of the sequences s and t. A TREE-INDEXING is a set T of sequences satisfying the following conditions:

(1) T is a set of sequences of ordinals; (2) T is closed under the taking of initial segments (including the empty segment); and (3) whenever s is a sequence and k, n ordinals such that $s^\frown \langle n \rangle \in T$ and $k < n$, the sequence $s^\frown \langle k \rangle$ is also a member of T. A TREE is a function of which the domain is a tree-indexing.[14] (Here a FUNCTION is understood in the usual way, as a set of ordered pairs satisfying the 'many-one condition'; and if f is a function, then $\langle x, y \rangle \in f$ if and only if x is a member of the domain of f and $f(x) = y$.)

For instance, the two trees f and g displayed above have as their domain the same tree-indexing — indeed, the set of which the members are Λ, $\langle 0 \rangle$, $\langle 1 \rangle$, $\langle 2 \rangle$, $\langle 0,0 \rangle$, $\langle 0,1 \rangle$, $\langle 0,2 \rangle$, $\langle 0,0,0 \rangle$, $\langle 0,0,1 \rangle$, and $\langle 0,0,2 \rangle$ — these correspond to the nodes in the displays above, reading from top to bottom, and within a line from left to right. In most cases, however, the values of f and g differ. For example, $f(\Lambda) = \langle \varphi, 9 \rangle$, but $g(\Lambda) = \langle \varphi, 10 \rangle$; and $f(\langle 1 \rangle) = \langle v_1, 0 \rangle$, but $g(\langle 1 \rangle) = \langle v_0, 0 \rangle$.

By an ANALYSIS is understood a finite, nonempty tree h such that every value of h is an ordered pair, and, further, whenever $\langle s, \langle \delta, k \rangle \rangle \in h$ one of the following conditions holds: (1) k is a natural number less than 9, $\delta \in B_k$, and $s^\frown \langle 0 \rangle$ is not in the domain of h; or (2) k is a natural number, $2 \le k \le 17$, and there exist natural numbers n, $p_0, ..., p_{n-1}$ and expressions $a_0, ..., a_{n-1}$ such that $\langle a_0, ..., a_{n-1}, \delta \rangle \in R_k$, the pairs $\langle s^\frown \langle 0 \rangle$, $\langle a_0, p_0 \rangle \rangle, ..., \langle s^\frown \langle n-1 \rangle$, $\langle a_{n-1}, p_{n-1} \rangle \rangle$ are all members of h, and the sequence $s^\frown \langle n \rangle$ is not in the domain of h. (The condition that h be finite is actually superfluous here, and, in view of the particular character of the syntactical rules S1–S17, follows from the other conditions. It is possible, however, to imagine systems of syntactical rules in connection with which this could not be said. It is obvious that every finite tree, and hence every analysis, is such that its domain is a finite set of finite sequences of finite ordinals (that is, natural numbers).)

An ANALYSIS of an expression δ is an analysis h such that, for some k, $\langle \Lambda, \langle \delta, k \rangle \rangle \in h$. It is easily seen that an expression is a denoting expression if and only if there is an analysis of it. Also, each analysis of a denoting expression assigns to that expression an intended syntactic category, as follows: if h is an analysis of δ, then the CATEGORY INDEX OF δ ACCORDING TO h is the unique natural number k such that either (1) $\langle \Lambda, \langle \delta, k \rangle \rangle \in h$ and $\langle 0 \rangle$ is not in the domain of h, or (2) $\langle 0 \rangle$ is in the

---

[14] What we have called TREE-INDEXINGS are customarily called TREES; and no term is generally reserved for what we have called trees, despite the fact that the latter form an important class of mathematical objects. For a lucid exposition of the customary mathematical notions see Gaifman and Specker (1964). Our tree-indexings form a special case of what Gaifman and Specker call SEQUENTIAL TREES. The specialization consists in imposing conditions (1) and (3), but is not seriously restrictive: every sequential tree is isomorphic to a tree-indexing.

domain of h, either $\langle \Lambda, \langle \delta, 2 \rangle \rangle$, $\langle \Lambda, \langle \delta, 3 \rangle \rangle$, $\langle \Lambda, \langle \delta, 4 \rangle \rangle$, $\langle \Lambda, \langle \delta, 8 \rangle \rangle$, $\langle \Lambda, \langle \delta, 9 \rangle \rangle$, $\langle \Lambda, \langle \delta, 10 \rangle \rangle$, $\langle \Lambda, \langle \delta, 11 \rangle \rangle$, or $\langle \Lambda, \langle \delta, 17 \rangle \rangle$ is in h, and $k = 1$, or (3) $\langle 0 \rangle$ is in the domain of h, $\langle \Lambda, \langle \delta, 5 \rangle \rangle \in h$, and $k = 2$, or (4) $\langle 0 \rangle$ is in the domain of h, $\langle \Lambda, \langle \delta, 6 \rangle \rangle \in h$, and $k = 3$, or (5) $\langle 0 \rangle$ is in the domain of h, $\langle \Lambda, \langle \delta, 7 \rangle \rangle$, $\langle \Lambda, \langle \delta, 12 \rangle \rangle$, $\langle \Lambda, \langle \delta, 13 \rangle \rangle$, $\langle \Lambda, \langle \delta, 14 \rangle \rangle$, $\langle \Lambda, \langle \delta, 15 \rangle \rangle$, or $\langle \Lambda, \langle \delta, 16 \rangle \rangle$ is in h, and $k = 4$.

Because a denoting expression may, like φ above, have two or more essentially different analyses, we cannot assign to each denoting expression a unique denotation function corresponding to a given model, but rather a denotation function corresponding to a given model and a given analysis. It is obvious, however, that for each analysis there is exactly one expression of which it is an analysis. We may therefore speak of THE DENOTATION FUNCTION, CORRESPONDING TO A MODEL ζ AND AN ANALYSIS h, OF THE EXPRESSION OF WHICH h IS AN ANALYSIS, or, more briefly, $D(\zeta, h)$.

Before defining, '$D(\zeta, h)$', it is necessary to introduce a little more auxiliary terminology. If a is an ordered pair, then by $1[a]$ and $2[a]$ are understood the first and second constituents, respectively, of a. If h is a tree and the 1-place sequence $\langle k \rangle$ is in the domain of h, then by $h_{(k)}$, or THE kth IMMEDIATE SUBTREE OF h, is understood the set of pairs $\langle s, a \rangle$ for which s is a sequence of ordinals and $\langle \langle k \rangle \hat{\ } s, a \rangle \in h$. By the RANK of a tree h is understood the least upper bound of the lengths of sequences in the domain of h. Every analysis, being finite, will have a finite rank. In such a case — that is, when the tree h has a finite rank — it is clear that the rank of each immediate subtree of h will be one less than the rank of h.

Assume henceforth that ζ is a model, that $\zeta = \langle A, I, G_0, \ldots, G_8 \rangle$, and that h is an analysis. We can now define $D(\zeta, h)$ recursively as follows. (The recursion is on the rank of the analysis h.)

(1) If the rank of h is 0, then $D(\zeta, h) = G_{2[h(\Lambda)]}(1[h(\Lambda)])$.

(2) If the rank of h is not 0, then $D(\zeta, h) = F_{2[h(\Lambda)]}$. $(D(\zeta, h_{(0)}), \ldots, D(\zeta, h_{(n)}))$, where $\{0, \ldots, n\}$ is the set of natural members k for which $\langle k \rangle$ is in the domain of h.

The following theorem is completely straightforward.

Theorem. Suppose that h is an analysis of δ, and that k is the category index of δ according to h. (1) $D(\zeta, h) \in U_k{}^{A\omega}$. (2) If $x, y \in A^\omega$ and $x_n = y_n$ for all n such that v_n occurs in δ, then $D(\zeta, h)(x) = D(\zeta, h)(y)$. Hence: (3) If δ is a sentence and $k = 1$, then $D(\zeta, h) \in (2^I)^{A\omega}$ and for all $x, y \in A^\omega$, $D(\zeta, h)(x) = D(\zeta, h)(y)$.

8. TRUTH AND LOGICAL TRUTH

The third part of the last theorem indicates that we may define a true sentence of our fragment in the manner suggested in Tarski [1] for mathematical languages, as one 'satisfied' by every infinite sequence (or, equivalently, by SOME infinite sequence). For convenience, however, we define truth not only for sentences but for arbitrary formulas; variables will behave as though universally quantified: if $\zeta = \langle A, I, G_0, ..., G_8 \rangle$, then φ is TRUE with respect to ζ, the analysis h, and the possible world i if and only if h is an analysis of φ, the category index of φ according to h is 1, $i \in I$, and, for every $x \in A^{\omega}$, $D(\zeta, h)(x)(i) = 1$.

A formula φ is LOGICALLY TRUE WITH RESPECT TO an analysis h if and only if h is an analysis of φ, the category index of φ according to h is 1, and for every model $\langle A, I, G_0, ..., G_8 \rangle$ and every $i \in I$, φ is true with respect to $\langle A, I, G_0, ..., G_8 \rangle$, h, and i. If φ, ψ are sentences having f, g respectively as analyses, then φ LOGICALLY IMPLIES ψ WITH RESPECT TO f and g if and only if the category index of φ with respect to f, as well as that of ψ with respect to g, is 1, and for every model $\langle A, I, G_0, ..., G_8 \rangle$ and every $i \in I$, if φ is true with respect to $\langle A, I, G_0, ..., G_8 \rangle$, f, and i, then ψ is true with respect to $\langle A, I, G_0, ..., G_8 \rangle$, g, and i. (This notion can be extended in an obvious way to the case in which φ is replaced by several, even infinitely many, sentences.) If α, β are denoting expressions having f, g respectively as analyses, then α is LOGICALLY EQUIVALENT TO β WITH RESPECT TO f and g if and only if the category index of α according to f is the same as the category index of β according to g, and, for every model ζ, $D(\zeta, f) = D(\zeta, g)$.

Professor Partee and Mr. Cooley have pointed out a reasonable way of removing the relativization to f and g. We might call two denoting expressions α and β simply LOGICALLY EQUIVALENT if for every analysis f of α there is an analysis g of β such that α is logically equivalent to β with respect to f and g, and, conversely, for every analysis g of β there is an analysis f of α such that α is equivalent to β with respect to f and g.

A denoting expression α is AMBIGUOUS WITH RESPECT TO a model ζ if and only if there are analyses f and g of α such that $D(\zeta, f) \neq D(\zeta, g)$. A denoting expression is called STRUCTURALLY AMBIGUOUS if there is a model with respect to which it is ambiguous. (I use the qualification 'structurally' rather unhappily, and wish I could think of a better term. In particular, I do not use 'syntactically', because an expression may have several 'essentially different' ANALYSES but still not be ambiguous in the sense given here. Yet some qualification is needed, for there is a type of ambiguity (rather uninteresting, to be sure) that is not covered by the present notion. I refer to LEXICAL ambiguity, or, roughly, that ambiguity of complex expressions that stems from the ambiguity of basic expressions occurring within them. Such ambiguity could be formally construed as follows. The use of a language would ideally involve not only the determination of the collection of ALL models of the language (a determination sufficient for the LOGICAL notions, that is, logical truth, logical implication, logical equivalence), but also the specification of a particular, ACTUAL model; this would be involved in characterizing ABSOLUTE truth (as opposed to truth WITH RESPECT TO a model).[15] But in connection with ordinary English there are SEVERAL equally natural choices of the actual model, arising from the fact that certain basic expressions (most prominently, certain common nouns and verbs) have several alternative denotations. We are thus led to consider a SET of actual models, and not a single actual model. If the denotation of a denoting expression varies from one actual model to another (with respect to a fixed analysis), then the expression may be considered LEXICALLY AMBIGUOUS (with respect to the analysis in question). It should, perhaps, be pointed out that throughout our development models play the role of POSSIBLE DICTIONARIES, with the one oddity that alternative definitions are never allowed within a single dictionary, but instead involve the consideration of several dictionaries.[16])

9. REMARKS ON THE PRESENT FRAGMENT

(i) Some linguists roughly sharing the main goal of the present paper, that is, to define the notion of a TRUE SENTENCE OF ENGLISH (or ENGLISH SENTENCE TRUE WITH RESPECT TO A GIVEN INTERPRETATION), have proposed that syntax — that is, the analysis of the notion of a (correctly formed) sentence — be attacked first, and that only after the completion of a syntactical theory consideration be given to semantics, which would then be developed on the basis of that theory. Such a program has almost no prospect of success. There will often be many ways of syntactically generating a given set of sentences, but only a few of them will have semantic relevance; and these will sometimes be less simple, and hence less superficially appealing, than certain of the semantically uninteresting

---

[15]   To be specific, a sentence would be considered TRUE WITH RESPECT TO AN ANALYSIS *h* AND A POSSIBLE WORLD *i* if it were true (in the sense given earlier) with respect to the actual model, *h*, and *i*. The relativization to *i* would be eliminable in the same way once we were able to single out the actual world among all possible worlds.

[16]   Notice that the use of an expression, like our ⌜walks⌝, that belongs to more than one basic category will not in itself produce either lexically or structurally ambiguous formulas, even though several denotations may be associated with the expression, depending on the category under which it is considered. In such cases we would informally speak of "ambiguity that is resolved by context".

modes of generation. Thus the construction of syntax and semantics must proceed hand in hand.

As a very simple example, observe that the set of formulas, and hence of sentences, of our fragment would remain unchanged if we deleted S12–S15 from the syntactical rules. The corresponding semantics, however, would be inadequate; it would provide, for instance, no account of the intuitive ambiguity of the sentence ⌜every brother of a man in Amsterdam loves Jane⌝.

(ii) The denotation of an adjective phrase is always a function from properties to properties. (This was one of the proposals advanced by Kamp and Parsons.) The standard denotations of many adjectives — for instance, ⌜green⌝ and ⌜married⌝ — may be taken as INTERSECTION FUNCTIONS, that is, functions H such that, for some property P, $H(Q)$ is, for every property Q, the property possessed by a given individual with respect to a given possible world if and only if the individual possesses both P and Q with respect to that possible world. It would be a mistake, however, to suppose that all adjectives could be so interpreted. Compare the common noun phrases ⌜big flea⌝ and ⌜big entity⌝. If the denotation of ⌜big⌝ were an intersection function, then there would be a single set B of individuals such that the extension of ⌜big flea⌝ with respect to the actual world (that is, the set of big fleas) would be the intersection of B with the set of fleas, and the extension of ⌜big entity⌝, again with respect to the actual world (that is, the set of big entities), would be the intersection of B with the set of entities (that is, the set B itself). But this is impossible, because not all big fleas (indeed, probably no big fleas) are big entities. (A big flea is, roughly, a flea bigger than most FLEAS, and a big entity an entity bigger than most ENTITIES.)

It would also be a mistake to impose in general the weaker assumption, satisfied by ⌜green⌝, ⌜married⌝, and ⌜big⌝, that the denotation of an adjective is a function that always assigns to a property one of its SUB-PROPERTIES; for consider ⌜false friend⌝, ⌜reputed millionaire⌝, ⌜ostensible ally⌝, ⌜possible president⌝, ⌜alleged intruder⌝.

(iii) Accordingly, the sentence ⌜every big flea is big⌝ is not logically true (under any analysis). Indeed, it is logically equivalent to ⌜every big flea is a big entity⌝ (with respect to the most natural analysis of the latter), and the latter probably not even true.

It appears that everyday usage is not quite decided as to the truth-conditions of sentences having adjectives like ⌜big⌝ in predicative position. Other conventions than ours (which is due to Kamp) are possible, but would be more complicated. The fact that our convention is in accordance with at least some varieties of ordinary usage is indicated by the plausibility of simultaneously maintaining the two sentences ⌜no flea is big⌝ and ⌜Jones finds a big flea⌝. On the other hand, ⌜every married man is married⌝ is certainly true; but it is not logically true, because its truth depends on the special circumstance that ⌜married⌝ denotes an intersection function. (Still less can we ascribe logical truth to the celebrated example ⌜every husband is married⌝.)

It would of course be possible to single out two special classes of basic adjective phrases, one a subclass of the other, and require the members of the larger class always to denote functions satisfying the subproperty condition and those of the smaller always to denote intersection functions. Then if δ is a one-word basic adjective phrase and ζ a common noun phrase, ⌜every $\delta \zeta$ is a ζ⌝ would be logically true if δ is in the larger class, and so would ⌜every $\delta \zeta$ is δ⌝ if δ is in the smaller. Such a course would, however, somewhat detract from the conceptual simplicity of our treatment. We should have to countenance as universes not only $U_{0,A,I}, \ldots$, $U_{8,A,I}$ but also the set of members of $U_{8,A,I}$ that satisfy the subproperty assumption and the set of intersection functions in $U_{8,A,I}$; and the last two universes cannot be constructed in the same simple manner as the others.

Rather than altering the notion of logical truth, as under this proposal, we could perhaps more conveniently consider the logical consequences of certain POSTULATES, in particular, the formulas

$$\ulcorner \text{every } \delta \zeta \text{ is a } \zeta \urcorner,$$

where ζ is a common noun phrase and δ a one-word adjective phrase in the larger class mentioned above, as well as

$$\ulcorner \text{every } \delta \zeta \text{ is a } \zeta \text{ such that that } \zeta \text{ is } \delta \urcorner$$

and

$$\ulcorner \text{every } \zeta \text{ such that that } \zeta \text{ is } \delta \text{ is a } \delta \zeta \urcorner,$$

where ζ is again a common noun phrase and δ is a one-word adjective phrase in the smaller class mentioned above, as well as certain obvious analogues appropriate to the case in which δ is an adjective phrase of more than one word. To be a little more explicit, we might call a sentence φ ANALYTIC with respect to one of its analyses h if φ is a logical consequence of the set of postulates given above, with respect to h and the most natural analyses of those postulates (that is, analyses according to which the postulates are understood as universal rather than existential generalizations); and for some purposes we might be more concerned with analyticity than with logical truth.

(iv) Adverbial phrases are interpreted in very much the same way as adjective phrases, and remarks analogous to those in (ii) and (iii) are applicable to them. Notice, for instance, that ⌜Jones kills Smith in a dream⌝ does not logically imply ⌜Jones kills Smith⌝; hence neither does ⌜Jones kills Smith with a knife⌝, even though ⌜necessarily if Jones kills Smith with a knife, then Jones kills Smith⌝ might well turn out to be TRUE (though not logically true) once we provide a proper analysis of ⌜if ... then⌝.

(v) Examples above reveal that the ⌜is⌝ of such formulas as ⌜v_0 is a horse⌝ may be identified with the ⌜is⌝ of identity, and the indefinite singular term ⌜a horse⌝ treated, as usual, existentially. The same point was tentatively suggested in Quine (1960) and emphasized in Bohnert and Backer (1967). Our examples also show that the ⌜is⌝ of ⌜John is big⌝, though not IDENTIFIABLE with the ⌜is⌝ of identity, is very simply REDUCIBLE to it; for instance, ⌜John is big⌝ is logically equivalent to ⌜John is a big entity⌝.

(vi) For simplicity I have treated only the restrictive use of adjectives, relative clauses, adformulas, and adverbs, though ordinary English recognizes also a nonrestrictive use. For instance, the sentence ⌜Mary loves the esteemed doctor⌝ is within our treatment unambiguous, whereas intuitively it could be regarded as having roughly the same meaning as either the restrictive ⌜Mary loves the doctor such that that doctor is esteemed⌝ or the non-restrictive ⌜Mary loves the doctor, and that doctor is esteemed⌝. It would not be too difficult to introduce such ambiguities in a formal way.

As far as relative clauses are concerned, we have confined ourselves to a ⌜such that⌝ locution, as in ⌜Mary loves the doctor such that that doctor is esteemed⌝, which is unambiguously synonymous with ⌜Mary loves the doctor who is esteemed⌝. The non-restrictive ⌜Mary loves the doctor, who is esteemed⌝ has no direct counterpart in our fragment.

Adformulas also may sometimes be intuitively construed as non-restrictive, though again we must go beyond our fragment for examples. For instance, ⌜the man such that that man fortunately loves Mary is tall⌝ may be understood either restrictively as ⌜the man such that it is fortunate that that man loves Mary is tall⌝ or unrestrictively as ⌜the man such that that man loves Mary is tall, and it is fortunate that that man loves Mary⌝. It is probable that nonrestrictive uses of adverbial phrases also exist, but I have been unable to find any clear-cut examples.

(vii) It appears to be purely a matter of taste whether certain additional syntactic (and corresponding semantic) categories should be recognized. I have in mind such categories as those of ONE-PLACE ADJECTIVAL PREP-

OSITIONS (for instance, $\ulcorner$in$\urcorner$), which would denote functions in $U_8{}^u{}_0$, and of TWO-PLACE ADJECTIVAL PREPOSITIONS (for instance, $\ulcorner$between$\urcorner$), which would designate functions in $U_8{}^u{}_0 \times {}^u{}_0$. To introduce these categories would not enlarge the compass of the present fragment, though there are other categories (such as those of ADADJECTIVE PHRASES, ADAD-ONE-VERB PHRASES, ADAD-TWO-VERB PHRASES, and BINARY CONJUNCTION PHRASES, interpreted by functions in $U_8{}^{U_8}$, $U_6{}^{U_6}$, $U_7{}^{U_7}$ and $U_1{}^{U_1 \times U_1}$ respectively) of which this could not be said.

(viii) Our fragment is rich in structural ambiguities, all roughly describable as arising from the various possible orders in which the 'syntactic operations' R_2–R_{17} may be applied; but in this respect I believe our fragment captures the character of ordinary English in a rather revealing way. For instance, the *de re* and *de dicto* interpretations of $\ulcorner$necessarily the father of Cain is Adam$\urcorner$ (of which the former is true and the latter false) correspond to two ways of generating the sentence in question; the *de re* interpretation is obtained when the syntactical rule S4 is applied (in connection with $\ulcorner$necessarily$\urcorner$) before S11 and the *de dicto* interpretation when the opposite order is adopted. (A related suggestion, concerned with modal and belief contexts, was made in Russell (1905) and amplified in Smullyan (1948), but seems not to have received adequate attention. I should point out one drawback, of both my treatment and that of Russell: one must either prohibit the existence of two genuine proper names of the same individual (so that, say, $\ulcorner$Samuel Clemens$\urcorner$ would be allowed in the language, but the purported name phrase $\ulcorner$Mark Twain$\urcorner$ would be replaced by the common noun phrase $\ulcorner$person called 'Mark Twain'$\urcorner$) or else reconcile oneself to the unambiguous truth of such sentences as $\ulcorner$necessarily Samuel Clemens is Mark Twain$\urcorner$. Since descriptive phrases are not affected and the intuition is a little vague on the issues raised, this appears to me to be a price it is possible to pay for the simple semantics outlined above. It is nevertheless possible to circumvent these paradoxes, and to do so with only minor departures from the present treatment; the procedure, because of its intimate connection with the treatment of indexical features of language, will be described in Part II of this paper.)

English has, however, certain (by no means complete) devices for reducing ambiguity. These include the use of several different styles of quantification having various scopes — for instance, the use of $\ulcorner$any$\urcorner$ and $\ulcorner$a certain$\urcorner$ as universal and existential 'quantifiers' of wide scope. The scope of quantifiers can also sometimes be resolved by word order (though not always according to the naive rule that the 'quantificational phrase' occurring first be given the widest scope) and sometimes by the relative length of the "quantified" common noun phrases. Such features of

English could be accounted for in precisely the style of our present treatment, but would require more complicated syntactical relations than R_2–R_{17}. For instance, if we were to include $\ulcorner$any$\urcorner$, we should have to make the following changes, among others: we should add rules precisely analogous to S9 and S13, but with $\ulcorner$every$\urcorner$ replaced by $\ulcorner$any$\urcorner$; corresponding semantical operations, identical with F_9 and F_{13}, would be added; R_9, R_{10}, R_{13}, and R_{14}, by which $\ulcorner$every$\urcorner$ and $\ulcorner$a$\urcorner$ are introduced, would be modified in such a way as not to apply to formulas or common noun phrases in which $\ulcorner$any$\urcorner$ already occurs; similarly, R_4 would be modified so as not to allow the appending of $\ulcorner$not$\urcorner$ to a formula containing $\ulcorner$any$\urcorner$. Such rules would restrict the variety of possible analyses of sentences containing $\ulcorner$any$\urcorner$; exact details must be postponed to another occasion.

(ix) I have deliberately, and for the sake of simplicity, ignored another source of ambiguity. We have taken the indefinite article $\ulcorner$a$\urcorner$ as always indicating existential quantification, but in some situations it may also be used universally, and indeed, in precisely the same way as $\ulcorner$any$\urcorner$; such is the case with one reading of the ambiguous sentence $\ulcorner$a woman loves every man such that that man loves that woman$\urcorner$.

(x) Considerable discussion has taken place as to what theory of descriptions best mirrors ordinary usage. It is therefore perhaps of some interest to see how $\ulcorner$the$\urcorner$ really and literally functions in English, and I believe the treatment above provides a correct description. $\ulcorner$The$\urcorner$ turns out to play the role of a quantifier, in complete analogy with $\ulcorner$every$\urcorner$ and $\ulcorner$a$\urcorner$, and does NOT generate (in combination with common noun phrases) denoting expressions. (This does not mean that it would not be POSSIBLE to assign complex and artificial denotations to such phrases as $\ulcorner$the $\zeta\urcorner$, $\ulcorner$every $\zeta\urcorner$, and $\ulcorner$a $\zeta\urcorner$, but in no case would the denotation be an individual).[17]

Two special points should be noted. Within our treatment $\ulcorner$the$\urcorner$ introduces ambiguities of scope (or of order of construction) of exactly the same sort as those associated with $\ulcorner$every$\urcorner$ and $\ulcorner$a$\urcorner$. Further, English sentences contain no variables, and hence no such locutions as $\ulcorner$the v_0 such that v_0 walks$\urcorner$; $\ulcorner$the$\urcorner$ is always accompanied by a common noun phrase. In these two features virtually all artificial theories of descriptions differ from English, as well they might: it is sometimes desirable to avoid ambiguity, and the introduction of bound variables in place of property names permits a first-order treatment of a good deal of what would otherwise require nonelementary second-order methods.

The moral for artificial languages ought I think to be this. If such a

---

[17] It is in fact sometimes important to assign such denotations, in particular, in connection with intensional verbs; see Montague (in preparation).

language is to avoid ambiguity completely, or is to fit within a first-order framework, then it should not attempt in its theory of descriptions to mirror English too closely; it should rather be influenced by other considerations, for instance, simplicity. Such an attitude is already customary in connection with artificial theories of quantification, but for reasons not at all clear to me is still resisted in some quarters in connection with descriptive phrases.

(xi) It is wrong to maintain — as Frege (1892) possibly did — that an analysis of ordinary English (or German) requires a notion of SENSE as well as one of DENOTATION. The fact that we have been able to do with denotation alone depends on two novelties of our treatment — our theory of descriptions, according to which descriptive phrases do not denote individuals (or anything else, for that matter; recall that Frege's famous example involves ⌜THE morning star⌝); and our decision to regard sentences as denoting propositions rather than truth values (and hence to regard verbs as denoting relations-in-intension rather than relations-in-extension), Frege's 'argument' that sentences cannot denote propositions depend of course on the assumption that descriptive phrases denote individuals.

I should not be understood as suggesting that it is IMPOSSIBLE to apply a sense-denotation distinction to English according to which formulas will denote truth values. Further, I believe that a treatment like Frege's, involving both sense and denotation, is the best way of dealing with certain interesting ARTIFICIAL languages; see Montague (1970).

It would be pointless to dispute whether what I have called denotation should instead be called sense. Perhaps the only real point that can be made in this connection is the following. Our basic objective, like Frege's, is to assign truth values to sentences. Like Frege, we seek to do this by assigning extra-linguistic entities to all expressions involved in the generation of sentences (including, among these, sentences themselves) in such a way that (*a*) the assignment to a compound will be a function of the entities assigned to its components, and (*b*) the truth-value of a sentence can be determined from the entity assigned to it. But whereas Frege's approach involves assigning at least two (and perhaps infinitely many) entities to each expression, we have done with one — what I prefer to call the denotation.

I should point out that the situation need not change even when (as in Part II of this paper) we admit context-dependent names of individuals; but the reader cannot be expected to accept this claim until he has seen the details in Part II.

(xii) It may not be quite clear why, within our treatment, formulas could not be taken as denoting truth values, verbs as denoting relations-in-extension, and common nouns as denoting sets. The reason should, however, become clear if one considers the effect of modifiers on such expressions, as in ⌜necessarily the father of Cain is Adam⌝, ⌜walks rapidly⌝, and ⌜possible president⌝. The denotations of the compound — whether taken as we have taken them or taken as such extensional entities as truth values or sets — could not be obtained from the truth values or sets corresponding to the components.[18]

(xiii) It is a little ugly to include ⌜v_0 believes that⌝ among our adformulas without giving a more comprehensive account of the various uses of ⌜believes⌝ and grammatically analogous verbs; and some of the presentation, particularly in Part II, would be smoother without that adformula. The reason for its inclusion is to indicate that such locutions, though sometimes regarded as serious obstacles to an adequate treatment of natural language, can be accommodated within our framework. I should point out, however, that if φ and ψ are logically equivalent sentences (with respect to given analyses f and g), then ⌜John believes that φ⌝ and ⌜John believes that ψ⌝ will turn out also to be logically equivalent (with respect to analyses that contain f and g as parts). This may at first appear strange, but is a conclusion that I believe we should accept; for a brief discussion of the issues involved, in connection with an artificial rather than a natural language, see Montague (1970).

(xiv) The method of presentation adopted here has been influenced by a general algebraic theory of languages and their interpretations recently constructed by the author, and exhibits the present fragment and those in Part II as special cases. The general theory contains, for instance, theorems according to which the syntactic categories of a very wide class of languages will be recursive (that is, decidable); the recursiveness of the categories $C_0, ..., C_8$ of our fragment, though independently rather obvious, is a consequence.

10. EXTENDING THE PRESENT FRAGMENT

Certain extensions, comprehending larger portions of English (for instance, indexical or context-dependent portions), will be given in Part II; and still wider extensions are known. In no case need one abandon the essential features of the treatment above, and in most cases the semantics remains simple.

---

[18] Let me spell out what is meant, in, say, the case of ⌜possible⌝. One can find two common nouns ζ and η corresponding to the same set of individuals — or having, as we should ordinarily say, the same extension (with respect to the actual world and the standard model) — but such that ⌜possible ζ⌝ and ⌜possible η⌝ have different extensions.

Often, however, the syntax becomes more complicated and requires the introduction of additional devices beyond those contemplated above. For instance, if we wish to include modern negation (rather than, or in addition to, the archaic negation employed above), we must be able to single out the MAIN VERB OCCURRENCE within a formula; this would also be required for the formation of tenses other than the present. The word ⌜all⌝ would behave very much like ⌜every⌝, but its syntax would require the ability to single out (for purposes of pluralization) both the main verb occurrence of a formula and the MAIN COMMON NOUN OCCURRENCE of a common noun phrase. (Once we can do this, the treatment of CARDINALS, as in ⌜three men walk⌝, presents no problem. Because there are infinitely many cardinals, we might wish to introduce a syntactic category of QUANTIFIERS, to which ⌜every⌝ and ⌜a⌝ would also belong, and each member of which would designate a function in $U_1^{u_4 u_2}$).[19] The introduction of ADADJECTIVES (that is, modifiers of adjective phrases) would require the ability to single out the MAIN ADJECTIVE OCCURRENCE of an adjective phrase. For then the simple syntactical rule S7 could no longer be maintained; the general rule seems to be that an adjective phrase δ should be placed before or after the common noun phrase it modifies according as the main occurrence of an adjective in δ stands at the end of δ or not. If binary connectives are included, we must be able to tell whether a given formula is (according to every possible analysis) compounded by means of a connective, and what that connective is; for there are some compounds (as with 'and' and 'or') that are not susceptible of negation. But I shall reserve for another occasion the detailed discussion of these and other extensions.

[19] For instance, a model would assign to ⌜every⌝ (as its denotation function) that function d in $(U_1^{U_4} {}^{\times U_2}{}^{A\omega})$ such that, for all $x \in A^\omega$, all $z \in U_4$, all $w \in U_2$, and all $i \in I$, $d(x)(z, w)(i) = 1$ if and only if $w(u)(i) = 1$ for all $u \in A$ for which $z(u)(i) = 1$. Quantifiers would enter formulas by way of the following syntactical rule: if φ is a formula, a a name phrase (and in particular a variable), δ a quantifier, and ζ a common noun phrase, and $\langle \varphi, a, \delta, \zeta, \psi \rangle \in R$, then ψ is a formula, where R is a syntactical relation containing such quintuples as $\langle ⌜v_0$ walks⌝, v_0, ⌜every⌝, ⌜man⌝, ⌜every man walks⌝$\rangle$ and $\langle ⌜v_0$ walks⌝, v_0, ⌜two⌝, ⌜man⌝, ⌜two men walk⌝$\rangle$. The corresponding semantical operation F would be characterized as follows: $F(p, a, d, z)$ is that function $q \in U_1^{A\omega}$ such that, for all $x \in A^\omega$, $q(x) = d(x)(z(x), w)$, where w is the set of all pairs $\langle u, p(x^{au}) \rangle$ such that $u \in A$, where n is the index of the variable represented by a. One would of course require also syntactical rule (with a corresponding semantical operation) whereby quantifiers could enter common noun phrases.

BIBLIOGRAPHY

K. Ajdukiewicz
1960   *Język i poznanie* (Warsaw).
H. G. Bohnert and P. O. Backer
1967   *Automatic English-to-logic translation in a simplified model* (IBM Research Paper RC-1744).
D. Davidson
1967a   "The logical form of action sentences", in N. Rescher (ed.), *The logic of decision and action* (Pittsburgh).
1967b   "Causal relations", *The Journal of Philosophy* 64, 691-703.
1970   "Semantics for Natural Languages", in Bruno Visentini et al., *Linguaggi nella societa e nella tecnica* (Milan), 177-88.
G. Frege
1892   "Über Sinn und Bedeutung", *Zeitschrift für Philosophie und philosophische Kritik* 100, 25-50.
H. Gaifman and E. P. Specker
1964   "Isomorphism types of trees", *Proceedings of the American Mathematical Society*, 15, 1-7.
S. Kripke
1963   "Semantical considerations on modal logic", *Acta Philosophica Fennica* 16, 83-94.
R. Montague
1970   "Pragmatics and intensional logic", *Synthese* 22, 68-94. Reprinted in D. Davidson and G. Harman (eds.), *Semantics of Natural Language* (Dordrecht, 1972).
in preparation   *Intensional verbs, indefinite terms, and unconceived trees.*
W. V. Quine
1940   *Mathematical logic* (New York). Revised edition (Cambridge, Mass., 1951).
1960   *Word and object*, (Cambridge, Mass.).
B. Russell
1905   "On denoting", *Mind* 14, 479-93.
A. F. Smullyan
1948   "Modality and description", *The Journal of Symbolic Logic* 13, 31-37.
A. Tarski
1936   "Der Wahrheitsbegriff in den formalisierten Sprachen", *Studia Philosophica* 1, 261-405.
1952   "Some notions and methods on the borderline of algebra and metamathematics", *Proceedings of the 1950 International Congress of Mathematicians* 1, 705-20.
1954   "Contributions to the theory of models, Part I", *Indagationes Mathematicae* 16, 572-81.

Hans Reichenbach

ANALYSIS OF CONVERSATIONAL LANGUAGE

§51. THE TENSES OF VERBS

A particularly important form of token-reflexive symbol is found in the tenses of verbs. The tenses determine time with reference to the time point of the act of speech, i.e. of the token uttered. A closer analysis reveals that the time indication given by the tenses is of a rather complex structure.

Let us call the time point of the token the POINT OF SPEECH. Then the three indications, 'before the point of speech', 'simultaneous with the point of speech', and 'after the point of speech', furnish only three tenses; since the number of verb tenses is obviously greater, we need a more complex interpretation. From a sentence like 'Peter had gone' we see that the time order expressed in the tense does not concern one event, but two events, whose positions are determined with respect to the point of speech. We shall call these time points the POINT OF THE EVENT and the POINT OF REFERENCE. In the example the point of the event is the time when Peter went; the point of reference is a time between this point and the point of speech. In an individual sentence like the one given it is not clear which time point is used as the point reference. This determination is rather given by the context of speech. In a story, for instance, the series of events recounted determines the point of reference which in this case is in the past, seen from the point of speech; some individual events lying outside this point are then referred, not directly to the point

Reprinted from: Hans Reichenbach, *Elements of Symbolic Logic* (McMillan, New York, 1947), 287-310.

of speech, but to this point of reference determined by the story. The following example, taken from W. Somerset Maugham's *Of Human Bondage*, may make these time relations clear:

> But Philip ceased to think of her a moment after he had settled down in his carriage. He thought only of the future. He had written to Mrs. Otter, the *massière* to whom Hayward had given him an introduction, and had in his pocket an invitation to tea on the following day.

The series of events recounted here in the simple past determine the point of reference as lying before the point of speech. Some individual events, like the settling down in the carriage, the writing of the letter, and the giving of the introduction, precede the point of reference and are therefore related in the past perfect.

Another illustration for these time relations may be given by a historical narrative, a quotation from Macaulay:

> In 1678 the whole face of things had changed ... eighteen years of misgovernment had made the ... majority desirous to obtain security for their liberties at any risk. The fury of their returning loyalty had spent itself in its first outbreak. In a very few months they had hanged and half-hanged, quartered and emboweled, enough to satisfy them. The Roundhead party seemed to be not merely overcome, but too much broken and scattered ever to rally again. Then commenced the reflux of public opinion. The nation began to find out to what a man it had intrusted without conditions all its dearest interests, on what a man it had lavished all its fondest affection.

The point of reference is here the year 1678. Events of this year are related in the simple past, such as the commencing of the reflux of public opinion, and the beginning of the discovery concerning the character of the king. The events preceding this time point are given in the past perfect, such as the change in the face of things, the outbreaks of cruelty, the nation's trust in the king.

In some tenses, two of the three points are simultaneous. Thus, in the simple past, the point of the event and the point of reference are simultaneous, and both are before the point of speech; the use of the simple past in the above quotation shows this clearly. This distinguishes the simple past from the present perfect. In the statement 'I have seen Charles' the event is also before the point of speech, but it is referred to a point simultaneous with the point of speech; i.e. the points of speech and reference coincide. This meaning of the present perfect may be illustrated by the following quotation from Keats:

> Much have I traveled in the realms of gold,
> And many goodly states and kingdoms seen;
> Round many western islands have I been
> Which bards in fealty to Apollo hold.

Comparing this with the above quotations we notice that here obviously the past events are seen, not from a reference point situated also in the past, but from a point of reference which coincides with the point of speech. This is the reason that the words of Keats are not of a narrative type but affect us with the immediacy of a direct report to the reader. We see that we need three time points even for the distinction of tenses which, in a superficial consideration, seem to concern only two time points. The difficulties which grammar books have in explaining the meanings of the different tenses originate from the fact that they do not recognize the three-place structure of the time determination given in the tenses.[1]

We thus come to the following tables, in which the initials '*E*', '*R*', and '*S*' stand, respectively, for 'point of the event', 'point of reference', and 'point of speech', and in which the direction of time is represented as the direction of the line from left to right:

Past Perfect	*Simple Past*	*Present Perfect*
I had seen John	I saw John	I have seen John
$E \quad R \quad S$	$R, E \quad S$	$E \quad S, R$

Present	*Simple Future*	*Future Perfect*
I see John	I shall see John	I shall have seen John
S, R, E	$S, R \quad E$	$S \quad E \quad R$

In some tenses, an additional indication is given concerning the time extension of the event. The English language uses the present participle to indicate that the event covers a certain stretch of time. We thus arrive at the following tables:

Past Perfect, *Extended*	*Simple Past,* *Extended*	*Present Perfect,* *Extended*
I had been seeing John	I was seeing John	I have been seeing John
$E \quad R \quad S$	$R, E \quad S$	$E \quad S, R$

---

[1] In J. O. H. Jespersen's excellent analysis of grammar (*The Philosophy of Grammar*, H. Holt, New York, 1924) I find the three-point structure indicated for such tenses as the past perfect and the future perfect (p. 256), but not applied to the interpretation of the other tenses. This explains the difficulties which even Jespersen has in distinguishing the present perfect from the simple past (p. 269). He sees correctly the close connection between the present tense and the present perfect, recognizable in such sentences as 'now I have eaten enough'. But he gives a rather vague definition of the present perfect and calls it 'a retrospective variety of the present'.

Present, Extended

I am seeing John

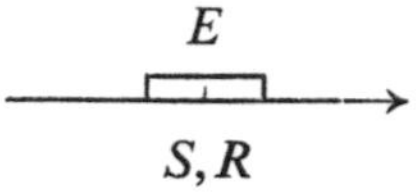

Simple Future, Extended

I shall be seeing John

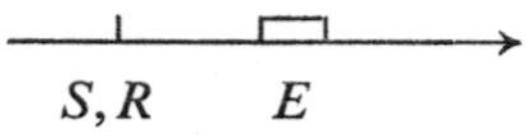

Future Perfect, Extended

I shall have been seeing John

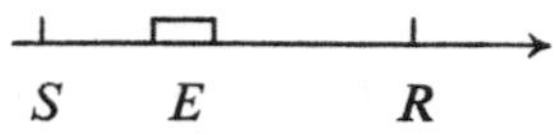

The extended tenses are sometimes used to indicate, not duration of the event, but repetition. Thus we say 'women are wearing larger hats this year' and mean that this is true for a great many instances. Whereas English expresses the extended tense by the use of the present participle, other languages have developed special suffixes for this tense. Thus the Turkish language possesses a tense of this kind, called *muzari*, which indicates repetition or duration, with the emphasis on repetition, including past and future cases. This tense is represented by the diagram

Turkish Muzari

görürüm

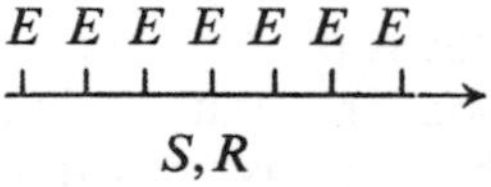

An example of this tense is the Turkish word *görürüm*, translatable as 'I usually see'. The syllable *gör* is the root meaning 'see', *ür* is the suffix expressing the *muzari*, and the *üm* is the suffix expressing the first person 'I'.[2] The sentence 'I see' would be in Turkish *görüyorum*; the only difference from the preceding example is given by the inflection *üyor* in the middle of the word, expressing the present tense. The Greek language uses the AORIST to express repetition or customary occurrence in the present tense. The aorist, however, is originally a nonextended past tense, and has assumed the second usage by a shift of meaning; in the sense of the extended tense it is called GNOMIC AORIST.[3]

German and French do not possess extended tenses, but express such meanings by special words, such as the equivalents of 'always', 'habitually', and so on. An exception is the French simple past. The French language possesses here two different tenses, the *imparfait* and the *passè défini*. They differ in so far as the *imparfait* is an extended tense, whereas the *passé défini* is not. Thus we have

[2] Turkish vowels with two dots are pronounced like the German vowels 'ö' and 'ü'.

[3] This shift of meaning is explainable as follows: One typical case of the past is stated, and to the listener is left the inductive inference that under similar conditions the same will be repeated in the future. A similar shift of meaning is given in the English 'Faint heart never won fair lady'. Cf. W. W. Goodwin, *Greek Grammar* (Ginn, Boston, 1930), 275.

126   *Hans Reichenbach*

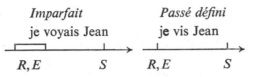

We find the same distinction in Greek, the Greek imperfect corresponding to the French *imparfait*, and the Greek aorist, in its original meaning as a past tense, corresponding to the French *passé défini*. Languages which do not have a *passé défini* sometimes use another tense in this meaning; thus Latin uses the present perfect in this sense (historical perfect).

We may add here the remark that the adjective is of the same logical nature as the present participle of a verb. It indicates an extended tense. If we put the word 'hungry', for instance, in the place of the word 'seeing' in our tables of extended tenses, we obtain the same extended tenses. A slight difference in the usage is that adjectives are preferred if the duration of the event is long; therefore adjectives can often be interpreted as describing permanent properties of things. The transition to the extended tense, and from there to the permanent tense, is seen in the examples 'he produces', 'he is producing', 'he is productive'.

When we wish to express, not repetition or duration, but validity at all times, we use the present tense. Thus we say 'two times two is four'. There the present tense expressed in the copula 'is' indicates that the time argument is used as a free variable; i.e. the sentence has the meaning 'two times two is four at any time'. This usage represents a second temporal function of the present tense.

Actual language does not always keep to the schemas given in our tables. Thus the English language uses sometimes the simple past where our schema would demand the present perfect. The English present perfect is often used in the sense of the corresponding extended tense, with the additional qualification that the duration of the event reaches up to the point of speech. Thus we have here the schema

English Present Perfect, Second Usage
I have seen him

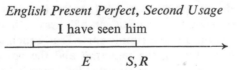

In the sense of this schema we say, for instance, 'I have known him for ten years'. If duration of the event is not meant, the English language then uses the simple past instead of the present perfect, as in 'I saw him ten years ago'. German and French would use the present perfect here.

When several sentences are combined to form a compound sentence, the tenses of the various clauses are adjusted to one another by certain rules which the grammarians call the rules for the SEQUENCE OF TENSES.

We can interpret these rules as the principle that, although the events referred to in the clauses may occupy different time points, the reference point should be the same for all clauses — a principle which, we shall say, demands THE PERMANENCE OF THE REFERENCE POINT. Thus, the tenses of the sentence, 'I had mailed the letter when John came and told me the news', may be diagramed as follows:

(1) 1st clause: $E_1 - R_1$ $- S$
    2nd clause: $R_2, E_2 - S$
    3rd clause: $R_3, E_3 - S$

Here the three reference points coincide. It would be incorrect to say, 'I had mailed the letter when John has come'; in such a combination the reference point would have been changed. As another example, consider the compound sentence, 'I have not decided which train I shall take'. That this sentence satisfies the rule of the permanence of the reference point is seen from the following diagram:

(2) 1st clause: $E_1 - S, R_1$
    2nd clause: $S, R_2 - E_2$

Here it would be incorrect to say: 'I did not decide which train I shall take'.

When the reference point is in the past, but the event coincides with the point of speech, a tense $R - S, E$ is required. In this sense, the form 'he would do' is used, which can be regarded as derived from the simple future 'he will do' by a back-shift of the two points R and E. We say, for instance, 'I did not know that you would be here'; this sentence represents the diagram:

(3) 1st clause: $R_1, E_1 - S$
    2nd clause: R_2 $- S, E_2$

The form 'I did not know that you were here' has a somewhat different meaning; it is used correctly only if the event of the man's being here extends to include the past time for which the 'I did not know' is stated, i.e. if the man was already here when I did not know it. Incidentally, in these sentences the forms 'would be' and 'were' do not have a modal function expressing irreality; i.e. they do not represent a conditional or a subjunctive, since the event referred to is not questioned. The nonmodal function is illustrated by the sentence 'I did not know that he was here', for which the form 'that he were here' appears incorrect.

When a time determination is added, such as is given by words like 'now' or 'yesterday', or by a nonreflexive symbol like 'November 7, 1944', it is referred, not to the event, but to the reference point of the sentence. We say, 'I met him yesterday'; that the word 'yesterday' refers here to the event obtains only because the points of reference and of event coincide. When we say, 'I had met him yesterday', what was yesterday is the reference point, and the meeting may have occurred the day before yesterday. We shall speak, therefore, of the POSITIONAL USE OF THE REFERENCE POINT; the reference point is used here as the carrier of the time position. Such usage, at least, is followed by the English language. Similarly, when time points are compared by means of words like 'when', 'before', or 'after', it is the reference points to which the comparison refers directly, not the events. Thus in the above example (1) the time points stated as identical by the word 'when' are the reference points of the three clauses, whereas the event of the first clause precedes that of the second and the third. Or consider the sentence, 'How unfortunate! Now that John tells me this I have mailed the letter'. The time stated here as identical with the time of John's telling the news is not the mailing of the letter but the reference point of the second clause, which is identical with the point of speech; and we have here the schema:

(4) 1st clause: S, R_1, E_1
    2nd clause: $E_2 - S, R_2$

For this reason it would be incorrect to say, 'Now that John tells me this I mailed the letter'.

If the time relation of the reference points compared is not identity, but time sequence, i.e. if one is said to be before the other, the rule of the permanence of the reference point can thus no longer be maintained. In 'he telephoned before he came' R_1 is said to be before R_2; but, at least, the tenses used have the same structure. It is different with the example, 'he was healthier when I saw him than he is now'. Here we have the structure:

(5) 1st clause: $R_1, E_1 - S$
    2nd clause: $R_2, E_2 - S$
    3rd clause: S, R_3, E_3

In such cases, the rule of the permanence of the reference point is replaced by the more general rule of the POSITIONAL USE OF THE REFERENCE POINT. The first rule, therefore, must be regarded as representing the special cases where the time relation between the reference points compared is identity.

Incidentally, the English usage of the simple past where other languages use the present perfect may be a result of the strict adherence to the principle of the positional use of the reference point. When we say, 'this is the man who drove the car', we use the simple past in the second clause because the positional principle would compel us to do so as soon as we add a time determination, as in 'this is the man who drove the car at the time of the accident'. The German uses here the present perfect, and the above sentence would be translated into *dies ist der Mann, der den Wagen gefahren hat*. Though this appears more satisfactory than the English version, it leads to a disadvantage when a time determination is added. The German is then compelled to refer the time determination, not to the reference point, but to the event, as in *dies ist der Mann, der den Wagen zur Zeit des Unglücksfalles gefahren hat*. In such cases, a language can satisfy either the principle of the permanence of the reference point or that of the positional use of the reference point, but not both.

The use of the future tenses is sometimes combined with certain deviations from the original meaning of the tenses. In the sentence 'Now I shall go' the simple future has the meaning $S, R-E$; this follows from the principle of the positional use of the reference point. However, in the sentence 'I shall go tomorrow' the same principle compels us to interpret the future tense in the form $S-R, E$. The simple future, then, is capable of two interpretations, and since there is no prevalent usage of the one or the other we cannot regard one interpretation as the correct one.[4] Further deviations occur in tense sequences. Consider the sentence: 'I shall take your photograph when you come'. The form 'when you will come' would be more correct; but we prefer to use here the present tense instead of the future. This usage may be interpreted as follows. First, the future tense is used in the first clause in the meaning $S-R, E$; second, in the second clause the point of speech is neglected. The neglect is possible because the word 'when' refers the reference point of the second clause clearly to a future event. A similar anomaly is found in the sentence, 'We shall hear the record when we have dined', where the present perfect is used instead of the future perfect 'when we shall have dined'.[5]

Turning to the general problem of the time order of the three points, we see from our tables that the possibilities of ordering the three time points are not exhausted. There are on the whole 13 possibilities, but the number of recognized grammatical tenses in English is only 6. If we wish to systematize the possible tenses we can proceed as follows. We choose the point of speech as the starting point; relative to it the point of reference can be in the past, at the same time, or in the future. This furnishes three possibilities. Next we consider the point of the event; it

---

[4] The distinction between the French future forms *je vais voir* and *je verrai* may perhaps be regarded as representing the distinction between the order $S, R-E$ and the order $S-R, E$.

[5] In some books on grammar we find the remark that the transition from direct to indirect discourse is accompanied by a shift of the tense from the present to the past. This shift, however, must not be regarded as a change in the meaning of the tense; it follows from the change in the point of speech. Thus 'I AM cold' has a point of speech lying before that of 'I said that I WAS cold'.

can be before, simultaneous with, or after the reference point. We thus arrive at $3 \cdot 3 = 9$ possible forms, which we call FUNDAMENTAL FORMS. Further differences of form result only when the position of the event relative to the point of speech is considered; this position, however, is usually irrelevant. Thus the form $S - E - R$ can be distinguished from the form S, $E - R$; with respect to relations between S and R on the one hand and between R and E on the other hand, however, these two forms do not differ, and we therefore regard them as representing the same fundamental form. Consequently, we need not deal with all the 13 possible forms and may restrict ourselves to the 9 fundamental forms.

For the 9 fundamental forms we suggest the following terminology. The position of R relative to S is indicated by the words 'past', 'present', and 'future'. The position of E relative to R is indicated by the words 'anterior', 'simple', and 'posterior', the word 'simple' being used for the coincidence of R and E. We thus arrive at the following names:

Structure	New Name	Traditional Name
$E - R - S$	Anterior past	Past perfect
$E, R - S$	Simple past	Simple past
$\left. \begin{array}{l} R - E - S \\ R - S, E \\ R - S - E \end{array} \right\}$	Posterior past	—
$E - S, R$	Anterior present	Present perfect
S, R, E	Simple present	Present
$S, R - E$	Posterior present	Simple future
$\left. \begin{array}{l} S - E - R \\ S, E - R \\ E - S - R \end{array} \right\}$	Anterior future	Future perfect
$S - R, E$	Simple future	Simple future
$S - R - E$	Posterior future	—

We see that more than one structure obtains only for the two RETRO-GRESSIVE tenses, the posterior past and the anterior future, in which the direction $S - R$ is opposite to the direction $R - E$. If we wish to distinguish among the individual structures we refer to them as the first, second, and third posterior past or anterior future.

The tenses for which a language has no established forms are expressed by transcriptions. We say, for instance, 'I shall be going to see him' and thus express the posterior future $S - R - E$ by speaking, not directly of the event E, but of the act of preparation for it; in this way we can at least express the time order for events which closely succeed the point of reference. Languages which have a future participle have direct forms for the posterior future. Thus the Latin *abiturus ero* represents this tense, meaning verbally 'I shall be one of those who will leave'. For the posterior past $R-E-S$ the form 'he would do' is used, for instance in 'I did not expect that he would win the race'. We met with this form in an above example where we interpreted it as the structure $R-S$, E; but this structure belongs to the same fundamental form as $R-E-S$ and may therefore be denoted by the same name. Instead of the form 'he would do', which grammar does not officially recognize as a tense,[6] transcriptions are frequently used. Thus we say, 'I did not expect that he was going to win the race', or, in formal writing, 'the king lavished his favor on the man who was to kill him'. In the last example, the order $R-E-S$ is expressed by the form 'was to kill', which conceives the event E, at the time R, as not yet realized, but as a destination.

Incidentally, the historical origin of many tenses is to be found in similar transcriptions. Thus 'I shall go' meant originally 'I am obliged to go'; the future-tense meaning developed because what I am obliged to do will be done by me at a later time.[7] The French future tense is of the same origin; thus the form *je donnerai*, meaning 'I shall give', is derived from *je donner ai*, which means 'I have to give'. This form of writing was actually used in Old French.[8] The double function of 'have', as expressing possession and a past tense, is derived from the idea that what I possess is acquired in the past; thus 'I have seen' meant originally 'I possess now the results of seeing', and then was interpreted as a reference to a past event.[9] The history of language shows that logical categories were not clearly seen in the beginnings of language but were the results of long developments; we therefore should not be astonished if actual language does not always fit the schema which we try to construct in symbolic logic. A mathematical language can be coordinated to actual language only in the sense of an approximation. [Ex.]

---

[6]   It is sometimes classified as a tense of the conditional mood, corresponding to the French conditional. In the examples considered above, however, it is not a conditional but a tense in the indicative mood.

[7]   In Old English no future tense existed, and the present tense was used both for the expression of the present and the future. The word 'shall' was used only in the meaning of obligation. In Middle English the word 'shall' gradually assumed the function of expressing the future tense. Cf. *The New English Dictionary* (Oxford), Vol. VIII, Pt. 2, S-Sh (1914), p. 609, col. 3.

[8]   This mode of expressing the future tense was preceded by a similar development of the Latin language, originating in vulgar Latin. Thus instead of the form *dabo*, meaning the future tense 'I shall give', the form *dare habeo* was used, which means 'I have to give'. Cf. Ferdinand Brunot, *Précis de grammaire historique de la langue française* (Masson et Cie., Paris, 1899), 434.

[9]   This is even more apparent when a two-place function is used. Thus 'I have finished my work' means originally 'I have my work finished', i.e., 'I possess my work as a finished one'. Cf. *The New English Dictionary* (Oxford, 1901), Vol. V, Pt. I, H, p. 127, col. 1-2. The German still uses the original word order, as in *Ich habe meine Arbeit beendet*.

132 Hans Reichenbach

§52. CLASSIFICATION OF FUNCTIONS

The grammatical classification of functions into nouns, adjectives, and verbs, criticized by us in §45, has only a technical significance. The verb carries the tense and personal suffixes and is thus indicated as a propositional function. Nouns and adjectives are used as functions only in combination with the auxiliary verb 'to be'. A logical difference is combined with this linguistic distinction only so far as nouns can be regarded as terms denoting classes, whereas the adjective has the nature of a tense and is therefore better included with the verbs (cf. §51).

A logically relevant classification of functions can be constructed by the use of the concepts developed in §22; furthermore, the distinctions explained in §39 and §48 must be considered. We thus arrive at the following classification.

1. We begin by collecting in one group several forms of divisions, namely, all divisions of functions with respect to PLACE PROPERTIES. Here we have the division concerning the number of variables (where space-time arguments are usually not counted), concerning univocality, concerning the structure of the field (divided field, nondivided field, uniform functions, interconnective functions), concerning symmetry, transitivity, reflexivity. Each function has its category in each of these divisions; this rule holds, correspondingly, also for the following divisions. The reflexive verbs are, in our terminology, mostly mesoreflexive functions; for instance, 'I struck myself' may be true, but need not be true. The grammatical term 'reflexive' means the logical 'not irreflexive'. Incidentally, the English language frequently drops the reflexive pronoun and then construes reflexive verbs as one-place functions, as in 'the enemy surrendered'. Other languages do not have this usage; thus the sentence quoted would read in German: *der Feind ergab sich*, in French: *l'ennemi se rendit*.

2. The second form of classification is given by the division concerning the INNER STRUCTURE of a function. Here we have the distinction of simple and complex functions. We shall regard a function as simple if it it is expressed by an independent word not indicating a derivation from other functions. Thus we shall conceive, for instance, the function 'brother' always as a simple function. It is true that there is no logical necessity to do so. Thus we could regard the function '$\hat{x}$ is the brother of $\hat{y}$' as a complex function of the form 'there is a u and a v so that u is the father of $\hat{x}$ and $\hat{y}$ and v is the mother of $\hat{x}$ and $\hat{y}$, and $\hat{x}$ and $\hat{y}$ are not identical, and $\hat{x}$ is male'. We prefer, however, not to make a formal use of this definition. What we call a simple function, therefore, depends on the language used; when this language possesses a special term for the function it will appear convenient to regard it as a simple function. In expressions like 'a brother of William', on the other hand, the linguistic

composition indicates the structure of a complex function. It is easily divided into simple parts, namely, the function 'brother' and the argument 'William'. Sometimes we are compelled to speak of complex functions even when a division into linguistic parts is not possible, as for instance when the word through its relation to other words indicates the character of a contracted symbol. Certain tenses of verbs are of this form. For instance, the indication of the past tense in the strong conjugation is not given by a suffix, but by a change of the vowel of the verbal root; the resulting word then expresses simultaneously the function and its time argument. Thus 'broke' is a contracted term expressing in one word the function 'break' and a time argument in the past tense. We therefore cannot separate here a term expressing the function from a term expressing the time argument, as can be done in the past tense of a weak verb, like 'killed'. But here the complex character of the word is clear from its relation to the root 'break'. Another example is the word 'presidential', which in such combinations as 'the presidential yacht' means 'belonging to the president', and therefore includes a function, namely, 'belonging', and its specialized argument.

3. The third form of classification is given by the division with respect to the NATURE OF THE ARGUMENT, namely, the division into thing-functions and fact-functions (cf. §48). Most verbal roots expressing functions are thing-functions; and the transition to an event-function is usually achieved by means of a suffix, as in 'the beating'. There are, however, also other forms of event-functions that are not constructed by means of a suffix, such as 'the sale'. Historically, of course, such words may be reducible to thing-functions; thus 'sale' is derived from the thing-function 'to sell'. In words like 'coronation' the origin from a verb, i.e. a thing-function, is visible only in the Latin root of the word, the verb *coronare*. The English verb 'to crown', although also derived from this root, differs from it by a phonetic development to which the noun was not subjected, and therefore does not represent the logical root of the corresponding fact-function.

4. Finally, we shall use the classification with respect to TYPE, resulting in the distinction between lower and higher functions. This distinction requires a special analysis which we shall present in the following section.

§53. FUNCTIONS OF HIGHER TYPES

The necessity for the use of functions of higher types was made clear in §39. In a logistic grammar, we need functions of higher types in particular for the interpretation of FUNCTIONAL MODIFIERS. These terms are known in traditional grammar by the name of ADVERBS, or ADVERBIAL COMPLE-

MENTS. To understand the nature of these modifiers, let us compare the statement 'John drives slowly' with the statement 'Royce Hall is a red building'. The word 'slowly' is a modifier of the function 'drives'; the word 'red', however, is not a modifier of the function 'building', but is an independent function. The independence is evident when our second sentence is written in the form 'Royce Hall is a building and Royce Hall is red'; for the first sentence such a transformation is not possible. Traditional grammar is seriously mistaken in interpreting all adjectives as modifiers of nouns; most adjectives are independent functions, like nouns and verbs. The symmetrical nature of adjective and noun in sentences like the given one was seen by Leibniz, who conceived such propositions as conjunctions of two propositions.

However, not all adjectives are independent functions. Let us write, instead of the first sentence, 'John is a slow driver'. This sentence differs from the first only in so far as it asserts a constant property of John and therefore represents an extended tense; it is equivalent to the sentence 'John always drives slowly'. Therefore the word 'slow' is here also a modifier of the function 'driver'. This is clear, too, because we cannot divide the sentence into two sentences 'John is slow and John is a driver'. What is said is not that John is slow in general but only that John is slow in his driving; thus the word 'slow', as before, operates as a modifier of 'drive'. It would be logical, therefore, to say 'John is a slowly driver'. It is the tendency to equalization which prevents the English language (and other languages as well) from distinguishing two different usages of the adjective in combination with a noun, although English clearly indicates the modifier character in such words if they are used in combination with a verb, namely, by adding the suffix 'ly'. The German language, strangely enough, makes the opposite mistake. In general it drops the distinction between adjective and adverb when the adverb modifies a verb; but for some adjectives used as modifiers of nouns it indicates the modifier character by writing adjective and noun in one word. Thus the two forms of our sentence would be in German *Johann fährt langsam* and *Johann ist ein Langsamfahrer*, although in the second version also the form *Johann ist ein langsamer Fahrer* could be used in German. Usually only some established combinations are used in German in this way, such as *Schnellfahrer, Schwerverwundeter, Schwerarbeiter*, etc. This is an instance where a logically clear distinction has not found its full expression in conversational languages.

To understand the nature of modifiers we must realize that most predicates are used in such a way that they leave open some space for further specification. The function 'x moves', for instance, leaves open a specification of the speed, telling us only that the speed is not zero. The addition of an adverb like 'slowly' includes the speed in a narrower interval. We may consider the individual motion of x, determined as to speed, direction, and so on, as a property f, which we call a SPECIFIC PROPERTY; the various properties f of this kind then may be included in a class of motion-properties represented by a function $\mu(f)$. The statement 'x_1 moves' tells us that x_1 has one of the motion-properties; in symbols, with '$m(x)$' for 'x moves':

(1) $\quad m(x_1) =_{Df} (\exists f) f(x_1) \cdot \mu(f)$

We see that '$m(x)$' is a contracted symbol standing for a complex function which includes a predicate as a bound variable. m is the property every x has that has a property f belonging to μ; being a property of an object of the zero type, m is of the first type. In class terminology, the class M coordinated to m is the disjunct of all the classes F coordinated to functions f having the property μ.

We can now introduce the modifier 'slowly'. Writing '$msl(x)$' for 'x moves slowly', and '$\sigma(f)$' for 'f is slow', we obtain

(2) $\quad msl(x_1) =_{Df} (\exists f) f(x_1) \cdot \mu(f) \cdot \sigma(f)$

This analysis shows why adverbs can be constructed from adjectives by the addition of a suffix; they are predicates, like adjectives, not denoting properties of THINGS, however, but of PROPERTIES. The suffix 'ly' indicates this usage.[10]

The functions μ and σ used in (2) differ in one important point. The properties f comprehended in μ are MUTUALLY EXCLUSIVE; i.e. if a thing x_1 has one of these properties, it cannot have one of the others. Thus if x_1 moves at 30 miles an hour, it cannot move simultaneously at 40 miles an hour. The properties f comprised in σ, however, are NONEXCLUSIVE. Thus x_1 may move slowly and at the same time eat slowly, or think slowly.

Usually a first-type property is introduced in the form (1) only for higher functions pertaining to mutually exclusive properties, such as μ. If the higher function relates to nonexclusive properties, like the function σ, the corresponding first-type property is usually defined by the requirement that a great number of specific properties of x_1 belong to σ, or that those specific properties of x_1 which belong to a certain function κ are contained in σ. Here κ may mean, for instance, properties involving a change in time, or at least a group of RELEVANT properties of this sort. The first-type property then is defined in the form

(3) $\quad sl(x_1) =_{Df} (f)[\kappa(f) \cdot f(x_1) \supset \sigma(f)]$

---

[10] It is impossible to symbolize the sentence 'x_1 moves slowly' in the form '$m(x_1) \cdot \sigma(m)$' because the property MOVING in general is not slow; only the specific sort of moving which refers to x_1 is slow. This is the reason that the specific property f must be introduced, as shown in (2).

This, for instance, is the way in which the adjective 'slow' is defined. The statement 'x_1 is slow' is given by the expression '$sl(x_1)$' defined in (3). The rather complicated relation between $sl(x_1)$ and $\sigma(f)$, shown by (3), explains why the meaning of the first-type predicate 'sl', i.e. the adjective 'slow', and of the second-type predicate σ, i.e. the word root 'slow' used in the adverb 'slowly', do not strictly correspond to each other.

Most adverbs represent functions σ of the nonexclusive type. Thus adverbs like 'very', 'greatly', 'extremely', are of this sort. A man may have many specific properties to which the modifier 'very' applies; he may be very intelligent, very strong, very helpful. Not always does language possess a word for the first-type property defined in (3). Thus we do not say 'x is very', although this expression might be defined according to (3). Perhaps the term 'x_1 is outstanding' may be conceived as derived from the adverb 'very' by (3), when in this formula 'σ' is interpreted as 'very'.

Now let us compare an adverbial modification with a statement asserting two independent properties. The statement cited above, 'Royce Hall is a red building' can be written in the form

(4) $bl(x_1) \cdot r(x_1)$

where 'bl' stands for 'building' and 'r' for 'red'. As in the preceding instance it is permissible to regard each of these properties as including a number of specific properties; thus a building is capable of many forms and sizes, and the color red is divisible into many different shades of red. Therefore we can conceive these first-type properties as derived from second-type properties:

(5) $bl(x_1) =_{Df} (\exists f) f(x_1) \cdot \lambda(f)$ $r(x_1) =_{Df} (\exists f) f(x_1) \cdot \rho(f)$

Here λ corresponds to the class of specific sorts of buildings, and ρ to the class of shades of red. Inserting (5) in (4) we arrive at the statement

(6) $[(\exists f) f(x_1) \cdot \lambda(f)] \cdot [(\exists f) f(x_1) \cdot \rho(f)]$

Comparing this with (2) we see a remarkable difference as to structure: (6) says that there is a specific property f of x_1 belonging to λ, and likewise such a property belonging to ρ; (2) says that it is THE SAME SPECIFIC PROPERTY f which belongs to the functions μ and σ. The identity of specific properties, expressed by the adverbial suffix 'ly', may be regarded as formulating the difference between an adverbial qualification of a function and the use of two independent functions.

The relation between the two forms (2) and (6) is as follows. A form corresponding to (6), namely,

(7) $[(\exists f) f(x_1) \cdot \mu(f_1)] \cdot [(\exists f) f(x_1) \cdot \sigma(f)]$

can be derived from (2), although the reverse relation does not hold; (2) says more than (7). We therefore can derive from an adverbial qualification a statement asserting two independent properties. But only the first of these two properties is the same as that used in the adverbial statement; this is the property derived from the exclusive function μ, in our example the first bracket of (7), which according to (1) means 'x_1 moves'. The second independent property, derived from the nonexclusive function σ, does not represent the adjective corresponding to the adverb. In our example, the second bracket of (7) defines a first-type property for which there is no name in conversational language, since the adjective 'slow' is defined, not by this bracket, but by (3). This is the reason that the statement 'x_1 moves and x_1 is slow' is not derivable from the statement 'x_1 moves slowly'.

Similar considerations hold where other forms for the definition of the adjective are used. Thus the derivation of the adjective 'beautiful' from a corresponding function of the second type does not follow (3), but cannot be represented by the second bracket in (7) either. Consider the statement 'Annette dances beautifully'; it has the form

$$(8) \quad (\exists f) f(x_1)\, \delta(f) \cdot \beta(f)$$

where δ represents the function comprehending properties of dancing, and β the function comprising properties of beauty. The first-type statement 'Annette dances' is definable as

$$(9) \quad d(x_1) =_{Df} (\exists f) f(x_1) \cdot \delta(f)$$

But the first-type predicate 'beautiful' is not defined in the same way. When we say 'Annette is beautiful' we mean that a particular property of Annette, namely, her bodily form, is beautiful. This leads to the following definition of the adjective 'beautiful':

$$(10) \quad bt(x_1) =_{Df} (\exists f) f(x_1) \cdot a(f) \cdot \beta(f)$$

where a is the function comprehending all individual forms of human bodies such that each f belonging to it specifies the shape of the whole body. We see that this definition corresponds to (2), not to (1); it can be read in the form 'Annette is beautifully shaped'. This shows that, although a form corresponding to (7) is derivable from (8), statement (8) does not imply a statement of the form 'Annette dances and is beautiful'.

This analysis explains why, although expressions like (2) and (8) are symmetrical in the two functions of higher order, verb and adverb do not occupy symmetrical positions in conversational language. Only if we were to use a definition of the adjective 'beautiful' corresponding to (9), namely, in the form

$$(11) \quad bt(x_1) =_{Df} (\exists f) f(x_1) \cdot \beta(f)$$

could we give to (8) a symmetrical interpretation; namely, we then could read (8) also in the form 'Annette is beautiful dancingly'. But although such a terminology might not appear incorrect, it certainly does not correspond to actual usage.

Let us add here a remark about the necessity of introducing higher functions for the interpretation of adverbs. It might be suggested that such functions be avoided by the application of the relation of class inclusion. Instead of the function δ, we then would use the function d occurring in (9), or the corresponding class D; similarly, we would use the function bt defined in (11), or the corresponding class Bt. These classes then would not be defined by the definitions (9) and (11), but would be regarded by primitive terms, like δ and β in the other interpretation. Applying the relation of class inclusion instead of class membership, we then would write the sentence 'Annette dances beautifully' in the form:

$$(12) \quad (\exists F) \, (x_1 \in F) \cdot (F \subset D) \cdot (F \subset Bt)$$

This expression would replace (8). It can be shown, however, that such an interpretation cannot be carried through. Formula (12) is equivalent to the expression

$$(13) \quad (x_1 \in D) \cdot (x_1 \in Bt)$$

since when x_1 belongs to the common class of D and Bt, there is always a subclass F of both classes to which x_1 belongs. We therefore cannot distinguish here between the adverbial modifier and the genuine adjective. Whereas the use of higher functions enables us to construct, for this distinction, the two different forms (7) and (2), the two corresponding forms (12) and (13) are identical. Incidentally, this interpretation would not rid us of the higher calculus of functions since the occurrence of a class F as a bound variable, as in (12), represents an operation within this calculus.

On the other hand, we do not wish to say that functions of a higher type are always clearly distinguishable, in conversational language, from functions of the first type. The logistic interpretation of conversational language cannot be given without certain arbitrary restrictions of meanings. General predicates like 'color' and 'motion' are not always used in strictly the same sense. Thus when we say 'red is a color', we use 'color' as a second-type predicate; in the sentence 'a red thing is a colored thing' we use it as a first-type predicate.

Let us now turn to another interpretation of adverbs which, although it also applies higher functions, leads to the advantage that the adverb is reduced to a function of the first type. The adverb is construed, in this conception, not as a predicate of the argument of the sentence, but of the

FACT coordinated to it. Following this interpretation we write the sentence 'Annette dances beautifully' in the form

(14) $(\exists f) f(x_1) \cdot \delta(f) \cdot bt\{(w)[f(x_1)]^*(v)\}$

where δ, as before, comprises all specific properties of dancing, while '*bt*' is employed here as a primitive term not derived from a higher function. Formula (14) can be read in the form: 'Annette dances and her dancing is beautiful'. The phrase 'her dancing' is regarded here as the description of the event, and not as a description of the specific property. This interpretation offers the advantage of a very simple conception of adverbs, namely, as adjectives referred to the event indicated by the sentence.

It is necessary, however, to add a qualification. We wish to say that there is a connection between the way of dancing and the property of being beautiful; that is, the property of the event is meant to qualify the specific property f in such a way that it must have a certain specific character. This connection is not expressed in (14), since (14) will hold also when no such connection exists. For instance, the sentence 'x_1 was murdered and the murder of x_1 led to a war' can also be expressed in the form (14), when we interpret the symbol 'δ' as 'was murdered' and '*bt*' as meaning 'led to a war'. However, the fact that the event led to a war does not specify the manner in which the murder was committed; it only states a consequence which originated, not from the way the murder was committed, but from the political circumstances in which it occurred. This example shows that (14) does not convey the full meaning of the adverbial sentence about the dancing, and therefore must be supplemented by a qualification.

The addition to be made to (14) is given by the statement of a connection between f and bt, which can be expressed in the form

(15) $f(x_1) \stackrel{.}{\Rightarrow} bt\{(w)[f(x_1)]^*(v)\}$

This expression must be so added to (14) that the scope of the existential operator includes (15). The addition then states that the property f which x_1 has connectively implies the property bt of the event; in this way a specification of f is attained. We use here a connective implication of the synthetic kind in order to exclude the paradoxes of the adjunctive implication. The application of an adjunctive general implication would not suffice. When adverbial expressions are interpreted in the form (14), a qualification in the form (15) must therefore be understood.

Grammar places in the category of adverbs a great many terms which should not be regarded as adverbs, i.e., as modifiers of functions. The word 'not', for instance, is classified by many grammarians as an adverb; but it is a logical term. Neither are the so-called adverbs of time and place ADVERBS; they are terms specifying the time and space argument to which the sentence as a whole refers. There are also higher functions which are not adverbs. They occur, for instance, when classes of classes are referred to, as in the term 'United Nations', or in the definition of numbers. Language frequently uses numerical qualifications, such as the words 'frequently', 'seldom', and 'usually'; these terms, which grammar classifies as adverbs, are not modifiers of functions, but express frequency relations concerning the occurrence of objects or events. They therefore constitute higher functions used as NUMERICAL QUALIFIERS. Thus, in the sentence 'chemical reactions are frequently accompanied by a production of heat', the word 'frequently' does not modify the function 'accompany' since it does not delimit a specific form of accompaniment; it states rather that the class of events described by the sentence as a whole is large.

On the other hand, there are certain terms that are incorrectly classified as adjectives. To call a word like 'all' an adjective when it precedes a noun is a logical absurdity. It is a logical term, and not a function. It is incorrect, furthermore, to regard the first term in a noun compound as an adjective. Thus, in the compound 'door bell', the word 'door' is not used as an adjective, since the sentence '*x* is a door bell' cannot be split into the two sentences '*x* is a door' and '*x* is a bell'. But the word 'door' is not used as an adverb either. It constitutes, rather, a part of a complex function, as explained in (23, §22). If a suitable terminology is desired, we may call the first term, in our example the word 'door', the INDIRECT PART of the compound; the second term, the word 'bell' in our example, may be called the DIRECT PART, it being the function which applies directly to the argument of the sentence. There are other forms of complex functions which do not follow the pattern (23, §22). Thus the function 'the last Goths' is a complex function in which 'last' does not have the character of an adjective, since '*x* is a last Goth' cannot be split into the two statements '*x* is last' and '*x* is a Goth'; that is, *x* is last only in so far as it is a Goth. The word 'last' stands here as an abbreviation for a qualification saying that there were no later Goths; the qualification could be easily symbolized with the help of logical terms. The word 'last', therefore, cannot be construed as an independent function but must be regarded as an incomplete symbol which has a meaning only in combination with functions. The distinction between direct and indirect part may be applied also to complex functions of this kind. Such functions, incidentally, can be constructed for any type. 'The last integer below 100', for instance, is a description given by means of a complex function of a higher type.

Let us add a remark about the use of predicate adjectives after verbs other than the copula. We say, for instance, 'the wine seems good', using the adjective 'good' as qualifying the wine and not as modifying the property of seeming. This appears correct; in fact, the sentence means 'it seems that the wine is good'; or, in a more elaborate version, 'the wine has a certain appearance which makes the speaker believe that the wine is good'. Here the word 'good' occurs as a predicate of the argument, 'the wine'.

There are other forms which, although at first glance appearing to be of a similar construction, require a different explanation. We say, 'oranges taste good'; but we mean, obviously, that the taste is good. The word 'good', therefore, has here the character of an adverb, and it would appear preferable to say: 'oranges taste well'. The adjectival form presumably originates from a shift in the meaning of the word 'taste'. It was used originally in the transitive form 'I taste the orange'. From a transitive verb we can always derive an intransitive one by means of binding one variable by an existential operator. Thus we have the two forms 'I taste' in the sense of 'there is something that I taste', and 'the orange is tasted' in the sense of 'there is somebody who tastes the orange'. But the verb 'taste' as well as some others, like 'look' and 'feel', underwent an unusual development: the transition to the intransitive form was combined with a change in the place of the argument variables, and we say now 'the orange tastes'. The adverb 'well' was originally combined only with the transitive meaning; in the sentence 'I tasted the orange well' it modifies, not the taste of the orange, but the abilities of the taster. In the reversed intransitive meaning, the adjective 'good' was used; 'the orange tastes good' stands as an abbreviation for 'I tasted the orange and found it good to my taste'. But since the verb 'taste' has now fully assumed the reversed intransitive meaning, it would be logical to combine it also in this meaning with the adverb 'well'.

In phrases like 'looks good' we may distinguish two different meanings. When we say 'the meal looks good', we mean that the meal looks as though it were a good meal; here the adjectival form is correct. In speaking of a good-looking girl, however, we wish to say, not that the girl is presumably good, but that the way she looks is good; here 'good' is used as an adverb, and it would appear preferable to speak of a well-looking girl. What makes such usage inopportune is that the adverb 'well' has acquired, in relation to persons, the meaning of the adjective 'healthy'; to say that a girl looks well means that she looks as though she were healthy. The historical explanation for the use of the adjective may be found in the transition to the reversed intransitive form, as explained above.

Because of its reference to functions of a higher type, the study of the adverb represents a rather intricate chapter of grammar. We should not be astonished that this part of conversational language does not always stand up to the gauge of logic. It is amazing enough that conversational language possesses means to delimit a category of terms that belong in the higher calculus of functions. [Ex.]

Jaakko Hintikka

SEMANTICS FOR PROPOSITIONAL ATTITUDES

1. THE CONTRAST BETWEEN THE THEORY OF REFERENCE AND THE THEORY OF MEANING IS SPURIOUS

In the philosophy of logic a distinction is often made between the THEORY OF REFERENCE and the THEORY OF MEANING.[1] In this paper I shall suggest (*inter alia*) that this distinction, though not without substance, is profoundly misleading. The theory of reference is, I shall argue, the theory of meaning for certain simple types of language. The only entities needed in the so-called theory of meaning are, in many interesting cases and perhaps even in all cases, merely what is required in order for the expression of our language to be able to refer in certain more complicated situations. Instead of the theory of reference and the theory of meaning we perhaps ought to speak in some cases of the theory of simple and of multiple reference, respectively. Quine has regretted that the term 'semantics', which etymologically ought to refer to the theory of meaning, has come to mean the theory of reference.[2] I submit that this usage is happier than Quine thinks, and that large parts of the theory of meaning in reality are — or ought to be — but semantical theories for notions transcending the range of certain elementary types of concepts.

It seems to me in fact that the usual reasons for distinguishing between meaning and reference are seriously mistaken. Frequently, they are formu-

Reprinted from J. Davis (ed.), *Philosophical Logic* (Dordrecht, Reidel, 1969), 21-45.
[1] See e.g. W. V. Quine, *From a Logical Point of View* (Harvard University Press, Cambridge, Mass., 1953) (2nd ed.: 1961), 130-32.
[2] *Ibid.*

lated in terms of a first-order (i.e. quantificational) language. In such a language, it is said, knowing the mere references of individual constants, or knowing the extensions of predicates, cannot suffice to specify their meanings because the references of two individual constants or the extensions of two predicate constants 'obviously' can coincide without there being any identity of meaning.[3] Hence, it is often concluded, the theory of reference for first-order languages will have to be supplemented by a theory of the 'meanings' of the expressions of these languages.

The line of argument is not without solid intuitive foundation, but its implications are different from what they are usually taken to be. This whole concept of meaning (as distinguished from reference) is very unclear and usually hard to fathom. However it is understood, it seems to me in any case completely hopeless to try to divorce the idea of the meaning of a sentence from the idea of the INFORMATION that the sentence can convey to a hearer or reader, should someone truthfully address it to him.[4] Now what is this information? Clearly it is just information to the effect that the sentence is true, that the world is such as to meet the truth-conditions of the sentence.

Now in the case of a first-order language these truth-conditions cannot be divested from the references of singular terms and from the extensions of its predicates. In fact, these references and extensions are precisely what the truth-conditions of quantified sentences turn on. The truth-value of a sentence is a function of the references (extensions) of the terms it contains, not of their 'meanings'. Thus it follows from the above principles that a theory of reference is for genuine first-order languages the basis of a theory of meaning. Recently, a similar conclusion has in effect been persuasively argued for (from entirely different premises and in an entirely different way) by Donald Davidson.[5] The references, not the alleged meanings, of our primitive terms are thus what determine the meanings (in the sense explained) of first-order sentences. Hence the introduction

---

[3] For a simple recent argument of this sort (without a specific reference to first-order theories), see e.g. William P. Alston, *Philosophy of Language* (Prentice-Hall, Inc., Englewood Cliffs, N.J., 1964), 13. Cf. also Quine, *From a Logical Point of View*, 21-22.

[4] In more general terms, it seems to me hopeless to try to develop a theory of sentential meaning which is not connected very closely with the idea of the information which the sentence can convey to us, or a theory of meaning for individual words which would not show how understanding them contributes to appreciating the information of the sentences in which they occur. There are of course many nuances in the actual use of words and sentences which are not directly explained by connecting meaning and information in this way, assuming that this can be done. However, there do not seem to be any obstacles in principle to explaining these nuances in terms of pragmatic, contextual, and other contingent pressures operating on a language-user. For remarks on this methodological situation, see my paper "Epistemic Logic and the Method of Philosophical Analysis", *Australasian Journal of Philosophy* 46 (1968) 37-51.

[5] Donald Davidson, "Truth and Meaning", *Synthese* 17 (1967), 304-23.

of the 'meanings' of singular terms and predicates is strictly useless: In any theory of meaning which serves to explain the information which first-order sentences convey, these 'meanings' are bound to be completely idle.

What happens, then, to our intuitions concerning the allegedly obvious difference between reference and meaning in first-order languages? If these intuitions are sound, and if the above remarks are to the point, then the only reasonable conclusion is that our intuitions do not really pertain to first-order discourse. The 'ordinary language' which we think of when we assert the obviousness of the distinction cannot be reduced to the canonical form of an applied first-order language without violating these intuitions. How these other languages enable us to appreciate the real (but frequently misunderstood) force of the apparently obvious difference between reference and meaning I shall indicate later (see Section VI *infra*).

2. FIRST-ORDER LANGUAGES

I conclude that the traditional theory of reference, suitably extended and developed, is all we need for a full-scale theory of meaning in the case of an applied first-order language. All that is needed to grasp the information that a sentence of such a language yields is given by the rules that determine the references of its terms, in the usual sense of the word. For the purposes of first-order languages, to specify the meaning of a singular term is therefore nearly tantamount to specifying its reference, and to specify the meaning of a predicate is for all practical purposes to specify its extension. As long as we can restrict ourselves to first-order discourse, the theory of truth and satisfaction will therefore be the central part of the theory of meaning.

A partial exception to this statement seems to be the theory of so-called 'meaning postulates' or 'semantical rules' which are supposed to catch non-logical synonymies.[6] However, I would argue that whatever non-logical identities of meaning there might be in our discourse ought to be spelled out, not in terms of definitions of terms, but by developing a satisfactory semantical theory for the terms which create these synonymies. In those cases in which meaning postulates are needed, this enterprise no longer belongs to the theory of first-order logic.

In more precise terms, one may thus say that to understand a sentence of first-order logic is to know its interpretation in the actual world. To know this is to know the interpretation function φ. This can be characterized as a function which does the following things:

6   See Quine, *From a Logical Point of View*, 33-37.

(1.1) For each individual constant a of our first-order language, $\varphi(a)$ is a member of the domain of individuals l.

The domain of individuals l is of course to be thought of as the totality of objects which our language speaks of.

(1.2) For each constant predicate Q (say of n terms), $\varphi(Q)$ is a set of n-tuples of the members of l.

If we know φ and if we know the usual rules holding of satisfaction (truth), we can in principle determine the truth-values of all the sentences of our first-order language. This is the cash value of the statement made above that the extensions of our individual constants and constant predicates are virtually all that we need in the theory of meaning in an applied first-order language.[7]

These conditions may be looked upon in slightly different ways. If φ is considered as an arbitrary function in (1.1)–(1.2), instead of the particular function which is involved in one's understanding of a language, and if l is likewise allowed to vary, we obtain a characterization of the concept of interpretation in the general model-theoretic sense.

3. PROPOSITIONAL ATTITUDES

We have to keep in mind the possibility that φ might be only a partial function (as applied to free singular terms), i.e. that some of our singular terms are in fact empty. This problem is not particularly prominent in the present paper, however.[8] If what I have said so far is correct, then the emphasis philosophers have put on the distinction between reference and meaning (e.g. between *Bedeutung* and *Sinn*) is motivated only in so far as they have implicitly or explicitly considered concepts which go beyond the expressive power of first-order languages.[9] Probably the most important type of such concept is a propositional attitude.[10] One purpose of this paper is to sketch some salient features of a semantical theory of

---

[7] The main reason why the truth of these observations is not appreciated more widely seems to be the failure to consider realistically what the actual use of a first-order language (say for the purpose of conveying information to another person) would look like.

[8] The basic problems as to what happens when this possibility is taken seriously are discussed in my paper, "Studies in the Logic of Existence and Necessity I", *The Monist* 50 (1966), 55-76, reprinted (with changes) in J. Davis (ed.), *Philosophical Logic* (Dordrecht, Reidel, 1969) under the title "Existential Presuppositions and Their Elimination".

[9] This is certainly true of Frege. His very interest in oblique contexts seems to have been kindled by the realization that they cannot be handled by means of the ideas he had successfully applied to first-order logic.

[10] The term seems to go back to Bertrand Russell, *An Inquiry into Meaning and Truth* (George Allen and Unwin, London, 1940).

such concepts. An interesting problem will be the question as to what extent we have to assume entities other than the usual individuals (the members of I) in order to give a satisfactory account of the meaning of propositional attitudes. As will be seen, what I take to be the true answer to this question is surprisingly subtle, and cannot be formulated by a simple 'yes' or 'no'.

What I take to be the distinctive feature of all use of propositional attitudes is the fact that in using them we are considering more than one possibility concerning the world.[11] (This consideration of different possibilities is precisely what makes propositional attitudes propositional, it seems to me.) It would be more natural to speak of different possibilities concerning our 'actual' world than to speak of several possible worlds. For the purpose of logical and semantical analysis, the second locution is much more appropriate than the first, however, although I admit that it sounds somewhat weird and perhaps also suggests that we are dealing with something much more unfamiliar and unrealistic than we are actually

---

[11] An important qualification here is that for deep logical reasons one cannot usually distinguish effectively between what is 'really' a logically possible world and what merely 'appears' on the face of one's language (or thinking) to be a possibility. This, in a sufficiently sharp analysis, is what destroys the pleasant invariance of propositional attitudes with respect to logical equivalence. Even though p and q are equivalent, i.e. even though the 'real' possibilities concerning the world that they admit and exclude are the same,

$$a \quad \begin{array}{l} \text{knows} \\ \text{believes} \\ \text{remembers} \\ \text{hopes} \\ \text{strives} \end{array} \quad \text{that } p$$

and

$$a \quad \begin{array}{l} \text{knows} \\ \text{believes} \\ \text{remembers} \\ \text{hopes} \\ \text{strives} \end{array} \quad \text{that } q$$

need not be equivalent, for the apparent (to a) possibilities admitted by p and q need not be identical.

I have studied this concept of an 'apparent' possibility and its consequences at some length elsewhere, especially in the second and third paper printed in *Deskription, Analytizität und Existenz* (ed. by Paul Weingartner) (Pustet, Salzburg and Munich 1966), in "Are Logical Truths Analytic?", *Philosophical Review* 74 (1965), 178-203, in "Surface Information and Depth Information", in *Information and Inference* (ed. by K. J. J. Hintikka and P. Suppes) (D. Reidel Publishing Co., Dordrecht, 1969), and in "Are Mathematical Truths Synthetic A Priori?", *Journal of Philosophy* 65 (1968), 640-51.

It is an extremely interesting concept to study and to codify. However, it is not directly relevant to the concerns of the present paper, and would in any case break its confines. Hence it will not be taken up here, except by way of this *caveat*.

doing. In our sense, whoever has made preparations for more than one course of events has dealt with several 'possible courses of events' or 'possible worlds'. Of course, the possible courses of events he considered were from his point of view so many alternative courses that the actual events might take. However, only one such course of events (at most) became actual. Hence there is a sense in which the others were merely 'possible courses of events', and this is the sense on which we shall try to capitalize.

Let us assume for simplicity that we are dealing with only one propositional attitude and that we are considering a situation in which it is attributed to one person only. Once we can handle this case, a generalization to the others is fairly straightforward. Since the person in question remains constant throughout the first part of our discussion, we need not always indicate him explicitly.

4. PROPOSITIONAL ATTITUDES AND 'POSSIBLE WORLDS'

My basic assumption (slightly oversimplified) is that an attribution of any propositional attitude to the person in question involves a division of all the possible worlds (more precisely, all the possible worlds which we can distinguish in the part of language we use in making the attribution) into two classes: into those possible worlds which are in accordance with the attitude in question and into those which are incompatible with it. The meaning of the division in the case of such attitudes as knowledge, belief, memory, perception, hope, wish, striving, desire, etc. is clear enough. For instance, if what we are speaking of are (say) a's memories, then these possible worlds are all the possible worlds compatible with everything he remembers.

There are propositional attitudes for which this division is not possible. Some such attitudes can be defined in terms of attitudes for which the assumptions do hold, and thus in a sense can be 'reduced' to them. Others may fail to respond to this kind of attempted reduction to those 'normal' attitudes which we shall be discussing here. If there really are such recalcitrant propositional attitudes, I shall be glad to restrict the scope of my treatment so as to exclude them. Enough extremely important notions will still remain within the purview of my methods.

There is a sense in which in discussing a propositional attitude, attributed to a person, we can even restrict our attention to those possible worlds which are in accordance with this attitude.[12] This may be brought

[12] There is a distinction here which is not particularly relevant to my concerns in the present paper but important enough to be noted in passing, especially as I have not made it clear in my earlier work. What precisely are the worlds 'alternative to' a given

out e.g. by paraphrasing statements about propositional attitudes in terms of this restricted class of all possible worlds. The following examples will illustrate these approximate paraphrases:

a believes that p = in all the possible worlds compatible with what *a* believes, it is the case that p;

a does not believe that p (in the sense 'it is not the case that *a* believes that p') = in at least one possible world compatible with what *a* believes it is not the case that p.

5. SEMANTICS FOR PROPOSITIONAL ATTITUDES

What kind of semantics is appropriate for this mode of treating propositional attitudes? Clearly what is involved is a set Ω of possible worlds or of models in the usual sense of the word. Each of them, say $\mu \in \Omega$, is characterized by a set of individuals $I(\mu)$ existing in that 'possible world'. An interpretation of individual constants and predicates will now be a two-argument function $\varphi(a, \mu)$ or $\varphi(Q, \mu)$ which depends also on the possible world μ in question. Otherwise an interpretation works in the same way as in the pure first-order case, and the same rules hold for propositional connectives as in this old case.

Simple though this extension of the earlier semantical theory is, it is in many ways illuminating. For instance, it is readily seen that in many cases earlier semantical rules are applicable without changes, *Inter alia*, in so far as no words for propositional attitudes occur inside the scope of a quantifier, this quantifier is subject to the same semantical rules (satisfaction conditions) as before.

6. MEANING AND THE DEPENDENCE OF REFERENCE ON 'POSSIBLE WORLDS'

A new aspect of the situation is the fact that the reference $\varphi(a, \mu)$ of a singular term now depends on μ — on what course the events will take, one might say. This enables us to appreciate an objection which you probably felt like making earlier when it was said that in a first-order

---

one, say μ? A moment's reflection on the principles underlying my discussion will show, I trust, that they must be taken to be worlds compatible with a certain person's having a definite propositional attitude in μ, and not just compatible with the content of his attitude, for instance, compatible with someone's knowing something in μ and not just compatible with what he knows. I failed to spell this out in my *Knowledge and Belief* (Cornell Univ. Press, Ithaca, N.Y., 1962), as R. Chisholm in effect pointed out in his review article, "The Logic of Knowing", *Journal of Philosophy* 60 (1963), 773-95.

language the theory of meaning is the theory of reference. What really determines the meaning of a singular term, you felt like saying, is not whatever reference it happens to have, but rather the way in which this reference is determined. But in order for this to make any difference, we must consider more than one possibility as to what the reference is, depending on the circumstances (i.e. depending on the course events will take). This dependence is just what is expressed by $\varphi(a, \mu)$ when it is considered as a function of μ. (This function IS the meaning of a, one is tempted to say.) Your objection thus has a point. However, it does not show that more is involved in the theory of meaning for first-order languages than the references of its terms. Rather, what is shown is that in order to spell out the idea that the meaning of a term is the way in which its reference is determined we have to consider how the reference varies in different possible worlds, and therefore go beyond first-order languages, just as I suggested above. Analogous remarks apply of course to the extensions of predicates.

Another novelty here is the need of picking out one distinguished possible world from among them all, viz. the world that happens to be actualized ('the actual world').

7. DEVELOPING AN EXPLICIT SEMANTICAL THEORY: ALTERNATIVENESS RELATIONS

How are these informal observations to be incorporated into a more explicit semantical theory? According to what I have said, understanding attributions of the propositional attitude in question (let us assume that this is expressed by 'B') means being able to make a distinction between two kinds of possible worlds, according to whether they are compatible with the relevant attitudes of the person in question. The semantical counterpart to this is of course a function which to a given individual person assigns a set of possible worlds.

However, a minor complication is in order here. Of course, the person in question may himself have different attitudes in the different worlds we are considering. Hence this function in effect becomes a relation which to a given individual AND TO A GIVEN POSSIBLE WORLD μ associates a number of possible worlds which we shall call the ALTERNATIVES to μ. The relation will be called the alternativeness relation. (For different propositional attitudes, we have to consider different alternativeness relations.) Our basic apparatus does not impose many restrictions on it. The obvious requirement that ensues from what has been said is the following:

(S.B.) $B_a p$ is true in a possible world μ if and only if p is true in all the alternatives to μ.

$B_a p$ may be thought of as a shorthand for '*a* believes that *p*'. We can write this condition in terms of an interpretation function φ. What understanding B means is to have a function φ_B which to a given possible world μ and to a given individual a associates a set of possible worlds $\varphi_B(a, \mu)$, namely, the set of all alternatives to μ.[13] Intuitively, they are the possible worlds compatible with the presence of the attitude expressed by B in the person a in the possible world μ.

In terms of this extended interpretation function, (S.B.) can be written as follows:

$B_a p$ is true in μ if and only if p is true in every member of $\varphi_B(a, \mu)$.

8. RELATION TO QUINE'S CRITERION OF COMMITMENT

The interesting and important feature of this truth-condition is that it involves quantification over a certain set of possible worlds. By Quine's famous criterion, we allegedly are ontologically committed to whatever we quantify over.[14] Thus my semantical theory of propositional attitudes seems to imply that we are committed to the existence of possible worlds as a part of our ontology.

This conclusion seems to me false, and I think that it in fact constitutes a counter-example to Quine's criterion of commitment *qua* a criterion of ontological commitment. Surely we must in some sense be COMMITTED to whatever we quantify over. To this extent Quine seems to be entirely right. But why call this a criterion of ONTOLOGICAL commitment? One's ontology is what one assumes to exist in one's world, it seems to me. It is, as it were, one's census of one's universe. Now such a census is meaningful only in some particular possible world. Hence Quine's criterion can work as a criterion of ONTOLOGICAL commitment only if the quantification it speaks of is a quantification over entities belonging to some one particular world. To be is perhaps to be a value of a bound variable. But to exist in an ontologically relevant sense, to be a part of the furniture of the world, is to be a value of a special kind of a bound variable, namely one whose

[13]   As the reader will notice, I am misusing (in the interest of simplicity) my terminology systematically by speaking elliptically of 'the person *a*' etc. when 'the person referred to by a' or some such thing is meant. I do not foresee any danger of confusion resulting from this, however.

[14]   E.g. Quine, *From a Logical Point of View*, 1-14, W. V. Quine, *Word and Object* (The MIT Press, Cambridge, Mass., and John Wiley, New York and London, 1960), 241-43. It is not quite clear from Quine's exposition, however, precisely how much emphasis is to be put on the word 'ontology' in his criterion of ontological commitment. My discussion which focuses on this word may thus have to be taken as a qualification to Quine's criterion rather than as outright criticism.

values all belong to the same possible world. Thus the notion of a possible world serves to clarify considerably the idea of ontological commitment so as to limit the scope of Quine's dictum.

Clearly, our quantification over possible worlds does not satisfy this extra requirement. Hence there is a perfectly good sense in which we are not ontologically committed to possible worlds, however important their role in our semantical theory may be.

Quine's distinction between ONTOLOGY and IDEOLOGY, somewhat modified and put to a new use, is handy here.[15] We have to distinguish between what we are committed to in the sense that we believe it to exist in the actual world or in some other possible world, and what we are committed to as a part of our ways of dealing with the world conceptually, committed to as a part of our conceptual system. The former constitute our ontology, the latter our 'ideology'. What I am suggesting is that the possible worlds we have to quantify over are a part of our ideology but not of our ontology.

The general criterion of commitment is a generalization of this. Quantification over the members of one particular world is a measure of ontology, quantification that crosses possible worlds is often a measure of ideology. Quine's distinction thus ceases to mark a difference between two different types of studies or two different kinds of entities within one's universe. It now marks, rather, a distinction between the objects of reference and certain aspects of our own referential apparatus. Here we can perhaps see what the so-called distinction between theory of reference and theory of meaning really amounts to.

It follows, incidentally, that if we could restrict our attention to ONE-possible world only, Quine's restriction would be true without qualifications. Of course, the restriction is one which Quine apparently would very much like to make; hence he has a legitimate reason for disregarding the qualifications for his own purposes.

Our 'ideological' commitment to possible worlds other than the actual one is neither surprising nor disconcerting. If what we are dealing with are the things people do — more specifically, the concepts they use — in order to be prepared for more than one eventuality, it is not at all remarkable that in order to describe these concepts fully we have to speak of courses of events other than the actual one.

9. SINGULAR TERMS AND QUANTIFICATION IN THE CONTEXT
OF PROPOSITIONAL ATTITUDES

Let us return to the role of individual constants (and other singular terms). Summing up what was said before, we can say that what the understand-

[15] Quine, *From a Logical Point of View*, 130-32.

ing of an individual constant amounts to in a first-order language is knowing which individual it stands for. Now it is seen that in the presence of propositional attitudes this statement has to be expanded to say that one has to know what the singular term stands for in the different possible worlds we are considering.

Furthermore, in the same way as these individuals (or perhaps rather the method of specifying them) may be said to be what is 'objectively given' to us when we understand the constant, in the same way what is involved in the understanding of a propositional attitude is precisely that distinction which in our semantical apparatus is expressed by the function which serves to define the alternativeness relation. This function is what is 'objectively given' to us with the understanding of a word for a propositional attitude.

These observations enable us to solve almost all the problems that relate to the use of identity in the context of propositional attitudes. For instance, we can at once see why the familiar principle of the substitutivity of identity is bound to fail in the presence of propositional attitudes when applied to arbitrary singular terms.[16] Two such terms, say a and b, may refer to one and the same individual in the actual world ($\varphi(a, \mu_0) = \varphi(b, \mu_0)$ for the world μ_0 that happens to be actualized), thus making the identity '$a = b$' true, and yet fail to refer to the same individual in some other (alternative) possible world. (I.e. we may have $\varphi(a, \mu_1) \neq \varphi(b, \mu_1)$ for some $\mu_1 \in \varphi_B(c, \mu_0)$ where c is the individual whose attitudes are being discussed and B the relevant attitude.) Since the presence of propositional attitudes means (if I am right) that these other possible worlds have to be discussed as well, in their presence the truth of the identity '$a = b$' does not guarantee that the same things can be said of the references of a and b without qualification, i.e. does not guarantee the intersubstitutivity of the terms a and b.

Our observations also enable us to deal with quantification in contexts governed by words for propositional attitudes as long as we do not quantify INTO them. However, as soon as we try to do so, all the familiar difficulties which have been so carefully and persuasively presented by Quine and others will apply with full force.[17] An individual constant occurring within the scope of an operator like B which expresses a propositional attitude does not specify a unique individual. Rather, what it does is to specify an individual in each of the possible worlds we have to

---

[16] For a discussion of the problems connected with the substitutivity principle, see my exchange with Føllesdal: Dagfinn Føllesdal, "Knowledge, Identity, and Existence", *Theoria* 33 (1967), 1-27; Jaakko Hintikka, "Existence and Identity in Epistemic Contexts", ibid., 138-47.

[17] See Quine, *From a Logical Point of View*, ch. 8; *Word and Object*, ch. 6; *The Ways of Paradox and Other Essays* (Random House, New York, 1966), chapters 13-15.

consider. Replace it by an individual variable, and you do not get anything that you could describe by speaking of the individuals over which this variables ranges. There are (it seems) simply no uniquely defined individuals here at all.

It is perhaps thought that the way out is simply to deny that one can ever quantify into a non-extensional context. However, this way out does not work.[18] As a matter of fact, in our ordinary language we often quantify into a grammatical construction governed by an expression for a propositional attitude. Locutions like 'knows who', 'sees what', 'has an opinion concerning the identity of' are cases in point, and so is almost any (other) construction in which pronouns are allowed to mix with words for propositional attitudes. Beliefs about 'oneself' and 'himself' yield further examples, and an account of their peculiarities leads to an interesting reconstruction of the traditional distinction between so-called modalities *de dicto* and *de re*.[19]

Another general fact is that we obviously have beliefs about definite individuals and not just about whoever happens to meet a certain description. I want to suggest that such beliefs (and the corresponding attitudes in the case of other propositional attitudes) are precisely what one half of the *de dicto* — *de re* distinction amounts to.[20]

Furthermore, it does not do to try to maintain that in these constructions the propositional attitude itself has to be taken in an unusual extensional or 'referentially transparent' sense. Such senses can in fact be defined in terms of the normal senses of propositional attitudes. However, these definitions already involve the objectionable quantification into opaque contexts, and if one tries to postulate the defined senses as irreducible primitive senses, they do not have the properties which they ought to have in order to provide the resulting quantified statements with the logical powers they in fact have in ordinary language. For instance, Quine's attempt to postulate a sense of (say) knowledge in which

---

[18] Some arguments to this effect were given in *Knowledge and Belief* (ref. 11 above), 142-46. The only informed criticism of this criticism that I have seen has been presented by R. L. Sleigh, in a paper entitled "A Note on an Argument of Hintikka's", *Philosophical Studies* 18 (1967), 12-14. As I point out in my reply, "Partially Transparent Senses of Knowing" (forthcoming), Sleigh's argument turns on an ambiguity in my original formulation which is easily repaired. Neither the ambiguity nor its elimination provides any solace to the adherents of the view I have criticized, however.

[19] One thing at which this old distinction aims is obviously the distinction (which I am about to explain) between statements about whoever or whatever meets a description and statements about the individual who in fact does so. For the distinction, cf. Jaakko Hintikka, "Individuals, Possible Worlds, and Epistemic Logic", *Nous* 1 (1967), 32-62, especially 46-49, as well as "'Knowing Oneself' and Other Problems in Epistemic Logic", *Theoria* 32 (1966), 1-13.

[20] Cf. below (Section XII).

one is allowed to quantify into a context governed by a transparently construed construction 'knows that' has the paradoxical result that

(Ex) Jones knows that $(x = a)$

is implied by any (transparently interpreted) statement of the form

Jones knows that $(b = a)$

and even by a similarly interpreted sentence

Jones knows that $(a = a)$.

This I take to show that the first of these three sentences can scarcely serve as a formulation of 'Jones knows who (or what) a is' in our canonical idiom. Yet no other paraphrase of this ubiquitous locution has been proposed, and none is likely to be forthcoming. (For what else can there be to Jones' knowing who a is than his knowing of some well-defined individual that Jones is that very individual? And it is Quine who always insists as strongly as anyone else that the values of bound variables have to be well-defined individuals.) It is not much more helpful to try to maintain that no true sentences of the form

Jones knows that $(b = a)$

(with the transparent sense of 'knows') are forthcoming whenever Jones fails to know who a is. The transparent sense in which this would be the case has never been explained in a satisfactory way, and I do not see how it can be done in a reasonable way without falling back to my own analysis. (What can it conceivably mean e.g. for Jones not to know in the transparent sense that an a, whom he knows to exist, is not self-identical? Can this self-identity fail to be true in a possible world compatible with everything Jones knows?)

Hence we have to countenance quantification into a context governed by an expression for an (opaquely construed) propositional attitude. Our semantical theory at once suggests a way of handling these problems. For instance, in order for existential generalization to be applicable to a singular term b occurring, say, in a context where a's beliefs are being discussed, it has to be required that b refers to the SAME individual in the different possible worlds compatible with what a believes (plus, possibly, in the actual world). This, naturally, will be expressed by a statement of the form

(*) $(Ex)[B_a(x = b) \ \& \ (x = b)]$

or, if we do not have to consider the actual world, of the form

$(Ex) B_a(x = b)$.

10. METHODS OF CROSS-IDENTIFICATION

This solution is simple, straightforward, and workable. It generalizes easily to other propositional attitudes. However, it hides certain interesting conceptual presuppositions. With what right do we speak of individuals in the different possible worlds as being IDENTICAL? This is the problem to which we have to address ourselves.

It is not difficult to see what more there is given to us with our ordinary understanding of propositional attitudes that we have not yet dealt with. For instance, consider a man who has a number of beliefs as to what will happen tomorrow to himself and to his friends. Consider, on his behalf, a number of possible courses of events tomorrow. If I know what our man believes, I can sort these into those which are compatible with his beliefs as distinguished from those which are incompatible with them. But this is not all that is involved. Surely the same or largely the same individuals must figure in these different sequences of events. Under different courses of events a given individual may undergo different experiences, entertain different beliefs and hopes and fears; he may behave rather differently and perhaps even look somewhat different. Nevertheless our man can be (although he need not be) and usually is completely confident that, whatever may happen, he is going to be able to recognize (re-identify) his friends under these various courses of events, at least in principle. He may admit that courses of events are perhaps logically possible under which he would fail to do so; but these would not be compatible with his beliefs as to what will happen. Given full descriptions of two different courses of events tomorrow, both compatible with what our man believes ('believes possible', we sometimes say with more logical than grammatical justification), he will be able to recognize which individuals figuring in one of these descriptions are identical with which individual in the other, even if their names are being withheld. (Of course our man need not believe all this but my point is merely that he CAN and very often DOES believe it.)

The logical moral of this story is that together with the rest of our beliefs we are often given something more than we have so far incorporated into our semantical theory. We are given ways of CROSS-IDENTIFYING individuals, that is to say, ways of understanding questions as to whether an individual figuring in one possible world is or is not identical with an individual figuring in another world.[21]

This is one point at which the obviousness of my claim may be partially obscured by my terminology. Let us recall what these 'possible worlds' are in the case of a propositional attitude. They are normally possible

---

[21] Cf. here my paper, "On the Logic of Perception" in *Perception and Personal Identity*, ed. by N. Care and R. Grimm (Case Western Reserve Univ. Press, Cleveland, 1969).

states of affairs or courses of events compatible with the attitude in question in some specified person. Now normally these attitudes may be attitudes toward definite persons or definite physical objects. But how is it that we may be sure, sight unseen, that the attitudes are directed toward the right persons or objects? Only if in all the possible worlds compatible with the attitude in question we can pick out the recipient of this attitude, i.e. the individual at its receiving end. Although in many concrete situations the possibility of doing so is obvious, it has not been built into our semantical apparatus so far. There is so far nothing in our semantical theory which enables us to relate to each other the members of the different domains of individuals $I(\mu)$. In many, though not necessarily all, applications of such relations are given to us as a part of our understanding of the concepts involved. For such cases, we have to build a richer semantical theory.

The way to do so is to postulate a method of making cross-identifications. One possible way to do so is to postulate a set of functions F each member f of which picks out at most one individual $f(\mu)$ from the domain of individuals $I(\mu)$ of each given model μ. We must allow that there is no such value for some models μ. In other words, $f \in F$ may be a partial function. Furthermore, we must often require that, given $f_1, f_2 \in F$, if $f_1(\mu) = f_2(\mu)$ then $f_1(\lambda) = f_2(\lambda)$ for all alternatives λ to μ. In other words, an individual cannot 'split' when we move from a world to its alternatives. This question may seem to be a mere matter of detail, but it is easily seen that the question whether an individual can split in the sense just explained is tantamount to the question whether the substitutivity of identity can fail for bound (individual) variables, i.e. to the question whether a sentence

$$(Ux)(Uy)(x = y \supset B_a(x = y))$$

can fail to be logically true. This, again, is tantamount to the question whether a sentence of the form

$$(Ux)(Uy)(x = y \supset (Q(x) \supset Q(y)))$$

(with just one layer of operators for propositional attitudes in Q) can fail to be logically true.

In terms of the set F, the question whether $a \in I(\mu)$ is identical with $b \in I(\lambda)$ amounts to the question whether there is a function of $f \in F$ such that $f(\mu) = a, f(\lambda) = b$.

11. THE ROLE OF INDIVIDUATING FUNCTIONS

Instead of speaking of a set of functions correlating to each other the individuals existing in the different possible worlds, it is often more appropriate to speak of these domains of individuals as being partly identical (overlapping). Then there would be no need to speak of correlations at all. This point of view is useful in that it illustrates the fact that the apparently different individuals which are correlated by one of the functions $f \in F$ is just what we ordinarily mean by one and the same individual. It is the concrete individual which we speak about, which we give a name to, etc. In fact, the members of F might in fact be thought of as names or individual constants of a certain special kind, namely those having a unique reference in all the different worlds we are speaking of and hence satisfying formulas of the form (*). Indeed, I shall assume in the sequel that a constant of this kind can be associated with each function $f \in F$.

However, emphasizing the role of the functions $f \in F$ is useful for several purposes. First and foremost, it highlights an extremely important non-trivial part of our native conceptual skills, namely, our capacity to recognize one and the same individual under different circumstances and under different courses of events. What the set F of functions embodied is just the totality of ways of doing this. The non-trivial character of the possibility of this recognition would be lost if we should simply speak of the members of the different possible worlds as being partly identical.

For another thing, the structure formed by the relations of cross-world identity (David Kaplan calls them "trans world heir lines") may be so complex as to be indescribable by speaking simply of partial identities between the domains of individuals of the different possible worlds. Above, it was said that in the case of many propositional attitudes an individual cannot 'split' when we move from a world to its alternatives. Although this seems to me to be the case with all the propositional attitudes I have studied in any detail, it is not quite clear to me precisely why this should always be the case. At any rate, there seem to be reasons for suspecting that the opposite 'irregularity' can occasionally take place with some modalities: individuals can 'merge together' when we move from a world to its alternatives. An analogy with temporal modalities may be instructive here.[22] If we presuppose some suitable system of cross-identifications between individuals existing at different times which turn on continuity, it seems possible in principle that a singular term should refer to the same physical system at all the different moments of time we are considering although this system 'merges' with others at times

[22] For temporal modalities, see e.g. A. N. Prior, *Past, Present and Future*, (Clarendon Press, Oxford, 1967). — I am not saying that our actual methods of cross-identification in the case of temporal modalities (i.e. on ordinary methods of re-identification) turn on continuity quite as exclusively as I am about to suggest. It suffices for my purposes to present an example of methods of cross-identification that allows both 'branching' and 'merging', and it seems to me at least conceivable that temporal modalities might under suitable circumstances create such a situation.

and occasionally 'splits up' into several. Some of these complications seem to be impossible to rule out completely in the case of some propositional attitudes, and because of them the idea of partly overlapping domains seems to me seriously oversimplified.

An extremely important further reason why we cannot reify the members of **F** into ordinary individuals is the possibility of having two different methods of cross-identification between the members of the same possible worlds, i.e. two different sets of 'individuating functions' although we are dealing with precisely the same sets of possible worlds. I have argued elsewhere that this kind of situation is not only possible to envisage but is actually present in our own ways with perceptual contexts.[23] It would take us too far to show precisely what is involved in such cases. Suffice it to point out that this claim, if true, would strikingly demonstrate the dependence of our methods of cross-identification on our own conceptual schemes and hence on things of our own creation. The apparent simplicity of our idea of an 'ordinary' individual, safe as it may seem in its solid commonplace reality, is thus seen to be merely a reflection of the familiarity and relatively deep customary entrenchment of one particular method of cross-identification, which *sub specie aeternitatis* (i.e. *sub specie logicae*) nevertheless enjoys but a relative privilege as against a host of others.

The methods of cross-identification represented by the set **F** of 'individuating functions', as we might call them, also call for several further comments.

The main function of this part of our semantical apparatus is to make sense of quantification into contexts of propositional attitudes. The truth-conditions of statements in which this happens can be spelled out in terms of membership in **F**. As an approximation we can say the following: A sentence of the form $(Ex) Q(x)$ is true in μ if and only if there is an individual constant (say b) associated with some $f \in F$ such that $Q(b)$ is true in μ. This approximation shows, incidentally, how close we can stick to the simple-minded idea that an existentially quantified sentence is true if and only if it has a true substitution instance. The only additional requirement we need is that the substitution-value of the bound variable has to be of the right sort, to wit, has to specify the same individual in all the possible worlds we are speaking of in the existential sentence in question. This is what is meant by the requirement that b has to be associated with one of the functions $f \in F$.

This approximation, although not unrepresentative of the general situation, requires certain modifications in order to work in all cases. The set **F** has to be relativized somewhat in the same way the unrestricted notion of a possible world was relativized by the notion of alternative in the truth-criterion (S.B.) above. (Not everyone is in all situations 'famil-

---

[23]   This is argued in 'On the Logic of Perception' (ref. 20 above).

iar with' all the relevant methods of individuation, it might be said.) I shall not discuss the ensuing complications here, however, for they do not change the overall picture in those respects which are relevant in the rest of this paper.

12. STATEMENTS ABOUT DEFINITE INDIVIDUALS VS. STATEMENTS ABOUT WHOEVER OR WHATEVER IS REFERRED TO BY A TERM

The possibility of quantifying across an operator which expresses a propositional attitude enables us to explicate the logic of the locutions in which we need this possibility in the first place. Perhaps the most important thing we can do here is to make a distinction between propositional attitudes directed to whoever (whatever) happens to be referred to by a term and attitudes directed toward a certain individual, independently of how he happens to be referred to. This distinction was hinted at above. Now it is time to explain it more fully. For instance, someone may have a belief concerning the next Governor of California, whoever he is or may be, say, that he will be a Democrat. This is different from believing something about the individual who, so far unbeknownst to all of us, in fact is the next Governor of California.

In formal terms, the distinction is illustrated by the pair of statements

$$B_a(g \text{ is a Democrat})$$
$$(Ex)\,((x = g)\ \&\ B_a(x \text{ is a Democrat})).$$

Notice, incidentally, that my way of drawing this distinction implies that one can have (say) a belief concerning the individual who in fact is *a* only if such an individual really exists, whereas one can in principle have a belief concerning *a*, 'whoever he is', even though there is no such person. This, of course, is just as it ought to be.

The naturalness of our semantical conditions, and their close relation to the realities of actual usage, can be illustrated by applying them to what I have called a statement about a definite individual. As an example, we can use

'*a* believes of the man who in fact is Mr. Smith that he is a thief',

in brief,

$$(Ex)\,(x = \text{Smith}\ \&\ B_a(x \text{ is a thief})).$$

In order for this to be true, there has to be some $f \in F$ such that the value of f in the actual world (call it μ_0) exists and is Smith and that $f(\mu)$ has the property of being a thief whenever $\mu \in \varphi_B(a, \mu_0)$, i.e. in all the alternatives to the actual world.

What the requirement of the existence of f amounts to is clear enough. If it is true to say that a has a belief about THE PARTICULAR INDIVIDUAL who in fact is Smith, then a clearly must believe that he can characterize this individual uniquely. In other words, he must have some way of referring to or characterizing this individual in such a way that one and the same individual is in fact so characterized in all the worlds compatible with what he believes. This is precisely what the existence of f amounts to. If no such function existed, a would not be able to pick out the individual who in fact is Smith under all the courses of events he believes possible, and there would not be any sense in saying that a's belief is ABOUT the particular individual in question.

13. INDIVIDUATING FUNCTIONS VS. INDIVIDUAL CONCEPTS

One important consequence of my approach is that not every function which from each μ picks out an individual can be said to specify a unique individual. In fact, many perfectly good free singular terms fail to do so in the context of many propositional attitudes. Even proper names fail to do so in epistemic contexts, for one may fail to know who the bearer of a given proper name is.

Such arbitrary functions may be important for many purposes. They are excellent approximations in our theory to the 'individual concepts' which many philosophers have postulated.[24] (In Section VI above we already met a number of such 'individual concepts' in the form of the functions $\varphi(a, \mu)$ with a fixed a.) Each such individual concept specifies or "contains", as Frege would say, not just a reference (in the actual world) but also the way in which this reference is given to us. Each of them would thus qualify for a sense (*Sinn*) of a singular term *à la* Frege.[25] However, we do not need the totality of such arbitrary functions in the semantics which I am building up and which (I want to argue) is largely implicit in our native conceptual apparatus. Quine's criterion, however misleading it may be as a criterion of ontological commitment, still works as a criterion of commitment. If it is applied here, it shows that we are not committed (ontologically or 'ideologically') to these arbitrary functions, since we do not have to quantify over them, only over the members of the much narrower class **F**.

The other side of the coin is that in our semantical apparatus we do have to quantify over the members of **F**. Does it follow that they 'exist'

[24] Cf. e.g. R. Carnap, *Meaning and Necessity*, (University of Chicago Press, Chicago, 1947) (2nd ed.: 1956), pp. 41, 180-81, and Section VI *supra*.
[25] Cf. Gottlob Frege, 'Über Sinn und Bedeutung', *Zeitschrift für Philosophie und philosophische Kritik* 100 (1892), 25-50, especially p. 26, last few lines.

or 'are part of our ontology'? An answer to this question can be given along the same lines as to the corresponding question concerning 'possible worlds'. The members of F are not members of any possible world; they are not part of anybody's count of 'what there is'. They may 'subsist' or perhaps 'exist', and they are certainly 'objective', but they do not have any ontological role to play. The need to distinguish between ontology and 'ideology' is especially patent here.

The functions that belong to F may of course be considered special cases of the 'individual concepts' postulated by some philosophers of logic or as special cases of Frege's 'senses' (*Sinne*). No identification is possible between the two classes, however, for we saw earlier that not every arbitrary singular term (say b) which picks out an individual from each $I(\mu)$ we are considering goes together with an $f \in F$, although every such term is certainly meaningful and hence has a Fregean 'sense' and perhaps even given us an 'individual concept'. As I have put it elsewhere, members of F do not only involve a 'way of being given' as Frege's senses do, but also A WAY OF BEING INDIVIDUATED.[26] The primary care is in our approach devoted to ordinary concrete individuals. Singular terms merit a special honorary mention only if they succeed in picking out a unique individual of this sort.

Let us say that an $f \in F$ is (gives us) an individuating concept, and let us say that a term b does INDIVIDUATE (in the context of discussing a's beliefs) in so far as

$$(Ex)\ B_a(x = b)$$

is true. Then we could have individuation without reference and reference without individuation: Both

$$(Ex)\ B_a(x = b)\ \&\ \sim (Ex)\ (x = b)$$

and

$$(Ex)\ (x = b)\ \&\ \sim (Ex)\ B_a(x = b)$$

can be true. We could even have both, but without matching:

$$(Ex)\ (x = b)\ \&\ (Ex)\ B_a(x = b)\ \&\ \sim (Ex)\ ((x = b)\ \&\ B_a(x = b))$$

is satisfiable. Only if

$$(Ex)\ ((x = b)\ \&\ B_a(x = b))$$

is true does the successful individuation give us the individual which the term b actually refers to.

---

[26] Cf. 'On the Logic of Perception' (ref. 21 above).

14. THE THEORY OF REFERENCE AS REPLACING THE THEORY OF
MEANING

Here we are perhaps beginning to see what I meant when I said at the beginning of this paper that what is often called the theory of meaning is better thought of as the theory of reference for certain more complicated conceptual situations. Some of the most typical concepts used in the theory of meaning, such as Frege's *Sinne* and the 'individual concepts' of certain other philosophers of logic were in the first place introduced to account for such puzzles as the failure of the substitutivity of identity and the difficulty of quantifying into opaque contexts (e.g. into a context governed by a word for a propositional attitude). I have argued, however, that a satisfactory semantical theory which clears up these puzzles can be built up without using Frege's *Sinne* and without any commitment to individual concepts in any ordinary sense of the word. Instead, what we need are the individuating functions, i.e. the members of **F**. And what these functions do is not connected with the ideas of the traditional theory of meaning. What they do is precisely to give us the individuals which we naively think our singular statements to be about and which we think our singular terms as referring to. This naive point of view is essentially correct, it seems to me. The functions of $f \in \mathbf{F}$ are the prime vehicles of our references to individuals when we discuss propositional attitudes. What is not always realized, however, is how much goes into our ordinary concepts of an individual and a reference. These are not specified in a way which works only under one particular course of events. They are in fact specified in a way which works under a wide variety of possible courses of events. But, in order to spell out this idea, we are led to consider several possible worlds, with all the problems with which we have dealt in this paper, including very prominently the problem of cross-identifying individuals.

The function of our 'individuating functions', i.e. the members of the set **F**, is to bring out these hidden — or perhaps merely overlooked — aspects of our concept of an individual (definite individual). This close connection between the set **F** and the concept of an individual appears in a variety of ways. One may for instance think of the role which the membership in **F** plays in the truth-conditions which we set up above for quantification into modal contexts. When it is asked in such a context whether there exists an individual of a certain kind, a singular term specifies such an individual only if its references match the values of a unique member of **F** in all the relevant possible worlds. Thus it is these functions that in effect give us the individuals which can serve as values of bound variables. As we saw above, it is mainly the possible subtlety and multiplicity of relations of cross-identity that prevent us from simply making the domains of the different possible worlds partly identical and thus hypostatizing my individuating functions into commonplace individuals.

This connection between individuating functions and the concept of an individual is part of what justifies us in thinking that in the traditional dichotomy their theory would belong primarily to the theory of reference, in spite of the fact that their main function in our semantical theory is to solve some of the very problems which the traditional theory of meaning was calculated to handle. This role is perhaps especially clear in connection with the substitutivity of identity. As we have seen, this principle does not hold for arbitrary singular terms *a*, *b*. However, if it is required in addition that both of these terms specify a well-defined individual, i.e. satisfy expressions like (*), depending on the context, then the substitutivity of identicals is easily seen to hold, presupposing of course here the prohibition against splitting that was mentioned above. What this observation shows is clear enough. The failure of the substitutivity of identity poses one of the most typical problems for the treatment of which meanings, individual concepts and other paraphernalia of the theory of meaning were introduced in the first place. If the substitutivity of identity fails, clearly we cannot be dealing with ordinary commonplace individuals, it was alleged, for if two such individuals are in fact identical, surely precisely same things can be said of them. This is what prompts the quest for individuals of some non-ordinary sort, capable of restoring the substitutivity principle when used as references of our terms. (This is almost precisely Frege's strategy.) We have seen, however, that the (apparent) failure of the substitutivity is due simply to the failure of some free singular terms to specify the same individual in the different 'possible worlds' we have to consider. Moreover, we have seen that this apparent failure is automatically corrected in precisely those cases in which it ought to be corrected, viz. in the cases where the two terms in question really do specify a UNIQUE individual. (That this depends on certain specific requirements concerning our methods of cross-identification, viz. on a prohibition against 'splitting', does not affect my point.) Substitutivity of identity is restored, in brief, not by requiring that our singular terms refer to the entities postulated by the so-called theory of meaning, but by requiring (in the form of an explicit premise) that they really succeed in specifying uniquely the kind of ordinary individual with which the theory of reference typically deals. One can scarcely hope to find a more striking example of the breakdown of the distinction between a theory of meaning and a theory of reference.[27]

[27] Views closely resembling some of those which I am putting forward here (and in some cases anticipating them) have been expressed by David Kaplan, Richard Montague, Dagfinn Føllesdal, Stig Kanger, Saul Kripke, and others. Here I am not trying to

15. TOWARDS A SEMANTIC NEOKANTIANISM

The aspect of my observations most likely to upset many contemporary philosophers is the ensuing implicit dependence of our concept of an individual on our ways of cross-identifying members of different 'possible worlds'. These 'possible worlds' and the supply of individuating functions which serve to interrelate their respective members may enjoy, and in my view do enjoy, some sort of objective reality. However, their existence is not a 'natural' thing. They may be as solidly objective as houses or books, but they are as certainly as these created by men (however unwittingly) for the purpose of facilitating their transactions with the reality they have to face. Hence my reasoning ends on a distinctly Kantian note. Whatever we say of the world is permeated throughout with concepts of our own making. Even such *prima facie* transparently simple notions as that of an individual turn out to depend on conceptual assumptions dealing with different possible states of affairs. As far as our thinking is concerned, reality cannot be in principle wholly disentangled from our concepts. A *Ding an sich*, which could be described or even as much as individuated without relying on some particular conceptual framework, is bound to remain an illusion.

relate my own ideas to theirs. It is only fair, however, to emphasize my direct and indirect debts to these writers.

Jaakko Hintikka

KNOWLEDGE, BELIEF, AND LOGICAL CONSEQUENCE

One of the most lively debated questions in the logical analysis of the notions of knowledge and belief today might be called the problem of CONSERVATION LAWS for these notions.[1] The term is apt because one of the more or less equivalent formulations of the problem is to ask whether knowledge and belief (in some suitably strong and possibly idealized sense) is invariant with respect to logical equivalence. This invariance may in turn be taken to amount to the validity of the rules of inference

$$(1) \quad \frac{p \equiv q}{K_a p \equiv K_a q} \qquad\qquad \frac{p \equiv q}{B_a p \equiv B_a q}$$

where '$K_a p$' is to be read 'a knows that p' and '$B_a p$' 'a believes that p'.

Perhaps a more usual formulation pertains to the corresponding implicational rules of inference

$$(2) \quad \frac{p \supset q}{K_a p \supset K_a q} \qquad\qquad \frac{p \supset q}{B_a p \supset B_a q}$$

Their import may be expressed, somewhat roughly, by saying that whenever someone knows (or believes) anything, he knows (or believes) all its logical consequences.

It is obvious that the rules of inference (2) imply (1). The converse is

Reprinted from *Ajatus* 32 (1970), 32-47. Revised.
[1] The contribution to this debate which prompted the present note are Richard L. Purtill, "Believing the Impossible", *Ajatus* 32 (1970), 18-24; Kathleen G. Johnson Wu, "Hintikka and Defensibility", *Ajatus* 32 (1970), 25-31.

true if we assume in addition the relatively unproblematic distributive principles

(3) $\vdash K_a(p\ \&\ q) \supset K_a q$
    $\vdash B_a(p\ \&\ q) \supset B_a q$

For if $\vdash p \supset q$, then $\vdash p \equiv (p\ \&\ q)$, hence by (1) $\vdash K_a p \equiv K_a(p\ \&\ q)$, and hence by (3) $\vdash K_a p \supset K_a q$. For belief, the argument is analogous.

One consequence of the assumptions (2) (or (1) and (3)) for the concept of belief is that no one can believe the impossible. For p's being logically inconsistent means that $\vdash p \supset (q\ \&\ \sim q)$, which by (2) implies

(4) $\vdash B_a p \supset B_a(q\ \&\ \sim q)$.

If we assume — as it seems natural to do — that no one can believe an explicitly contradictory proposition on the form $q\ \&\ \sim q$, then (4) implies that no one can believe an inconsistent statement, however hidden its inconsistency may be. What has been dubbed 'Alice's Law' (viz. the thesis that one cannot believe what is impossible) is thus a natural concomitant of the doxastic part (1) or (2), and it is indeed implied by (2) if we assume in addition that

(5) $\vdash \sim B_a(q\ \&\ \sim q)$.

This assumption comes very close to ruling out believing the impossible while knowing it to be impossible, for the impossibility of a proposition which is the explicit form $q\ \&\ \sim q$ surely cannot escape anyone's attention who understands what he is saying.

At first blush, the assumptions (1)–(2) undoubtedly look blatantly unrealistic. Surely each of us, at the very least anyone who has ever been trying to trace the logical implications of an intricate set of assumptions, has often believed and even known things whose distant consequences are beyond the ken both of his knowledge and of his belief. We do not like to say that Euclid already knew all that there is to know about elementary geometry (apart from the imperfections of his axiomatics). However obvious a logical implication from p to q may be, some sufficiently dense person may in principle fail to recognize it, and hence might believe (know) that p without believing (knowing) that q.

The first answer usually given to these objections to (1)–(2) is that 'some idealization is necessary in doxastic and epistemic logic: we cannot get a consistent system and at the same time take account of the vagaries of infants or idiots'. The problem is nevertheless more serious than this, for there does not seem to be any guarantee that even the most acute mathematician can see all the logical consequences of the axioms he is studying without a great deal of mental exertion.

Or is there perhaps such a guarantee? There would be, it seems to me, if certain widely discussed and widely held philosophical doctrines were correct. Insignificant-looking problems in epistemic and doxastic logic thus turn out to have a significant connection with much wider issues. It has sometimes been held that all logical inference is analytical or 'tautological', that all information that the conclusion of such an inference gives us is 'objectively' contained already in the premises, and that all increase of information in a logical inference is therefore purely psychological.[2] If these interesting claims were true, there would not be any reason to modify the rules of inference (1)–(2). In every 'objective' sense, a man who believes that p already believes that q whenever $\vdash(p \supset q)$, if these claims are right. What prevents him from assenting to q can only be a psychological block or an ignorance of the meaning of his own symbols. If this were the case, the idealization involved (1)–(2) would not only be admissible but inevitable.

However, I have all along been suspicious of these claims, and recently I have sought to disprove in some detail their theoretical basis.[3] It simply is not true that there are no objective senses of information in which logical inference can add to our information. Hence (1)–(2) do present a genuine — and serious — problem. To this extent at least, the present surge of papers dealing with them is justified.

Several different lines of thought may be attempted here. One is to stick to (1)–(2) but to reinterpret the metalogical notions of provability, disprovability, etc. in some new way. This is the course I followed in my book *Knowledge and Belief.*[4] The upshot of the ensuing discussion[5] seems to be that although the details of my account can be tightened up so as to bar all specific criticisms, the reinterpretation tends to limit seriously the applicability of this approach. Something else thus seems to be needed, in other words, a different approach to (1) and (2) seems highly

[2] This was one of the most characteristic theses of logical positivists. See e.g. A. J. Ayer, *Language, Truth, and Logic* (London, 1936), chapter iv, "The A Priori"; Carl G. Hempel, "Geometry and Empirical Science", *American Mathematical Monthly* 52 (1945), 7-17, reprinted in Herbert Feigl and Wilfrid Sellars, editors, *Readings in Philosophical Analysis* (New York, 1949), 238-48; Hans Hahn, *Logik, Mathematik und Naturerkennen* (= *Einheitswissenschaft*, vol 2) (Vienna, 1933).
[3] See the following papers of mine: "Are Logical Truths Analytic?", *Philosophical Review* 74 (1965), 178-203; "Are Logical Truths Tautologies?" and "Kant Vindicated" in Paul Weingartner, editor, *Deskription, Analytizität und Existenz* (Salzburg and Munich, A. Pustet, 1966), 215-33 and 234-53, respectively; "Are Mathematical Truths Synthetic A Priori?", *Journal of Philosophy* 65 (1968), 640-51; "Information, Deduction, and the A Priori", vol. 4 (1970), 135-52; "Surface Information and Depth Information" in Jaakko Hintikka and Patrick Suppes, editors, *Information and Inference* (Dordrecht, D. Reidel, 1970), 263-97.
[4] Contemporary Philosophy Series (See, for instance, Ithaca, Cornell University Press, N.Y., 1962. See especially pp. 29-39.)
[5] Leonard Linsky, "Interpreting Doxastic Logic", *Journal of Philosophy* 65 (1968), 500-02.

desirable. If leaving these laws unmodified results in too unrealistic a treatment, it lies close at hand to try to restrict (1) and (2) in some suitable way.

What would such a course look like? *Prima facie*, it may seem hopeless to impose any sharp boundaries between admissible and inadmissible uses of (1)–(2). What causes the breakdown of these rules is after all the fact that one cannot usually see all the logical consequences of what one knows or believes. Now it may seem completely impossible to draw a line between the implications one sees and those one does not see by means of general logical considerations alone. A genius might readily see quite distant consequences while another man may almost literally 'fail to put two and two together'. Even for one and the same person, the extent to which one follows the logical consequences of what one believes varies with one's mood, training, and degree of concentration. How can anyone hope to impose strict, uniform limits on these logical insights which so obviously are not only ephemeral but also idiosyncratic?

By way of an answer, a general methodological point can be made. Of course we cannot set sharp limits on people's logical acumen or lack thereof. What one can do is to isolate those objective, structural factors which contribute most to the difficulty of perceiving relations of logical consequence. Making them the only relevant factors may involve some idealization, but it may also result in an interesting theoretical model of people's 'deductive behavior' which facilitates the description and analysis of the inferences they draw as well as their failures to draw certain inferences. A quick comparison may not be entirely misleading. No one is likely to behave precisely so as to maximize one's expected utility. But the 'expected utility hypothesis' postulating such behavior has given rise to extensive and interesting theories of human behavior in certain situations.[6] It may be hoped that a logical theory which isolates the most salient obstacles to perceiving deductive relationships will perform similar services to a student of the logical inferences people actually draw and fail to draw.

Now what are the crucial factors that limit our 'deductive omniscience'? Many plausible-looking candidates spring to mind: the number of steps of inference, the length of the propositions involved, and so on. Important as these parameters may be, most of them are by no means peculiar to human information processing, and are not invariant with respect to relatively trivial changes from one deductive system to another. Something more central to our spontaneous processes of information processing has to be found.

---

[6] See e.g. R. Duncan Luce and Patrick Suppes, "Preference, Utility, and Subjective Probability", in Luce, Bush, and Galanter, editors, *Handbook of Mathematical Psychology*, vol. 3 (New York, John Wiley & Sons, 1965).

It seems to me that some of the deepest remarks on the peculiarities of human information processing have been made by John von Neumann. In his Silliman Lectures[7] he introduces the concept of ARITHMETICAL DEPTH. He does this primarily for languages dealing with numerical computations. In them, arithmetical depth indicates the maximal nesting of the basic operations in a function. Can this notion be extended to the languages in connection with which (1)–(2) have been considered? These are typically first-order (quantificational) languages with operators like K, B added, but without function symbols. Now it is well known how quantifiers can be replaced by the so-called Skolem functions.[8] When they are considered as primitives, von Neumann's definition applies. If we then go back to the original first-order proposition, the nesting of functions becomes the nesting of quantifiers, and arithmetical depth is converted into the number of layers of quantifiers in our first-order expression.

Apart from certain niceties in the notion of nesting (such as the question: When precisely is an operation independent of earlier ones and hence irrelevant to nesting and when does it depend on it so as to contribute to nesting?), this will then be the extension of von Neumann's notion to quantification theory: the number of layers of quantifiers in a proposition at its deepest or, which amounts to the same, the length of the longest chain of nested quantifiers. We shall call this the QUANTIFICA-TIONAL DEPTH or simply the DEPTH of the proposition in question.[9]

In addition to arithmetical depth, von Neumann considers what he calls the logical depth of a function. Since this notion is tied to the breakdown of functions into operations that a computer can actually perform, and thus to the peculiarities of one particular way of realizing the functions in question on a computer, it need not concern us here.

What von Neumann emphasizes is that 'whatever language the central nervous system is using, it is characterized by less logical and arithmetical depth than what we are normally used to' (p. 81). 'Thus logics and mathematics in the central nervous system, when viewed as languages, must structurally be essentially different from those languages to which our human experience refers' (p. 82).

---

[7] John von Neumann, *The Computer and the Brain* (New Haven, Yale University Press, 1958). (See especially pp. 23-28, 80-82.)

[8] For instance, $(x)(Ey)F(x,y)$ is true in a model if and only if there exists a function $f(z)$ such that $(x)F(x,f(x))$ is true in that model. This function $f(z)$ is an example of Skolem functions.

[9] A minor qualification is needed here because some of the apparently nested quantifiers may not really be connected with each other. (This corresponds to a situation in which one of the Skolem functions inside does not really depend on some of the outer variables.) The necessary minor adjustment is indicated e.g. in my article "Information, Deduction, and the A Priori", *Noûs* 4 (1970), 135-52, note 11.

Thus the crucial parameter which according to von Neumann apparently presents the greatest resistance to such information processing as takes place in our central nervous system is, in the case of (modalized or unmodalized) first-order languages, the depth of its expressions. In order to catch 'the logic in our nervous system' we therefore have to pay special attention to this parameter.

Even apart from von Neumann, the importance of quantificational depth is easy to appreciate. For simplicity, we may consider closed sentences in some suitable first-order language, i.e. sentences without individual constants and other free singular terms. In other words, all the individuals the sentence invites us to consider are introduced by the quantifiers. (That each of them asks us to consider an individual is seen from the very meaning of quantifiers: '(Ex)' means 'for at least one individual, call it x, it is the case that', and '(x)' 'for each individual, call it x, it is the case that'.) Then the quantificational depth of a sentence s will be the maximal complexity of the configurations of individuals considered in it at any time, measured by the number of individuals involved. Of course, it is only to be expected that the complexity of the configurations involved in a sentence is one of the prime factors limiting our insights into its logical relations to other sentences. The deeper sentences a chain of inferences involves, the harder it presumably is (*ceteris paribus*) to perceive.

It may be shown that in a certain sense such increase of depth is frequently involved in quantificational (first-order) deductions, even in the sense that to derive q from p one has to go by way of propositions deeper than either p or q. In the light of von Neumann's observations on the 'logics in the central nervous system', it is not surprising that relatively few non-trivial quantificational inferences can be found in ordinary discourse, as some perceptive logicians have rightly emphasized. It is also significant that the tremendous subtlety and power of first-order deduction is virtually hidden by most introductory textbooks of logic.[10] Furthermore, the naturalness of the so-called natural deduction methods is obvious due to the fact that in them the depth of one's expressions (although not the depth, suitably defined, of the whole argument) is kept as small as possible. The importance of our unconscious strategy of minimizing depth for understanding the behavior of quantifying expressions of ordinary language has not been fully realized by linguists,

---

[10] Examples may convey a feeling of this triviality of textbook logic. Hao Wang has shown that most of the propositions of the purely logical part of *Principia Mathematica* fall within the scope of extremely simple decision methods. Almost all logical truths (of first-order logic) that are found in textbooks are "surface tautologies" in the sense of my paper "Surface Information and Depth Information" (note 3 above), and probably all of them admit of proof in which the increase is very small, at most 1 or 2.

something very much like probabilistic concepts also in the area of deductive relationships.[12] (We may, for instance, speculate how likely it is that this or that putative theorem can be proved, and choose our deductive strategies accordingly.) Now these quasi-probabilities cannot obey all the usual laws of probability calculus, for they require that the probability-measure (on the sentences of our language) be invariant with respect to logical equivalence, and that all logically inconsistent sentences be assigned zero probability. These assumptions are remarkably similar to (1) and (5). They will have to be given up if probabilistic notions are to be applied to deductive relationships. However, we clearly want to preserve most of the other axioms of probability calculus. (What will otherwise remain of the idea of probability, anyway?) This is impossible (or at least extremely difficult) if the number of deductive steps, the maximal length of a deductive branch, or any similar parameter is used as an index of the difficulty of perceiving a deductive relationship (viz. the one established by these deductive steps or these interrelated branches of deduction). In this respect, the restriction I am proposing to impose on (1)–(2) is superior to its more obvious-looking competitors. We may perhaps say that it leaves propositional relationships intact, affecting only quantificational ones. Since the latter play no role in the axioms of probability calculus, the changes needed in these axioms are minimal.

   Although the restriction on (2) which can be formulated in terms of distributive normal forms is clumsy to apply, this particular way of formulating the restriction serves to throw some interesting light on Purtill's suggestions. In order to save (1)–(2) unmodified, he proposes a strong sense of belief in which

   (6) *a* believes that *p*

implies

   (7) *a* understands *p*

and

   (8) *a* is disposed to act as if it were the case that *p*.

   Here 'acting' will mean, on the intended interpretation, nonverbal behavior — that is, not only sincerely SAYING that *p* is the case but also actually taking some non-verbal measures not incompatible with the truth of *p*.

   Purtill suggests that no such non-verbal behavior can be consistent with the truth of an inconsistent proposition, and that no one can therefore believe what is impossible in the intended strong sense of belief.

12 Some such probabilistic notions are developed in the papers listed above in note 3.

By the same token, no form of behavior can fail to be consistent with a logically true proposition. Thus we seem to have

(9) $\vdash B_a p$

whenever p is logically true. But (9) implies (together with certain relatively unproblematic assumptions) the doxastic part of (1)–(2). For if $\vdash (p \supset q)$, then by (9) $\vdash B_a(p \supset q)$, and hence by a well-known principle of doxastic logic $\vdash (B_a p \supset B_a q)$. For knowledge, the situation would be parallel. However, this defence of (1)–(2) does not work.

One highly interesting observation we can make by means of distributive normal forms is that Purtill's assumption is in fact incorrect and that it often makes perfectly good sense to speak of acting (non-verbally) as if a logically inconsistent sentence were true. In order to see how this is possible, we have to recall the structure of constituents.[13] A brief intuitive explanation is to say that a constituent $C^{(d)}$ of depth d is as full a description of a (kind of) possible world as one can give without considering more than d individuals in their relation to each other. This description takes the form of a ramified list of all the different sequences of individuals (of length d) that one can find in a world in which $C^{(d)}$ is true. By 'ramified', I refer to the fact that this list specifies which sequences are possible completions of an initial segment of a given sequence. A constituent thus has the structure of a finite set of trees. At each node of each tree, it is specified what properties the corresponding (kind of) individual has and how it is related to individuals lower in the same branch. The different branches from bottom to top specify the different kinds of sequences of individuals that one can come upon in a world in which $C^{(d)}$ is true.

A finite set of such trees may fail to describe a possible world, for obvious reasons. All the sequences have to be drawn from one and the same supply of individuals. This creates obvious similarities between the several parts of the trees. For instance, the same result (apart from the order of the trees and branches) must be obtained by truncating the trees at any one level, that is, by cutting off the tops, the bottoms, or any intermediate layer of nodes. Constituents failing these simple tests of consistency I have called TRIVIALLY INCONSISTENT.

The remarkable fact is that the inconsistency of some constituents cannot be perceived in this way. Such a constituent tells a story as to what kinds of individuals one might come upon one after another in the

---

[13] The following explanation is similar to the one given in "Information, Deduction, and the A Priori" (note 3 above). Constituents are studied systematically in my paper, "Distributive Normal Forms in First-Order Logic" in J. N. Crossley and M. A. E. Dummett, editors, *Formal Systems and Recursive Functions* (North-Holland Publishing Company, Amsterdam, 1965), 47-90.

world, a story which cannot be disproved by comparing the different parts of the story with one another but which nevertheless cannot describe any actualizable world. The inconsistency of a constituent of this kind can only be seen by considering longer sequences of individuals than the ones considered in it — sequences whose length can be very large and cannot in general be predicated on the basis of the given constituent by recursive methods.

Given such a constituent, it makes perfectly good sense to speak of someone's acting as if it were true. For instance, the constituent might say that individuals of two different kinds (defined by specifying what further kinds of individuals there are in relation to them) exist in the world. Then one can perfectly well make preparations for meeting both of them, unaware that they cannot co-exist in the same world, although each kind of individual can exist in a suitable possible world. To gain some feeling for the situation, we may think of someone asserting that a's father was an only child and that a has first cousins on his father's side. Whatever the case may be, no one will be able to find both these individuals — a's father who is an only child AND one of a's first cousins on father's side — in the same world, although there is no impossibility in either's existing alone. And surely one can think, say, of a hopeful legatee who acts as if he should inherit both these relatives of his. In general, acting on the truth of a first-order proposition is in any case to act on the assumption that one can only come upon certain ramified sequences of individuals in the world, and not upon others. Even if there are hidden discrepancies in the list of acceptable sequences, this does not make any essential difference to the kinds of preparations one can — or perhaps has to — make for the eventuality that the constituent in question should turn out to be true: they are similar in both cases.

Notice that this sense of 'acting on' is quite a concrete one. It means acting on a specific expectation as to what kinds of individuals, and in what combinations, one may encounter in examining the world, hence in a sense what possible experiences one might have in a world as described by the constituent in question.

It seems to me that this possibility of being disposed to act on the truth of an inconsistent proposition undercuts Purtill's defense of the unmodified rules (1)-(2). I do not see any difficulty whatsoever in someone's believing the impossible (though not any old impossibility) even in Purtill's strong sense.

It also seems to me that another aspect of Purtill's definition of the strong sense of belief can be turned to a defense of my restriction on (1)–(2) rather than of the unrestricted form of these rules. That is the requirement (7) to the effect that the believer has to understand the proposition in question. I am not sure whether this requirement can be considered as a sign of a strong sense of belief, for one can scarcely be said to believe a proposition in any normal sense of the word unless one understands it.

This may of course depend somewhat on the elusive notion of understanding. When can one be said to understand a proposition? There may be some temptation to try to identify understanding p with capturing all its logical consequences. If we could assent to this identification, we could leave (1)–(2) unmodified, for whoever believes that p (sc. with understanding) will surely believe any logical consequence of q, for he could not then have 'understood' p without being aware of these consequences. However, already in the case of non-trivial first-order propositions, this involves a most unrealistic standard of understanding. Surely one can understand perfectly well (say) the axioms of elementary geometry without knowing all the theorems.

A much more interesting (although still somewhat idealized) standard of understanding can be based on my earlier observations. Surely the the most concrete sense imaginable of understanding what a first-order proposition p says is to know which sequences of individuals in which combination one can expect to hit upon if it is true — sequences no longer than those already considered in p. Now this is just what the distributive normal form of p (at the depth of p) spells out as fully as possible. The elimination of trivially inconsistent constituents, which I shall assume to have been accomplished, does not spoil this interpretation.

But if so, one can defend the restriction I proposed to impose on (1)–(2) in an interesting way. The question really is not when one can believe p without believing q while $\vdash (p \supset q)$. The question really is when this can happen while one fully understands p (and perhaps also to the same extent q). In the former sense, people may indeed fail to see the most elementary logical connections, whereas in the latter case it is much less obvious that they can fail to believe that q in the case of any relatively simple consequence q of p. If the concept of understanding is now delineated along the lines just suggested, understanding p implies knowing (in principle) its distributive normal form minus trivially inconsistent constituents, and this is enough to perceive all surface tautologies of the form $p \supset q$ at the depth of p. But this means that whoever believes that p AND UNDERSTANDS p will believe all surface consequences of p (at the same depth). This of course amounts to saying that the restricted forms of (1)–(2) are valid. If I am right, they are valid as soon as we merely add the requirement of understanding, suitably interpreted, to our concept of belief.

Notice that I am not saying that nobody will be found who will sincerely say that he fails to believe that q even when he believes that p and when

$(p \supset q)$ is a surface tautology, at the depth of p. What I have done is to provide a sense of understanding in which such a failure *ipso facto* shows that he does not fully understand what he is saying.

These observations provide in my opinion interesting further reasons for restricting (1)–(2) in the way I have proposed. We may perhaps say that although knowledge and belief are not invariant with respect to logical equivalence, they are invariant with respect to those logical equivalences necessary for understanding what is being believed.

Academy of Finland
Stanford University

Dov M. Gabbay

TENSE LOGICS AND THE TENSES OF ENGLISH

0. INTRODUCTION

In this paper we outline the kind of modal logic and semantics that is suitable for the representation and analysis of a non-trivial body of tensed statements in English. We shall also make some remarks concerning further possible complexities, and thus suggest problems that need further investigation.

To achieve our goal, we shall need to depart radically from traditional tense-logics, with regard to both semantic and syntactic concepts. The new concepts introduced will hopefully help with the clarification of the question of whether tense-logic can provide a useful framework for the empirical study of the tenses of English that linguists undertake.

We begin with a brief description of traditional tense-logics. We shall then proceed, step by step, to show the need for further development, by using as illustrations certain sentences of English. On this basis we shall devise a semantics and syntax that is more adequate for representing the tense-system of natural languages than the traditional framework.

To be sure, what is known as the tense-system of English incorporates more than what is accounted for in our system, since it involves also the factors of aspect and mood. But at least we can claim that our system analyzes some of the complexities of the tense-system that are the result of temporal references alone. If and when mood and aspect will receive

Partially supported by NSF grant NSF GJ-443X. I am grateful to Professor J. M. E. Moravcsik for most valuable criticism and remarks. The observations of §5 are due to him.

a clear and rigorous analysis, a consolidation of our efforts with the analysis of these other factors should represent fully the structure of the relevant class of English sentences.

1. TRADITIONAL TENSE LOGICS

The language of traditional tense (and for the sake of simplicity) propositional logic is the following:

(1) A set $\P = [p_1, p_2, \ldots]$ of atomic propositions.
(2) The classical connectives $\sim$, $\wedge$, $\vee$, $\rightarrow$.
(3) A set C of tense connectives, usually with F (FA reads: A will be true), P (PA reads: A was true) and sometimes J (JA reads: A is true now), T (TA reads: A will be true tomorrow) and Y (YA reads: A was true yesterday).

The traditional semantical interpretation for the tense language is the following: we imagine a set of S of moments of time, with a relation $R \subseteq S^2$ on it, representing the 'flow' of time or the earlier-later relation. So for t, $s \in S$, tRs reads, s is in the future of t or t is in the past of s. With each moment of time t, we associate the function $D_t : \P \rightarrow [o, 1]$, giving truth values to the atomic propositions (i.e. $D_t(p) = 1$ iff p is true at the moment t).

One may consider several possible properties for the flow of time. R may be transitive, or (S, R) may be linear, or rational time ($R =$ smaller than) or real numbers time, S may be the set of integers, or (S, R) may be branching time etc.

Generally, given an (S, R, D_t), we can define the notion of the truth value of a statement A at a point $t \in S$, denoted by $\|A\|_t$, by induction as follows:

$\|A\|_t = 1$ iff $D_t(A) = 1$, for A atomic.
$\|A \wedge B\|_t = 1$ iff $\|A\|_t = 1$ and $\|B\|_t = 1$.
$\|\sim A\|_t = 1$ iff $\|A\|_t = 0$.
$\|A \vee B\|_t = 1$ iff $\|A\|_t = 1$ or $\|B\|_t = 1$.
$\|A \rightarrow B\|_t = 1$ iff $\|A\|_t = 0$ or $\|B\|_t = 1$.
$\|FA\|_t = 1$ iff $\|A\|_s = 1$, for some s such that tRs.
$\|PA\|_t = 1$ iff $\|A\|_s = 1$, for some s such that sRt.

In case we have integer time, and T and Y in the language we take

$\|TA\|_t = 1$ iff $\|A\|_{t+1} = 1$.
$\|YA\|_t = 1$ iff $\|A\|_{t-1} = 1$.

The case of J (now) will be discussed later.

Given a condition on (S, R) (e.g. time is linear etc.) we ask ourselves: what is the set X of all the statements A such that $\|A\|_t = 1$, for all t, for all (S, R, D_t) fulfilling this condition (e.g. that (S, R) is linear)? We seek to axiomatize X. Axiom systems have been presented corresponding to many possible conditions on the flow of time (S, R).

Traditional tense logic is mainly concerned with the problem of axiomatizing the sets X *of valid statements for various possible 'flows' of time.*

Example: An axiom system $(K_t$, due to Lemmon) for the most general flow of time (i.e. no restriction on R).

(1) axioms and rules of classical logic.
(2) $G(A \to B) \to (GA \to GB)$
$H(A \to B) \to (HA \to HB)$
(3) $\dfrac{\vdash A}{\vdash GA} \ , \ \dfrac{\vdash A}{\vdash HA}$
(4) $\sim A \to G \sim HA$
$\sim A \to H \sim GA$

Where GA is $\sim F \sim A$ and HA is $\sim P \sim A$.

For example adding the axioms $GA \to GGA$ and $HA \to HHA$ corresponds to a condition on R, that R is transitive.

Generally it turns out that there is a remarkable correspondence between axioms and conditions (on (S, R)).

From now on we assume that R is transitive.

Traditional tense logic is not suitable for expressing tense statements of English. We do not speak by saying *PFPFFA* and the like. (Indeed, Prof. Bar-Hillel, and I suppose others as well, have long been speaking against the name TENSE logics.)

There are more, less obvious reasons, for the unsuitability of traditional tense logics for the analysis of the tenses of English. In order to be able to see this more clearly, let us enumerate the tacit assumptions and properties of traditional tense logic.

Properties of Traditional Tense Logics

I. Choice of language (i.e. what tense operators to take).
II. Choice of semantics (i.e. the fact that each atomic proposition has a truth value at a point t of time and not e.g. an interval of time or a sequence of points etc.).
III. Choice of truth tables (i.e. the fact that we evaluate the truth value of A at a point and not something else).

IV. The choice of the inductive definition of the truth table for the tense operators.

2. TROUBLES WITH J

Suppose we want to take a language with $C = [P, F]$ and want to add J to it (the 'now' tense operator); what kind of semantics do we need to have for J? Look at:

(1) I am going now.
(2) It is now the case that I will later be glad that I am going now.

Sentence (1) suggests that we should in our semantics distinguish a point $o \in S$ to be the present and take JA to mean "A is true at O". In (2) the two 'now's' refer to the same point and so we may want to take the table for J to be

$$\|JA\|_t = 1 \text{ iff } \|A\|_0 = 1.$$

(i.e. whenever 'A is true now' is uttered, at any time t, this means that A is true at o).

This gives rise to a perfectly adequate logical system, but does not seem to allow for the possibility of saying something at time t and referring by 'now' to the same time t. Or e.g.

(3) It is now the case that I will be glad that I am going then.

In (3) again we need a now operator that refers to t, when evaluated at t.

This suggests that we have to keep track of when a statement B was uttered, so that when we encounter a subformula of the form JA we evaluate the truth value of A at the time of utterance of B.

Thus we get the following semantics:
We imagine time structures of the form (S, R, D_t, U, O) where (S, R, D_t) are as before, O is the real present, U is the time of utterance. We evaluate $\|A\|$ at a pair of points, i.e. $\|A\|_t^s$, s is the time that A was uttered and t is the time that A is evaluated. The table is as follows:

$\|A\|_t^s = 1$ iff $D_t(A) = 1$, A atomic.
$\|A \wedge B\|_t^s = 1$ iff $\|A\|_t^s = 1$ and $\|B\|_t^s = 1$.

The cases of $\sim$, $\vee$, $\rightarrow$ are similar to $\wedge$, i.e. taken classically.

$\|FA\|_t^s = 1$ iff $\|A\|_{t'}^s = 1$, for some t' such that tRt'.
$\|PA\|_t^s = 1$ iff $\|A\|_{t'}^s = 1$, for some t' such that $t'Rt$.
$\|JA\|_t^s = 1$ iff $\|A\|_s^s = 1$.

This table is essentially due to D. Kaplan.

3. TROUBLE WITH P AND F

We saw that we need have tables of the form $\|A\|_t^s$, because we wanted to represent 'now' and 'then' and so had to record the point of utterance. But don't we record the point of utterance when we use F (will) and P (was) as well?

(4) John will find out that Mary was killed.

Don't we keep in mind the present, and that the 'was killed' was in the past of the present? I.e. if we evaluate according to the table of §1, we get $\|FPA\|_o = 1$ iff for some t, such that oRt, $\|PA\|_t = 1$. So to make $\|PA\|_t = 1$, we need an s, such that sRt and $\|A\|_s = 1$. But according to our meaning, we must find an s in the past of o, i.e. when we evaluate $\|PA\|_t$, we must remember that the original statement was uttered at o, i.e. we must look at $\|PA\|_t^o$.

Similarly with $\|PFA\|_o$, e.g.:

(5) A child was born that will be king.

The 'will' is in the future of 'now'. Actually, we use the 'would' and the 'will have' to express two other future and past tenses that supplement the 'will' and 'was'.

4. 'WILL, 'WAS', 'WOULD', AND 'WILL HAVE'

Take the English sentence:

(6) John told me that he will not come to the meeting.

This sentence means that at some time t, in the past of O, John said that he will not come at some time s IN THE FUTURE OF O.

Compare (6) with the following:

(7) Why didn't John come?
Well, he told me he would be busy.

There is a certain ambiguity here (we will have better examples later) but by and large, if the meeting has already taken place one would use 'would' and if not — 'will'.

The iteration FPA has similar properties. Consider the following:

(8) If you will not be generous with your child, he will hate you for the hard time you will have given him.

(9) If you will not compensate your child he will hate you for the hard time you gave him.

In (8) the future perfect is used to indicate that the 'hard time' is in the past of 'hate' but still in the future of 'now'. While ordinary past takes us back to the past of 'now'.

Notice that both the 'future perfect' and the 'would' although do not 'jump' over 'now' do not go all the way but still remain BOUNDED by the present (compare with 14 below).

Consider more complex examples:

    (10) I knew that by the time the criminal is brought to trial, he will have realised that his best policy will be to deny that he owned the gun.

    (11) I will not admit that it was I who told him that the price will change.

    (12) I will not admit that it was I who told him that the price would change.

The above examples show that there are two types of tense operators involved:

    (a) $F_w A$ ('A will be true')
    (b) $F_d A$ ('A would be true')
    (c) $P_w A$ ('A was true')
    (d) $P_d A$ ('A will have been true')
        (i.e. future perfect).

The examples suggest that the truth values of the tense operators cannot be evaluated simple mindedly 'at a point s' (i.e. 'the value of A at s') because:

    (1) The present, O, is involved (i.e. with F_w and P_w that jump)
    (2) We have to know the point of reference of time that preceded s.

To understand (2) look at the following example:

    (13) He will realise, that by the time he will graduate, the draft will have been cancelled.

(By the way, compare (13) with

    (14) He will realise that the draft was cancelled)

In (13) the 'will have been' refers to the time between his 'realisation' and 'graduation'. So we must keep record of the time of his 'realisation'. THE ABOVE DISCUSSION SUGGESTS THE TRUTH DEFINITION GIVEN BELOW.

We assume our structures are of the form (S, R, O, D_t) with R transitive and irreflexive and fulfilling the property that for all t, ORt or tRO holds. Let us also add to the language the operator:

       JA ('A is true now')

and give the definition:

DEFINITION: The truth value of a formula A at a pair of points t,s (t may not appear!) is denoted by $\|A\|_{t,s}$ and is defined by the following clauses:

(a) $\|A\|_{t,s}$ is defined if and only if one of the conditions below is satisfied:

    (1) $\|A\|_o$ is defined.
    (2) $\|A\|_{o,s}$ (for $s \neq o$), is defined.
    (3) $\|A\|_{t,s}$ (for $t \neq s$ and ORt, ORs and either tRs or sRt hold) is defined.
    (4) $\|A\|_{t,s}$ (for $t \neq s$ and tRO and sRO and either tRs or sRt) is defined.

(b)   In case $\|A\|_{t,s}$ is defined then the value is given by $\|p\|_{t,s} = D_t\,(p)$, for atomic p, and for the other cases the value is given by the table below; where (*) abbreviates the phrase 'THERE EXISTS A u SUCH THAT'.

For example: "(*) $\|A\|_{s,u} = 1$ $tRuRs$" means: 'There exists a u such that $\|A\|_{s,u} = 1$ and tRu and uRs'.

value at t,s in case / operator	CASE I: oRt and oRs		CASE II: tRo and sRo		CASE III
	subcase I 1 tRs or $t=0$	subcase I 2 sRt	subcase II 1 tRs	subcase II 2 sRt or $t=0$	Value at 0
$F_w\,A$	(*) sRu and $\|A\|_{s,u}=1$	(*) sRu and $\|A\|_{s,u}=1$	(*) oRu and $\|A\|_{o,u}=1$	(*) oRu and $\|A\|_{o,u}=1$	(*) oRu and $\|A\|_{o,u}=1$
$P_w\,A$	(*) uRo and $\|A\|_{o,u}=1$	(*) uRo and $\|A\|_{o,u}=1$	(*) uRs and $\|A\|_{s,u}=1$	(*) uRs and $\|A\|_{s,u}=1$	(*) uRo and $\|A\|_{o,u}=1$
$F_d\,A$	(*) sRu and $\|A\|_{s,u}=1$	(*) sRu and uRt and $\|A\|_{s,u}=1$	(*) sRu and uRo and $\|A\|_{s,u}=1$	(*) sRu and uRo and $\|A\|_{s,u}=1$	(*) oRu and $\|A\|_{o,u}=1$
$P_d\,A$	(*) tRu and uRs and $\|A\|_{s,u}=1$	(*) uRs and oRu and $\|A\|_{s,u}=1$	(*) tRu and uRs and $\|A\|_{s,u}=1$	(*) uRs and $\|A\|_{s,u}=1$	(*) uRo and $\|A\|_{o,u}=1$

The table shows the definition of the truth value for F_w and P_w is symmetrical with respect to cases I and II while the definition for F_d is not (i.e. F_d case I 1 and F_d case II 2). This is because of the following:

(15) 'I was told that John said he would come.'

The 'would' does not refer to the time between 'I was told' and 'he said' but between 'he said' and the present 'o'. Compare with (B).

The table given in this section is only a suggestion. The main point we make is that we need at LEAST something of this nature. Do we need more?

5. FURTHER COMPLEXITIES OF TENSE ITERATION[1]

Up till now we assumed that the only point that needs to be kept on record through the sequences is the point of utterance, along with the immediately preceding point. There are, however, grounds for supposing that even this added feature will not take care of all of the complexities of iteration. (To be sure, we must be careful when we talk of iteration in this context. We don't have English sentences like: "it is the case that it will be the case that it was the case that ... etc." Rather, the tenses affect a sequence of events. In this respect the tense operators in English differ from the modal operators.)

While in the previous sections we recorded point 0, and then computed the various P's and F's by using the table, we shall now consider sentences that seem to involve the consideration of points that are not 0, or are not immediately preceding the point to be computed. For example:

(16) She regretted that she married the man who was to become an officer of the bank where she had had her account.

The regret was prior to the time of utterance, the marriage prior to the regret, the promotion to the status of office of the bank came after the marriage but prior to the point of utterance. Still, the period during which she had her account with the bank must have been prior to the marriage. Thus in order to calculate the last temporal reference point we must jump back to the last past, which is neither the starting point, nor the immediately preceding temporal point. (We are jumping over a future, so to speak.)

It is far from clear what sort of rule would take care of this phenomenon. For one thing, it is not clear that the interpretation of the sequence of temporal references is independent of the particular verbs used. Let us consider

(16a) She regretted that she married the man who was to become an officer of the bank where she had opened her account.

Syntactically and referentially we have the same structure; but the substitution of the verb 'open' seems to cast doubt on whether the last event must be prior to the marriage, or merely prior to the point of utterance.

Perhaps a clearer example would be:

(17) She will go to the school, that was her mothers' alma mater, and it will become better than Harvard.

Here the going to school is in the future of the point of utterance, the mother's attendance is in the past of the point of utterance, but in order

---

[1] We wish to acknowledge the help of Joan Bresnan and William Leben with some of the considerations brought forth in this section, without attributing to them agreement with any of what is proposed here.

to calculate the time at which the school overtakes Harvard we must consider the last future reference, and thus we jump over one point, the past reference to mother's attendance, without going all the way back to the original point of utterance.

Cases like (17) might be explained on syntactic grounds. We have here a coordinate structure, and what we "jump over" is a relative clause of the first conjunct. Thus one explanation for the "jumpings" might be that in a sequence of conjunctions the temporal reference points form a sequence that bypasses the sequence built into any possible relative clause. If this is so, it would show that one cannot formulate detailed rules for the complete semantics of tense iterations without taking into account the syntactic structures that make up the sequence. This is suggested also by

(16b) She regretted that the man who was to become an officer of the bank where she had had her account married her.

Clearly here too, the having of the account must be prior to the marriage, even though the latter is only mentioned at the end of the sentence. We can explain this by pointing out that (16b) is transformationally related to (16). Once more we see that syntactic structure other than mere left-to-right ordering must be taken into account in the computation of the tense sequence.

In the meantime, the tentative conclusion is that we must give tables for evaluating sentences $\|A\|_{(u, t_1, t_2, t_3, \ldots)}$ i.e. we must keep record of the entire sequence of points and not only that, but also keep track of the kind of operators used (i.e. whether t_3 was introduced because of an F or not, because if we have another F, the next point may have to be chosen in the future of t_3!).

Doubts: (1) We must make sure that in the examples above we use only the structure of the sequence of P's and F's and not the meaning of the verbs.

Doubts: (2) We don't speak like $PFPA$ but introduce an event with each tense operator. E.g.: 'He THOUGHT I will FIND OUT that she was KILLED'. Is this significant for our purposes?

6. DO WE TAKE TRUTH VALUES AT POINTS?

Up to now we evaluated $\|A\|$ either at a point of time or a sequence of points of time. The original underlying tense structure, (S, R, D_t) was not changed. $D_t(p)$ gave for each t and p the value of P at t. Is this O.K.?

(18) Yesterday she worked in the garden for ten hours.

(19) This castle was built during the 17th Century.

(20) He won the game in the 17th Century.

We see that some verbs can be evaluated at a moment of time (e.g. 'win') while others need a period of time! This means that $D_t(p)$ should be replaced by $D_T(p)$, T is an interval. We have no idea what table to give to the tense operators F, P, J, etc.

7. CONCLUSIONS

The preceding sections showed that in order to present an adequate semantics and syntax for tensed English one must go beyond traditional tense logics. We have also seen, however — in the last two sections — that the complications arising with regard to certain types of sentences as of now resist adequate treatment. Even so, our explorations of the last two sections at least helped to set the level of adequacy for the treatments of tense in English. For only a system that can fully account for the data surveyed briefly in the past two sections can claim descriptive adequacy. At the same time, the data in question indicate the possibility of uncovering interesting results concerning the interaction of the tense system with prior syntactic structure and analysis, as well as possible criteria of complexity of the semantics of natural languages. The thorough investigation of these matters lies beyond the scope of the present enterprise.

Part II

ALTERNATIVE APPROACHES TO MEANING

— — — — — — — — — — — — — — — — — —

J. L. Austin

THE MEANING OF A WORD

SPECIMENS OF SENSE

1.1.   What-is-the-meaning-of (the word) 'rat'?
1.11. What-is-the-meaning-of (the word) 'word'?
1.21. What is a 'rat'?
1.211. What is a 'word'?
1.22. What is the 'muzzle' of a rat?
2.1.   What-is-the-meaning-of (the phrase) 'What-is-the-meaning-of'?
2.11. What-is-the-meaning-of (the sentence) 'What-is-the-meaning-of (the word) "*x*"?'?

SPECIMENS OF NONSENSE

1.1.   What-is-the-meaning-of a word?
1.11. What-is-the-meaning-of any word?
1.12. What-is-the-meaning-of a word in general?
1.21. What is the-meaning-of-a-word?
1.211. What is the-meaning-of-(the-word)-'rat'?
1.22. What is the 'meaning' of a word?
1.221. What is the 'meaning' of (the word) 'rat'?
2.1.   What-is-the-meaning-of (the phrase) 'the-meaning-of-a word'?

Reprinted from: J. L. Austin, *Philosophical Papers* ed. by J. Urmson and G. Warnock (Oxford, Oxford Univ. Press, 1961), 23-43.

2.11. What-is-the-meaning-of (the sentence) 'What is the-meaning-of-
(the-word)-"*x*"?'?
2.12. What-is-the-meaning-of (the sentence) 'What is the "meaning"
of "the word" "*x*"?'?

This paper is about the phrase 'the meaning of a word'. It is divided into
three parts, of which the first is the most trite and the second the most
muddled: all are too long. In the first, I try to make it clear that the
phrase 'the meaning of a word' is, in general, if not always, a dangerous
nonsense-phrase. In the other two parts I consider in turn two questions,
often asked in philosophy, which clearly need new and careful scrutiny if
that facile phrase 'the meaning of a word' is no longer to be permitted to
impose upon us.

                                        I

I begin, then, with some remarks about 'the meaning of a word'. I think
many persons now see all or part of what I shall say: but not all do,
and there is a tendency to forget it, or to get it slightly wrong. In so far
as I am merely flogging the converted, I apologize to them.

A preliminary remark. It may justly be urged that, properly speaking,
what alone has meaning is a *sentence*. Of course, we can speak quite
properly of, for example, 'looking up the meaning of a word' in a
dictionary. Nevertheless, it appears that the sense in which a word or a
phrase 'has a meaning' is derivative from the sense in which a sentence
'has a meaning': to say a word or a phrase 'has a meaning' is to say that
there are sentences in which it occurs which 'have meanings': and to
know the meaning which the word or phrase has, is to know the meanings
of sentences in which it occurs. All the dictionary can do when we 'look
up the meaning of a word' is to suggest aids to the understanding of
sentences in which it occurs. Hence it appears correct to say that what
'has meaning' in the primary sense is the sentence. And older philosophers
who discussed the problem of 'the meaning of words' tend to fall into
special errors, avoided by more recent philosophers, who discuss rather
the parallel problem of 'the meaning of sentences'. Nevertheless, if we
are on our guard, we perhaps need not fall into these special errors, and
I propose to overlook them at present.

There are many sorts of sentences in which the words 'the meaning of
the word so-and-so' are found, e.g. 'He does not know, or understand,
the meaning of the word *handsaw*': 'I shall have to explain to her the
meaning of the word *pikestaff*': and so on. I intend to consider primarily
the common question, 'What is the meaning of *so-and-so*?' or 'What is
the meaning of *the word so-and-so*?'

Suppose that in ordinary life I am asked: 'What is the meaning of the word *racy*?' There are two sorts of thing I may do in response: I may reply *in words*, trying to describe what raciness is and what it is not, to give examples of sentences in which one might use the word *racy*, and of others in which one should not. Let us call this *sort* of thing 'explaining the syntactics' of the word 'racy' in the English language. On the other hand, I might do what we may call 'demonstrating the semantics' of the word, by getting the questioner to *imagine*, or even actually to *experience*, situations which we should describe correctly by means of sentences containing the words 'racy' 'raciness', etc., and again other situations where we should *not* use these words. This is, of course, a simple case: but perhaps the same two *sorts* of procedure would be gone through in the case of at least most ordinary words. And in the same way, if I wished to find out 'whether he understands the meaning of the word *racy*', I should test him at some length in these two ways (which perhaps could not be entirely divorced from each other).

Having asked in this way, and answered, 'What is the meaning of (the word) "rat"?', 'What is the meaning of (the word) "cat"?', 'What is the meaning of (the word) "mat"?', and so on, we then try, being philosophers, to ask the further *general* question, 'What is the meaning of a word?' But there is something spurious about this question. We do not intend to mean by it a certain question which would be perfectly all right, namely, 'What is the meaning of (the word) "word"?': *that* would be no more general than is asking the meaning of the word 'rat', and would be answered in a precisely similar way. No: we want to ask rather, 'What is the meaning of a-word-in-general?' or 'of *any* word' — not meaning 'any' word *you like to choose*, but rather *no particular* word *at all*, just 'any word'. Now if we pause even for a moment to reflect, this is a perfectly absurd question to be trying to ask. I can only answer a question of the form 'What is the meaning of "*x*"?' if "*x*" is some *particular* word you are asking about. This supposed *general* question is really just a spurious question of a type which commonly arises in philosophy. We may call it the fallacy of asking about 'Nothing-in-particular' which is a practice decried by the plain man, but by the philosopher called 'generalizing' and regarded with some complacency. Many other examples of the fallacy can be found: take, for example, the case of 'reality' — we try to pass from such questions as 'How would you distinguish a real rat from an imaginary rat?' to 'What is a real thing?', a question which merely gives rise to nonsense.

We may expose the error in our present case thus. Instead of asking 'What is the meaning of (the word) "rat"?' we might clearly have asked 'What is a "rat"?' and so on. But if our questions have been put in *that* form, it becomes very difficult to formulate any *general* question which could impose on us for a moment. Perhaps 'What is anything?'? Few philosophers, if perhaps not none, have been foolhardy enough to pose such a question. In the same way, we should not perhaps be tempted to generalize such a question as 'Does he know the meaning of (the word) "rat"?' 'Does he know the meaning of a word?' would be silly.

Faced with the nonsense question 'What is the meaning of a word?', and perhaps dimly recognizing it to be nonsense, we are nevertheless not inclined to give it up. Instead, we transform it in a curious and noteworthy manner. Up to now, we had been asking '*What-is the meaning-of* (the word) "rat"?', etc.; and ultimately '*What-is-the-meaning-of* a word?' But now, being baffled, we change so to speak, the hyphenation, and ask 'What is *the-meaning-of-a-word*?' or sometimes, 'What is the "meaning" of a word?' (1.22): I shall refer, for brevity's sake, only to the other (1.21). It is easy to see how very different this question is from the other. At once a crowd of traditional and reassuring answers present themselves: 'a concept', 'an idea', 'an image', 'a class of similar sensa', etc., all of which are equally spurious answers to a pseudo-question. Plunging ahead, however, or rather retracing our steps, we now proceed to ask such questions as 'What is the-meaning-of-(the-word) "rat"?' which is as spurious as 'What-is-the-meaning-of (the word) "rat"?' was genuine. And again we answer 'the idea of a rat' and so forth. How quaint this procedure is, may be seen in the following way. Supposing a plain man puzzled, were to ask me 'What is the meaning of (the word) "muggy"?', and I were to answer, 'The idea or concept of "mugginess"' or 'The class of sensa of which it is correct to say "This is muggy"': the man would stare at me as at an imbecile. And that is sufficiently unusual for me to conclude that that was not at all the sort of answer he expected: nor, in plain English, *can* that question *ever* require that sort of answer.

To show up this pseudo-question, let us take a parallel case, where perhaps no one has yet been deluded, though they well might be. Suppose that I ask 'What is the point of doing so-and-so?' For example, I ask Old Father William 'What is the point of standing on one's head?' He replies in the way we know. Then I follow this up with 'What is the point of balancing an eel on the end of one's nose?' And he explains. Now suppose I ask as my third question 'What is the point of doing *anything* — not anything *in particular*, but just *anything*?' Old Father William would no doubt kick me downstairs without the option. But lesser men, raising this same question and finding no answer, would very likely commit suicide or join the Church. (Luckily, in the case of 'What is the meaning of a word?' the effects are less serious, amounting only to the writing of books.) On the other hand, more adventurous intellects would no doubt take to asking 'What is the-point-of-doing-a-thing?' or 'What is the "point" of doing a thing?': and then later 'What is the-point-of-eating-suet?' and so on. Thus we should discover a whole new universe of a kind of entity called 'points', not previously suspected of existence.

To make the matter clearer, let us consider another case which is precisely *unlike* the case of 'What is the meaning of?' I can ask not only the question, 'What is the square root of 4?', of 8, and so on, but also 'What is the square root of a number?': which is either nonsense or equivalent to 'What is the "square root" of a number?' I then give a definition of the 'square root' of a number, such that, for any given number x, 'the square root of x' is a definite description of another number y. This differs from our case in that 'the meaning of p' is not a definite description of any entity.

The general questions which we want to ask about 'meaning' are best phrased as, 'What-is-the-meaning-of (the phrase) "what-is-the-meaning-of (the word) 'x'?"?' The *sort* of answer we should get to these quite sensible questions is that with which I began this discussion: viz. that when I am asked 'What-is-the-meaning-of (the word) "x"?', I naturally reply by explaining its syntactics and demonstrating its semantics.

All this must seem very obvious, but I wish to point out that it is fatally easy to forget it: no doubt I shall do so myself many times in the course of this paper. Even those who see pretty clearly that 'concepts', 'abstract ideas', and so on are fictitious entities, which we owe in part to asking questions about 'the meaning of a word', nevertheless themselves think that there *is something* which is 'the meaning of a word'. Thus Mr. Hampshire[1] attacks to some purpose the theory that there is such a thing as '*the* meaning of a word': what *he* thinks is wrong is the belief that there is a *single* thing called *the* meaning: 'concepts' are nonsense, and no single particular 'image' can be *the* meaning of a general word. So, he goes on to say, the meaning of a word must really be 'a *class* of similar particular ideas'. 'If we are asked "What does this mean?" we point to (!) a class of particular ideas.' But a 'class of particular ideas' is every bit as fictitious an entity as a 'concept' or 'abstract idea'. In the same way Mr. C. W. Morris (in the *Encyclopaedia of Unified Science*) attacks, to some purpose, those who think of 'a meaning' as a definite something which is 'simply located' somewhere: what *he* thinks is wrong is that people think of 'a meaning' as a kind of entity which can be described wholly without reference to the total activity of 'semiosis'. Well and good. Yet he himself makes some of the crudest possible remarks about 'the designatum' of a word: every sign has a designatum, which is not a particular thing but a *kind* of object or *class* of object. Now this is quite as fictitious an entity as any 'Platonic idea': and is due to precisely the same fallacy of looking for 'the meaning (or designatum) of a word'.

[1] "Ideas, Propositions and Signs", in the *Proceedings of the Aristotelian Society* (1939-40).

Why are we tempted to slip back in this way? Perhaps there are two
main reasons. First, there is the curious belief that all words are *names*,
i.e. in effect *proper* names, and therefore stand for something or designate
it in the way that a proper name does. But this view that general names
'have denotation' in the same way that proper names do, is quite as odd
as the view that proper names 'have connotation' in the same way that
general names do, which is commonly recognized to lead to error.
Secondly, we are afflicted by a more common malady, which is this.
When we have given an analysis of a certain sentence, containing a
word or phrase '*x*', we often feel inclined to ask, of our analysis, 'What
in it, is "*x*"?' For example, we give an analysis of 'The State owns this
land', in sentences about individual men, their relations and transactions:
and then at last we feel inclined to ask: well now, *what*, in all that, *is* the
State? And we might answer: the State *is* a collection of individual men
united in a certain manner. Or again, when we have analysed the statement 'trees can exist unperceived' into statements about sensing sensa,
we still tend to feel uneasy unless we can say *something* '*really does*' 'exist
unperceived': hence theories about 'sensibilia' and what not. So in our
present case, having given all that is required, viz. an account of 'What-is-
the-meaning-of "What is-the-meaning-of (the word) '*x*'?"' we *still* feel
tempted, wrongly supposing our original sentence to contain a constituent 'the-meaning-of (the-word)-"*x*"', to ask 'Well now, as it turns
out, what *is* the meaning of the word "*x*", after all?' And we answer, 'a
class of similar particular ideas' and what not.

Of course, all my account of our motives in this matter may be only a
convenient didactic schema: I do not think it is — but I recognize that
one should not impute motives, least of all rational motives. Anyhow,
what I claim in clear, is that there is *no* simple and handy appendage of a
word called 'the meaning of (the word) "*x*"'.

II

I now pass on to the first of the two points which need now a careful
scrutiny if we are no longer to be imposed upon by that convenient
phrase 'the meaning of a word'. What I shall say here is, I know, not as
clear as it should be.

Constantly we ask the question, 'Is *y* the meaning, or *part* of the
meaning, or *contained* in the meaning, of *x*? — or is it *not*?' A favourite
way of putting the question is to ask, 'Is the judgement "*x* is *y*" analytic
or synthetic?' Clearly, we suppose, *y* must be *either* a part of the meaning
of *x*, *or* not any part of it. And, if *y is* a part of the meaning of *x*, to say
'*x* is not *y*' will be self-contradictory: while if it is *not* a part of the mean-

ing of x, to say 'x is not y' will present no difficulty — such a state of affairs will be readily 'conceivable'. This seems to be the merest common sense. And no doubt it *would* be the merest common sense *if* 'meanings' were things in some ordinary sense which contained parts in some ordinary sense. But they are *not*. Unfortunately, many philosophers who know they are not, still speak as though y must either be or not be 'part of the meaning' of x. But this is the point: *if* 'explaining the meaning of a word' is really the complicated sort of affair that we have seen it to be, and *if* there is really nothing to call 'the meaning of a word' — *then* phrases like 'part of the meaning of the word x' are completely undefined; it is left hanging in the air, we do not know what it means at all. *We are using a working-model which fails to fit the facts that we really wish to talk about.* When we consider what we really do want to talk about, and not the working-model, what would really be meant at all by a judgement being 'analytic or synthetic'? We simply do not know. Of course, we feel inclined to say 'I can easily produce examples of analytic and synthetic judgements; for instance, I should confidently say "Being a professor is *not* part of the meaning of being a man" and so forth.' 'A is A is analytic.' Yes, but it is when we are required to give a *general definition* of what we mean by 'analytic' or 'synthetic', and when we are required to justify our dogma that *every* judgement is either analytic or synthetic, that we find we have, in fact, nothing to fall back upon *except our working-model*. From the start, it is clear that our working-model fails to do justice, for example, to the distinction between syntactics and semantics: for instance, talking about the contradictory of every sentence having to be either self-contradictory or not so, is to talk as though all sentences which we are prohibited from saying were sentences which offended against *syntactical* rules, and could be formally reduced to verbal self-contradictions. But this overlooks all semantical considerations, which philosophers are sadly prone to do. Let us consider two cases of some things which we simply *cannot say*: although they are *not* 'self-contradictory' and although — and this of course is where many will have axes to grind — we cannot possibly be tempted to say that we have 'synthetic *a priori*' knowledge of their contradictions.

Let us begin with a case which, being about *sentences* rather than *words*, is not quite in point, but which may encourage us. Take the well-known sentence 'The cat is on the mat, and I do not believe it'. That seems absurd. On the other hand 'The cat is on the mat, and I believe it' seems trivial. If we were to adopt a customary dichotomy, and to say *either* a proposition p implies another proposition r, or p is perfectly compatible with not-r, we should at once in our present case be tempted to say that 'The cat is on the mat' *implies* 'I believe it': hence both the triviality of adding 'and I believe it' and the absurdity of adding 'and I do not believe it'. But of course 'the cat is on the mat' does *not* imply 'Austin believes the cat is on the mat': nor even 'the speaker believes the cat is on the mat' — for the speaker may be lying. The doctrine which is produced in this case is, that not *p* indeed, but *asserting p* implies 'I (who assert *p*) believe *p*'. And here 'implies' must be given a special sense: for of course it is not that 'I assert *p*' implies (in the ordinary sense) 'I believe *p*', for I may be lying. It is the sort of sense in which by asking a question I 'imply' that I do not know the answer to it. By asserting *p* I *give it to be understood* that I believe *p*.

Now the reason why I cannot say 'The cat is on the mat and I do not believe it' is not that it offends against syntactics in the sense of being in some way 'self-contradictory'. What prevents my saying it, is rather some semantic convention (implicit, of course), about the way we use words *in situations*. What precisely is the account to be given in this case we need not ask. Let us rather notice one significant feature of it. Whereas '*p* and I believe it' is somehow trivial, and '*p* and I do not believe it' is somehow nonsense, a third sentence '*p* and *I might not have* believed it' makes perfectly good sense. Let us call these three sentences Q, not Q, and 'might not Q'. Now what prohibits us from saying '*p*' implies 'I believe *p*' in the ordinary sense of 'implies', is precisely shown by the fact that although not-Q is (*somehow*) absurd, 'might not Q' is not at all absurd. For in ordinary cases of implication, not merely is not Q absurd, but 'might not Q' is *also* absurd: e.g. 'triangles are figures and triangles have no shape' is no more absurd than 'triangles are figures and triangles might have had no shape'. Consideration of the sentence 'might not Q' will afford a rough test as to whether *p* 'implies' *r* in the *ordinary* sense, or in the special sense, of 'implies'.

Bearing this in mind, let us now consider a sentence which, as I claim, cannot possibly be classified as *either* 'analytic' *or* 'synthetic'. I refer to the sentence, 'This *x* exists', where *x* is a sensum, e.g. 'This noise exists'. In endeavouring to classify it, one party would point to the triviality of 'This noise exists', and to the absurdity of 'This noise does not exist'. They would say, therefore, that *existence* is 'part of the meaning of' *this*. But another party would point out, that 'This noise might not have existed' makes perfectly good sense. *They* would say, therefore, that *existence* cannot be 'part of the meaning of' *this*.

Both parties, as we are now in a position to see, would be correct in their *arguments*, but incorrect in their *conclusions*. What seems to be true is that *using the word 'this'* (not: the word 'this') *gives it to be understood that* the sensum referred to 'exists'.

Perhaps, historically', this fact about the sentence-trio, 'This noise exists', 'This noise does not exist', and 'This noise might not have existed', was pointed out before any philosopher had had time to pronounce that

'This noise exists' is analytic, or is synthetic. But such a pronouncement might well have been made: and *to this day*, even when the fact has been pointed out, many philosophers *worry* about the case, supposing the sentence *must* be one or the other but painfully aware of the difficulties in choosing either. I wish to point out that consideration of the analogy between this case and the other, should cure us once and for all of this bogy, and of insisting on classifying sentences as *either* analytic *or* synthetic. It may encourage us to consider again what the facts in their actual complexity really are. (One thing it suggests is a reconsideration of 'Caesar is bald' and similar propositions: but I cannot go into that.)

So far, however, we have scarcely begun in earnest: we have merely felt that initial trepidation, experienced when the firm ground of prejudice begins to slip away beneath the feet. Perhaps there are other cases, or other sorts of cases, where it will not be possible to say either that *y* is a 'part of the meaning' of *x* or that it is not, without being misleading.

Suppose we take the case of 'being thought good by me' and 'being approved of by me'. Are we to rush at this with the dichotomy: *either* 'being approved of by me' *is* part of the meaning of 'being thought good by me' *or* it is *not*? Is it *obvious* that 'I think *x* good but I do not approve of it' is self-contradictory? Of course it is not *verbally* self-contradictory. That it either is or is not 'really' self-contradictory would seem to be difficult to establish. Of course, we think, it must be one or the other — only 'it's difficult to decide *which*': or 'it depends on how you use the words'. But are those really the difficulties which baffle us? Of course, *if* it were certain that every sentence *must* be either analytic or synthetic, those *must* be the difficulties. But then, it is not certain: no account even of what the distinction means, is given except by reference to our shabby working-model. I suggest that 'I think *x* good but I do not approve of it' may very well be neither self-contradictory nor yet 'perfectly good sense' in the way in which 'I think *x* exciting but I do not approve of it' *is* 'perfectly good sense'.

Perhaps this example does not strike you as awkward. It cannot be expected that all examples will appeal equally to all hearers. Let us take some others. Is 'What is good ought to exist' analytic or synthetic? According to Moore's theory, this must be 'synthetic': yet he constantly in *Principia Ethica* takes its truth for granted. And that illustrates one of the main drawbacks of insisting on saying that a sentence *must* be either analytic or synthetic: you are almost certain to have left on your hands some general sentences which are certainly not analytic but which you find it difficult to conceive being false: i.e. you are landed with 'synthetic *a priori* knowledge'. Take that sentence of ill fame 'Pink is more like red than black'. It is rash to pronounce this 'synthetic *a priori* knowledge' on the ground that 'being more like red than black' is not 'part of the meaning' or 'part of the definition' of 'pink' and that it is not 'conceivable' that pink should be more like black than red: I dare say, so far as these phrases have any clear meaning, that it *is not*: but the question is: *is* the thing therefore 'synthetic' *a priori* knowledge?

Or, again, take some examples from Berkeley: is *extended* 'part of the meaning' of *coloured* or of *shaped*, or *shaped* 'part of the meaning' of *extended*? is 'est sed non percipitur' self-contradictory (when said of a sensum), or is it not? When we worry thus, is it not worth considering the possibility that we are oversimplifying?

What we are to say in these cases, what even the possibilities are, I do not at present clearly see. (1) Evidently, we must throw away the old working-model as soon as we take account even of the existence of a distinction between syntactics and semantics. (2) But evidently also, our *new* working-model, the supposed 'ideal' language, is in many ways a most inadequate model of any *actual* language: its careful separation of syntactics from semantics, its lists of explicitly formulated rules and conventions, and its careful delimitation of their spheres of operation — all are misleading. An *actual* language has few, if any, explicit conventions, no sharp limits to the spheres of operation of rules, no rigid separation of what is syntactical and what semantical. (3) Finally, I think I can see that there are difficulties about our powers of imagination, and about the curious way in which it is enslaved by words.

To encourage ourselves in the belief that this sort of consideration may play havoc with the distinction 'analytic or synthetic', let us consider a similar and more familiar case. It seems, does it not, perfectly obvious that every proposition must have a contradictory? Yet it does not turn out so. Suppose that I live in harmony and friendship for four years with a cat: and then it delivers a philippic. We ask ourselves, perhaps, 'Is it a real cat? or is it *not* a real cat?' Either it *is*, or it *is not*, but we cannot be sure which. Now actually, that is not so: *neither* 'It is a real cat' *nor* 'it is not a real cat' fits the facts semantically: each is designed for other situations than this one: you could not say the former of something which delivers philippics, nor yet the latter of something which has behaved as this has for four years. There are similar difficulties about choosing between 'This *is* a hallucination' and 'This is *not* a hallucination'. With sound instinct, the plain man turns in such cases to Watson and says 'Well now, *what would you* say?' 'How would you *describe* it? The difficulty is just that: there is *no* short description which is not misleading: the only thing to do, and that can easily be done, is to set out the description of the facts at length. Ordinary language breaks down in extraordinary cases. (In such cases, the cause of the breakdown is semantical.) Now no doubt an *ideal* language would *not* break down, whatever happened. In doing physics, for example, where our language is tightened up in order precisely to describe complicated and unusual cases concisely, we *prepare linguistically for the worst*. In ordinary language we do not: *words fail us*. If we talk as though an ordinary must be like an ideal language, we shall misrepresent the facts.

Consider now 'being extended' and 'being shaped'. In ordinary life we never get into a situation where we learn to say that anything is extended but not shaped nor conversely. We have all learned to use, and have used, the words only in cases where it is correct to use both. Supposing now someone says '*x* is extended but has no shape'. Somehow we cannot see what this 'could mean' — there are no semantic conventions, explicit or implicit, to cover this case: yet it is not prohibited in any way — there are no limiting rules about what we might or might not say *in extraordinary cases*. It is not *merely* the difficulty of imagining or experiencing extraordinary cases, either, which causes worry. There is this too: we can only describe what it is we are trying to imagine, by means of words which precisely describe and evoke the *ordinary* case, which we are trying to think away. Ordinary language *blinkers* the already feeble imagination. It would be difficult, in this way, if I were to say 'Can I think of a case where a man would be neither at home nor not at home?' This is inhibiting, because I think of the *ordinary* case where I ask 'Is he at home?' and get the answer, 'No': when certainly he is not at home. But supposing I happen *first* to think of the situation when I call on him just after he has died: then I see at once it would be wrong to say either. So in our case, the only thing to do is to imagine or experience all kinds of odd situations, and then suddenly round on oneself and ask: there, *now* would I say that, being extended it must be shaped? A new idiom might in odd cases be demanded.

I should like to say, in concluding this section, that in the course of stressing that we must pay attention to the facts of *actual* language, what we can and cannot say, and *precisely* why, another and converse point takes shape. Although it will not do to force actual language to accord with some preconceived model: it *equally* will not do, having discovered the facts about 'ordinary usage' *to rest content* with that, as though there were nothing more to be discussed and discovered. There may be plenty that might happen and does happen which would need new and better language to describe it in. Very often philosophers are only engaged on this task, when they seem to be perversely using words in a way which makes no sense according to 'ordinary usage'. There may be extraordinary facts, even about our everyday experience, which plain men and plain language overlook.

III

The last, and perhaps least unimportant point I have to make is the following: it seems to me that far more *detailed* attention ought to be given to that celebrated question, the posing of which has given birth to, and still keeps alive, so many erroneous theories, namely: why do we call different things by the same name? In reply to this, the philoprogenitive invent theories of 'universals' and what not: some entity or other to be that of which the 'name' is the name. And in reply to *them*, the more cautious (the 'nominalists') have usually been content to reply simply that: the reason why we call different things by the same name is simply that the things are *similar*: there is nothing *identical* present in them. This reply is inadequate in many respects: it does not, for example, attack the misleading form in which the question is posed, nor sufficiently go into the peculiarities of the word 'similar'. But what I wish to object to in it tonight is rather this: that *it is not in the least true* that all the things which I 'call by the same (general) name' *are* in general 'similar', in any ordinary sense of that much abused word.

It is a most strange thing that 'nominalists' should rest content with this answer. Not merely is it untrue to the facts; but further, if they had examined the facts, which are, in themselves, interesting enough, they could have produced with little trouble a far more formidable case against their opponents. So long as they say the things *are similar*, it will always be open to someone to say: 'Ah yes, similar *in a certain respect*: and that can only be explained by means of universals' (or whatever the name may be that they prefer for that well-tried nostrum): or again to maintain that similarity is only 'intelligible' as partial *identity*: and so on. And even those who are not persuaded entirely, may yet go so far as to allow that the 'similarity' and 'identity' languages are *alternatives*, the choice between which is indifferent. But surely, if it were made evident that we often 'call different things by the same name', and for perfectly 'good reasons',[2] when the things are not even in any ordinary sense 'similar', it will become excessively difficult to maintain that there is something 'identical' present in each — and after all, it is in *refuting* that position that the nominalist is really interested. Not, of course, that we can really *refute* it, or hope to cure those incurables who have long since reached the tertiary stage of universals.

Leaving historical disputes aside, it is a matter of urgency that a doctrine should be developed about the various kinds of good reasons for which we 'call' different things[3] 'by the same name'. This is an absorbing question, but habitually neglected, so far as I know, by philologists as

---

[2] We are not interested in mere equivocation, of course.
[3] Strictly, *sorts* of things rather than *particular* things.

well as by philosophers. Lying in the no man's land between them, it falls between two schools, to develop such a doctrine fully would be very complicated and perhaps tedious: but also very useful in many ways. It demands the study of *actual* languages, *not* ideal ones. That the Polish semanticists have discussed such questions I neither know nor believe. Aristotle did to a quite considerable extent, but scrappily and inexactly.

I shall proceed forthwith simply to give some of the more obvious cases where the reasons for 'calling different sorts of things by the same name' are not to be dismissed lightly as 'similarity'. And show how consideration of these facts may warn us against errors which are constant in philosophy.

1. A very simple case indeed is one often mentioned by Aristotle: the adjective 'healthy': when I talk of a healthy body and again of a healthy complexion, of healthy exercise: the word is *not* just being used *equivocally*. Aristotle would say it is being used 'paronymously'.[4] In this case there is what we may call a *primary nuclear* sense of 'healthy': the sense in which 'healthy' is used of a healthy body: I call this *nuclear* because it is 'contained as a part' in the other two senses which may be set out as 'productive of healthy bodies' and 'resulting from a healthy body'.

This is a simple case, easily understood. Yet constantly it is forgotten when we start disputing as to whether a certain word *has* 'two senses' or has *not* two senses. I remember myself disputing as to whether 'exist' has two senses (as used of material objects and again of sensa), or only one: actually we were agreed that 'exist' is used paronymously, only he called that 'having two senses', and I did not. Prichard's paper[5] on ἀγαθόν (in Aristotle) contains a classic instance of misunderstanding about paronymity, and so worrying about whether a word really 'has always the same meaning' or 'has several different meanings'.

Now are we to be content to say that the exercise, the complexion, and the body are all called 'healthy' 'because they are similar'? Such a remark cannot fail to be misleading. Why make it? And why not direct attention to the important and actual facts?

2. The next case I shall take is what Aristotle calls 'analogous' terms. When $A:B::X:Y$ and A and X are often called by the same name, e.g. the foot of a mountain and the foot of a list. Here there is a good reason for calling the things both 'feet' but are we to say they are 'similar'? Not in any ordinary sense. We may say that the relations in which they stand to B and Y respectively are similar relations. Well and good: but

---

4   But there are other varieties of paronymity of course.
5   "The Meaning of ΑΓΑΘΟΝ in the *Ethics* of Aristotle", by H. A. Prichard. Reprinted in his *Moral Obligation* (Oxford, 1949).

A and *X* are not the relations in which they stand: and anyone simply told that, in calling *A* and *X* both 'feet' I was calling attention to a 'similarity' in them, would probably be misled. Anyhow, it is most necessary to remember that 'similarity' covers such possibilities if it is to do so. (An especially severe case of 'analogy' arises when a term is used, as Aristotle says 'in different categories': e.g. when I talk about 'change' as qualitative change, change of position, place, etc., how far is it true to say these 'changes' are 'similar'?)

3. Another case is where I call B by the same name as A, because it resembles *A*, C by the same name because it resembles *B*, *D* ... and so on. But ultimately *A* and, say, *D* do not resemble each other in any recognizable sense at all. This is a very common case: and the dangers are obvious, when we search for something 'identical' in all of them!

4. Another case which is commonly found is this. Take a word like 'fascist': this originally connotes, say, a great many characteristics at once: say *x*, *y*, and *z*. Now we will use 'fascist' subsequently of things which possess only *one* of these striking characteristics. So that things called 'fascist' in these senses, which we may call 'incomplete' senses, need not be similar at all to each other. This often puzzles us most of all when the original 'complete' sense has been forgotten: compare the various meanings of 'cynicism': we should be puzzled to find the 'similarity' there! Sometimes the 'incompleteness' of the resemblance is coupled with a positive lack of resemblance, so that we invent a phrase to mark it as a warning, e.g. 'cupboard love'.

5. Another better-known case is that of a so-called determinable and its determinates: colour and red, green, blue, etc., or rather 'absolutely specific' reds, greens, blues, etc. Because this is better known, I shall not discuss it, though I am as a matter of fact rather sceptical about the accounts usually given. Instead, it should be pointed out how common this sort of relationship is and that it should be suspected in cases where we are prone to overlook it. A striking example is the case of 'pleasure': pleasures we may say not merely resemble each other in being pleasant, but also *differ* precisely in the way in which they are pleasant.[6] No greater mistake could be made than the hedonistic mistake (copied by non-hedonists) of thinking that pleasure is always a single similar feeling, somehow isolable from the various activities which 'give rise' to it.

6. Another case which often provides puzzles, is that of words like 'youth' and 'love': which sometimes mean the object loved, or the thing which is youthful, sometimes the passion 'Love' or the quality (?) 'youth'. These cases are of course easy (rather *like* 'healthy'?). But suppose we take the noun 'truth': here is a case where the disagreements between

---

[6] If we say that they are all called 'pleasures' 'because they are similar', we shall overlook this fact.

different theorists have largely turned on whether they interpreted this as a name of a substance, of a quality, or of a relation.

7. Lastly, I want to take a specially interesting sort of case, which is perhaps commoner and at the bottom of more muddles than we are aware of. Take the sense in which I talk of a cricket bat and a cricket ball and a cricket umpire. The reason that all are called by the same name is perhaps that each has its part — its *own special* part — to play in the activity called cricketing: it is no good to say that cricket *simply* means 'used in cricket': for we cannot explain what we mean by 'cricket' *except* by explaining the special parts played in cricketing by the bat, ball, etc. Aristotle's suggestion was that the word 'good' might be used in such a way: in which case it is obvious how far astray we should go if we look for a 'definition' of the word 'good' in any ordinary simple sense: or look for the way in which 'good' things are 'similar' to each other, in any ordinary sense. If we tried to find out by such methods what 'cricket' meant, we should very likely conclude that it too was a simple unanalysable supersensible quality.

Another thing that becomes plain from such examples is that the apparently common-sense distinction between 'What is the meaning of the word *x*' and 'What particular things *are x* and to what degrees?' is not of universal application by any means. The questions cannot be distinguished in such cases. Or a similar case would be some word like 'golfing': it is not sensible to ask 'What is the meaning of golfing?' 'What things are golfing?' Though it *is* sensible to ask what component activities go to constitute golfing, what implements are used in golfing ('golf' clubs, etc.) and in what ways. Aristotle suggests 'happiness' is a word of this kind: in which case it is evident how far astray we shall go if we treat it as though it were a word like 'whiteness'.

These summarily treated examples are enough to show how essential it is to have a thorough knowledge of the different reasons for which we call different things by the same name, before we can embark confidently on an inquiry. If we rush up with a demand for a definition in the simple manner of Plato or many other philosophers, if we use the rigid dichotomy 'same meaning, different meaning', or 'What *x* means', as distinguished from 'the things which are *x*', we shall simply make hashes of things. Perhaps some people are now discussing such questions seriously. All that is to be found in traditional Logics is the mention that there are, besides univocal and equivocal words, 'also analogous words': which, without further explanation, is used to lump together all cases where a word has not always absolutely the same meaning, nor several absolutely different meanings. All that 'similarity' theorists manage is to say that all things called by some one name are similar to some one pattern, or all are more similar to each other than any of them is to anything else; which is *obviously* untrue. Anyone who wishes to see the complexity of the problem, has only got to look in a (good) dictionary under such a word as 'head': the different meanings of the word 'head' will be related to each other in all sorts of different ways at once.

To summarize the contentions of this paper then. Firstly, the phrase 'the meaning of a word' is a spurious phrase. Secondly and consequently, a re-examination is needed of phrases like the two which I discuss, 'being a part of the meaning of' and 'having the same meaning'. On these matters, dogmatists require prodding: although history indeed suggests that it may sometimes be better to let sleeping dogmatists lie.

Michael Dummett

TRUTH

Frege held that truth and falsity are the references of sentences. Sentences cannot stand for propositions (what Frege calls 'thoughts'), since the reference of a complex expression depends only on the reference of its parts; whereas if we substitute for a singular term occurring in a sentence another singular term with the same reference but a different sense, the sense of the whole sentence, i.e. the thought which it expresses, changes. The only thing which it appears MUST in these circumstances remain unchanged is the truth-value of the sentence. The expressions 'is true' and 'is false' look like predicates applying to propositions, and one might suppose that truth and falsity were properties of propositions; but it now appears that the relation between a proposition and its truth value is not like that between a table and its shape, but rather like that between the sense of a definite description and the actual object for which it stands.

To the objection that there are non-truth-functional occurrences of sentences as parts of complex sentences, e.g. clauses in indirect speech, Frege replies that in such contexts we must take ordinary singular terms as standing, not for their customary reference, but for their sense, and hence we may say that in such a context, and only then, a sentence stands for the proposition it usually expresses.

If someone asks, 'But what kind of entities are these truth-values supposed to be?' we may reply that there is no more difficulty in seeing what the truth-value of a sentence may be than there is in seeing what the direction of a line may be; we have been told when two sentences have

From *Proceedings of the Aristotelian Society* 59 (1958-59), 141-62. Reprinted by courtesy of the author and the Editor of the Aristotelian Society, with the author's new postscript.

the same truth-value — when they are materially equivalent — just as we know when two lines have the same direction— when they are parallel. Nor need we waste time on the objection raised by Max Black that on Frege's theory certain sentences become meaningful which we should not normally regard as such e.g. 'If oysters are inedible, then the False'. If sentences stand for truth-values, but there are also expressions standing for truth-values which are not sentences, then the objection to allowing expressions of the latter kind to stand wherever sentences can stand and vice versa is grammatical, not logical. We often use the word 'thing' to provide a noun where grammar demands one and we have only an adjective, e.g. in 'That was a disgraceful thing to do'; and we could introduce a verb, say 'trues', to fulfil the purely grammatical function of converting a noun standing for a truth-value into a sentence standing for the same truth-value. It may be said that Frege has proved that a sentence does not ordinarily stand for a proposition, and has given a plausible argument that IF sentences have references, they stand for truth-values, but that he has done nothing to show that sentences do have references at all. This is incorrect; Frege's demonstration that the notions of a concept (property) and a relation can be explained as special cases of the notion of a function provides a plausible argument for saying that sentences have a reference.

What IS questionable is Frege's use of the words 'truth' and 'falsity' as names of the references of sentences; for by using these words rather than invented words of his own he gives the impression that by taking sentences to have a reference, with material equivalence as the criterion of identity, he has given an account of the notions of truth and falsity which we are accustomed to employ. Let us compare truth and falsity with the winning and losing of a board game. For a particular game we may imagine first formulating the rules by specifying the initial position and the permissible moves; the game comes to an end when there is no permissible move. We may then distinguish between two (or three) kinds of final positions, which we call 'Win' (meaning that the player to make the first move wins), 'Lose' (similarly), and, possibly, 'Draw'. Unless we tacitly appeal to the usual meanings of the words 'win', 'lose' and 'draw', this description leaves out one vital point — that it is the object of a player to win. It is part of the concept of winning a game that a player plays to win, and this part of the concept is not conveyed by a classification of the end positions into winning ones and losing ones. We can imagine a variant of chess in which it is the object of each player to be checkmated, and this would be an entirely different game; but the formal description we imagined would coincide with the formal description of chess. The whole theory of chess could be formulated with reference only to the formal description; but which theorems of this theory interested us would depend upon whether we wished to play chess or the variant game. Likewise, it is part of the concept of truth that we aim at making true statements; and Frege's theory of truth and falsity as the reference of sentences leaves this feature of the concept of truth quite out of account. Frege indeed tried to bring it in afterwards, in his theory of assertion — but too late; for the sense of the sentence is not given in advance of our going in for the activity of asserting, since otherwise there could be people who expressed the same thoughts but went in instead for denying them.

A similar criticism applies to many accounts of truth and falsity or of the meanings of certain sentences in terms of truth and falsity. We cannot in general suppose that we give a proper account of a concept by describing those circumstances in which we do, and those in which we do not, make use of the relevant word, by describing the USAGE of that word; we must also give an account of the POINT of the concept, explain what we use the word FOR. Classifications do not exist in the void, but are connected always with some interest which we have, so that to assign something to one class or another will have consequences connected with this interest. A clear example is the problem of justifying a form of argument, deductive or inductive. Classification of arguments into (deductively or inductively) valid and invalid ones is not a game played merely for its own sake, although it COULD be taught without reference to any purpose or interest, say as a school exercise. Hence there is really a problem of showing that the criteria we employ for recognizing valid arguments do in fact serve the purpose we intend them to serve: the problem is not to be dismissed — as it has long been fashionable to do — by saying that we use the criteria we use.

We cannot assume that a classification effected by means of a predicate in use in a language will always have just ONE point. It may be that the classification of statements into true ones, false ones, and, perhaps, those that are neither true nor false, has one principal point, but that other subsidiary ends are served by it which make the use of the words 'true' and 'false' more complex than it would otherwise be. At one time it was usual to say that we do not call ethical statements 'true' or 'false', and from this many consequences for ethics were held to flow. But the question is not whether these words are in practice applied to ethical statements, but whether, if they were so applied, the point of doing so would be the same as the point of applying them to statements of other kinds, and, if not, in what ways it would be different. Again, to be told that we say of a statement containing a singular term which lacks reference that it is neither true nor false is so far only to be informed of a point of usage; no philosophical consequences can yet be drawn. Rather, we need to ask whether describing such a statement as neither true nor false accords better with the general point of classifying statements as true or false than to describe it as false. Suppose that we learn that in a particular language such statements are described as 'false': how are we to tell whether this shows that they use such statements differently from ourselves or merely that 'false' is not an exact translation of their word? To say that we use singular statements in such a way that they are neither true nor false when the subject has no reference is meant to characterize our use of singular statements; hence it ought to be possible to describe when in a language not containing words for 'true' and 'false' singular statements would be used in the same way as we use them, and when they would be used so as to be false when the subject had no reference. Until we have an account of the general point of the classification into statements that they are neither true nor false; and until we have an account of how the truth-conditions of a statement determine its meaning the description of the meaning by stating the truth conditions is valueless.

A popular account of the meaning of the word 'true', also deriving from Frege, is that ⌜It is true that P⌝ has the same sense as the sentence P. If we then ask why it is any use to have the word 'true' in the language, the answer is that we often refer to propositions indirectly, i.e. without expressing them, as when we say 'Goldbach's conjecture' or 'what the witness said'. We also generalize about propositions without referring to any particular one, e.g. in 'Everything he says is true'. This explanation cannot rank as a definition in the strict sense, since it permits elimination of 'is true' only when it occurs attached to a that-clause, and not when attached to any other expression standing for a proposition or to a variable; but, since every proposition can be expressed by a sentence, this does not refute its claim to be considered as determining uniquely the sense of 'is true'. It might be compared with the recursive definition of '+', which enables us to eliminate the sign '+' only when it occurs in front of a numeral, and not when it occurs in front of any other expression for a number or in front of a variable; yet there is a clear mathematical sense in which it specifies uniquely what operation '+' is to signify. Similarly, our explanation of 'is true' determines uniquely the sense, or at least the application, of this predicate: for any given proposition there is a sentence expressing that proposition, and that sentence states the conditions under which the proposition is true.

If, as Frege thought, there exist sentences which express propositions but are neither true nor false, then this explanation appears incorrect. Suppose that P contains a singular term which has a sense but no reference: then, according to Frege, P expresses a proposition which has no truth-value. This proposition is therefore not true, and hence the statement ⌜It is true that P⌝ will be FALSE. P will therefore not have the same sense as ⌜It is true that P⌝, since the latter is false while the former although it is vital for understanding the behavior of quantifying expressions in ordinary language.

The main non-trivial example of quantificational reasoning which has traditionally been considered by philosophers of mathematics is found in axiomatic geometry. It is probably not accidental that there is 'the logic of the central nervous system' helped by the 'logic' of our perceptual apparatus.

When free singular terms are admitted to our sentences, the important parameter will be the sum of the number of these terms and the quantificational depth of a sentence. This again indicates the maximal complexity of the configurations one has to consider in order to understand the sentence. However, all the interesting problems come up already in the case of closed sentences, and I shall therefore restrict my attention to them.

In first-order languages, the depth of sentences is therefore one of the most important obstacles to perceiving their logical relations, perhaps the most important one. This observation may be brought to bear on our problem concerning (1)–(2). The obvious way of doing so is to restrict (2) to those cases in which the implication from p to q can be proved without going beyond the depth of p.

This restriction is of course relative to the method of proof involved. If this method is the one that relies on distributive normal forms and on the elimination of trivially inconsistent constituents, the restriction amounts to requiring that $p \supset q$ be a surface tautology at the depth of p. This is a well-defined restriction, which I already have put forward earlier as a solution to the problems of 'deductive omniscience' (or lack thereof).[11] It seems to me to accomplish very well the purpose a restriction was to serve in the first place.

The main disadvantage it apparently has is its dependency on one particular method of deduction. Moreover, this method of deduction is so laborious as to be practically useless. It can nevertheless be shown — although no specific results have reached the print yet — that the restriction on (2) we just obtained is essentially the same as one would have obtained by considering what can be proved by the standard deductive techniques without increasing the depth of one's expressions (plus the total number of free singular terms involved in the deduction). Hence the restriction mentioned seems to have a great deal of intrinsic interest, as might indeed be expected on the basis of the role distributive normal forms play in the logical structure of first-order languages.

Other reasons can be given for this type of restriction on (1)–(2). One is the fact — as it seems to me to be — that we spontaneously apply

---

[11] See the papers listed in note 3 above, especially the last one, as well as "'Knowing Oneself' and Other Problems in Epistemic Logic", *Theoria* 32 (1966), 1-13.

is not. It is not possible to plead that ⌜It is true that P⌝ is itself neither true nor false when the singular term occurring in P lacks a reference, since the *oratio obliqua* clause ⌜that P⌝ stands for the proposition expressed by P, and it is admitted that P does have a sense and express a proposition; the singular term occurring in P has in ⌜It is true that P⌝ its indirect reference, namely its sense, and we assumed that it did have a sense. In general, it will always be inconsistent to maintain the truth of every instance of 'It is true that p if and only if p' while allowing that there is a type of sentence which under certain conditions is neither true nor false. It would be possible to evade this objection by claiming that the 'that'-clause in a sentence beginning 'It is true that' is not an instance of *oratio obliqua*; that the word 'that' here serves the purely grammatical function of transforming a sentence into a noun-clause without altering either its sense or its reference. We should then have to take phrases like 'Goldbach's conjecture' and 'what the witness said' as standing not for propositions but for truth-values. The expression 'is true' would then be exactly like the verb 'trues' which we imagined earlier; it would simply convert a noun-phrase standing for a truth-value into a sentence without altering its sense or its reference. It might be objected that this variant of Frege's account tallies badly with his saying that it is the THOUGHT (proposition) which is what is true or false; but we can express this point of Frege's by saying that it is the THOUGHT, rather than the SENTENCE, which primarily stands for a truth-value. A stronger objection to the variant account is that it leans heavily on the theory of truth-values as references of sentences, while the original version depends only on the more plausible view that clauses in indirect speech stand for propositions. In any case, if there are meaningful sentences which say nothing which is true or false, then there must be A use of the word 'true' which applies to propositions; for if we say ⌜It is neither true nor false that P⌝, the clause ⌜that P⌝ must here be in *oratio obliqua*, otherwise the whole sentence would lack a truth-value.

Even if we do not wish to say of certain statements that they are neither true nor false, this account cannot give the WHOLE meaning of the word 'true'. If we are to give an explanation of the word 'false' parallel to our explanation of 'true' we shall have to say that ⌜It is false that P⌝ has the same sense as the negation of P. In logical symbolism there exists a sign which, put in front of a sentence, forms the negation of that sentence; but in natural languages we do not have such a sign. We have to think to realize that the negation of 'No-one is here' is not 'No-one is not here' but 'Someone is here'; there is no one rule for forming the negation of a given sentence. Now according to what principle do we recognize one sentence as the negation of another? It is natural to answer: The negation of a sentence P is that sentence which is true if and only if P is false and false if and only if P is true. But this explanation is ruled out if we want to use the notion of the negation of a sentence in order to explain the sense of the word 'false'. It would not solve the difficulty if we did have a general sign of negation analogous to the logical symbol, for the question would then be: How in general do we determine the sense of the negation, given the sense of the original sentence?

We encounter the same difficulty over the connective 'or'. We can give an account of the meaning of 'and' by saying that we are in a position to assert $\ulcorner P$ and $Q \urcorner$ when and only when we are in a position to assert P and in a position to assert Q. (This is not circular: one could train a dog to bark only when a bell rang AND a light shone without presupposing that it possessed the concept of conjunction.) But, if we accept a two-valued logic, we cannot give a similar explanation of the meaning of 'or'. We often assert $\ulcorner P$ or $Q \urcorner$ when we are not either in a position to assert P or in a position to assert Q. I use the word 'we' here, meaning mankind, advisedly. If the history master gives the schoolboy a hint, saying, 'It was either James I or Charles I who was beheaded', then the schoolboy is in a position to assert, 'Either James I or Charles I was beheaded' without (perhaps) being in a position to assert either limb of the disjunction; but it is not this sort of case which causes the difficulty. The ULTIMATE source of the schoolboy's knowledge derives from something which justifies the assertion that Charles I was beheaded; and this is all that would be required for the proposed explanation of the word 'or' to be adequate. Likewise, the explanation is not impugned by cases like that in which I remember that I was talking either to Jean or to Alice, but cannot remember which. My knowledge that I was talking either to Jean or to Alice derives ultimately from the knowledge that I had at the time that I was talking to (say) Jean; the fact that the incomplete knowledge is all that survives is beside the point. Rather, the difficulty arises because we often make statements of the form $\ulcorner P$ or $Q \urcorner$ when the ultimate evidence for making them, in the sense indicated, is neither evidence for the truth of P nor evidence for the truth of Q. The most striking instance of this is the fact that we are prepared to assert ANY statement of the form $\ulcorner P$ or not $P \urcorner$, even though we may have no evidence either for the truth of P or for the truth of $\ulcorner$not $P \urcorner$.

In order to justify asserting $\ulcorner P$ or not $P \urcorner$, we appeal to the truthtable explanation of the meaning of 'or'. But if the whole explanation of the meanings of 'true' and 'false' is given by 'It is true that p if and only if p' and 'It is false that p if and only if not p', this appeal fails. The truthtable tells us, e.g. that from P we may infer $\ulcorner P$ or $Q \urcorner$ (in particular, $\ulcorner P$ or not $P \urcorner$); but THAT much we already knew from the explanation of 'or' which we have rejected as insufficient. The truth-table does not show us that we are entitled to assert $\ulcorner P$ or not $P\urcorner$ in every possible case, since this is to assume that every statement is either true or false; but, if our explanation of 'true' and 'false' is all the explanation that can be given, to say that every statement is either true or false is just to say that we are always justified in saying $\ulcorner P$ or not $P\urcorner$.

We naturally think of truth-tables as giving the explanation of the sense which we attach to the sign of negation and to the connectives, an explanation which will show that we are justified in regarding certain forms of statement as logically true. It now appears that if we accept the redundancy theory of 'true' and 'false' — the theory that our explanation gives the whole meaning of these words — the truth-table explanation is quite unsatisfactory. More generally, we must abandon the idea which we naturally have that the notions of truth and falsity play an essential role in any account either of the meaning of statements in general or of the meaning of a particular statement. The conception pervades the thought of Frege that the general form of explanation of the sense of a statement consists in laying down the conditions under which it is true and those under which it is false (or better: saying that it is false under all other conditions); this same conception is expressed in the *Tractatus* in the words, 'In order to be able to say that "p" is true (or false), I must have determined under what conditions I call "p" true, and this is how I determine the sense of the sentence' (4.063). But in order that someone should gain from the explanation that P is true in such-and-such circumstances an understanding of the sense of P, he must already know what it means to say of P that it is true. If when he inquires into this he is told that the only explanation is that to say that P is true is the same as to assert P, it will follow that in order to understand what is meant by saying that P is true, he must already know the sense of asserting P, which was precisely what was supposed to be being explained to him.

We thus have either to supplement the redundancy theory or to give up many of our preconceptions about truth and falsity. It has become a commonplace to say that there cannot be a criterion of truth. The argument is that we determine the sense of a sentence by laying down the conditions under which it is true, so that we could not first know the sense of a sentence and then apply some criterion to decide in what circumstances it was true. In the same sense there could not be a criterion for what constitutes the winning of a game, since learning what constitutes winning it is an essential part of learning what the game is. This does not mean that there may not be in any sense a theory of truth. For a particular bounded language, if it is free of ambiguity and inconsistency, it must be possible to characterize the true sentences of the language; somewhat as, for a given game, we can say which moves are winning moves. (A language is bounded if we may not introduce into it new words or new senses for old words.) Such a characterization would be recursive, defining truth first for the simplest possible sentences, and then for sentences built out of others by the logical operations employed in the language; this is what is done in formalized languages by a truth-definition. The redundancy theory gives the general form of such a truth-definition, though in particular cases more informative definitions might be given.

Now we have seen that to say for each particular game what winning it consists in is not to give a satisfactory account of the concept of winning a game. What makes us use the same term 'winning' for each of these various activities is that the point of every game is that each player tries to do what for that game constitutes winning; i.e. what constitutes winning always plays the same part in determining what playing the game consists in. Similarly, what the truth of a statement consists in always plays the same role in determining the sense of that statement, and a theory of truth must be possible in the sense of an account of what that role is. I shall not now attempt such an account; I claim, however, that such an account would justify the following. A statement, so long as it is not ambiguous or vague, divides all possible states of affairs into just TWO classes. For a given state of affairs, either the statement is used in such a way that a man who asserted it but envisaged that state of affairs as a possibility would be held to have spoken misleadingly, or the assertion of the statement would not be taken as expressing the speaker's exclusion of that possibility. If a state of affairs of the first kind obtains, the statement is false; if all actual states of affairs are of the second kind, it is true. It is thus prima facie senseless to say of any statement that in such-and-such a state of affairs it would be neither true nor false.

The sense of a statement is determined by knowing in what circumstances it is true and in what false. Likewise the sense of a command is determined by knowing what constitutes obedience to it and what disobedience; and the sense of a bet by knowing when the bet is won and when it is lost. Now there may be a gap between the winning of a bet and the losing of it, as with a conditional bet; can there be a similar gap between obedience and disobedience to a command, or between the truth and falsity of a statement? There is a distinction between a conditional bet and a bet on the truth of a material conditional; if the antecedent is unfulfilled, in the first case the bet is off — it is just as if no bet had been made — but in the second case the bet is won. A conditional command where the antecedent is in the power of the person given the order (e.g. a mother says to a child, 'If you go out, wear your coat') is always like a bet on the material conditional; it is equivalent to the command to ensure the truth of the material conditional, viz. 'Do not go out without your coat'. We cannot say that if the child does not go out, it is just as if no command had been given, since it may be that, unable to find his coat, he stayed in in order to comply with the command.

Can a distinction parallel to that for bets be drawn for conditional commands where the antecedent is not in the person's power? I contend that the distinction which looks as if it could be drawn is in fact void of significance. There are two distinct kinds of consequence of making a bet, winning it and losing; to determine what is to involve one of these is not yet to determine completely what is to involve the other. But there is only kind of consequence of giving a command, namely that, provided one had the right to give it in the first place, one acquires a right to punish or at least reprobate disobedience. It might be thought that punishment and reward were distinct consequences of a command in the same sense that paying money and receiving it are distinct consequences of a bet; but this does not tally with the role of commands in our society. The right to a reward is not taken to be an automatic consequence of obedience to a command, as the RIGHT to reproach is an automatic consequence of disobedience; if a reward is given, this is an act of grace, just as it is an act of grace if the punishment or reproach is withheld. Moreover, any action deliberately taken in order to comply with the command (to avoid disobedience to it) has the same claim to be rewarded as any other; hence to determine what constitutes disobedience to the command is thereby to determine what sort of behaviour might be rewarded, without the need for any further decision. If the child stays in because he cannot find his coat, this behaviour is as meritorious as if he goes out remembering to wear it; and if he forgets all about the order, but wears his coat for some other reason, this behaviour no more deserves commendation than if he chooses, for selfish reasons, to remain indoors. Where the antecedent is not in the person's power, it is indeed possible to regard the conditional command as analogous to the conditional bet; but since obedience to a command has no consequence of its own other than that of avoiding the punishment due for disobedience, there is not for such commands any significant distinction parallel to that between conditional bets and bets about a material conditional. If we regarded obedience to a command as giving a right to a reward, we could then introduce such a distinction for commands whose antecedent was in the person's power. Thus the mother might use the form, 'If you go out, wear your coat', as involving that if the child went out with his coat he would be rewarded, if he went out without it he would be punished, and if he stayed indoors — even in order to comply with the command — he would be neither punished nor rewarded; while the form, 'Do not go out without your coat', would involve his being rewarded if he stayed indoors.

Statements are like commands (as we use them) and not like bets; the making of a statement has, as it were, only one kind of consequence. To see this, let us imagine a language which contains conditional statements but has no counterfactual form (counterfactuals would introduce irrelevant complications). Two alternative accounts are suggested of the way in which conditionals are used in this language: one, that they are used to make statements conditionally; the other, that they represent the material conditional. On the first interpretation, a conditional statement is like a conditional bet: if the antecedent is fulfilled, then the statement is treated as if it had been an unconditional assertion of the consequent, and is said to be true or false accordingly; if the antecedent is not fulfilled, then it is just as if no statement, true or false, had been made at all. On the second interpretation, if the antecedent is not fulfilled, then the statement is said to be true. How are we to settle which of these two accounts is the correct one? If statements are really like bets and not like commands; if there are two distinct kinds of consequence which may follow the making of a statement, those that go with calling the statement 'true' and those that go with calling it 'false', so that there may be a gap between these two kinds of consequence; then we ought to be able to find something which decides between the two accounts as definite as the financial transaction which distinguishes a bet on the truth of the material conditional from a conditional bet. It is no use asking whether these people SAY that the man who has made a conditional statement whose antecedent turns out false said something true or that he said nothing true or false: they may have no words corresponding to 'true' and 'false'; and if they do, how could we be sure that the correspondence was exact? If their using the words 'true' and 'false' is to have the slightest significance, there must be some difference in their behaviour which goes with their saying 'true' or 'neither true nor false' in this case.

It is evident on reflection that there is nothing in what they do which could distinguish between the two alternative accounts; the distinction between them is as empty as the analogous distinction for conditional commands whose antecedent is not in the person's power. In order to fix the sense of an utterance, we do not need to make two separate decisions — when to say that a true statement has been made and when to say that a false statement has been made; rather, any situation in which nothing obtains which is taken as a case of its being false may be regarded as a case of its being true, just as someone who behaves so as not to disobey a command may be regarded as having obeyed it. The point becomes clearer when we look at it in the following way. If it makes sense in general to suppose that a certain form of statement is so used that in certain circumstances it is true, in others false, and in yet others nothing has been said true or false, then we can imagine that a form of conditional was used in this way (von Wright actually holds that WE use conditionals in this way). If P turns out true, then ⌜If P, then Q⌝

is said to be true or false according as Q is true or false, while if P turns out false we say that nothing was said true or false. Let us contrast this with what Frege and Strawson say about the use in our language of statements containing a singular term. If there is an object for which the singular term stands, then the statement is true or false according as the predicate does or does not apply to that object, but if there is no such object, then we have not said anything true or false. Now do these accounts tell us the sense of sentences of these two kinds? — that is, do they tell us how these statements are used, what is DONE by making statements of these forms? Not at all, for an essential feature of their use has not yet been laid down. Someone uttering a conditional statement of the kind described may very well have no opinion as to whether the antecedent was going to turn out true or false; that is, he is not taken as having misused the statement or misled his hearers if he envisages it as a possibility that that case will arise in which he is said not to have made a statement true or false. All that he conveys by uttering the conditional statement is that he excludes the possibility that the case will arise in which he is said to have said something false, namely that antecedent is true and consequent false. With the case of a singular statement it is quite different. Here someone is definitely either misusing the form of statement or misleading his hearers if he envisages it as a possibility that that case will arise in which what he said will be said to be neither true nor false, namely that the singular term has no reference. He conveys more by making the statement than just that he excludes the possibility of its being false; he commits himself to its being true.

Are we then to say that laying down the truth-conditions for a sentence is not sufficient to determine its sense, that something further will have to be stipulated as well? Rather than say this we should abandon the notions of truth and falsity altogether. In order to characterize the sense of expressions of our two forms, only a twofold classification of possible relevant circumstances is necessary. We need to distinguish those states of affairs such that if the speaker envisaged them as possibilities he would be held to be either misusing the statement or misleading his hearers, and those of which this is not the case: and ONE way of using the words 'true' and 'false' would be to call states of affairs of the former kind those in which the statement was false and the others those in which the statement was true. For our conditional statements, the distinction would be between those states of affairs in which the statement was said to be false and those in which we said that it would either be true or else neither true nor false. For singular statements, the distinction would be between those states of affairs in which we said that the statement would either be false or else neither true nor false, and those in which it was true. To grasp the sense or use of these forms of statement, the twofold classification is quite sufficient; the threefold classification with which we started is entirely beside the point. Thus, on ONE way of using the words 'true' and 'false', we should, instead of distinguishing between the conditional statement's being true and its being neither true nor false, have distinguished between two different ways in which it could be true; and instead of distinguishing between the singular statement's being false and its being neither true nor false, we should have distinguished between two different ways in which it could be false.

This gives us a hint at a way of explaining the role played by truth and falsity in determining the sense of a statement. We have not yet seen what point there may be in distinguishing between different ways in which a statement may be true or between different ways in which it may be false, or, as we might say, between degrees of truth and falsity. The point of such distinctions does not lie in anything to do with the sense of the statement itself, but has to do with the way in which it enters into complex statements. Let us imagine that in the language of which the conditional statements we considered form a part there exists a sign of negation, i.e. a word which, placed in front of a statement, forms another statement; I call it a sign of negation because in most cases it forms a statement which we should regard as being used as the contradictory of the original statement. Let us suppose, however, that when placed in front of a conditional statement ⌜If P, then Q⌝, it forms a statement which is used in the same way as the statement ⌜If P, then not Q⌝. Then if we describe the use of the conditionals by reference to a twofold classification only, i.e. in the same way as we describe a material conditional, we shall be unable to give a truth-functional account of the behaviour of their sign 'not'. That is, we should have the tables:

P	Q	⌜If P, then Q⌝	⌜Not: if P, then Q⌝
T	T	T	F
T	F	F	T
F	T	T	T
F	F	T	T

in which the truth-value of ⌜Not: if P, then Q⌝ is not determined by the truth-value of ⌜If P, then Q⌝. If, on the other hand, we revert to our original threefold classification, marking the case in which we said that no statement true or false had been made by 'X', then we have the tables:

P	Q	⌜If P, then Q⌝	⌜Not: if P, then Q⌝
T	T	T	F
T	F	F	T
F	T	X	X
F	F	X	X

which can be quite satisfactorily accounted for by giving the table for 'not':

R	$\ulcorner\text{Not } R\urcorner$
T	F
X	X
F	T

(I have assumed that the statements P and Q take only the values T and F.) It now becomes quite natural to think of 'T' as representing 'true', 'F' 'false' and 'X' 'neither true nor false'. Then we can say that their symbol 'not' really is a sign of negation, since $\ulcorner\text{Not } P\urcorner$ is true when and only when P is false and false when and only when P is true. We must not forget, however, that the justification for distinguishing between the cases in which a conditional was said to have the value T and the cases in which it was said to have the value X was simply the possibility, created by this distinction, of treating 'not' truth-functionally. In the same way if we have in a language an expression which normally functions as a sign of negation, but the effect of prefacing a singular statement with this expression is to produce a statement whose utterance still commits the speaker to there being an object for which the singular term stands, it is very natural to distinguish between two kinds of falsity a singular statement may have: that when the singular term has a reference, but the predicate does not apply to it, and that when the singular term lacks a reference. Let us represent the case in which the singular term has no reference by the symbol 'Y', and let us suppose S to be a singular statement. Then we have the table:

S	$\ulcorner\text{Not } S\urcorner$
T	F
Y	Y
F	T

Here again it is natural to think of 'T' as representing 'true'. 'F' 'false' and 'Y' 'neither true nor false'.

There is no necessity to use the words 'true' and 'false' as suggested above, so that we have to interpret X as a kind of truth and Y as a kind of falsity. Logicians who study many-valued logics have a term which can be employed here: they would say that T and X are 'designated' truth-values and F and Y 'undesignated' ones. (In a many-valued logic those formulas are considered valid which have a designated value for every assignment of values to their sentence-letters.) The points to observe are just these: (i) The sense of a sentence is determined wholly by knowing the case in which it has a designated value and the cases in which it has an undesignated one. (ii) Finer distinctions between different designated values or different undesignated ones, however naturally they come to us, are justified only if they are needed in order to give a truth-functional account of the formation of complex statements by means of operators. (iii) In MOST philosophical discussions of truth and falsity, what we really have in mind is the distinction between a designated and an undesignated value, and hence choosing the names 'truth' and 'falsity' for particular designated and undesignated values respectively will only obscure the issue. (iv) Saying that in certain circumstances a statement is neither true nor false does not determine whether the statement is in that case to count as having an undesignated or a designated value, i.e. whether someone who asserts the statement is or is not taken as excluding the possibility that that case obtains.

Baffled by the attempt to describe in general the relation between language and reality, we have nowadays abandoned the correspondence theory of truth, and justify our doing so on the score that it was an attempt to state a CRITERION of truth in the sense in which this cannot be done. Nevertheless, the correspondence theory expresses one important feature of the concept of truth which is not expressed by the law 'It is true that p if and only if p' and which we have so far left quite out of account: that a statement is true only if there is something in the world IN VIRTUE OF WHICH it is true. Although we no longer accept the correspondence theory, we remain realists *au fond*; we retain in our thinking a fundamentally realist conception of truth. Realism consists in the belief that for any statement there must be something in virtue of which either it or its negation is true; it is only on the basis of this belief that we can justify the idea that truth and falsity play an essential role in the notion of the meaning of a statement, that the general form of an explanation of meaning is a statement of the truth-conditions.

To see the importance of this feature of the concept of truth, let us envisage a dispute over the logical validity of the statement 'Either Jones was brave or he was not'. *A* imagines Jones to be a man, now dead, who never encountered danger in his life. *B* retorts that it could still be true that Jones was brave, namely, if it is true that if Jones HAD encountered danger, he would have acted bravely. *A* agrees with this, but still maintains that it does not need to be the case that either 'Jones was brave' = 'If Jones had encountered danger, he would have acted bravely' nor 'Jones was not brave' = 'If Jones had encountered danger, he would not have acted bravely' is true. For, he argues, it might be the case that however many facts we knew of the kind which we should normally regard as grounds for asserting such counterfactual conditionals, we should still know nothing which would be a ground for asserting either. It is clear that *B* cannot agree that this is a possibility and yet continue to insist that all the same either 'Jones was brave' or

'Jones was not brave' is true; for he would then be committed to holding that a statement may be true even though there is nothing whatever such that, if we knew of it, we should count it as evidence or as a ground for the truth of the statement, and this is absurd. (It may be objected that there are assertions for which it would be out of place to ask one who made them for his evidence or grounds; but for SUCH assertions the speaker must always either be in a position to make or in a position to deny them.) If *B* still wishes to maintain the necessity of 'Either Jones was brave or he was not', he will have to hold either that there must be some fact of the sort to which we usually appeal in discussing counterfactuals which, if we knew it, would decide us in favour either of the one counterfactual or of the other; or else that there is some fact of extraordinary kind, perhaps known only to God. In the latter case he imagines a kind of spiritual mechanism — Jones' character — which determines how he acts in each situation that arises; his acting in such-and-such a way reveals to us the state of this spiritual mechanism, which was however already in place before its observable effects were displayed in his behaviour. *B* would then argue thus: If Jones HAD encountered danger, he would either have acted bravely or have acted like a coward. Suppose he had acted bravely. This would then have shown us that he was brave; but he would ALREADY have been brave before his courage was revealed by his behaviour. That is, either his character included the quality of courage or it did not, and his character determines his behaviour. We know his character only indirectly, through its effects on his behaviour; but each character-trait must be THERE within him independently of whether it reveals itself to us or not.

Anyone of a sufficient degree of sophistication will reject *B*'s belief in a spiritual mechanism; either he will be a materialist and substitute for it an equally blind belief in a physiological mechanism, or he will accept *A*'s conclusion that 'Either Jones was brave or he was not' is not logically necessary. His ground for rejecting *B*'s argument is that if such a statement as 'Jones was brave' is true, it must be true in virtue of the sort of fact we have been taught to regard as justifying us in asserting it. It cannot be true in virtue of a fact of some quite different sort of which we can have no direct knowledge, for otherwise the statement 'Jones was brave' would not have the meaning that WE have given it. In accepting *A*'s position he makes a small retreat from realism; he abandons a realist view of character.

In order, then, to decide whether a realist account of truth can be given for statements of some particular kind, we have to ask whether for such a statement *P* it must be the case that if we knew sufficiently many facts of the kind we normally treat as justifying us in asserting *P*, we should be in a position either to assert *P* or to assert ⌐Not *P*⌐: if so, then it can truly be said that there must either be something in virtue of which P is true or something in virtue of which it is false. It is easy to overlook the force of the phrase 'sufficiently many'. Consider the statement 'A city will never be built on this spot'. Even if we have an oracle which can answer every question of the kind, 'Will there be a city here in 1990?' 'In 2100?' etc., we might never be in a position either to declare the statement true or to declare it false. Someone may say: That is only because you are assuming the knowledge of only finitely many answers of the oracle; but if you knew the oracle's answers to ALL these questions, you would be able to decide the truth-value of the statement. But what would it mean to know infinitely many facts? It could mean that the oracle gave a direct answer 'No' to the question, 'Will a city ever be built here?': but to assume this is just like B's assumption of the existence of a hidden spiritual mechanism. It might mean that we had an argument to show the falsity of $\ulcorner$A city will be built here in the year $N\urcorner$ irrespective of the value of N, e.g. if 'here' is the North Pole: but no one would suggest that it must be the case that either the oracle will give an affirmative answer to some question of the form 'Will there be a city here in the year ...?' or we can find a general argument for a negative answer. Finally, it could mean that we were ABLE to answer every question of the form, 'Will there be a city here in the year...?': but having infinite knowledge in THIS sense will place us in no better position than when we had the oracle.

We thus arrive at the following position. We are entitled to say that a statement P must be either true or false, that there must be something in virtue of which either it is true or it is false, only when P is a statement of such a kind that we could in a finite time bring ourselves into a position in which we were justified either in asserting or in denying P; that is, when P is an effectively decidable statement. This limitation is not trivial: there is an immense range of statements which, like 'Jones was brave', are concealed conditionals, or which, like 'A city will never be built here', contain — explicitly or implicitly — an unlimited generality and which therefore fail the test.

What I have done here is to transfer to ordinary statements what the intuitionists say about mathematical statements. The sense of e.g. the existential quantifier is determined by considering what sort of fact makes an existential statement true, and this means: the sort of fact which we have been taught to regard as justifying us in asserting an existential statement. What would make the statement that there exists an odd perfect number true would be some particular number's being both odd and perfect; hence the assertion of the existential statement must be taken as a claim to be able to assert some one of the singular statements. We are thus justified in asserting that there is a number with a certain property only if we have a method for finding a particular number with that property. Likewise, the sense of a universal statement is given by the sort of consideration we regard as justifying us in asserting it: namely we can assert that every number has a certain property if we have a general method for showing, for any arbitrary number, that it has that property. Now what if someone insists that either the statement 'There is an odd perfect number' is true, or else every perfect number is even? He is justified if he knows of a procedure which will lead him in a finite time either to the determination of a particular odd perfect number or to a general proof that a number assumed to be perfect is even. But if he knows of no such procedure, then he is trying to attach to the statement 'Every perfect number is even' a meaning which lies BEYOND that provided by the training we are given in the use of universal statements; he wants to say, as *B* said of 'Jones was brave', that its truth may lie in a region directly accessible only to God, which human beings can never survey.

We learn the sense of the logical operators by being trained to USE statements containing them, i.e., to assert such statements under certain conditions. Thus we learn to assert $\ulcorner P$ and $Q \urcorner$ when we can assert P and can assert Q; to assert $\ulcorner P$ or $Q \urcorner$ when we can assert P or can assert Q; to assert $\ulcorner$For some n, $F(n) \urcorner$ when we can assert $\ulcorner F(0) \urcorner$ or can assert $\ulcorner F(1) \urcorner$ or .... We learn to assert $\ulcorner$For every n, $F(n) \urcorner$ when we can assert $\ulcorner F(0) \urcorner$ and $\ulcorner F(1) \urcorner$ and ...; and to say that we can assert all of these means that we have a general method for establishing $\ulcorner F(x) \urcorner$ irrespective of the value of x. Here we have abandoned altogether the attempt to explain the meaning of a statement by laying down its truth-conditions. WE NO LONGER EXPLAIN THE SENSE OF A STATEMENT BY STIPULATING ITS TRUTH-VALUE IN TERMS OF THE TRUTH-VALUES OF ITS CONSTITUENTS, BUT BY STIPULATING WHEN IT MAY BE ASSERTED IN TERMS OF THE CONDITIONS UNDER WHICH ITS CONSTITUENTS MAY BE ASSERTED. The justification for this change is that this is how we in fact learn to use these statements: furthermore, the notions of truth and falsity cannot be satisfactorily explained so as to form a basis for an account of meaning once we leave the realm of effectively decidable statements. One result of this shift in our account of meaning is that, unless we are dealing only with effectively decidable statements, certain formulas which appeared in the two-valued logic to be logical laws no longer rank as such, in particular the law of excluded middle: this is rejected, not on the ground that there is a middle truth-value, but because meaning, and hence validity, is no longer to be explained in terms of truth-values.

Intuitionists speak of mathematics in a highly anti-realist (anti-platonist) way: for them it is WE who construct mathematics; it is not already THERE waiting for us to discover. An extreme form of such constructivism is found in Wittgenstein's REMARKS ON THE FOUNDATIONS

OF MATHEMATICS. This makes it appear as though the intuitionist rejection of an account of the meaning of mathematical statements in terms of truth and falsity could not be generalized for other regions of discourse, since even if there is no independent mathematical reality answering to our mathematical statements, there is an independent reality answering to statements of other kinds. On the other hand the exposition of intuitionism I have just given was not based on a rejection of the Fregean notion of a mathematical reality waiting to be discovered, but only on considerations about meaning. Now certainly someone who accepts the intuitionist standpoint in mathematics will not be inclined to adopt the platonist picture. Must he then go to the other extreme, and have the picture of our creating mathematics as we go along? To adopt this picture involves thinking with Wittgenstein that we are FREE in mathematics at every point; no step we take has been forced on us by a necessity external to us, but has been freely chosen. This picture is not the only alternative. If we think that mathematical results are in some sense imposed on us from without, we could have instead the picture of a mathematical reality not already in existence but as it were coming into being as we probe. Our investigations bring into existence what was not there before, but what they bring into existence is not of our own making.

Whether this picture is right or wrong for mathematics, it is available for other regions of reality as an alternative to the realist conception of the world. This shows how it is possible to hold that the intuitionist substitution of an account of the USE of a statement for an account of its truth-conditions as the general form of explanation of meaning should be applied to all realms of discourse without thinking that we create the world; we can abandon realism without falling into subjective idealism. This substitution does not, of course, involve dropping the words 'true' and 'false', since for most ordinary contexts the account of these words embodied in the laws 'It is true that p if and only if p' and 'It is false that p if and only if not p' is quite sufficient: but it means facing the consequences of admitting that this is the WHOLE explanation of the sense of these words, and this involves dethroning truth and falsity from their central place in philosophy and in particular in the theory of meaning. Of course the doctrine that meaning is to be explained in terms of use is the cardinal doctrine of the later Wittgenstein; but I do not think the point of this doctrine has so far been generally understood.

Postscript (1972) to Truth

The article still seems to me substantially correct, but I should like to add the following emendations and glosses:

(1) The remark about Frege at the end of the third paragraph is quite misleading. The really questionable part of Frege's doctrine is not that sentences have references, nor that these references are truth-values, but that truth-values are objects. If truth-values are not objects, then the relation between a sentence and its truth-value is only analogous to, not identical with, the relation between a name and its bearer, just as is the relation between a predicate and the concept for which it stands. It is true that the notion of the incompleteness of a function is more readily intelligible than, and can be used to illuminate, that of the incompleteness of a concept or relation; but that does not require that concepts and relations be taken as actually special cases of functions, rather than merely analogues of them.

(2) The comparison between the notion of truth and that of winning a game still seems to me a good one. The text as it stands might, however, give rise to a certain misunderstanding, though this would be a misinterpretation of what I intended as the time of writing. Suppose that we have, for each of a large range of games, a characterisation of the conditions under which one player or side is said to have won the game. Now we ask whether it is sufficient, in order to convey to someone previously quite unacquainted with it what the notion of winning is, to add to this characterisation the mere observation that the participants in a game play with the intention of winning. The correct answer is, I think, that there is a wider and a narrower sense to the expression "to play a game", and that, in the context of the wider sense, this simple supplementation is sufficient, while, in that of the narrower sense, it is not. Someone who came from a culture from which the practice of playing games was entirely lacking could hardly understand the bare remark that the intention of the players is to win, since he would want to know what further purpose this intention subserved: we should therefore have to explain to him the character of games as a social institution, which is a complicated matter. (A child who thinks that there is no point in playing a game unless he wins may be said not yet to have grasped fully the concept of a GAME; yet to say that the intention of the players is to win does not allow for there being any such point.) All this relates, however, only to the narrower, i.e. strict, sense of 'game'. Suppose that two countries, engaged in a political dispute, were to agree to resolve it, on precise terms, not by war, but by a contest between their respective chess champions. The two champions could then naturally be said to play a game of chess; but, since the usual social surroundings of a game would be absent, in the narrower sense it would also be correct to say that they weren't PLAYING and that it was not a mere game that they were engaged in. When we are thinking of games in that wider sense of 'game' which would allow such a contest to be called a 'game', ALL that can be said about winning,

beyond the characterisation of what counts as winning, is that it is what each player has the intention to do.

In this respect, truth is an enormously more complicated notion than that of winning. The misunderstanding to which I referred would be the idea that all that had to be added to a characterisation of the conditions under which a sentence of each of a number of languages was true, in order to explain the notion of truth, would be the flat observation that, in uttering a sentence assertorically, a speaker did so with the intention of uttering a true sentence. We have seen that, looked at in one way, the corresponding thesis for the notion of winning may be held to be correct; but there is no way in which the thesis could be held correct for the notion of truth, and it was not my aim to suggest this. What has to be added to a truth-definition for the sentences of a language, if the notion of truth is to be explained, is a description of the linguistic activity of making assertions; and this is a task of enormous complexity. What we can say is that any such account of what assertion is must introduce a distinction between correct and incorrect assertions, and that it is in terms of that distinction that the notion of truth has first to be explained.

(3) It should be noted that stipulating that every instance of 'It is true that p if and only if p' is to hold will not succeed in determining, even for one who already understands the language relative to which the stipulation is made, the application of the predicate 'true' to sentences of that language unless the language is such as to confer a definite meaning on every conditional formed by taking any arbitrary sentence of the language as antecedent, since, obviously, in order to apply the stipulation to some sentence P, we must be able to understand the conditional ⌜If P, then it is true that P⌝. Hence, when P is a sentence such that we attach no determinate sense to conditionals having P as antecedent, the stipulation will not succeed in telling us when P is true. For instance, we have virtually no use in English for conditionals whose antecedents are themselves conditionals: so we can obtain no help towards resolving the disputed question when an indicative conditional ⌜If Q, then R⌝ of English should be considered true by appeal to the principle that we should accept ⌜If, if Q, then R, then it is true that if Q, then R⌝.

(4) In the text it is argued (quite correctly, I still believe) that uses of 'true' and 'false' which involve that, in recognisable circumstances, a sentence (assumed to be neither ambiguous nor vague) will be neither true nor false relate only to the behaviour of that sentence as a constituent of compound sentences, and, in particular, to the sense of its negation. There is, however, a distinct but prior consideration of the same kind. We are accustomed, in general, to distinguish between an assertion's being CORRECT and the speaker's having a WARRANT for making it: the text assumes implicitly that this distinction has already been drawn.

But we need to ask on what basis we make any such distinction. For instance, a sentence in the future tense used to express the intention of the speaker contrasts with the corresponding declaration of intention (in the form 'I intend to ...'). The same contrast exists between the genuine future tense used to make a prediction, and the future tense used to express present tendencies. (This latter occurs, e.g. in an announcement of the form, 'The wedding accounced between *A* and *B* will not now take place'. Such an announcement cancels, but does not falsify, the earlier announcement, and is not itself falsified if the couple later make it up and get married after all; if this were not so, the 'now' would be superfluous.) With both pairs, the conditions under which an assertion of either form would be warranted coincide: but the conditions for their truth differ. In both pairs, the first member may actually be false, although the assertion was warranted; or, conversely, be true, although it was not warranted. I should maintain that this distinction also derives its significance from the behaviour of sentences as constituents of more complex ones. Thus, for each pair, a conditional which has one member of the pair as antecedent has a quite different sense from one having the other member as antecedent; or, again, the sense of the past future ('was going to ...') varies accordingly as we take the future ingredient as constituting the plain future tense or the future tense which expresses the existence of a present intention or tendency. If we are concerned with an assertoric sentence which cannot appear as a constituent of a more complex sentence, we have no need of a distinction between cases in which an assertion made by means of it would be warranted and those in which it would be correct. As already noted, the conditionals of natural language are, or approximate to being, just such sentences; it is for just that reason that philosophers have found it so hard to say what should be reckoned as part of the truth-condition for such a conditional, and what as merely part of the grounds for asserting it.

(5) Some people have been surprised by my characterising the content of an assertion in terms of what it excludes, i.e. what would show it to be wrong, rather than in terms of what establishes it as correct. I find their surprise surprising in its turn, since the example shows so clearly why the former approach is better. It is obvious that one who makes a conditional assertion does not wish to rule out the antecedent's being false, and that one who asserts a singular statement does not wish to allow for the term's lacking a reference: but, if we tried to contrast the two cases in terms of what established the assertions as correct, we should quickly find ourselves involved in disputes about when a conditional statement is to be said to be true. Of course, we can talk instead about what is required to be the case by an assertion; but this notion relates, once again, to how we recognise the assertion as incorrect. The reason is

similar to what is said in the text about obedience and disobedience: our notions of right and wrong, for assertions as for actions, are asymmetrical, and it is the apparently negative notion which is primary. There is a well-defined consequence of an assertion's proving incorrect, namely that the speaker must withdraw it, just as there is a well-defined consequence of disobedience; there is not in the same way a well-defined consequence of an assertion's proving correct, or of obedience. When we talk of a previous assertion having been right, we are usually primarily concerned with the speaker's having been justified in making it, just as, when obedience is in question, it is always a matter of deliberate compliance.

(6) 'The making of a statement has, as it were, only one kind of consequence'. This remark is essentially correct, but the 'as it were' is important: assertions do not have the same kind of relation to determinate consequences that commands and bets do.

(7) It is the final section of the article which stands most in need of revision. In this section I am concerned with deep grounds for rejecting the law of excluded middle as applied to certain statements, whereas, in the earlier part, I had been concerned with superficial grounds for rejecting it. The superficial case is that in which it is held that, in certain RECOGNISABLE circumstances, a statement will be neither true nor false. The upshot of the preceding discussion was that, whenever some recognisable circumstance is regarded as settling the truth-value of the statement, that circumstance must determinately confer on the statement either a designated or an undesignated value, and that that is all that is relevant to the content of an assertion of the statement on its own; the point of describing the sentence as neither true nor false whenever some recognisable circumstance obtains can, therefore, only relate to the content of more complex sentences in which the given sentence occurs as a constituent.

The deep case is that in which it is agreed, for all recognisable circumstances, whether they determine the statement as true or as false (and there are none in which it is held to be neither); but no effective method exists which will in all cases bring about circumstances of one or the other kind. The text describes the principle that a statement can be true only if there is something in virtue of which it is true as a realist one: but the point of the dispute over 'Jones was brave' is that both parties accept the principle. The anti-realist uses it to infer that the statement is not necessarily either true or false; the realist uses it to infer that that which makes it true or false cannot be identified with that by which we recognise it as true or as false, when we are able to do so. For the realist, our understanding of the statement consists in our grasp of its truth-conditions, which determinately either obtain or fail to obtain, but which cannot be recognised by us in all cases as obtaining whenever they do; for the anti-realist, our understanding consists in knowing what recognisable circumstances determine it as true or as false.

The text stigmatises as absurd the proposition that a statement might be true even though there was nothing such that, if we knew of it, we should count as evidence of its truth. This was intended to mean 'nothing of the sort which we ordinarily use as evidence for the truth or falsity of such a statement'. The claim in the text is a very bold one, and should be rejected by a realist, who might, and I think ought, to agree to the following weaker principle: that a statement cannot be true unless it is in principle capable of being known to be true. This principle is closely connected with the first one: for that in virtue of which a statement is true is that by which the statement might be known to be true. The fundamental difference between the anti-realist and the realist lies in this: that, in the second principle, the anti-realist interprets "capable of being known" to mean 'capable of being known *by us*', whereas the realist interprets it to mean 'capable of being known by some hypothetical being whose intellectual capacities and powers of observation may exceed our own'. The realist holds that we give sense to those sentences of our language which are not effectively decidable by appealing tacitly to means of determining their truth-values which we do not ourselves possess, but which we can conceive of by analogy with those which we do. The anti-realist holds that such a conception is quite spurious, an illusion of meaning, and that the only meaning we can confer on our sentences must relate to those means of determining their truth-values which we actually possess. Hence, unless we have a means which would in principle decide the truth-value of a given statement, we do not have for it a notion of truth and falsity which would entitle us to say that it must be either true or false.

The text of the article espouses a frankly anti-realist position; it says, in effect, that a realist interpretation is possible only for those statements which are in principle effectively decidable (i.e. those for which there is no serious issue between the realist and anti-realist). I am no longer so unsympathetic to realism: the realist has a lot more to say for himself than is acknowledged in the article. The dispute is still a long way from resolution. On the one hand, it is unclear whether the realist's defence of his position can be made convincing; on the other, it is unclear whether the anti-realist's position can be made coherent. I remain convinced, however, that the issue between realism and anti-realism, construed roughly along the present lines, is one of the most fundamental of all the problems of philosophy; convinced also that very few people are thinking about it in the terms which seem to me to be the right ones.

J. O. Urmson

CRITERIA OF INTENTIONALITY

In the eleventh chapter of his book, *Perceiving*, Mr. Chisholm offers three criteria of intentionality. A sentence is intentional, according to Chisholm, if it satisfies any one of these criteria. In this paper I inquire carefully neither what intentionality is nor whether Chisholm's criteria are satisfactory criteria of it. Chisholm's criteria, especially the first and third, are interesting in their own right, whatever they are criteria of. I propose, taking each in turn, to attempt to find a representative range of examples which satisfy them and to explain why they do so. Many points discussed already by Quine, Linsky and others will arise, but detailed documentation seems unnecessary.

Chisholm states and illustrates his first criterion as follows:

First let us say that a simple declarative sentence is intentional if it uses a substantival expression — a name or a description — in such a way that neither the sentence nor its contradictory implies either that there is or there isn't anything to which the substantival expression truly applies. 'Diogenes looked for an honest man' is intentional by this criterion. Neither 'Diogenes looked for an honest man' nor its contradictory — 'Diogenes did *not* look for an honest man' — implies either that there are, or that there are not, any honest men. But 'Diogenes sits in his tub' is not intentional by this criterion, for it implies that there *is* a tub in which he sits.

Perceiving, 170.

I have no desire to raise pedantic difficulties about the wording of this criterion; but the following points do seem relevant:

(a) I do not believe that there is any simple declarative sentence which

Reprinted from: *Proceedings of the Aristotelian Soc. Supplementary* 42 (1968), 108-22.

has to be used in the way that Chisholm has in mind. The following dialogue is possible:

A. Diogenes looked for an honest man.
B. Who was that?
A. The man who anonymously returned the purse he had lost.

If the sentence "Diogenes looked for an honest man" is used in the way that Chisholm has in mind, Diogenes' search will be merely vain if there is no honest man. But if the sentence is used as in the foregoing dialogue, then, if there is no such man (Diogenes merely mislaid his purse and nobody has returned it), Diogenes' search is misconceived rather than unsuccessful. The specific dialogue is unplausible, but if a detective were to approach us and say "I am looking for a man with a hare lip and a limp" it would be more natural to suppose the question "Who is he and what has he done?" in order, than that the detective was frivolously interested in finding a specimen answering to his description, if there was one. When the description is used referringly, that is, when the question "Who (what) is that?" is appropriate, I should prefer to say that the existence of what is referred to in the utterance is presupposed rather than implied. When the description is used so that the question is inappropriate, the existence of nothing is implied or presupposed; these, I take it, are the cases in which Chisholm and we ourselves are interested.

Let us then emend Chisholm's criterion to read 'a use of a simple declarative sentence' instead of 'a simple declarative sentence' · with appropriate consequential changes, and to read 'implies or presupposes' where Chisholm has only 'implies'.

(b) The criterion apparently covers such cases as 'Tom behaves like an honest man', though they are quite different from those that Chisholm appears to have in mind. I shall presume that the criterion can be revised to exclude them, but do not undertake the revision.

(c) It would be well to add 'whether real or imaginary' (giving a generous scope to 'imaginary') after 'there isn't anything' in Chisholm's formulation. I take it that "I admire Pickwick" is no more intentional than is "I admire you". If someone worships Zeus or looks for Sherlock Holmes's violin, he is no doubt grievously in error. But he is mistaking the mythical or fictional for the real, which is a factual error; whereas if one mistakes an inexistent for an existent object, by asking who was the honest man sought by Diogenes, one is misunderstanding discourse. There are philosophical problems about the imaginary, but they are quite different from those with which we are now concerned. The point is that Diogenes might equally well have sought for an honest character in fiction without it being implied either that there were or were not any.

If we supply a natural context, the three utterances

(1) I am looking for an honest man,
(2) I am looking for Sherlock Holmes,
(3) I am looking for the present King of France,

raise quite different problems. The first is our present concern; the second is the problem of the fictional and the real; the third is that of the ostensibly referring expression which has no referent, even a fictional one. Traditional discussions often neglect these distinctions, for example with regard to Russell's theory of descriptions. Thus "The (well-known) labours of Hercules are impossible" is just true, whereas if someone says "The labours of the present King of France are impossible" I simply do not know what he is talking about. Again, the defect of the classical analysis of "Dragons do not exist" as (roughly) "There is nothing which has wings, breathes fire, etc." is that in the analysandum I am denying the (real) existence of certain fictional objects, whereas the analysans no more does this than does "there is nothing made of gold that rusts". Again, if asked whether the present King of France is bald I should not say "No", nor that the question did not arise; I simply do not know what is being talked about. It may be that the speaker turns out to be a newly aroused Rip Van Winkle who is referring to Louis the Fourteenth in this inaccurate way, in which case I shall know what to say. Otherwise the question does not (for me) make a successful reference, so that I cannot consider even whether it arises. Maybe the question where Sherlock Holmes' violin is nowadays does not arise; I know what the question is about, and see that it does not arise because the violin is fictional.

Let us take Criterion I to have been emended on the lines indicated. We may now list some (only some) of the verbs and verbal expressions which, with some such object as a common name in the plural ('tigers') or an indefinite description in Russell's sense ('an honest man'), may occur in simple declarative sentences used in a way which satisfies the criterion: 'look for', 'dig a trap for', 'take precautions against', 'listen for', 'test for', 'hunt', 'take out an insurance policy against'. It is noteworthy that 'look for' is in the list, but not 'find', 'dig a trap for' but not 'catch in a trap', 'take precautions against (burglars)' but not 'foil'. It is equally noteworthy that the verbal expressions 'try to catch in a trap', 'try to find' and 'try to foil' can be added to the list, which can be further extended by use of such auxiliaries as 'set about' and 'take steps to'.

Lest we get too excited about our being able to stand in a relation (of looking for, or hunting) toward an object or objects which may not exist, we may pause to observe that we can stand in equally commonplace relationships to objects which, if we are to stand in that relationship to them, must positively not exist. Thus it can be true that I am building a house only if the house does not exist. No doubt, if I am building a house, something between foundations and a complete house must exist, but what I am building is a complete house, and if that already exists I cannot be building it. This painfully obscurantist way of putting the conceptual truth about construction and manufacture is no worse than, and even parallel to, the traditional jargon of intentional inexistence.

We may undertake tasks which fall under the general rubric of getting into a relation R with an object Y. We may fail in such tasks because, though there are Y's available, we cannot get into relation R with any of them (I have the task of picking an apple, but, though there are apples on the tree, I can reach none). Equally we may fail because there are no Y's, or no available Y's, to get into relation R with (there are no apples on the tree). It is possible to describe a task in a way which implies or presupposes the existence of Y's, thus eliminating the latter of these two modes of failure from consideration. Thus if we say that Tom is trying to ride (R) a bicycle (Y), we describe his task in a way which presupposes that a Y is available and leaves open only the question whether Tom will succeed in getting into relation R with it. Manufacturing and construction tasks presuppose or imply the non-existence of the Y since the relation R into which one is trying to get is that of having brought into existence. But the most general case is that in which success depends on both there being Y's and the agent's getting into relation R with one or more of them. If Tom is trying to find a proof of Goldbach's conjecture he may fail either because there is no proof or because he cannot find it, though there is one.

Evidently a great many of the uses of simple declarative sentences which satisfy Criterion I are simply accounts of tasks of getting into relation R with a Y which admit of failure through there being no Y's. To look for an honest man is to undertake a task the success of which is finding an honest man, where failure may result from there being no honest men. This account seems to me, rightly or wrongly, to remove any legitimate philosophical perplexity about such cases.

Certainly there are complications of and variations upon this simple theme. Thus in the cases of taking precautions against, insuring against and building barricades against, our task is not to get into a relation R with a Y, but to do so if there are any Y's. I may take precautions against burglars; then my task is successfully accomplished if I foil burglars, if there are burglars, unsuccessfully accomplished if I fail to foil burglars, if there are any. What we are to say about success or failure if there are no burglars is a problem of unfulfilled conditionals rather than intentionality and needs no discussion here. Such complications of the task and success model are unproblematical. The simple truth is that we do not have to know whether there is a stud in the box before opening it in the hope of finding one.

In the examples so far considered the traditional connexion between intentionality and mentality has not been much in evidence. Clearly there is the tenuous connexion that tasks can only be undertaken by beings with minds. But this applies equally to tasks like trying to ride a bicycle, where the existence of the Y is presupposed, and to building, where the non-existence of the Y is presupposed or implied. So this aspect of mentality is not a distinguishing mark of the intentional cases. But there seems to be little else conspicuously mental about digging traps for wild pigs and building stockades against lions, both of which are intentional by Criterion I, since they leave open the question of the existence of wild pigs and lions.

One need hardly add that to look for an honest man is not to be in a relationship with a psychic object, hoping sooner or later to get into another relation, finding, with a physical one. The expression 'an honest man' is not being used here referentially, no more to psychic than to physical objects. To take 'an honest man' as referring to a psychic object is as ridiculous as to suppose that in building one operates on a psychic entity which turns into a physical one on completion.

But so far we have considered only some examples, ones deliberately selected to fit the account given. They have all embodied verbs of action, since task verbs are verbs of action. But it is possible to give examples which satisfy the criterion which do not embody verbs of action. Here are a few:

> Blackcurrants require a generous supply of nitrogen,
> This book deserves a lifetime's study,
> This picture is worth a king's ransom,
> I want an orange,
> He needs a shave.

Chisholm says on page 173 of *Perceiving* that

in describing nonpsychological phenomena we do, on occasion, use sentences which are intentional by one or more of the above criteria. One may say, 'This weapon, suitably placed, is capable of causing the destruction of Boston' and 'The cash register knows that 7 and 5 are 12'. But although these sentences are intentional according to our criteria, we can readily transform them into others which are not: 'If this weapon were suitably placed, then Boston would be destroyed' and 'If you press the key marked 7 and the one marked 5, the cash register will yield a slip marked 12'.

Since I have been, in effect, claiming to show how many of Chisholm's 'psychological' examples can be readily transformed, in the strict sense of providing an equivalence, on the model that 'A is looking for B' is equivalent to '*A* is engaged in a task the success of which is finding *B*', it would ill become me to protest at the suggestion that the nonpsychological examples can also be transformed. But I do not find Chisholm's specimens of transformation persuasive, and I believe that the examples given above are in principle to be dealt with in a manner parallel to our treatment of the first batch of examples.

Requiring, deserving, needing, being worth, and wanting are not tasks, of which getting is the success; but in each case the getting is clearly envisaged as some sort of goal or success, the detailed distinction of the cases being beyond our present scope. The non-intentional situations of blackcurrants getting nitrogen, the book getting study, the picture fetching a king's ransom, my getting an orange and his getting a shave are all represented as in some way appropriate. Further, each appropriate situation may fail to arise either because the object (e.g., the supply of nitrogen) does not exist or because the subject fails to get into the required relationship to it. The analogy with the task success example is thus very close.

One can find examples which require a more complicated treatment to fit them into the general teleological interpretation which I have offered for uses of sentences satisfying criterion I. There is a range of cases typified by '*A* is (consciously) taking a risk of *Y*' and '*A* is (whether he knows it or not) incurring the risk of *Y*'. There is not space to deal with these cases thoroughly, but I suggest that they involve a sort of negative teleology, the likelihood of a specified form of failure or undesirable outcome.

One final remark before we leave this criterion. It is often suggested that '*A* is thinking about *Y*' is a prime case of intentionality. If '*Y*' be a name or description, as criterion I requires, then this is not so, if we rely on this criterion. If *A* is thinking about Pickwick, then there must be a (fictional) Pickwick for him to think about; '*A* is thinking about his next meal' implies that *A* will get another meal — we shall have to revise our account of the matter to '*A* was thinking about the meal he had hoped to get' if he is cut off in his prime before he gets it. But this implies the non-existence of the meal and so does not satisfy criterion I. In thinking about my next holiday I may well realise that things may not turn out as I envisage them, but the thoughts will not be even inaccurate thoughts about the holiday unless it occurs. Of course, we shall not say, retrospectively, that my earlier statement 'I am thinking about my next holiday' was false, if I do not get the holiday; but the referring expression will turn out to have been inaccurate. As is argued more fully later in the paper (and Linsky has already pointed out), an inaccurate reference does not necessarily make the statement in which it occurs false. No doubt, 'I am thinking about a holiday' is colloquially permissible and formally satisfies criterion I; but it clearly falls under the teleological model.

Chisholm's second criterion of intentionality is:

Secondly, let us say of any noncompound sentence which contains a propositional clause, that it is intentional provided that neither the sentence nor its
contradictory implies that the propositional clause is true or that it is false.
'James believes that there are tigers in India' is intentional by this criterion,
because neither it nor its contradictory implies either that there are, or that there
are not, any tigers in India.

Perceiving, 171.

Wishing for generous space to discuss the third criterion, I shall say
little about this one. I merely remark that, since it is of the nature of a
proposition to admit the two possibilities of truth and falsehood, if a
propositional clause is introduced into speech there will be these two
possibilities unless one is excluded. We can exclude one by simply denying
or asserting p. We also exclude one by prefacing 'that p' by 'A knows'
or 'it is noteworthy', etc.; these cases do not therefore satisfy Criterion II.
Though such examples as 'It is possible that p' leave both possibilities
open their contradictories do not and therefore they do no satisfy the
criterion. Here, however, is a sufficiently motley collection of examples
that satisfy Criterion II by the simple device of giving no clue whether
p is true or false:

He believes that p.	He explained how to p.
It says on page 3 that p.	It is illegal to p.
Nobody has ever claimed that p.	Nobody could say that p.
It would be wise to p.	without laughing.
	I was invited to p.

I regret that I can find nothing in common to these examples save that
they were constructed to fit the criterion, which is not in itself of high
philosophical significance.

Chisholm's third criterion of intentionality is this:

Suppose there are two names or descriptions which designate the same things
and that E is a sentence obtained merely by separating these two names or
descriptions by means of 'is identical with' (or 'are identical with' if the first
word is plural). Suppose also that A is a sentence using one of those names or
descriptions and that B is like A except that, where A uses the one, B uses the
other. Let us say that A is intentional if the conjunction of A and E does not
imply B.

Perceiving, 171

Some general remarks about so-called 'opacity of reference' seem
necessary before we discuss this criterion.

If *X* makes a communication to *Y* which includes a referring expression, three distinct questions (at least) arise:
(a) Is the reference successful; that is, does *Y* take *X* to be referring to the object to which he is in fact referring?
(b) Is the reference accurate; that is, does the referring expression properly apply to the object or objects to which *X* applies it?
(c) Is the reference apt; that is, is the referring expression suitably chosen in relation to the total content and context of the communication? I say nothing about questions (a) and (b), except to note that a reference may well be successful but inaccurate. We often refer successfully to a non-insect by using the referring expression 'that insect'. We do not usually regard such inaccurate reference as rendering the statement in which it occurs false.

More important for my purposes is the fact that a reference may be accurate but inept. Thus I may know someone well, both as the local bank manager and as Tom the husband of Mary, whom I also know well. If I meet Mary and tell her truly and accurately "The bank manager is on his way home" my reference is so inept that, unless clearly jocular in tone, it may not be immediately successful. "The bank manager — do you mean Tom?", Mary may ask, and when I answer "Yes" she may properly complain "Well, why didn't you say Tom in the first place?" In this example the reference is inept because of the status of the auditor. Still more obviously the reference in "The man I met five minutes ago is on his way home" is inept if the communication is made to a person who was not with me five minutes ago.

There are many principles of aptness of reference. Apart from considerations of politeness and social acceptability (refer to developing, not to underdeveloped, countries) and matters of literary taste (it is pompous to refer to Aristotle as the sage of Stagira), here are three principles of aptness of greater relevance to philosophical issues:

(1) Other things being equal, it is best to use the referring expression most likely to secure successful identification by the person(s) to whom the communication is addressed. (Call a man 'Tom' or 'your husband' to his wife, 'the bank manager' to business acquaintances, 'the man we just met' to a companion to whom he is a stranger, and so on.)

(2) Other things being equal, when using a descriptive referring expression, it is best to use the one whose meaning is most apposite to the topic of discourse. This is obscure, but readily clarified by examples. If the local postman is also the local darts champion, it is more apt to say 'The postman is late' if he is late with the letters, and more apt to say 'The champion is late' if he is not at the pub in time for the darts match. Again, it is apt enough to say 'That large mass of metal is inter-

fering with my compass', but it is better to call that same object a motor car if you wish to say that it has a good turning-circle.

When this principle of aptness is particularly relevant Quine is accustomed to say that the referring expression is not used purely referentially.

(3) Other things being equal, it is better in reported speech to use the referring expression which was used by the speaker reported.

One of the points of putting 'other things being equal' into the formulation of each principle of aptness is that the principles can conflict and one may be overridden by considerations derived from another. Since my third principle of aptness is often exalted into a principle of accuracy rather than aptness, it is particularly relevant to observe how easily it can be overridden by other considerations. Let us suppose that Smith says to me "The bank manager has just parked his car in the market place", and that I then meet the bank manager's wife, Mary. I can aptly say to her "Mr. Smith tells me that Tom (or "your husband") has just parked in the market place". I should certainly not say to her, in accordance with the third principle of aptness, "Mr. Smith tells me that the bank manager has just parked in the market place". Moreover, my choice of referring expression would not for one moment lead Mary to suppose that I was suggesting, let alone stating, that Smith had used some such referring expression as "Mary's husband". Similarly, if Smith had said "I believe (know, think, etc.) that the bank manager has just parked in the market place", I should naturally report to Mary that Smith believed (knew, thought, etc.) that Tom (her husband) had parked there.

In the foregoing examples the first principle overrode the third. Similarly the second principle, that of appositeness, can override it. I might have been at school with the present Prime Minister and have been then prepared to say "I know that Harold is the brightest boy in the form"; of course, I could not then have said "I know the future Prime Minister is the brightest boy in the form", unless "the future P.M." had been his nick-name, for prophetic reference is inept except in the mouths of professional prophets. But I might well say now "Even when we were at school I knew that the present Prime Minister was the brightest boy in the form, though I never guessed that he would rise to such dizzy heights". It would be absurd to deny that I could have known what is asserted in the first clause, adducing the second clause in proof.

But the supreme consideration in choosing a referring expression is that it should be one which will be successful with one's audience. This normally overrides all other considerations of aptness and even of accuracy; when talking to a non-gardener one should always refer to a pelargonium as a geranium.

Thus, while it is often reasonable to suppose that the referring expression used in a report of speech is that used in the speech reported, and the report might otherwise be inept, we can now state the following general truth: to ascribe to a person the statement that *A* is *B*, where '*A*' is a referring expression, is not positively to ascribe to him the use of that referring expression, or even the knowledge that *A* is a suitable expression for referring to the object in question. The same principle holds for the ascription of knowledge, belief, etc.

If what I have just claimed is true, it is very hard indeed to think of any examples that satisfy Criterion III. Thus, let the proposition *A* be 'Jones says (knows, believes, etc.) that the local bank manager is a crook', and let *E* be 'The local bank manager is identical with Tom'; then *A* and *E* seem to me to entail *B*: 'Jones says (knows, believes, etc.) that Tom is a crook'. Further the entailment holds whether or not Jones knows the truth of *E*. Of course, it would be very inept to report Jones in the *B* form except to a person who knows Tom as Tom. But it would be very inept NOT to report Jones in something like the *B* form to, say, Tom's father, wife or brother.

In general, when philosophers have claimed to find examples that satisfy criterion III, any plausibility in their claim has had nothing to do with the general form. They have taken cases where to use the referring expression of *B* would be notably inept. The most plausible examples are those where the additional information is provided that the speaker reported is not merely ignorant of the truth of *E*, but would deny it. Thus let *A* be 'Tom knows that Tully wrote the *Offices*' and let *E* be 'Tully is identical with Cicero'; then it will be grossly inept to say *B*: 'Tom knows that Cicero wrote the *Offices*', if we know that Tom thinks that Cicero is a different person from Tully.

But let us take a formally analogous example:

A: Jones believes that the bank manager is a crook,
E: The bank manager is identical with Mary's husband.

Let us grant that Jones believes that Mary is married to someone else altogether. Once again, reporting the matter to most parties, it would be an offence against both the second and the third principles of aptness to say (*B*) 'Jones believes that Mary's husband is a crook'. But if I am talking to Mary herself, the ineptitude of referring to her husband except by name or as her husband will surely override these considerations. I may well say "Jones believes that your husband is a crook", though I might add "but he doesn't realise that he is your husband". In the light of this, it seems that it is not the form of the example but the ineptitude of the reference which can make us unwilling to accept *B*. *B* is sometimes unacceptable, but not because it goes beyond the premises *A* and *E*.

Chisholm's main example seems to me to illustrate ineptitude of reference, not non-entailment. He says: "most of us knew in 1944 that Eisenhower was the one in command (A); but although he was (identical with) the man who was to succeed Truman (E), it is not true that we knew in 1944 that the man who was to succeed Truman was the one in command (B)". I can only say that I think that B is true; the reference is indeed inept, because there is much to be said against it and nothing for it; but, as my earlier example about the Prime Minister shows, it is not inevitably inept, and certainly is not false, merely because we did not know in 1944 that Eisenhower would succeed Truman, and could not have referred to him then as 'the one who is to succeed Truman'.

One can, of course, construct examples, or quasi-examples, where expressions of a type suitable to be referring expressions in fact occur as predicates. Let us suppose that Bill is Alice's natural father, that Alice was adopted as a baby, and that Alice believes her adoptive-father to be her natural father. Then from A, 'Alice knows that Bill is the owner of the car outside' and E, 'The owner of the car outside is identical with Alice's father', we cannot infer B, 'Alice knows that Bill is her father'. But this is a bogus example, which shows only that you can know some facts about something without knowing all the facts about it. The referring expressions in E do not function as such in A and B. For similar reasons, we can say that Alice does not know that her father is her father without attributing to her any obtuseness about the principle of identity. We can reword our premiss A as 'Alice knows that Bill owns the car outside' and B as 'Alice knows that Bill begat her'. E has vanished and no one will find it perplexing that though the same man owns the car and begat Alice A may be true and B false.

I find it hard, therefore, to find examples which satisfy Criterion III. Perhaps the incorporation of such expressions as 'Said in so many words' and 'Inscribed on a monument' might seem to given plausible examples. Thus if A is 'Tom said in so many words that Mary was a fool' and E is 'Mary is Alice's daughter', do they together entail B, 'Tom said in so many words that Alice's daughter was a fool'? I am inclined to think that they do; it seems that the expression 'in so many words' guarantees the literal accuracy only of the predicate. I might say B to you if you knew Alice, but did not know the name of her daughter.

We do have techniques at our disposal for faithfully reporting a speaker's referring expression in indirect speech — techniques which would be superfluous if we always did so. The most obvious thing to do is to use two referring expressions — that of the speaker and our own one more apt to the context — thus:

He said Mary was a hypocrite, calling her a cunning little vixen.

He said of Mary that the cunning little vixen was a hypocrite.
He said that the cunning little vixen, meaning Mary, was a hypocrite.

We may also suggest that the referring expression is not our own but that of the reported speaker by imitating his accent while uttering it and similar histrionic devices. But usually there is no point in preserving such referring expressions as 'that chap over there' in new speech contexts where they would be inept, and we make no effort to do so. The devices just illustrated and mentioned are for occasions when a laudatory, abusive or otherwise noteworthy referring expression has been used by the speaker reported.

In fact the most plausible examples of the satisfaction of criterion III that I can find are not cases of reported speech, knowledge and belief, but ones which incorporate such expressions as 'it is remarkable that' and 'it is evident that'. Consider this example:

A: It is remarkable that this experienced driver is driving so badly.
E: This experienced driver is identical with this man who has just drunk four whiskies.

I find it hard to believe that these together entail:

B: It is remarkable that this man who has just drunk four double whiskies is driving so badly.

Here what is being found remarkable (and could in parallel examples be found evident) is that a certain predicate attaches to some particular reference, so that the substitution is out of order. Still more obviously, if it is obscene to say that *a* is *f*, and *a* is identical with *b*, it does not follow that it is obscene to say that *b* is *f*. But I do not suppose that Chisholm will thank me for offering such cases as prime examples of intentionality.

I have no general morals to draw. I thought it interesting to examine Chisholm's criteria and I have done so. But I am obliged to say that I find them to have little connexion with each other. Moreover, none appears to have any particular connexion with psychological matters. I have never acquired the concept of an intentional object; I begin to believe, but do not assert, that there is none to acquire. But, as when Diogenes looked for an honest man, we may look for a concept of intentionality even if there is none to be found.

Part III

PHILOSOPHERS ON GRAMMAR

--- --- --- --- --- --- --- --- --- --- --- --- --- --- --- --- ---

P. T. Geach

A PROGRAM FOR SYNTAX

The program for syntax which I describe here is not one I can claim as specially my own. The two basic ideas are due to Frege: analysis of an expression into a main functor and its argument(s), and distinction among categories of functors according to the categories of arguments and values. The development of a handy notation for categories, and of an algorithm to test whether a string of expressions will combine into a complex expression that belongs to a definite category, is due to the Polish logicians, particularly Ajdukiewicz. My own contribution has been confined to working out details. So my program is not original, but I think it is right in essentials; and I am making propaganda for it by working it out in some particular instructive examples. I think this is all the more called for because some recent work in syntax seems to have ignored the insights I am trying to convey.

I shall begin with some thoughts from Aristotle's pioneering treatise on syntax, the *De Interpretatione*. Aristotle holds that the very simplest sort of sentence is a two-word sentence consisting of two heterogeneous parts — a name and a predicative element (rhēma). For example, 'petetai Sōkratēs', 'Socrates is flying'. This gives us an extremely simple example for application of our category theory:

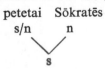

petetai Sōkratēs
s/n   n

s

The two-word Greek expression as a whole belongs to the category s of

Reprinted from: Synthese 22 (1970) 3-17.

sentences; 'petetai' is a functor that takes a single name (of category n) 'Sōkratēs' as argument and yields as a result an expression of category s. Ajdukiewicz represented functorial categories by a fractional notation: a/β would be the category of a function that operates upon a single argument of category β to yield an expression of category a, so that we have a "multiplying out" of category indices. This notation becomes awkward to print when indices become complex; so following a suggestion of my Leeds colleague Dr. T. C. Potts I shall henceforth rather write ': $a\beta$' for such a functorial category. (This device makes bracketing theoretically superfluous, but in practice I shall insert parentheses sometimes to facilitate reading.) Our first rule then is the multiplying-out rule:

$$: a\beta \ \beta \to a$$

For instance, :sn n→s.

Aristotle observed that one may get a sentence from a rhēma like 'petetai' not only by combining it with a name but also by combining it with a quantified phrase like 'pās anthrōpos', 'every man'. He further observed that these two types of sentence behave quite differently under negation; the negation of 'petetai Sōkratēs' is 'ou petetai Sōkratēs', when the negation 'ou' attaches to the rhēma 'petetai'; the negation of 'pās anthrōpos petetai' is 'ou pās anthrōpos petetai', where the negative attaches to the quantified phrase 'pās anthrōpos'. This is a profound insight, ignored by those who would lump together proper names and phrases like 'every man' as Noun Phrases; we have two different syntactical categories. It is easy to find in the Ajdukiewicz scheme another category that will yield the category s when combined with the category :sn; for we shall have, by the general rule, ::s:sn :sn → s. But this is not enough to exhaust the Aristotelian insight. We should wish to make 'ou petetai' 'does not fly' a syntactically coherent sub-string of 'ou petetai Sōkratēs', and on the other hand to make 'ou pās anthrōpos' 'not every man' a syntactically coherent sub-string of 'ou pās anthrōpos petetai'. But by the Ajdukiewicz criteria for a string's being syntactically coherent (SC), neither string will come out as SC. To negation 'ou', we must assign the category :ss of a sentence-forming operator upon sentences; and neither the category-indices ':ss :sn' of 'ou petetai' nor the indices ':ss :s:sn' of 'ou pās anthrōpos' multiply out by Ajdukiewicz' rule to a single index of the whole expression. These are two particular cases of a general fact, noticed by medieval logicians: that a sentence may contain a *formale*, formal element — Ajdukiewicz' main functor — negation of which is negation of the whole proposition.

Intuitions about the SC nature of sub-strings are fallible, but are *pro tanto* evidential; we need to check our general theories of syntax against such intuitions, and also to correct our intuitions against wider insights.

By the two-way process we may hope to get steadily closer to truth. In this case, we can satisfy the demands of intuition if we supplement the Ajdukiewicz multiplying-out rule with a recursive rule:

If $a\beta \to \gamma$, $a : \beta\delta \to : \gamma\delta$.

This already covers the Aristotelian and medieval cases. For suppose the main functor of a sentence is of category $:s\beta$, so that we have a sentence by adding a β expression. We then have by our recursive rule:

Since $:ss\ s \to s$, $:ss$, $:ss\ :s\beta \to :s\beta$.

And this covers all cases in which negation, of category $:ss$, operates upon a sentence of structure $:s\beta\ \beta$. The string of expressions categorized as:

$:ss\ :s\beta\ \beta$,

may be split up in two ways into SC sub-strings; namely, we may regard negation $(:ss)$ as operating on the whole sentence categorized as $:s\beta\ \beta$; or, we may regard it as combining with the $:s\beta$ expression to form a complex $:s\beta$ expression, which then combines with the β expression to form a sentence. The two Aristotelian examples are covered by this account if we take $\beta = :sn$ and $\beta = :s:sn$.

Such possibilities of multiple analysis do not mean that we have a syntactically ambiguous string. We have a single "proper series of indices", as Ajdukiewicz calls it, for a given sentence; the different ways of multiplying out the indices reveal two different but equally legitimate ways of dissecting out an SC sub-string from a larger SC string.

The Ajdukiewicz scheme allows for functors that take more than one argument. In the present discussion it will be enough to consider functors that take two arguments of the same category: if this category is β and a is the category of the functor plus its two arguments, I give the functor the category $:a(2\beta)$. We get in Ajdukiewicz the rule for multiplying out with such category indices:

$:a(2\beta)\ \beta\ \beta \to a$.

Once again I add a recursive rule:

If $a\ \beta\ \beta \to \gamma$,   then $a :\beta\delta\ :\beta\delta \to :\gamma\delta$.

A medieval example may serve to illustrate the newly introduced categories. 'John or James came' need not be transformed into 'John came or James came' before we investigate its SC character; we can show it to be SC as it stands. But we cannot treat it as having the same simple subject-predicate structure as 'John came', only having a complex subject 'John or James' instead of the single name 'John'. For whereas the negation of 'John came' attaches to the predicate 'came', 'John or James came' has to be negated by negating 'or' — '*neither* John *nor* James came'.

So my medieval writer justly took 'or' to be here the *formale* or main functor. 'John or James' may be regarded as a restricted existential quantification — 'for some x in the universe {John, James}, x...'; so we assign to it, just as we do to 'pās anthrōpos' or 'every man', the category :s:sn. The functor 'or' will then be assigned the category :(:s:sn) (2n), which combines with two names of category n to yield an :s:sn expression; and this in turn combines with the predicate 'came' of category :sn to yield a sentence. Negation, of category :ss, will combine with a functor of category :(:s:sn) (2n) to yield a functor of the same category; we see this by twice applying our recursive rule:

> :ss s → s
> *ergo*, :ss :s:sn → :s:sn
> *ergo*, :ss :(:s:sn) (2n) → :(:s:sn) (2n).

I shall now briefly sketch how the traditional apparatus of Parts of Speech get reshaped in an Ajdukiewicz grammar. I shall consider only some of the traditional list.

I. VERBS

Intransitive verbs like 'come' or 'petetai' may be categorized as :sn. A transitive verb along with its noun-object, a phrase like 'loves Socrates', will likewise be of category :sn; 'loves' itself is thus most conveniently categorized as ::snn. 'Every Greek loves Socrates' then admits of a double dissection into SC sub-strings; we need this, because we need to recognize both 'loves Socrates' and 'every Greek loves' as SC expressions that may recur in other contexts e.g. in the relative clauses 'who loves Socrates' and 'that every Greek loves'. (When symbolizing a piece of argument stated in the vernacular, we might find it convenient to represent either recurrent phrase by the same one-place predicate letter each time it occurred.) In fact, 'loves Socrates' gets categorized as ::snn n, which multiplies out to :sn by the Ajdukiewicz rule; and then 'Every Greek loves Socrates' will be categorized as :s:sn :sn, which multiplies out to s. On the other hand, 'every Greek loves' gets categorized as :s:sn ::snn; this multiplies out to :sn by our recursive rule:

> Since   :s:sn :sn → s,   :s:sn ::snn → :sn.

So 'Every Greek loves Socrates' comes out as :sn n, and thus again as s. Once again, we have two equally legitimate analyses, not a syntactic ambiguity.

II. CONJUNCTIONS

The term 'connective' is preferable, since 'conjunction' is indispensable as a name for one of the truth-functions. Traditional grammar distinguishes subordinating and coordinating connectives; in one case, e.g. with 'if', the connective is felt to go with the clause that follows it; in the other case, e.g. 'and', 'or', the connective is felt to be joining two clauses, not going with one rather than the other. No such distinction is needed for the binary sentence-connectives in a formal system, which may very well be taken to be all of one category; but for analysis of the vernacular it seems better to recognize a syntactical distinction between the two sorts of connectives. A subordinating connective would be of category $::sss$; so such a connective together with the clause following it would be of category $::sss$ s, i.e. $:ss$, which is the category of a sentence-forming operator upon a sentence. A coordinating connective, on the other hand, would be of category $:s(2s)$. A string categorizable as $:s(2s)$ s s has as a whole the category s; but just as the category indices $':s(2s)$ s' do not multiply out to a single index, so we need not take either 'John ran and' or 'and Jane rode' to be an SC substring of 'John ran and Jane rode'.

Grammarians have often taken sentences in which a coordinating connective joins expressions other than sentences to be derived from sentences in which the same connective joins sentences. I regard this view as wholly erroneous. Our theory of categories does not restrict the possible arguments of an $:s(2s)$ connective to a pair of sentences; on the contrary, by our recursive rule we have that a pair of the category $:s\beta$ may also be so connected to form a third:

> Since $:s(2s)$ s s → s, $:s(2s)$ $:s\beta$ $:s\beta$ → $:s\beta$, whatever category β may be.

And so we obtain a correct analysis of a sentence like:

> All the girls admired, but most boys detested, one of the saxophonists.

This is not equivalent, as a moment's thought shows, to:

> All the girls admired one of the saxophonists, but most boys detested one of the saxophonists,

and cannot sensibly be regarded as a transformation of it. The expressions 'all the girls admired' and 'most boys detested' are in fact each assignable to the category $:sn$, as we saw before regarding 'every Greek loved'; so the coordinating connective 'but' can combine them to form a single string of category $:sn$. Since 'one of the saxophonists' is plainly a quantifying expression like 'every man', it is of category $:s:sn$; this is the main functor, operating upon 'All the girls admired, but most boys detested', of category :sn, to yield a sentence. The change of intonation pattern marked by the second comma, as contrasted with the smooth run in the sentence:

> All the girls were thrilled, but most boys detested one of the saxophonists,

is easily explained: 'most boys detested one of the saxophonists' is an SC substring (in fact a sentence) in the latter example but not in the former, and the change of intonation shows our feeling for this. (Just as 'Plato was bald' has a different intonation pattern when it stands by itself and when it comes as part of 'The man whose most famous pupil was Plato was bald'; in the latter context it is patently not an SC string.)

Similarly, a subordinating connective along with the clause following it will come out, as I said, in the category :ss, that of a sentence-forming operator upon sentences; but it does not follow that such a unit can be read only as attached to an entire main clause; on the contrary, we must sometimes so regard it as attached to an expression of another category. A good medieval example of syntactical ambiguity brings out this point:

> Every man dies when just one man dies.

This could be true (and was once, in this sense, a presumption of English law) as denying the possibility of quite simultaneous deaths; in the other possible sense, it could be true only if there were just one man, so that his death was the death of every man. The first sense requires us to take the subordinating connective plus its clause, 'when just one man dies', as going not with 'Every man dies' but just with 'dies', as we may see from the paraphrase:

> It holds of every man that he dies when just one man dies (namely he himself and nobody else).

The second sense affirms that the universal death of mankind happens along with the death of one and only one man; here, the whole sentence 'Every man dies' is operated on by the sentence-forming operator 'when just one man dies'.

III. ADVERBS

Some adverbs, as the name suggests, are verb-forming operators upon verbs, and are thus of category :(:sn) (:sn). Thus 'passionately protested' comes out as of the same category with 'protested' (I am taking this as an intransitive verb of category :sn) but also 'passionately loved' comes out as of the same category with 'loved', namely ::snn, for we have:

Since :(:sn) (:sn) :sn → :sn, :(:sn) (:sn) ::snn → ::snn.

And as in the other example we have a double possibility of analysis that corresponds to no syntactical ambiguity: 'passionately/loved Mary' and 'passionately loved/Mary' alike work out as SC, and here once more we are just picking out subordinate SC strings in alternative ways from an SC string.

Two adverbs can be joined by a coordinating connective — 'passionately and sincerely', 'improbably but presumably'. On the other hand a combination like 'passionately and presumably' sounds like nonsense. It is nonsense; it involves a confusion of syntactical categories. For an adverb like 'improbably' or 'presumably' is to be taken, in at least some cases, not as modifying the verb, but as modifying the whole sentence — its category must thus be :ss. Two adverbs of category :ss can be joined with the connective 'but' of category :s(2s); for by our recursive rule:

Since :s(2s) s s → s, :s(2s) :ss :ss → :ss.

So 'improbably but presumably' comes out as a complex adverb of category :ss. Again, by our recursive rule:

Since :s(2s) s s → s, :s(2s) :sn :sn → :sn
Since :s(2s) :sn :sn → :sn, :s(2s) :(:sn) (:sn) :(:sn) (:sn)
→ :(:sn) (:sn).

So 'passionately and sincerely' comes out as of category :(:sn) (:sn), like its component adverbs. But an operator of category :s(2s) can take only two arguments of like category; so if we attempt to join with 'and' the adverbs 'passionately', of category :(:sn) (:sn), and 'presumably', of category :ss, we get syntactical nonsense.

IV. PREPOSITIONS

A prepositional phrase may be an adverb of category :(:sn) (:sn), like 'in London' in 'Raleigh smoked in London'; if so the preposition in the phrase is of category ::(:sn) (:sn)n. On the other hand, in the sentence 'Nobody except Raleigh smoked', 'nobody except Raleigh', like plain 'nobody', is a quantifying expression, of category :s:sn. So 'except Raleigh' is a functor turning one quantifying expression into another — thus, of category :(:s:sn) (:s:sn); and 'except' itself is of category ::(:s:sn) (:s:sn) n. As before, expressions of the same category can be joined with coordinating connectives but not expressions unlike in category; for example, we may assume that 'before' and 'after' are both of category ::(:sn)(:sn)n, so 'before or after' is well-formed, as we may see:

Since $:s(2s) s s \rightarrow s$, $:s(2s) :sn :sn \rightarrow :sn$
    ergo, $:s(2s) :(:sn) (:sn) :(:sn) (:sn)$
    $\rightarrow :(:sn) (:sn)$
    ergo, $:s(2s) ::(:sn) (:sn)n ::(:sn) (:sn)n$
    $\rightarrow ::(:sn) (:sn)n.$

But though 'Nobody smoked before or after Raleigh' is well-formed, 'Nobody smoked before or except Raleigh' is syntactical nonsense, because 'before' and 'except' differ in category.

The preposition 'by' is of different category, again, in the use it has with the passive construction; 'was hit by' must be regarded as formed by a logical operation upon 'hit', and the functor is of category $:(::snn)$ $(::snn)$, since $::snn$ is the category of 'hit'. The word "governed" by 'by' is thus not syntactically connected with it, since $':(::snn) (::snn)'$ and 'n' do not multiply out to give a single index. Why anyone should call a 'by' phrase an Adverbial of Manner I can only dimly imagine, calling to mind half-remembered school exercises in parsing. (How, in what manner, was Caesar killed? By Brutus. Very well then, 'by Brutus' is an Adverbial of Manner, just like 'brutally'!)

The categorizing of prepositions, however, raises very serious difficulties for our whole theory of categories — difficulties which I think can be overcome only by introducing a further powerful, recursive, procedure for establishing that an expression is SC. For example, 'some city' like 'every man' is of category $:s:sn$; but if we assign 'in' to category $::(:sn)$ $(:sn)n$, not only is the functor incapable of taking 'some city' as an argument as it can take 'London', but also the whole sentence 'Raleigh smoked in some city' cannot be made out to be SC by any way of multiplying out the category indices of 'Raleigh' (n), 'smoked' $(:sn)$, 'in', and 'some city'. The only arrangement of the indices that multiplies out to 's' is this:

$:s:sn$	$::(:sn) (:sn) n$	n	$:sn$
(some city)	(in)	(Raleigh)	(smoked)

but this gives rather the syntactical analysis of 'Some city smoked in Raleigh'.

Our recursive procedure is supplied by the well-known logical device — well expounded e.g. in Quine's *Methods of Logic* — of introducing a predicate as an interpretation of a schematic letter in a schema. If 'F' is of category $:sn$, the schema 'F(London)' will be SC and of category s. Now if 'F(London)' is SC, so will '(Some city)F' be — since $':s:sn :sn'$ gives 's'. We now reason thus: We have seen how to assign categories to the expressions in 'Raleigh smoked in London' so as to show it is SC and of category s. We may accordingly assign 'Raleigh smoked in —', as the interpretation of the one-place predicate letter 'F' in the SC schema

'F(London)'. But then also the corresponding interpretation of the SC schema '(Some city)F' will be SC; and this interpretation is the sentence 'Raleigh smoked in some city'; so this sentence is also SC.

Some quite short sentences require a number of steps like this to show they are SC. I shall give an example presently; but I must first explain how to categorize the reflexive pronouns in '-self'. Such a pronoun can be attached to a transitive verb of category ::snn to yield a one-place predicate of category :sn. We have already seen two ways of so attaching an expression to a transitive verb; both ':s:sn ::snn' and '::snn n' multiply out to ':sn'. But a reflexive pronoun plainly is not either a name, or a quantifying expression like 'every man'. Nor is it a mere proxy or substitute for an expression of one of these categories; we might take 'himself' in 'Judas hanged himself' to go proxy for 'Judas', but there is nothing 'himself' would be taken as proxy for in 'The Apostle who hanged himself went to Hell', and plainly 'hanged himself' is not syntactically different in the two sentences. The only category that gives the right result is ::sn::snn, since ::sn::snn ::snn→:sn. We may now consider our example, recalling ones of medieval vintage:

> Every number or its successor is even.

We begin with the clearly well-formed sentence: '8 or 3 is even'. If we give the numerals the category n of proper names (shades of Frege!) then 'is even' will be of category :sn and this sentence will be of the same syntax in essentials as our previous example 'John or James came'.

Since '8 or 3 is even' is SC, we may take '8 or ⊥ is even' as the interpretation of the one-place predicate letter 'F' (category :sn) in the SC schema 'F(3)'. Now if 'F(3)' is SC, then if we assign to '5's successor' the quantifier category :s:sn (there are arguments for doing this, but I omit them for simplicity of exposition), the schema '(5's successor) F' will be SC. But the corresponding interpretation of THIS schema will be the sentence:

> 8 or 5's successor is even.

So this sentence is SC.

We now treat '⊥ or ²'s successor is even' as the interpretation of the two-place predicate letter 'R' in the schema 'R(8,5)'. If 'R' is of category ::snn, and each of '8', '5' is of category n, this schema is SC. But then also the result of operating on 'R' with a reflexive pronoun, 'R(⊥, itself)', will be an SC ONE-place schematic predicate; since we just saw that is how the reflexive pronoun works, to turn a two-place predicate into a one-place predicate. And the corresponding interpretation of 'R(⊥, itself)' will be:

> ⊥ or itself's successor is even.

So this counts as an SC one-place predicate. English accidence of course demands that one rewrite 'itself's' as 'its'.

Finally, since we may treat '$\perp$ or its successor is even' as an interpretation of the one-place predicate letter G, and since with the quantifying expression 'Every number' prefixed we get an SC schema '(Every number) G', we get as the relevant interpretation of this schema:

Every number or its successor is even.

So THIS is an SC sentence; which was to be proved.

Grammarians may find my interpretation of this sentence extremely farfetched. They should consider, however, that it does correspond to the obvious correct paraphrase:

It holds of every number that it or its (own) successor is even.

Moreover, other analyses, more comfortable to the ideas that come natural to grammarians, lead us into a bog of absurdity. We cannot construe our sentence on the model of:

Every man or every woman will be shot.

For this is equivalent to 'Every man will be shot or every woman will be shot'; but no such equivalence holds in our case — the irrelevant falsehood 'Every number is even' has nothing to do with the syntax of our example. (Nor need 'Every man or every woman will be shot' itself be construed as SHORT FOR a disjunction of sentences, though it is EQUIVALENT to one; for it is easily shown by our rules that the two quantifying expressions 'every man' and 'every woman', of category :s:sn, can in their own right be joined by 'or', category :ss, to form an expression of that same category.) As for taking 'number or its successor' as a complex term, that lets us in at once, as many medieval predecessors noticed, for an absurd "syllogism":

Every number is a (number or its successor).
Every (number or its successor) is even.
ergo: Every number is even!

V. RELATIVE PRONOUNS

Quine and I have both repeatedly argued that the use of relative pronouns may fruitfully be compared to that of bound variables. The question is, though, which kind of expressions throws light on the syntax of the other kind; the syntax of bound variables is very complicated and unperspicuous, as we may see e.g. from the need for rules in logic books to guard against unintended "captures" of variables in formulas introduced by substitution. Ajdukiewicz attempted to modify his scheme of categories so as to assign categories to quantifiers that bind variables; but his theory is manifestly inadequate — it takes no account of the fact that a variable is bound to a quantifier containing an EQUIFORM variable: for Ajdukiewicz '(x) (Fxy)' would not differ syntactically from '(z) (Fxy)', so far as I can see.

It occurred to me that some light might be thrown on the matter by constructing a simple combinatory logic, on the lines of Quine's paper 'Variables explained away'. I cannot claim any algorithmic facility in working with combinators, but I have reached results encouraging enough to be worth reporting.

To translate into a combinatory notation the English sentence:

Anybody who hurts anybody who hurst him hurts himself.

I began with an obvious translation of this into quantifier notation (variables restricted to persons; '$H \underline{1} \underline{2}$' = '$\underline{2}$ hurts $\underline{1}$'):

$$(x) \, ((y) \, (Hxy \rightarrow Hyx) \rightarrow Hxx)$$

and then devised the following set of combinators:

'Univ': when a predicate followed by a string of variables has prefixed to it a universal quantifier binding just the last variable of the string, we may instead delete the last variable and prefix 'Univ'; e.g. '(x) (Fx)' becomes 'Univ F' and '(x) (Ryx)' becomes 'Univ Ry'.

'Imp': if the antecedent of a conditional consists of a predicate followed by a string of variables, and the consequent consists of a predicate followed by just the same string, then we may instead write 'Imp' followed by the two predicates followed by the string of variables. E.g. '$Rxy \rightarrow Sxy$' becomes 'Imp R S xy'; '$Fz \rightarrow Gz$' becomes 'Imp F G z'.

'Ref': if a predicate is followed by a string of variables ending with repetition of a variable, we may instead delete the repetition and prefix 'Ref' to the predicate. E.g. 'Rxx' becomes 'Ref Rx', and '$Syxx$' becomes 'Ref Syx'.

'Cnv': the result of prefixing 'Cnv' to a predicate followed by a string of two or more variables is tantamount to the result of switching the last two variables of the string. E.g. 'Ryx' may be rewritten as 'Cnv R xy', and '$Rxyx$' as 'Cnv R xxy'.

We now eliminate, step by step, the variables in the above formula. '$Hxy \rightarrow Hyx$' may be rewritten as '$Hxy \rightarrow$ Cnv H xy', and then as 'Imp H Cnv H xy'.

So '(y) $(Hxy \rightarrow Hyx)$' may be rewritten as '(y) (Imp H Cnv H xy)' and thus as 'Univ Imp H Cnv H x'.

'Hxx' may be rewritten as 'Ref H x'; so since '(y) $(Hxy \rightarrow Hyx)$' may be rewritten as 'Univ Imp H Cnv Hx', '$((y)$ $(Hxy \rightarrow Hyx) \rightarrow Hxx)$' may be rewritten as:

Imp Univ Imp H Cnv H Ref H x.

Finally, to get an equivalent of the whole formula, we get the effect of the prenex '(x)' by deleting the final 'x' and prefixing 'Univ':

Univ Imp Univ Imp H Cnv H Ref H.

It is fairly easy to see how the symbols of this string should be assigned to categories. 'Univ F', when 'F' is one-place, is a sentence of the same form as 'Everyone smokes'; 'Univ', like 'everyone', is of category :s:sn. 'H', like the transitive verb 'hurts' that it represents, is of category ::snn. 'Imp' is a connective that combines two predicates to form a predicate with the same number of places; it is thus of category ::sn(2:sn). 'Ref', like a reflexive pronoun, reduces a predicate of $n + 1$ places to a predicate of n places; it is thus of category ::sn(::snn). And 'Cnv' turns a many-place predicate into one of the same number of places; it is thus of category :(::snn)(::snn). (It might seem as if these assignments of categories were too restrictive of the arguments these functors would be allowed to operate on. But in view of our recursive rules this is not so. For example, 'Imp' could combine two predicates of category ::snn to form a third:

::sn(2:sn) :sn :sn → :sn
ergo, ::sn(2:sn) ::snn ::snn → ::snn.)

We may now check that the above string is, as Ajdukiewicz would say, well-formed throughout and of category s. 'Cnv H' is of category ::snn, since we have

:(::snn)(::snn) ::snn → ::snn.

So 'Imp H Cnv H' is of category ::snn, since we have:

::sn(2:sn) :sn :sn → :sn.

Hence, by the recursive rule:

::sn(2:sn) ::snn ::snn → ::snn.

So 'Univ Imp H Cnv H' is of category :sn, since we have:

:s:sn :sn → s
ergo, :s:sn ::snn → :sn.

Now also 'Ref H' is of category :sn, since we have:

::sn(::snn) ::snn → :sn.

Hence 'Imp Univ Imp H Cnv H Ref H' is of category sn

::sn(2:sn) :sn :sn → :sn.

Finally, since 'Univ' is of category :s:sn, the category of the whole works out as s.

Now this string of predicates and combinators can at once be translated, word for word, into pidgin English:

Univ	Imp	Univ	H	H	Cnv H	Ref H
anybody	who	anybody	who	hurt	get hurt by	hurt self.

(Some small changes of word order were made to improve this mock-up of English: 'Cnv' was rendered by 'get' before the argument of the functor and 'by' after it, and 'Ref' by 'self' after rather than before the argument of this functor.) I suggest, therefore, on the strength of this example (and of others I have not space for here) that we may hope to get a good mock-up of the use of relative pronouns in the vernacular by exercises in combinatory logic.

An interesting confirmation of this conjecture comes to us when we observe that in the above sentence 'Univ Imp' is an SC sub-string:

Univ   Imp
:s:sn   :(:sn) (2:sn) → :s(2:sn),

by our recursive rule since :s:sn :sn → s.

Accordingly, we could definitionally introduce a new combinator of category :s(2:sn), say 'Unimp', and rewrite our string as 'Unimp Unimp H Cnv H Ref H'. The new string may also be translated straight into pidgin English:

Unimp	Unimp	H	Cnv H	Ref H
Whoever	whoever	hurt	get hurt by	hurt self.

And this seems to give a correct account of the logical syntax of the relative pronoun 'whoever'. Of course these results are most unnatural from the point of view of school grammar; in 'anybody who hurts...' the major division would be taken to come not after 'who' but after 'anybody', and 'who hurts...' would be taken as an SC sub-string somehow "modifying" 'anybody'. But if we are to get a scientific insight into syntax we mustn't be afraid to break Priscian's head. As Descartes said, *manum ferulae subduximus* — we no longer need hold out our hand to be caned by pedants.

Such are some specimens of the work I have done to carry out this Polish program. Much more remains to be done; it is like fitting together a huge jig-saw puzzle. But I hope I may have persuaded some readers that further following of this path is worthwhile.

University of Leeds,
University of Pennsylvania

W. V. O. Quine

METHODOLOGICAL REFLECTIONS ON CURRENT LINGUISTIC THEORY

I want to make some broadly methodological remarks on a variety of issues. To begin with I'll talk of RULES, and dwell a while on the distinction between FITTING and GUIDING.

Imagine two systems of English grammar: one an old-fashioned system that draws heavily on the Latin grammarians, and the other a streamlined formulation due to Jespersen. Imagine that the two systems are EXTENSIONALLY EQUIVALENT, in this sense: they determine, recursively, the same infinite set of well-formed English sentences. In Denmark the boys in one school learn English by the one system, and those in another school learn it by the other. In the end the boys all sound alike. Both systems of rules FIT the behavior of all the boys, but each system GUIDES the behavior of only half the boys. Both systems FIT the behavior also of all us native speakers of English; this is what makes both systems correct. But neither system guides us native speakers of English; no rules do, except for some intrusions of inessential schoolwork.

My distinction between fitting and guiding is, you see, the obvious and flat-footed one. Fitting is a matter of true description; guiding is a matter of cause and effect. Behavior FITS a rule whenever it conforms to it; whenever the rule truly describes the behavior. But the behavior is not GUIDED by the rule unless the behaver knows the rule and can state it. This behaver OBSERVES the rule.

But now it seems that Chomsky and his followers recognize an intermediate condition, between mere fitting and full guidance in my flat-footed sense of the word. They regard English speech as in some sense

Reprinted from: *Synthese* 21 (1970), 386-98.

rule-GUIDED not only in the case of the Danish schoolboys, but also in our own case, however unprepared we be to state the rules. According to this doctrine, two extensionally equivalent systems of grammatical rules need not be equally correct. The right rules are the rules that the native speakers themselves have somehow implicitly in mind. It is the grammarian's task to find the right rules, in this sense. This added task is set by demanding not just any old recursive demarcation of the right totality of well-formed sentences, but rather a recursive demarcation of the right totality of trees. The trees used to be mere *ad hoc* scaffolding by the aid of which the grammarians, each in his own way, contrived to specify the objective totality of well-formed sentences. According to the new doctrine, the trees are themselves part of the objective linguistic reality to be specified.

We have all known that the native speaker must have acquired some recursive habit of mind, however unconscious, for building sentences in an essentially treelike way; this is evident from the infinitude of his repertoire. We can all go this far with Postal when, in his review of Dixon, he writes:

> The claim that there are linguistic rules is simply the claim that individuals know their language and have not learned each of its sentences separately.[1]

His word 'claim', even, seems ill suited to anything so uncontroversial. What is more than trivial, in the new doctrine that I speak of, is rather the following: it imputes to the natives an unconscious preference for one system of rules over another, equally unconscious, which is extensionally equivalent to it.

Are the unconscious rules the same, even, from one native speaker to the next? Let us grant that the generated infinitude of well-formed sentences is itself the same for two natives. There may then seem to be a presumption of sameness of generating rules — just because any appreciably different but extensionally equivalent system of rules is apt to be prohibitively complex and artificial. However, this suggestion gets us nowhere. Insofar as it is true, the grammarian can just follow his old plan, after all, of settling for ANY system of rules, naturally the simpler the better, that demarcates the right infinite set of well-formed sentences. If the new doctrine of the grammarian's added burden has any content, it owes it to there being appreciably unlike and still comparably manageable systems of rules for generating the same infinite totality of well-formed sentences. From experiences with axiom systems in mathematics, incidentally, we can easily believe in the existence of such alternatives. In my parable of the Danish schoolboys I have already assumed the existence of just such alternative systems for English; though it should of course be said, if we are to be fussy about the facts, that Jespersen's grammar and that of the

[1] Paul Postal, Review of Dixon, *Linguistic Science and Logic*, in *Language* 42 (1966), 84-93, specifically page 88.

old-fashioned textbooks really fall short of extensional equivalence at some points.

We see then that the new doctrine of the grammarian's added burden raises the problem of evidence whereby to decide, or conjecture, which of two extensionally equivalent systems of rules has been implicitly guiding the native's verbal behavior. Implicit guidance is a moot enough idea to demand some explicit methodology. If it is to make any sense to say that a native was implicitly guided by one system of rules and not by another extensionally equivalent system, this sense must link up somehow with the native's disposition to behave in observable ways in observable circumstances. These dispositions must go beyond the mere attesting to the well-formedness of strings, since extensionally equivalent rules are indistinguishable on that score. It could be a question of dispositions to make or accept certain transformations and not others; or certain inferences and not others.

Certainly I have no quarrel with dispositions. Nor do I question the notion of implicit and unconscious conformity to a rule, when this is merely a question of fitting. Bodies obey, in this sense, the law of falling bodies, and English speakers obey, in this sense, any and all of the extensionally equivalent systems of grammar that demarcate the right totality of well-formed English sentences. These are acceptably clear dispositions on the part of bodies and English speakers. The sticking point is this Chomskian midpoint between rules as merely fitting, on the one hand, and rules as real and overt guides on the other; Chomsky's intermediate notion of rules as heeded inarticulately. It is a point deserving of close methodological attention.

Ironically these same linguists have expressed doubt about the relatively clear and hundrum notion of a disposition to verbal behavior. Chomsky writes:

Presumably, a complex of dispositions is a structure that can be represented as a set of probabilities for utterances in certain definable "circumstances" ... But it must be recognized that the notion "probability of a sentence" is an entirely useless one ... On empirical grounds, the probability of my producing some given sentence of English ... is indistinguishable from the probability of my producing a given sentence of Japanese.[2]

I am puzzled by how quickly he turns his back on the crucial phrase "in certain definable 'circumstances'". Solubility in water would be a pretty idle disposition if defined in terms of the absolute probability of dissolving, without reference to the circumstance of being in water. Weight would be a pretty idle disposition if defined in terms of the ab-

---

[2] Noam Chomsky, "Quine's Empirical Assumptions", *Synthese* 19 (1968), 53-68, specifically p. 57.

solute probability of falling, without reference to the circumstance of removal of support. Verbal dispositions would be pretty idle if defined in terms of the absolute probability of utterance out of the blue. I, among others, have talked mainly of verbal dispositions in a very specific circumstance: a questionnaire circumstance, the circumstance of being offered a sentence for assent or dissent or indecision or bizarreness reaction.

Chomsky's nihilistic attitude toward dispositions is the more puzzling in that I find it again in the newspaper account of his recent lectures in England, despite an intervening answer of mine[3] to the earlier statement. I seem to detect an echo of it also in a footnote in Postal's review of Dixon.[4] This rejection of dispositions would be bewildering by itself. It is doubly so when contrasted with the rather uncritical doctrine just previously considered — the doctrine of unconscious preferences among extensionally equivalent grammars. I'd like to think that I am missing something.

Now some more remarks on the task of the grammarian. What I have said suggests, too simply, the following notion of the grammarians' classical task: that is the task of demarcating, recursively and in formal terms, the infinite totality of the well-formed strings of phonemes of the chosen language. It would seem from my remarks up to now that this is the basic or classical task, which, then, is added to if one insists further on some distinction between right and wrong rules, right and wrong trees subtending this same superficial mass of foliage. The trouble with thus stating the basic or classical task is that it presupposes some prior behavioral standard of what, in general, to aspire to include under the head of well-formed strings for a given community. What are the behavioral data of well-formedness? Passive observation of chance utterance is a beginning. The grammarian can extrapolate this corpus by analogical construction, and he can test these conjectures on an informant to see if they elicit only a manifestation of bewilderment. But of course the grammarian settles for no such criterion. Traditionally, at any rate, the grammarian has accepted a wide range of sentences as grammatical which an informant would reject as bizarre. I think of sentences such as Carnap's example, 'This stone is thinking about Vienna'.

A more realistic characterization of the grammarians' classical task is an open-ended one. He does not have a prior behavioral criterion of well-formedness; he just has some sufficient behavioral conditions. Strings heard from natives count as well-formed, at least provisionally. So do sentences which, when tried on an informant, elicit casual and unbewildered responses. What I then picture the grammarian as doing is to devise as simple a formal recursion as he can which takes in all these confirmably

3 W. V. Quine, "Replies", *Synthese* 19 (1968), 264-321, specifically p. 280.
4 Paul Postal, Review, note 12.

well-formed strings and excludes all strings that would bring really excessive bizarreness reactions. He rounds out and rounds off his data. Sometimes of course he will even reject a heard string as ill-formed, thus rejecting a datum, if he can appreciably simplify his system in so doing; but it would be regrettable to do much of this.

In this somewhat melancholy version of the grammarian's task, I have held Chomsky's doctrine in abeyance. Chomsky believes that the linguistic community itself has a sense of grammaticality which the grammarian can and should uncover; that grammaticality is not just the grammarian's rounding off of performance data. Up to a point I agree; the native's disposition to bizarreness reactions is an implicit sense of grammaticality of a sort. But Chomsky would of course credit the native with a full and precise sense of grammaticality, this being of a piece with the native's purported fund of tacit rules — the native's purported bias even among extensionally equivalent grammars. Now this doctrine is interesting, certainly, if true; let me only mention again the crying need, at this point, for explicitness of criteria and awareness of method.

An attitude that is closely linked to this doctrine is a readiness to recognize linguistic universals. The problem of evidence for a linguistic universal is insufficiently appreciated. Someone says, let us suppose, that the subject-predicate construction occurs in all the languages he has examined. Now of course all those languages have been translated, however forcibly, into English and *vice versa*. Point, then, in those languages to the translations of the English subject-predicate construction, and you establish the thesis; the subject-predicate construction occurs in all those languages. Or is it imposed by translation? What is the difference? Does the thesis say more than that basic English is translatable into all those languages? And what does even this latter claim amount to, pending some standard of faithfulness and objectivity of translation?

To make proper sense of the hypothesis that the subject-predicate construction is a linguistic universal, we need an unequivocal behavioral criterion of subject and predicate. It is not enough to say that if we take these and these as subjects and those and those as predicates then there are ways of so handling the rest of the language as to get general English translations. The trouble is that there are extensionally equivalent grammars. Timely reflection on method and evidence should tend to stifle much of the talk of linguistic universals.

Insofar, on the other hand, as one is prepared to impute to the native a specific and detailed though inarticulate grammatical system, one is apt to conceive of the notions of subject and predicate and similar notions as objective and as unequivocally apprehended by the native himself. To conceive of them thus is no more of a strain, surely, then to suppose that the native favors one of two extensionally equivalent grammars over another. In all this there is no folly, I feel sure, that conscientious reflection on method and evidence cannot cure; but the cure is apt to take time.

I think it is instructive, before leaving this topic, to fit an idea of Geach's into the picture. Besides singling out the well-formed strings, Geach argues, our grammar must distinguish between proper and spurious components of well-formed strings. One of this example of a spurious component was 'Plato was bald' in the context 'The philosopher whose most eminent pupil was Plato was bald'.[5] This demand is reminiscent of Chomsky's demand that the grammarian shows how to generate not only the well-formed strings but the right trees. Yet Geach is not committed to finding a bias in the native community between extensionally equivalent grammars. I expect Geach's demand is reconcilable even with the humdrum view of the grammarian's task as the task merely of generating the well-formed strings; for the thing that Geach demands, the marking of the proper components of each well-formed string, would doubtless be a valuable auxiliary to the rules for generating further well-formed strings. The same case can be made, more generally, for Chomsky's insistence that the grammarian's proper product is the whole tree rather than just the well-formed strings that it issues in. The argument is simply that rules for generating further well-formed strings (and trees) can then be formulated in terms of past trees and not just past well-formed strings. This is a strong argument, and it does not depend on any obscure doctrine to the effect that the natives tacitly prefer one system of grammar to another that is extensionally equivalent to it. It would be well to sort out these motives and benefits and see whether the obscure points of doctrine might not be cheerfully dropped.

Such an inquiry could, I suppose, convince us that there is indeed an unarticulated system of grammatical rules which is somehow implicit in the native mind in a way that an extensionally equivalent system is not. For me such a conviction would depend in part upon clarification of criteria.

To get down more nearly to cases, suppose again a language for which we have two extensionally equivalent systems of grammar; two extensionally equivalent recursive definitions of well-formed string. According to one of these systems, the immediate constituents of a certain sentence are 'AB' and 'C'; according to the other system they are 'A' and 'BC'. The enigmatic doctrine under consideration says that one of these analyses is right, and the other wrong, by tacit consensus of native speakers. How do we find out which is right?

An unimaginative suggestion might be: ask the natives. Ask them, in their language, whether the real constituents of 'ABC' are 'AB' and 'C'. Does this pose an embarrassing question of translation? Well, then let the native language be English. The essential problem remains; we do not really understand our own English question. We are looking for a criterion of what to count as the real or proper grammar, as over against an extensionally equivalent counterfeit. We are looking, in the specific case, for a test of what to count as the real or proper constituents of '*ABC*', as against counterfeit constituents. And now the test suggested is that we ask the native the very question which we do not understand ourselves: the very question for which we ourselves are seeking a test. We are moving in an oddly warped circle.

Better and more imaginative suggestions may be forthcoming for determining, less directly, what to regard as the real constituents of '*ABC*' from the point of view of tacit native grammar. I suggested some time ago that it could be a question of dispositions to make or accept certain transformations or inferences. But I want now to make use of the unimaginative suggestion as a point at which to take off on a tangent, leaving at last this whole question of a native bias toward one of two extensionally equivalent grammars.

The unimaginative suggestion was: ask the natives. The same question, and the same warped circle or one very much like it, are encountered from time to time in semantics. People like me challenge the notion of synonymy and ask for a criterion. What is synonymy? How do you tell whether two expressions are synonymous? Ask the natives. This essentially was Arne Næss's answer some decades ago, as I analyze it.[6] Moreover he suited the action to the word, disseminating questionnaires and claiming significantly uniform results. This was also essentially the answer more recently of Fodor and Katz,[7] as I analyze it; and I have sensed suggestions of it in Chomsky. Now a reason for pausing over this oddly warped circle is that an empirical investigation, however odd, that yields uniformities has a claim to attention. Grant for the sake of argument that Næss's questionnaire on synonymy yielded statistically significant uniformities; what do they mean? Do they show that Næss's laymen are pretty much alike on the score of their synonymy pairs, obscure though it be to us wherein synonymy consists? Do they show something also, or instead, about how Næss's laymen use the obscure word 'synonymy' or its paraphrases? Separation of these components presents an odd problem.

Essentially the same question is raised outside linguistics by work of Smith Stevens on subjective magnitudes.[8] For years he gathered subjective testimony of the pitch and loudness of sounds: whether this was twice as

---

[6] Arne Næss, *Interpretation and Preciseness* (Oslo, Dybwad, 1953).
[7] Jerry Fodor and Jerrold Katz, "The Structure of a Semantic Theory", *Language* 39 (1963), 170-210.
[8] S. S. Stevens, "On the Psychophysical Law", *Psychological Review* 64 (1957), 153-81.

high as that, or half again as loud as that. He plotted these findings against the physical frequencies and volumes, and came out with significant correlations — not linear, but logarithmic. Significant, but of what? Was it uniformity of error in his subjects' effort to estimate physical frequency and volume? Or was it uniformity of subjective experience, coupled with uniformity of meaning attached to enigmatically subjective expressions like 'twice as high' and 'half again as loud'? Or did the subjective experience vary from subject to subject, while the meaning attached to the subjective expressions varied in a compensatory way? The uniformities surprise me and I am prepared to find them instructive, but I am at a loss to sort them out. It is the same warped circle.

Turning back to synonymy, or to the semantical notion of analyticity which is interdefinable with synonymy, I might mention also a questionnaire experiment which avoided the warped circle. Apostel and others[9] in Geneva compiled various lists of sentences. One list contained only sentences that the experimenters regarded as analytic. Other lists had varied and irrelevant motifs. Subjects were given these lists, untitled, and were asked to sort various further sentences into the appropriate lists. The experiment, much the same as one proposed more recently by Katz,[10] sought evidence of a felt similarity among analytic sentences, without benefit of title. The outcome was reported as at best indecisive.

A controversy over semantical notions has simmered for twenty years. Some of us have criticized these notions as insufficiently empirical. Others have defended the notions without improving them. Their defense has been visibly motivated by a sense of the indispensability of these notions in various applications. We would have been spared much of this rearguard action if the defenders of semantical notions had taken the criticism of these notions to heart, and sought seriously to get along without them. In one, certainly, of its most conspicuous applications the notion of synonymy is not needed; namely, in the definition of the phoneme. According to the familiar definition, what shows that two sounds belong to distinct phonemes is that the substitution of one for the other changes the meaning of some expression. Surely, however, meaning enough for this purpose is afforded by the innocent and uncontroversial notion of stimulus meaning.

The behavioral definition of stimulus meaning is as follows, nearly enough: the stimulus meaning of a sentence, for a given speaker, is the class of all stimulatory situations in the presence of which he will assent to the sentence if queried. Stimulus meaning is at its best among observa-

---

[9] L. Apostel, W. Mays, A. Morf, and J. Piaget, *Les liaisons analytiques et synthétiques dans le comportement du sujet* (Paris, Presses Universitaires, 1937).
[10] Jerrold Katz, "Some Remarks on Quine on Analyticity", *Journal of Philosophy* **64** (1967), 36-52.

tion sentences. The behavioral definition of an observation sentence is as follows: an observation sentence is a sentence whose stimulus meaning is the same for just about all speakers of the language. Examples: 'It is raining', 'This is red', 'This is a rabbit'.

Sameness of stimulus meaning is no appreciable approximation to the general notion of synonymy to which semantics has aspired. Within observation sentences, however, sameness of stimulus meaning is synonymy enough. For distinguishing phonemes, consequently, it is enough; for surely, if two sounds belong to distinct phonemes, the meaning of some observation sentences will be changed by the substitution.

For that matter, phonemes can also no doubt be distinguished by appealing merely to well-formedness of expressions; by appealing, that is, to the capacity of a string of sounds to occur in the native stream of speech. Presumably, if two sounds belong to distinct phonemes, the substitution will render some coherent string of sounds incoherent. This way of defining the phoneme was proposed by Anders Wedberg,[11] and was already implicit, I think, in Zellig Harris. I wanted to bring in the definition in terms of stimulus meaning, however, as an example of how stimulus meaning can sometimes do the work that is desired of meaning or synonymy.

I turn, for the remainder of my remarks, to the notion of deep structure and its relation to logical analysis. Take, first, logical analysis. What do we do when we paraphrase a sentence by introducing logical symbols for truth functions and quantifiers? In principle it is the same as when in highschool algebra we were given some data about rowing up and down a river; we paraphrased the data into algebraic equations, with a view to solving these for the speech of the river. In principle it is the same also as programming a computer.

I find the phrase 'logical analysis' misleading, in its suggestion that we are exposing a logical structure that lay hidden in the sentence all along. This conception I find both obscure and idle. When we move from verbal sentences to logical formulas we are merely retreating to a notion that has certain technical advantages, algorithmic and conceptual. I mentioned the analogy of the computer; but essentially the same thing is happening in a more moderate way when in natural history we switch to the Latin binominals for genera and species, or when in relativity physics we paraphrase our temporal references into a spatial idiom using four dimensions. No one wants to say that the binominals of Linnæus or the fourth dimension of Einstein or the binary code of the computer were somehow implicit in ordinary language; and I have seen no more reason to so regard the quantifiers and truth functions.

[11] Anders Wedberg, "On the Principles of Phonemic Analysis", *Ajatus* 26 (1964), 235-53.

What now of deep structure? If we believe that native speakers have a detailed though inarticulate grammatical system, specific even as between extensionally equivalent systems, then certainly we believe that deep structure, whatever there may be of it, is there to be uncovered. How to tell whether we are getting it right, whether we are matching the inarticulate native analysis or just carving out an extensional equivalent, is a methodological question that I have mentioned already.

If on the contrary we hold every grammar to be as authentic as every extensionally equivalent grammar, and to be preferred only for its simplicity and convenience, then deep structure loses its objectivity but need not lose its place. Deep structure, and the transformations to and from it, might still qualify as auxiliaries to the simplest and most convenient system we know for demarcating the class of well-formed string. They would stay on in this role just as the trees would stay on, and Geach's discrimination of proper and improper ingredients.

Thus conceived, the grammarian's deep structure is similar in a way to logical structure. Both are paraphrases of sentences of ordinary language; both are paraphrases that we resort to for certain purposes of technical convenience. But the purposes are not the same. The grammarian's purpose is to put the sentence into a form that can be generated by a grammatical tree in the most efficient way. The logician's purpose is to put the sentence into a form that admits most efficiently of logical calculation, or shows its implications and conceptual affinities most perspicuously, obviating fallacy and paradox.

These different purposes, the grammarian's and the logician's, are not in general best served by the same paraphrases; and for this reason the grammarian's deep structure is not to be identified with logical structure, suggestive though the one may be for the other. I have two major examples in mind to bring out the divergence.

One example is the elimination of singular terms other than variables. Let 'a' represent such a singular term — perhaps a proper name, perhaps a complex singular term — and let 'Fa' represent a sentence containing it. We can paraphrase 'Fa', to begin with, as '$(\exists x)(Fx \cdot a = x)$'. In this way all singular terms, other than simple variables such as the 'x' here, can be confined to one specific manner of occurrence: occurrence to the left of '$=$'. Then, as a next step, we can reckon this identity sign to the singular term as an invariable suffix, thus re-parsing the singular term as a general term or predicate.

The advantages of this transformation are specific and limited. Laws of logic become simplified, through not having to provide for the instantiation of quantifications by terms other than variables. The simplification is the greater for the fact that the instantiations thus avoided were ones that depended awkwardly on existence assumptions. Certain gains in philosophical clarity ensue also. Variables, rather than names, come to be seen as the primary avenue of reference. Little puzzles about names that fail to name anything are swept aside.

This elimination of singular terms is not all good, however, even for logic and mathematics. Inference moves faster when we can instantiate quantifications directly by names and complex singular terms, rather than working through the variables and paraphrases. And complex singular terms are in practice vital for algebraic technique. An algebraist who was not free to substitute complex expressions directly for variables, or to substitute one side of a complex equality directly for the other, would soon give up.

The important point thus emerges that logical analysis itself — better, logical paraphrase — may go one way or another depending on one's specific logical purpose. The image of exposing an already present logical structure by analysis is a poor one. And when our interest turns to English grammar, again we are bound to find that the elimination of singular terms is to no purpose. Surely it yields no deep structure that would help to simplify an account of English grammar. Thus take the distinction between the referential and the non-referential use of singular terms. Work of Geach[12] and Strawson[13] suggests that this distinction is vital to an appreciation of English; but the logical paraphrase obliterates it utterly.

In my view the logical structure and the deep structure, or let me say the logician's paraphrases and the grammarian's paraphrase, differ not in kind but in detail and purpose. They differ in the same sort of way that the logician's two paraphrases differ from each other: one the austere and pellucid paraphrase containing no singular terms but variables, and the other the algorithmically efficient paraphrase bristling with complex singular terms.

The elimination of singular terms was one example of the difference between paraphrasing for logic and paraphrasing for grammar. Now the other example I have in mind is the treatment of time as a fourth dimension. A while ago I referred this to physics, but it is vital equally for logic and philosophy. A logic of tense is a towering triviality which we have no excuse to put up with if our concern is merely with the scientific use of language rather than with the scientific study of it. We program language into the simple neo-classical logic of truth functions and quantifiers, by eliminating tense and treating times on a par with places. The resulting simplification of formal logic may be sensed from this example, which I have used before: George V married Queen Mary; Queen Mary is a

[12] Peter Geach, *Reference and Generality* (Ithaca, N Y., Cornell University Press, 1962).
[13] P. F. Strawson, "Singular Terms and Predication", *Synthese* 19 (1968), 97-117.

widow; therefore George V married a widow. We cease to have to provide against this kind of thing, among others.

Philosophical clarification ensues as well. Thus consider the following puzzles. How can things be related that do not coexist at any one time? How can a variable range now over things that no longer exist? or range ever over things that never coexist? How can a class have members that never coexist? How can a class, which is an abstract object, be said to change, as it must when its members change or cease to exist? We make a clean sweep of all such puzzles by dropping tense and treating all past, present, and future bodies as four-dimensional substances tenselessly scattered about in spacetime.

This is a paraphrase which, we see, works wonders for logic, philosophy, and physics as well, but presumably is not wanted for English grammar. A deep structure without tense seems unpromising, at any rate, as a means of simplifying a grammatical account of an Indo-European language. Here again, evidently, is a wide divergence between the structure that the logician is after and what the grammarian wants under the head of deep structure. And yet, reading Postal's typescript "Coreferentiality and physical objects', I begin to wonder whether the four-dimensional view might be useful sometimes in grammar too.

My previous example, the elimination of singular terms, spoke for pluralism not just as between logical structure and grammatical deep structure, but within logical structure; one logical paraphrase served one logical purpose, another another. Perhaps now there is a case also for pluralism within grammatical deep structure: one paraphrase might serve one grammatical purpose, another. A paraphrase into the tenseless idiom of four dimensions might play an auxiliary role in connection with some grammatical twists, while a different deep structure, retaining tense, might still be exploited for other grammatical ends. So let me conclude with a plea against absolutism.

P. F. Strawson

GRAMMAR AND PHILOSOPHY[1]

1. One who speaks his native language fluently and correctly has acquired over a period of time that mastery of the language which he now has. During this period he was exposed, no doubt, to many sentences produced by others and to some correction of sentences he produced himself. But his mastery of the language does not consist merely in his being able to reproduce the sentences produced by others and, in their corrected forms, the sentences earlier produced by himself. It consists in his being able also to produce indefinitely many new sentences, knowing what they mean, and in being able to understand indefinitely many new sentences which are produced to him. It consists also in his being able to distinguish between sentences of his language which are fully 'correct' and literally significant sentences — however elaborate or stylistically unusual they may be — and sentences which deviate, in various ways or degrees, from full 'correctness' or literal significance; and perhaps to remark, with more or less explicitness, on how the sentences which deviate from correctness do so deviate.

It seems entirely reasonable to say that the possession, on the part of the fluent and correct speaker of a language, of these abilities to construct,

Reprinted from: G. Harman and D. Davidson (eds.), *Semantics of Natural Language* (Dordrecht, Reidel, 1972), 455-72.
[1] It will be obvious to any auditor of Professor Chomsky's John Locke lectures, delivered in Oxford this summer after the present paper was written, that he has moved from, or modified, some of the positions here attributed to him on the basis of his publications. However, with occasional qualifications, I have allowed the attributions to stand; the written, checkable word provides a firmer basis for discussion than the spoken, uncheckable word.

interpret and criticize sentences implies the existence of a set or system of rules which the speaker has, in some sense, mastered. This does not imply that he consciously constructs or interprets sentences by the light of any such rules, nor that he could even begin to formulate such rules with any approach to full explicitness or to the maximum of system. Such rules may 'govern' his exercise of his abilities of sentence-construction and interpretation, and even of sentence-criticism, without his approaching full consciousness of such rules as governing such exercise. We should not expect of the fluent and correct speaker of a language, just because he is one, that he can state the theory of his practice.

Nevertheless the practice is there. And so it should be possible, for those who are minded to do so, to extract the theory and to state it with full explicitness and the maximum of system. This is the aim which the new grammarians set themselves, the exponents of transformational generative grammar. A fully explicit and maximally systematic statement of the rules which 'govern' the fluent speaker's exercise of his capacities will supply the THEORY of that speaker's language. Such a theory may be called, in an extended sense of the word, a GRAMMAR of the language. It will contain three parts or components: a syntactic part; a semantic part; and a phonological part. Very roughly, and rather misleadingly, these parts may be said to be concerned respectively with structure, with sense and with sound; rather misleadingly, in so far as structure is itself quite largely determinant of sense. It is, on the whole, the syntactic or structural part which has received the most emphasis and aroused the most interest in the work of the transformational grammarians.

We are familiar, from traditional grammar, with some of the terms which are used in the new grammar to express facts about the structure of sentences. We are familiar, that is to say, with such grammatical CLASS- or CATEGORY-names as those of noun and noun-phrase, verb, preposition, adverb and adjective; and with the names of such grammatical RELATIONS as those of subject of sentence, subject of verb, object of verb, modifier of subject, modifier of verb and so on. Quite obviously a grasp of facts about structure, about grammatical relation in a sentence, enters into our understanding of sentences. To appreciate the difference in sense between 'John loves Mary' and 'Mary loves John' or between 'The old man sings a song' and 'The man sings an old song' IS to grasp those structural facts which are expressed in the terminology of grammar by saying that 'John' is the subject and 'Mary' the object of the verb in the first sentence and vice versa in the second or that the adjective 'old' stands in attributive combination with 'man' in the third sentence and with 'song' in the fourth. In the kind of grammatical analysis which we do (or did) at school, we set out, in a prescribed form, facts of this kind about the grammatical relations which hold within the sentences we analyse. To that extent we set out their structure. Of course we may be rather bad at this exercise while perfectly well appreciating the differences in sense between such sentences; which illustrates merely the point that grasp of structure is not the same thing as ability to state explicitly what is grasped.

Grammatical structure, then, as well as the senses of individual words, is determinant of the sense or semantic interpretation of sentences. The central thesis of the transformational grammarians, the step which conditions the whole character of their theories, is the insistence that any adequate grammatical theory must recognize a distinction between the superficial syntactic structure of a sentence and its basic structure, between its deep grammar and its surface grammar. The motivation of this distinction goes very deep indeed, as we shall see hereafter. But we can easily be induced to see reason for it by noting, for example, that two sentences may be very similar in their superficial syntactic structure while, so to speak, the structure of their sense is very different; that in our understanding of such sentences we allow for differences in the grammatical relations of their elements which are simply not marked in the sentences as they stand. Chomsky gives as an example of this the pair of sentences, 'They persuaded John to leave' and 'They expected John to leave'. In our understanding of these sentences 'John' has a subject-like relation to the verb 'leave' in both; but while it also has an object-like relation to the main verb ('persuaded') of the first sentence, it has no such relation to the main verb ('expected') of the second. Thus we understand the elements of the sentences as differently related in the two cases; but there is no MANIFEST structural difference between the sentences as they stand, corresponding to this understood difference. Again, a perhaps more striking way of making the distinction between deep and surface structure acceptable is to point to certain syntactically or structurally ambiguous sentences such as — to adapt an older example — 'The principal thing in his life was the love of women'. Though the ambiguity might well be removed by the context, the sentence, as it stands, leaves us uncertain as to whether it is his loving women or women loving him that is in question. Now both the unmanifest structural differences exemplified in the first kind of case and the syntactic ambiguities exemplified in the second would, it is held, be clearly and systematically exhibited in the representation of the deep, as opposed to the surface, structure of sentences. For EVERY syntactic or structural relation between sentence-elements would be represented with total explicitness. A grammar of the desired kind will therefore assign at least two different deep structures to a syntactically ambiguous sentence, and will assign patently different deep structures to sentences which have a merely superficial identity of structure.

Looking for a moment beyond the confines of a single language, we may glimpse another and older kind of motivation for such a distinction. Just as surface similarity may conceal deep difference, so surface difference may conceal deep identity. Given two sentences in different languages, the one an accurate and adequate translation of the other, we may easily find grammatical constructions in the one which are absent in the other. But may we not want to say that the FUNDAMENTAL structural relationships thus differently displayed on the surface are exactly the same in both? The question how far we are prepared to press this thought has a bearing on the question whether we are prepared to entertain, and, if so, how we are prepared to use, the notion of a universal grammar. Evidently such a thought cannot be without interest for philosophers.

But this is to anticipate. Let us turn now to the question how facts about structure are actually presented by the transformational grammarians. Any answer I can give to this question in the present context must necessarily be incomplete and grossly simplified; but not, I hope, misleadingly so in relation to the further questions I wish to raise.

The syntactic component, then, of a grammar or theory of a language consists of a system of rules, permissive or mandatory, which operate, finally, on certain elements. These terminal materials are to be thought of as the minimal meaning units of the language, the atoms to be structured, as it were, by the syntax of the language. Chomsky calls these items formatives. No easy identification of formatives with any familiar idea is possible; but we need not concern ourselves here with their exact nature. Formatives are of two kinds, lexical and non-lexical. The first we may think of as corresponding to those general terms or proper names of the language of which the meaning is not in any way syntactically derived — such as the verbs 'sing' or 'love', the adjective 'red', the name 'Mary'. The latter are a more heterogeneous bunch and will include, for example, a formative named *Past*, for Past Tense.

The rules which operate, finally, on these materials are such that, for any sentence of the language, there is a path through the application of these rules the following of which path will yield us a complete exhibition both of the deep structure and of the surface structure of that sentence. This must not be misunderstood. It means no more than it says. It does not mean, for example, that the grammar provides us with a mechanical procedure for FINDING the deep structure of an antecedently given sentence or for PRODUCING a given sentence.[2] It means only that, in a complete grammar of the kind in question, there IS some path through the rules which will yield these results. From what has already been said it will be clear that the rules are themselves of two kinds; those which yield deep structures and those which transform these into surface struc-

[2] See Chomsky, *Aspects of the Theory of Syntax*, 141.

tures. With rules of the latter kind I shall not be much concerned. But I must say a little more about deep structure rules or rules of the base.

The terms in which the fundamental type of base-rules are framed have reassuring familiarity. They are the names of grammatical CLASSES or CATEGORIES, such as Sentence, Noun-Phrase, Predicate-Phrase, Noun, Verb, Adjective, Verbal Auxiliary, Prepositional Phrase etc. The results of applying the rules can be most easily represented by a kind of inverted tree-structure, in producing which we start from the basic symbol S (for Sentence) and branch out into constituent grammatical categories, then into constituents of those constituents and so on until we reach a point at which all the terminal category names are such that we can enter formatives directly under them. The rules permit the production of very simple diagrams of this kind — such as the diagram, say, for 'John smiled' — and, again, of diagrams of any degree of complexity. For they permit the re-introduction of the symbol S under a suitable constituent structure heading, such as noun-phrase, where it acts, in turn, as the head of another, subordinate branching diagram. The deep or base structure diagram of some actual sentence of the language is completed when, under the terminal category headings are entered appropriate formatives, the resulting string or sequence of formatives constituting the terminal sequence of the structure. Thus the non-lexical formative *Past* can be entered under the category heading *Verbal Auxiliary*. Lexical formatives are listed in a lexicon which assigns them to lexical categories like Noun, Verb and Adjective.

From a completed diagram of this kind, setting out a terminal sequence together with the pattern of its derivation, we can read off, with total explicitness, all those facts of grammatical structure which bear on the interpretation of the sentence whose deep structure it represents. The reason why we can do so — and this is a point of absolutely central importance — is that all those syntactical RELATIONS which, as we already know, are so largely determinant of the sense (or semantic interpretation) of sentences are DEFINED in terms of the grammatical CATEGORIES or CLASSES and their permitted concatenations in deep structure diagrams. Chomsky is quite explicit on this important point. If we set aside the lexicon, the primary function of the rules of the base so far described is, he says, "that of defining the grammatical relations that are expressed in the deep structure and that therefore determine the semantic interpretation of a sentence".[3] Here, I repeat, we have a point of central importance. Most of the detail of what I have been saying can be safely forgotten if this is remembered.

The syntactic component of the theory, then, yields us both deep and surface structures of sentences. Now a word — no more — about their

[3] Chomsky, *Aspects*, 99. See also pp. 69, 117, 120, 141.

relations to the remaining components, the semantic and the phonological. The rules of the phonological component of the theory are applied to surface structures to yield the actual sound-rendering of a sentence. The information contained in the semantic component about the meanings of individual lexical items is supposed to combine with the structural information contained in the deep structure diagram to determine the full semantic interpretation of the sentence.[4]

2. So much by way of a sketch of the type of theory of a language envisaged by some transformational grammarians. Now I began this paper by summarising the linguistic ability of an ideally fluent and correct speaker of a language as the ability to understand, produce and criticize indefinitely many new sentences of his language. The theorists of transformational grammar, at least in their more cautious moments, do not claim that the possession of these linguistic abilities by an idealised speaker-hearer can be completely and adequately explained simply by crediting him with a 'tacit mastery' — or even by crediting him with an 'internal representation' — of such a system of rules as such a theory would provide. They concede, or, rather, insist, that more is required for an adequate explanation. Let us, for the moment, postpone consideration of the question how the grammarians themselves think the provision of such a theory needs supplementing if the demand for adequate explanation is to be met; and let us consider, instead, a condition in respect of which a non-specialist critic might find that such a theory fell short of HIS demands for understanding. I shall name this the condition of perspicuousness.

Here we must turn once more to the consideration of the deep structures of sentences, so decisive, as Chomsky says, for their semantic interpretation. Deep structures are generated by the base rules of the syntactic component. If we set aside that part of the base (including the lexicon) which allows the completion of deep structures with terminal sequences, we are left essentially with the branching rules which introduce grammatical categories (Noun-Phrase, Verb, Prepositional Phrase, etc.) in various permitted concatenations. As remarked, Chomsky says that the importance of these rules and of the grammatical categories which they introduce consists primarily in the fact that they supply the basis for the definition of those grammatical RELATIONS which, as far as structural con-

---

[4] This is one important point on which Chomsky has modified his views. He now allows that surface structure also may bear on semantic interpretation; so that two sentences with exactly the same deep structure diagram may nevertheless differ in meaning, the difference appearing only at the level of the transformations which yield surface structure. However, he adheres to his original view as regards those aspects of semantic interpretation which depend on the GRAMMATICAL RELATIONS; and it is with these that the present paper is concerned.

siderations go, are of decisive, though not exclusive, importance for the semantic interpretation of sentences. This is why the grammatical categories and the rules framed in terms of them MATTER. They matter because together they provide the terms in which the grammatical relations (subject-of, predicate-of, object-of, modifier-of etc.) can be defined for the given language. And these relations matter because of their decisive bearing on the semantic interpretation of sentences. But so far, if we keep the lexicon on one side, the grammar gives us no information about the significance of these grammatical relations independent of their definition in terms of the grammatical categories. The symbols for the grammatical categories, and the rules for framing structure diagrams containing them, are said to point forward to the grammatical relations, so important for understanding sentences; but the names of the grammatical relations point back, by definition, to the symbols for the grammatical categories and their arrangement; and, since the grammar is a fully explicit statement of rules, we must not suppose ourselves equipped with ANY understanding of EITHER of these kinds of term except such as is given by the explicit grammar itself.

Of course the grammar, or theory of the language, as a whole, provides a way out of this circle of technical terms. It provides a way out because it contains a lexicon which, in its syntactic part, assigns lexical formatives to grammatical categories; and because it contains a semantic component which we may think of as containing all the remaining information about elements of the language which anyone must possess who understands the language. Now it is true, as critics have urged and grammarians acknowledged, that no satisfactory theoretical account has yet been given of the semantic component. But this point, thus generally stated, is not one I wish to labour. Let us simply assume that grasp of the rules of the theory, including grasp of the semantic component, would carry with it a complete grasp of the sense of all formatives, lexical and non-lexical alike. Then, since the grammar assigns individual formatives to grammatical categories, we see that the grammar provides for the immediate linking of the senses of formatives with grammatical categories; and hence it provides, mediately, for the linking of the senses of formatives with possible grammatical relations in deep structure, the relations which help to determine the sense of sentences. But — and this is the point on which my criticisms bear — of this apparently crucial set of connexions there is, in the grammar, no general theory whatever. There is simply the list of items in the lexicon without any account of general principles determining the assignment of those items to grammatical categories. Yet it is above all of this set of connexions that we might expect a general theory if we hoped that the grammar might satisfy the condition of perspicuousness.

It is worth while dwelling once more on the reasons why we might expect this. We are to remember that the primary importance of the grammatical categories and their permitted orderings in the deep structures of a language lies in the fact that they provide the terms in which the underlying grammatical functions and relations of elements in sentences can be defined — for the given language. And these functions and relations are functions and relations which any ordinary speaker of the language grasps implicitly in understanding the sentences he hears and produces. He grasps them implicitly, having — we may suppose — no explicit training in the grammar. Now how is his implicit grasp of these functions and relations connected with his knowledge of the meaning of the elements of his language? It is not to be supposed that his knowledge of the meaning of these elements is something quite separate from his grasp of the power of these elements to figure in those grammatical functions and in those grammatical relations which he must have an implicit grasp of in order to understand the sense of the sentences he hears and produces. His grasp of the meanings of the elements of the language, it seems, must include at least some grasp of their potential roles in the grammatical relations of base structures. Suppose, then, there are intrinsic and general connexions between types of element-meaning and potentialities of grammatical role in deep, or base, structure. In stating the principles of such connexion, we should, obviously, be linking semantic and syntactic considerations. Might we not also be laying the foundations, or some part of the foundations, of a general theory of grammar? In any case, a grammar which rested on, or incorporated, such principles would have a better claim than one which did not, to satisfy the condition of perspicuousness.

3. Thus, at least, we might reason. A little later I shall have to refine on this notion of perspicuousness. First, let us return, briefly, to Chomsky. As I have already hinted, he himself is the first to acknowledge that what he calls a "DESCRIPTIVELY adequate" generative grammar of a language — such a theory as I described, in barest outline, in section 1 of this paper — would not by itself satisfy the condition of EXPLANATORY adequacy. To satisfy this condition we should need, he says, a theory of linguistic universals characteristic of human language in general; and we should need to show that this theory was related in a certain way to our descriptively adequate grammar, picking it out, as it were, from other possible grammars consistent with the "primary linguistic data". Now regarding these requirements we may be disposed to ask two questions. First, would their fulfilment finally yield a COMPLETE explanation of the idealised hearer-speaker's possession of his linguistic abilities — including it must be remembered, his ability to UNDERSTAND the indefinitely many sentences of the language? And, second, would their fulfilment involve —

besides, doubtless, much else — the linking of semantic and syntactic considerations in somewhat the way just alluded to?

To neither question is the official answer entirely clear. But, as regards the first question, we may suppose that the fulfilment of the stated requirements would take us at least nearer to a complete explanation of the speaker-hearer's abilities.[5] And, in view of this, we may be surprised by the character of Chomsky's answer to the second question. For though he admits that "there is no reason to rule out *a priori*" the possibility that "substantive characterizations" of "the universal vocabulary from which grammatical descriptions are constructed" might ultimately have to refer "to semantic concepts of one sort or another",[6] yet his references to any such possibility are markedly cool. Thus he speaks of "vague and unsupported assertions about the 'semantic basis for syntax'" which "make no contribution to the understanding of these questions."[7] Vague and unsupported assertions, of course, do not make much of a contribution to the understanding of anything. But if a general direction of inquiry seems promising, if indeed one can see no alternative to it, one should surely seek in that direction for assertions which are not vague and which one can support.

Chomsky himself remarks that it would be natural to expect that the ultimate framework for the characterization of the universal categories of grammar should be found in some features of the base. He has in mind what he calls FORMAL features of the base. But the base includes the lexicon. And the lexicon includes lists of items capable of being entered directly under lexical category-headings in base structures. These items will be far less numerous than the entries in an ordinary dictionary of the language. For example, they will not include, in the category of nouns, formatives corresponding to our ordinary abstract nouns, 'sincerity' and 'destruction'; 'sincerity' and 'destruction' appear in sentences only as a result of a nominalising transformation.[8] Would it not seem very natural,

---

[5] Leaving, one must suppose, a certain amount of work for psychologists and physiologists still to do.

[6] Chomsky, *Aspects*, 116-17.

[7] Chomsky, *Aspects*, 78.

[8] It appears from the John Locke lectures that Chomsky no longer holds (or holds for all cases) that such abstract nouns appear as the result of nominalising transformation. Rather, he holds that there are underlying semantic or lexical elements, in themselves neither nominal nor, e.g. verbal or adjectival, but capable of appearing in deep structures in either rôle. Nevertheless, there would appear to be grounds for awarding SOME KIND of syntactical primacy to the verbal, or adjectival, over the nominal, rôle in such cases; and such an award will serve my present purpose, in whatever theoretical terms it is ultimately to be understood. My own guess, for what it is worth, is in line with Chomsky's later position, in so far as I see no reason why we should not, and much reason why we should, have a use for a notion of NOMINALISATION which does not depend on that of TRANSFORMATION.

then, to survey the restricted list of items in the lexicon with a certain question in mind: viz. what semantical types of items are to be found in the lexicon, such that they can combine into sentences of which the deep structure requires minimum transformation to yield surface structure? And what correlations can be found between the semantical types of those items and the grammatical or syntactic categories to which they are there assigned? Or consider a more specific question. The grammatical category, Sentence, is basically divided, in the models of transformational grammar put forward by Chomsky, into Noun-Phrase and Predicate-Phrase, and this division immediately yields us, by definition, for basic structures, the relations of subject and predicate of a sentence. This point seems to bring us to the very brink of the question: What general semantic types of expression qualify for the basic subject- and predicate-rôles in simplest sentences? and why? An answer to this question, it might seem, could very well be at least a beginning towards a perspicuous characterization of this apparently fundamental grammatical relation; helping us, e.g. to understand its extension, via nominalisations, to other, less simple cases. Yet no move is made towards confronting these questions, either in the more general or a more specific form.

4. I have said that it would seem natural enough, given their ultimate theoretical concerns, for transformational grammarians to move in the direction I have indicated. Yet, on the other hand, there are reasons why it is natural that they should not. More than this: there are reasons why the questions I have just indicated as natural, though they are in the right spirit, are not yet in the right form. It is probably true that if genuinely explanatory foundations are to be provided for grammar, an attempt must be made to close the explanation-gap between semantico-logical features on the one hand and syntactic classifications and relations on the other. It is probably false that this attempt is best undertaken by first framing questions directly in terms of traditional syntactic categories and relations, such as those of noun and verb, object of the verb, etc. Let me first try to explain the grammarians' reluctance to undertake the necessary enterprise before explaining why the form of the enterprise is not to be so simply understood. The two points are closely, and subtly, interconnected.

First, let us recall that just as, on the one hand, the transformational grammarians tend to be severe critics of the philosophers of ordinary language for being insufficiently systematic, so, on the other, they are no less severe critics of those philosophers of language who derive their inspiration from formal logic and practise, or advocate, the construction of ideal languages; and their criticism of these last is that, though they are indeed systematic, they are insufficiently empirical.[9] For though the

9 See, for example, on both points, Katz, *Philosophy of Language*, Ch. 3.

approach of the transformational grammarians is in one way highly abstract and theoretical, it is in another way thoroughly empirical. They are empirical linguists, grammarians — though in aspiration generalising grammarians — of actually given languages, inclined to be suspicious of theoretical notions except in so far as they can be used in THE CONSTRUCTION OF SYSTEMS, OR MECHANISMS, OF RULES which will yield what is actually found in accepted sentences and will regularly mark the deviations in deviant ones. Thus, though it is characteristic of the transformational grammarian that he is willing to view the thought of a universal grammar, a general theory of language, with favour, yet he would — the example of Chomsky suggests — prefer to view the concepts which enter into such a theory as capable of being elucidated entirely in terms of the contribution they make to such working rule-mechanisms. Any other view of them is likely to be, from the grammarian's point of view, too vague and intuitive to satisfy his ideal of empirical clarity.

Thus the grammarian is apt to be inhibited from adopting an approach which the philosopher may be more ready to adopt, and which perhaps must be adopted if truly explanatory foundations are to be provided for grammar. Certain of the fundamental ideas of the transformational grammarians — the distinction between deep and surface structures, the notion of systematic transformational relations between them, the hint of a suggestion that the basic forms of functional relation are to be found in the simplest forms of deep structures — these will strike a responsive chord in the breast of any philosopher who has tried to reach through surface similarities of grammatical form to the semantico-logical differences which lie below them; that is, of any philosopher whatever. But when the question of explanatory foundations for grammar is raised against this background of shared ideas, the philosopher's response, it seems to me, should, at least at first, be to make the maximum use of his disreputable liberty from empirical constraints. Thus he need not be at all concerned, at least to begin with, with the actual formal arrangements by means of which functional relations are actually represented, whether in the base or at any other level, in a particular language. He will have, as the grammarian has, a conception of meaning-elements (the atoms to be structured) on the one hand; and of semantically significant modes of combination of them (syntactical relations) on the other. But he will be prepared from the start to use a vocabulary which is overtly semantic or, in a broad sense, logical, for the classification of elements, abstractly conceived; and this vocabulary will from the start stand in perspicuous connexion with his vocabulary of modes of combination or grammatical relations. Given these perspicuous connexions, he may next consider possible formal arrangements by means of which the combining functions might be discharged; and may finally relate these theoretical models of language to what is actually found in empirically given languages.

Here, then, is a programme for research in non-empirical linguistics, which may perhaps in the end pay empirical dividends. The procedure to be followed in pursuing such a programme will in some ways be reminiscent of the setting up of ideal languages by the logicians; but the purpose will be less restricted than that of the logicians. Quine says somewhere: don't expose more structure than you need expose. But the non-empirical grammarian will be concerned with every point at which structure is needed to contribute to overall meaning. Structure must be exposed at every point and understood at every point.

To say now a little more about details of procedure. Practically speaking it is inevitable that one should start with relatively simple models of language-types and work up to more complex ones. The vital distinction to be observed throughout is that between the intrinsic or essential grammar of a language-type and the alternative or variable grammars of that language-type. A language-type is defined by specifying (1) the semantic or broadly logical type of meaning-elements it contains and (2) the types of significant combinations into which they can enter to form sentences. These specifications determine *a priori* the essential grammar of the language-type, on the assumption that each sentence, at least in the base, must permit of a syntactically unambiguous reading. The rules of essential grammar will require that all combinations must somehow or other be indicated and, when necessary, differentiated; that if, e.g. a sentence contains a number of elements which could be significantly clustered into different attributive groupings, then it must somehow be indicated which elements are to be taken with which; or, again, that in the case of an element signifying a non-symmetrical relation in combination with elements or clusters signifying its terms, the ordering of the term-signifying elements or clusters must somehow be indicated. These are requirements of essential grammar. But the essential grammar of a language-type in no way stipulates HOW such requirements are to be fulfilled. There lies open a choice among different ways of using such various formal devices as those of, e.g. element-positioning, inflection, affixing or the use of special syntactic markers. In choosing one among various possible sets of formal arrangements adequate to the requirements of essential grammar, we should be choosing one of the possible variable or alternative grammars for the language-type in question. When such a choice is made and codified, we have a complete and completely perspicuous grammar (or form of grammar) for that language-type; at the cost, of course, of not having the grammar of an actual language at all, but only of an ideally simplified type of language.

If we press these researches even a little way, we find that we need quite an elaborate vocabulary, or set of interrelated vocabularies, of theoretical notions. Thus we need, first, what might be called an onto-logical vocabulary. We need, second, a semantic vocabulary, or vocabulary for naming semantic types of elements and even for describing individual elements (elements being throughout, as already said, rather abstractly conceived). Third, we need a functional vocabulary for naming the kinds of combination or relation into which elements may enter in sentences and the kinds of rôle which elements or combinations of elements may play in sentences. Fourth, and finally, we need a vocabulary of formal devices. Between, and within, the first three vocabularies, or batteries of notions, there are close interrelations and dependences. The fourth vocabulary stands rather apart from the rest in that we need to invoke it only when we move from essential to variable grammar. Specimen items belonging to the fourth vocabulary I have already mentioned, in referring to element-positioning, inflection, etc. Specimen items belonging to the ontological vocabulary might include space, time, particular continuant, situation, general character or relation; and some sub-classifications of these last, as, perhaps, of general characters into sorts, states, actions, properties, and of relations into, at least, sym-metrical and non-symmetrical. Readiness to employ some such notions as these is inseparable from the use of the functional and semantic vocabularies. The functional notions must include those of major linkage of major sentence-parts into sentences and, for any language-type which is not of an idiotic simplicity, the notion of minor linkage of elements into sentence-parts. Major and minor linkages alike will have to be further distinguished into kinds, as also will the rôles which elements or parts may play, and the different relations in which they may stand to each other, inside these different combinations. The internal relations, the interlockings and overlappings of the functional vocabulary are most complex, and I shall not attempt to illustrate them here. The semantic vocabulary for a fairly restricted language-type might include three main classes of elements: (1) proper names for continuant particulars; (2) elements signifying general characters and relations; and (3) deictic elements. At least the second and third classes would be subdivided for a language-type of any richness, the second on lines already indicated in the ontological vocabulary, the third perhaps into elements for tempo-ral deixis, for spatial deixis, for interlocutory deixis and for what might be called merely contextual deixis.

Now it will be noted that in listing these specimen items from the inter-related vocabularies of essential grammar, I have made no mention of of any of the traditional syntactic categories of noun, verb, adjective, preposition, etc. And this is no accident of selection or omission. The more complex the language-type, the more complex, certainly, will be the interrelated vocabularies necessary to specify the type and to state, as consequences of the specification, the requirements of its essential grammar. But, however complex those vocabularies become, they will never, so long as we remain at the level of essential grammar, include the traditional syntactic classifications I have mentioned. For those classifications, as understood by conventional modern grammarians, involve an essential reference to the formal arrangements by means of which grammatical relations are represented in variable grammar. The more rigorous the grammarian, the more he strives to explain such categories as noun and verb in terms of formal criteria: in terms of the types of inflection which expressions may undergo and their distribution in sentences, the positions they may standardly occupy in sentences relative to expressions of other categories. The statement of such criteria can, perhaps never be entirely purged of semantic notions; and it must be framed with some looseness if the traditional categories are to be applied over a range of languages. But the point remains that the conventional categories reflect the interaction, in actual languages, of semantic and functional factors with actually found formal factors; and therefore have no place in the study of essential grammars. This will not prevent the student of perspicuous grammar from observing how natural it is that certain types of formal arrangement, and hence perhaps certain conventional syntactic categories, should enter at the level of variable grammar. But it will be at that level that they will enter, and not before. And what holds for the conventional syntactic CATEGORIES will hold also for the conventional syntactic RELATIONS in so far as their characterisation is inseparable from that of the conventional syntactic categories.

It will now, I hope, be clear why I earlier remarked that the task of finding explanatory foundations for grammar is not best approached by trying to establish direct links between semantico-logical notions and such traditional, or at least traditionally named, syntactic categories as the transformational grammarians employ in imagining base structures. If the names have anything like their normal significance, we must go behind or below them, to essential functions and classifications; and if they do not, it would be better to drop them in favour of a more perspicuous nomenclature. Some incidental advantages of emancipating ourselves, as we must, from these traditional categories are indeed obvious. We shall be readier for the discovery that such categories cannot be readily forced on some (from our point of view) remote languages; and correspondingly less prone to draw from such a discovery romantic conclusions about profound differences between the conceptual schemes of speakers of such languages and our own.

Many questions arise about such a programme as I have sketched. The notion of an essential grammar is, evidently, a relative notion: an essential grammar is the essential grammar OF A SPECIFIED LANGUAGE-

TYPE. We may set aside the obvious fact that the only practicable way of proceeding is to start from relatively simple specifications and build up to more complex ones, essential and alternative grammars themselves becoming more complex at every stage. There are more fundamental questions to be faced regarding the specifications of relatively basic types of element and combination, the selection of basic functional and logico-semantic vocabularies. It is admitted that these selections cannot be wholly independent of each other, that every semantico-logical type carries with it a certain potentiality of syntactic function. Is it not to be feared (supposed) that any such selection as the theorist of perspicuous grammars will make is likely to be restrictively conditioned by features of those languages with which he is most familiar? that, at worst, the ontology which was to enter into the explanatory foundations of grammar will be nothing but the abstract reflection of the base of the ontologist's native and local grammar? And, if so, how does it stand with the idea of a GENERAL theory of human language — nothing less than which will satisfy the full demand for explanation?

To these questions I can give only dogmatic answers. First, even if such fears are to some extent justified, it by no means follows that there is nothing to be gained by pursuing the suggested approach. To achieve any fairly rich model of perspicuous grammar would, I think, be to achieve a great deal. Even though it did not directly supply us with substantive linguistic universals of a general theory, it might help us to look for them. It is no new thing to work towards a comprehensive theory by way of theories which are less than comprehensive, to reach an adequate explanation by way of discarding inadequate explanations. But, second, it seems to me that such fears are likely to be exaggerated. We are all animals of the same species with fundamentally similar nervous and cerebral organisations and it is not to be supposed either that the most general categories for the organisation of human experience are widely different or, correspondingly, that the basic logico-semantic types of element to be detected in human languages are so very widely different either. (This is not to say that detection will be easy.) The linguistic evidence may indeed SEEM to point to some fairly basic variations;[10] and it simply cannot be said, in advance of a much greater development of theory and research, what the best way of handling such apparent problems of variation will be. But no language could even set us a

---

[10] It may SEEM to suggest, for example, that in certain areas in which *we* are inclined to number concepts of sorts of objects among our PRIMARY concepts, the most nearly corresponding PRIMARY concepts of other language-speakers MAY be of a different and possibly more primitive kind, not yet determined either as concepts of certain sorts of objects or as concepts of sorts of activities or situations in which such objects may be typically involved.

definite problem unless it were UNDERSTOOD by some theorist of grammar; so it is scarcely to be feared (or hoped) that any which does set a definite problem could for ever escape the embrace of a unified theory.

One of the transformational grammarians suggests that a general theory of language, conceived as a quite self-contained empirical-linguistic study, would contain the solutions to a great range of traditional philosophical problems.[11] I have been suggesting that a general theory of language should not be above receiving help from philosophy as well as offering help to it. One of the most striking things about the transformational approach to grammar is that it does point so markedly in the direction I have indicated. To follow this direction does not seem to be a departure from empiricism, generously conceived, even though the proper title for such an endeavour might well be held to be, as I suggested earlier, Research in Non-Empirical Linguistics. Of course the empirical value of the constructions of the philosophical student of perspicuous grammars is finally subject to the checks of psychologists and linguists, working separately and in combination. But where these two very different studies meet, the philosopher, at least for a time, may also find a role; and that not the least promising which is at present available to him. And, finally, whatever the ultimate empirical value of his constructions, and even if they have none, he may be sure of finding them a fruitful source of a kind of question and answer which he characteristically prizes.

---

[11] See Katz, *Philosophy of Language.*

Part IV

THE THEORY OF KNOWLEDGE AND LINGUISTIC THEORY

— — — — — — — — — — — — — — — — — —

Gottlob Frege

THE THOUGHT: A LOGICAL INQUIRY

(translated by A. M. and Marcelle Quinton)

The word 'true' indicates the aim of logic as does 'beautiful' that of
aesthetics or 'good' that of ethics. All sciences have truth as their goal;
but logic is also concerned with it in a quite different way from this.
It has much the same relation to truth as physics has to weight or heat.
To discover truths is the task of all sciences; it falls to logic to discern
the laws of truth. The word 'law' is used in two senses. When we speak of
laws of morals or the state we mean regulations which ought to be obeyed
but with which actual happenings are not always in conformity. Laws of
nature are the generalization of natural occurrences with which the
occurrences are always in accordance. It is rather in this sense that I
speak of laws of truth. This is, to be sure, not a matter of what happens
so much as of what is. Rules for asserting, thinking, judging, inferring,
follow from the laws of truth. And thus one can very well speak of laws
of thought too. But there is an imminent danger here of mixing different
things up. Perhaps the expression 'law of thought' is interpreted by
analogy with 'law of nature' and the generalization of thinking as a
mental occurrence is meant by it. A law of thought in this sense would be a
psychological law. And so one might come to believe that logic deals
with the mental process of thinking and the psychological laws in
accordance with which it takes place. This would be a misunderstanding of the task of logic, for truth has not been given the place which
is its due here. Error and superstition have causes just as much as genuine
knowledge. The assertion both of what is false and of what is true takes

First written in 1918. From *Mind* 65 (1956), 289-311. Reprinted by permission of the
translators, A. M. and Marcelle Quinton, and the Editor of *Mind*.

place in accordance with psychological laws. A derivation from these and an explanation of a mental process that terminates in an assertion can never take the place of a proof of what is asserted. Could not logical laws also have played a part in this mental process? I do not want to dispute this, but when it is a question of truth possibility is not enough. For it is also possible that something not logical played a part in the process and deflected it from the truth. We can only decide this after we have discerned the laws of truth; but then we will probably be able to do without the derivation and explanation of the mental process if it is important to us to decide whether the assertion in which the process terminates is justified. In order to avoid this misunderstanding and to prevent the blurring of the boundary between psychology and logic, I assign to logic the task of discovering the laws of truth, not of assertion or thought. The meaning of the word 'true' is explained by the laws of truth.

But first I shall attempt to outline roughly what I want to call true in this connexion. In this way other uses of our word may be excluded. It is not to be used here in the sense of 'genuine' or 'veracious', nor, as it sometimes occurs in the treatment of questions of art, when, for example, truth in art is discussed, when truth is set up as the goal of art, when the truth of a work of art or true feeling is spoken of. The word 'true' is put in front of another word in order to show that this word is to be understood in its proper, unadulterated sense. This use too lies off the path followed here; that kind of truth is meant whose recognition is the goal of science.

Grammatically the word 'true' appears as an adjective. Hence the desire arises to delimit more closely the sphere in which truth can be affirmed, in which truth comes into the question at all. One finds truth affirmed of pictures, ideas, statements, and thoughts. It is striking that visible and audible things occur here alongside things which cannot be perceived with the senses. This hints that shifts of meaning have taken place. Indeed! Is a picture, then, as a mere visible and tangible thing, really true, and a stone, a leaf, not true? Obviously one would not call a picture true unless there were an intention behind it. A picture must represent something. Furthermore, an idea is not called true in itself but only with respect to an intention that it should correspond to something. It might be supposed from this that truth consists in the correspondence of a picture with what it depicts. Correspondence is a relation. This is contradicted, however, by the use of the word 'true', which is not a relation-word and contains no reference to anything else to which something must correspond. If I do not know that a picture is meant to represent Cologne Cathedral then I do not know with what to compare the picture to decide on its truth. A correspondence, moreover, can only be perfect if the corresponding things coincide and are, therefore, not distinct things at all. It is said to be possible to establish the authenticity of a bank-note by comparing it stereoscopically with an authentic one. But it would be ridiculous to try to compare a gold piece with a twenty-mark note stereoscopically. It would only be possible to compare an idea with a thing if the thing were an idea too. And then, if the first did correspond perfectly with the second, they would coincide. But this is not at all what is wanted when truth is defined as the correspondence of an idea with something real. For it is absolutely essential that the reality be distinct from the idea. But then there can be no complete correspondence, no complete truth. So nothing at all would be true; for what is only half true is untrue. Truth cannot tolerate a more or less. But yet? Can it not be laid down that truth exists when there is correspondence in a certain respect? But in which? For what would we then have to do to decide whether something were true? We should have to inquire whether it were true that an idea and a reality, perhaps, corresponded in the laid-down respect. And then we should be confronted by a question of the same kind and the game could begin again. So the attempt to explain truth as correspondence collapses. And every other attempt to define truth collapses too. For in a definition certain characteristics would have to be stated. And in application to any particular case the question would always arise whether it were true that the characteristics were present. So one goes round in a circle. Consequently, it is probable that the content of the word 'true' is unique and indefinable.

When one ascribes truth to a picture one does not really want to ascribe a property which belongs to this picture altogether independently of other things, but one always has something quite different in mind and one wants to say that that picture corresponds in some way to this thing. 'My idea corresponds to Cologne Cathedral' is a sentence and the question now arises of the truth of this sentence. So what is improperly called the truth of pictures and ideas is reduced to the truth of sentences. What does one call a sentence? A series of sounds; but only when it has a sense, by which is not meant that every series of sounds that has sense is a sentence. And when we call a sentence true we really mean its sense is. From which it follows that it is for the sense of a sentence that the question of truth arises in general. Now is the sense of a sentence an idea? In any case being true does not consist in the correspondence of this sense with something else, for otherwise the question of truth would reiterate itself to infinity.

Without wishing to give a definition, I call a thought something for which the question of truth arises. So I ascribe what is false to a thought just as much as what is true.[1] So I can say: the thought is the sense of the

[1] In a similar way it has perhaps been said 'a judgement is something which is

sentence without wishing to say as well that the sense of every sentence is a thought. The thought, in itself immaterial, clothes itself in the material garment of a sentence and thereby becomes comprehensible to us. We say a sentence expresses a thought.

A thought is something immaterial and everything material and perceptible is excluded from this sphere of that for which the question of truth arises. Truth is not a quality that corresponds with a particular kind of sense-impression. So it is sharply distinguished from the qualities which we denote by the words 'red', 'bitter', 'lilac-smelling'. But do we not see that the sun has risen and do we not then also see that this is true? That the sun has risen is not an object which emits rays that reach my eyes, it is not a visible thing like the sun itself. That the sun has risen is seen to be true on the basis of sense-impressions. But being true is not a material, perceptible property. For being magnetic is also recognized on the basis of sense-impressions of something, though this property corresponds as little as truth with a particular kind of sense-impressions. So far these properties agree. However, we need sense-impressions in order to recognize a body as magnetic. On the other hand, when I find that it is true that I do not smell anything at this moment, I do not do so on the basis of sense-impressions.

It may nevertheless be thought that we cannot recognize a property of a thing without at the same time realizing the thought that this thing has this property to be true. So with every property of a thing is joined a property of a thought, namely, that of truth. It is also worthy of notice that the sentence 'I smell the scent of violets' has just the same content as the sentence 'it is true that I smell the scent of violets'. So it seems, then, that nothing is added to the thought by my ascribing to it the property of truth. And yet is it not a great result when the scientist after much hesitation and careful inquiry, can finally say 'what I supposed is true'? The meaning of the word 'true' seems to be altogether unique. May we not be dealing here with something which cannot, in the ordinary sense, be called a quality at all? In spite of this doubt I want first to express myself in accordance with ordinary usage, as if truth were a quality, until something more to the point is found.

In order to work out more precisely what I want to call thought, I

---

either true or false'. In fact I use the word 'thought' in approximately the sense which 'judgement' has in the writings of logicians. I hope it will become clear in what follows why I choose 'thought'. Such an explanation has been objected to on the ground that in it a distinction is drawn between true and false judgements which of all possible distinctions among judgements has perhaps the least significance. I cannot see that it is a logical deficiency that a distinction is given with the explanation. As far as significance is concerned, it should not by any means be judged as trifling if, as I have said, the word 'true' indicates the aim of logic.

shall distinguish various kinds of sentences.[2] One does not want to deny sense to an imperative sentence, but this sense is not such that the question of truth could arise for it. Therefore I shall not call the sense of an imperative sentence a thought. Sentences expressing desires or requests are ruled out in the same way. Only those sentences in which we communicate or state something come into the question. But I do not count among these exclamations in which one vents one's feelings, groaning, sighing, laughing, unless it has been decided by some agreement that they are to communicate something. But how about interrogative sentences? In a word-question we utter an incomplete sentence which only obtains a true sense through the completion for which we ask. Word-questions are accordingly left out of consideration here. Sentence-questions are a different matter. We expect to hear 'yes' or 'no'. The answer 'yes' means the same as an indicative sentence, for in it the thought that was already completely contained in the interrogative sentence is laid down as true. So a sentence-question can be formed from every indicative sentence. An exclamation cannot be regarded as a communication on this account, since no corresponding sentence-question can be formed. An interrogative sentence and an indicative one contain the same thought; but the indicative contains something else as well, namely, the assertion. The interrogative sentence contains something more too, namely a request. Therefore two things must be distinguished in an indicative sentence: the content, which it has in common with the corresponding sentence-question, and the assertion. The former is the thought, or at least contains the thought. So it is possible to express the thought without laying it down as true. Both are so closely joined in an indicative sentence that it is easy to overlook their separability. Consequently we may distinguish:

(1) the apprehension of a thought–thinking,
(2) the recognition of the truth of a thought–judgement;[3]
(3) the manifestation of this judgement–assertion.

We perform the first act when we form a sentence-question. An advance

[2] I am not using the word 'sentence' here in a purely grammatical sense where it also includes subordinate clauses. An isolated subordinate clause does not always have a sense about which the question of truth can arise, whereas the complex sentence to which it belongs has such a sense.

[3] It seems to me that thought and judgement have not hitherto been adequately distinguished. Perhaps language is misleading. For we have no particular clause in the indicative sentence which corresponds to the assertion, that something is being asserted lies rather in the form of the indicative. We have the advantage in German that main and subordinate clauses are distinguished by the word-order. In this connexion it is noticeable that a subordinate clause can also contain an assertion and that often neither main nor subordinate clause expresses a complete thought by itself but only the complex sentence does.

in science usually takes place in this way, first a thought is apprehended, such as can perhaps be expressed in a sentence-question, and, after appropriate investigations, this thought is finally recognized to be true. We declare the recognition of truth in the form of an indicative sentence. We do not have to use the word 'true' for this. And even when we do use it the real assertive force lies, not in it, but in the form of the indicative sentence and where this loses its assertive force the word 'true' cannot put it back again. This happens when we do not speak seriously. As stage thunder is only apparent thunder and a stage fight only an apparent fight, so stage assertion is only apparent assertion. It is only acting, only fancy. In his part the actor asserts nothing, nor does he lie, even if he says something of whose falsehood he is convinced. In poetry we have the case of thoughts being expressed without being actually put forward as true in spite of the form of the indicative sentence, although it may be suggested to the hearer to make an assenting judgement himself. Therefore it must still always be asked, about what is presented in the form of an indicative sentence, whether it really contains an assertion. And this question must be answered in the negative if the requisite seriousness is lacking. It is irrelevant whether the word 'true' is used here. This explains why it is that nothing seems to be added to a thought by attributing to it the property of truth.

An indicative sentence often contains, as well as a thought and the assertion, a third component over which the assertion does not extend. This is often said to act on the feelings, the mood of the hearer or to arouse his imagination. Words like 'alas' and 'thank God' belong here. Such constituents of sentences are more noticeably prominent in poetry, but are seldom wholly absent from prose. They occur more rarely in mathematical, physical, or chemical than in historical expositions. What are called the humanities are more closely connected with poetry and are therefore less scientific than the exact sciences which are drier the more exact they are, for exact science is directed toward truth and only the truth. Therefore all constituents of sentences to which the assertive force does not reach do not belong to scientific exposition but they are sometimes hard to avoid, even for one who sees the danger connected with them. Where the main thing is to approach what cannot be grasped in thought by means of guesswork these components have their justification. The more exactly scientific an exposition is the less will the nationality of its author be discernible and the easier will it be to translate. On the other hand, the constituents of language, to which I want to call attention here, make the translation of poetry very difficult, even make a complete translation almost always impossible, for it is in precisely that in which poetic value largely consists that languages differ most.

It makes no difference to the thought whether I use the word 'horse' or 'steed' or 'cart-horse' or 'mare'. The assertive force does not extend over that in which these words differ. What is called mood, fragrance, illumination in a poem, what is portrayed by cadence and rhythm, does not belong to the thought.

Much of language serves the purpose of aiding the hearer's understanding, for instance the stressing of part of a sentence by accentuation or word-order. One should remember words like 'still' and 'already' too. With the sentence 'Alfred has still not come' one really says 'Alfred has not come' and, at the same time, hints that his arrival is expected, but it is only hinted. It cannot be said that, since Alfred's arrival is not expected, the sense of the sentence is therefore false. The word 'but' differs from 'and' in that with it one intimates that what follows is in contrast with what would be expected from what preceded it. Such suggestions in speech make no difference to the thought. A sentence can be transformed by changing the verb from active to passive and making the object the subject at the same time. In the same way the dative may be changed into the nominative while 'give' is replaced by 'receive'. Naturally such transformations are not indifferent in every respect; but they do not touch the thought, they do not touch what is true or false. If the inadmissibility of such transformations were generally admitted then all deeper logical investigation would be hindered. It is just as important to neglect distinctions that do not touch the heart of the matter as to make distinctions which concern what is essential. But what is essential depends on one's purpose. To a mind concerned with what is beautiful in language what is indifferent to the logician can appear as just what is important.

Thus the contents of a sentence often go beyond the thoughts expressed by it. But the opposite often happens too, that the mere wording, which can be grasped by writing or the gramophone does not suffice for the expression of the thought. The present tense is used in two ways: first, in order to give a date, second, in order to eliminate any temporal restriction where timelessness or eternity is part of the thought. Think for instance, of the laws of mathematics. Which of the two cases occurs is not expressed but must be guessed. If a time indication is needed by the present tense one must know when the sentence was uttered to apprehend the thought correctly. Therefore the time of utterance is part of the expression of the thought. If someone wants to say the same today as he expressed yesterday using the word 'today', he must replace this word with 'yesterday'. Although the thought is the same its verbal expression must be different so that the sense, which would otherwise be affected by the differing times of utterance, is readjusted. The case is the same with words like 'here' and 'there'. In all such cases the mere wording, as it is given in writing, is not the complete expression of the thought, but the knowledge of certain accompanying conditions of utterance, which are used as means of expressing the thought, are needed for its correct apprehension. The pointing of fingers, hand movements, glances may belong here too. The same utterance containing the word 'I' will express different thoughts in the mouths of different men, of which some may be true, others false.

The occurrence of the word 'I' in a sentence gives rise to some questions. Consider the following case. Dr. Gustav Lauben says, 'I have been wounded'. Leo Peter hears this and remarks some days later, 'Dr. Gustav Lauben has been wounded'. Does this sentence express the same thought as the one Dr. Lauben uttered himself? Suppose that Rudolph Lingens were present when Dr. Lauben spoke and now hears what is related by Leo Peter. If the same thought is uttered by Dr. Lauben and Leo Peter then Rudolph Lingens, who is fully master of the language and remembers what Dr. Lauben has said in the presence, must now know at once from Leo Peter's report that the same thing is under discussion. But knowledge of the language is a separate thing when it is a matter of proper names. It may well be the case that only a few people associate a particular thought with the sentence 'Dr. Lauben has been wounded'. In this case one needs for complete understanding a knowledge of the expression 'Dr. Lauben'. Now if both Leo Peter and Rudolph Lingens understand by 'Dr. Lauben' the doctor who lives as the only doctor in a house known to both of them, then they both understand the sentence 'Dr. Gustav Lauben has been wounded' in the same way, they associate the same thought with it. But it is also possible that Rudolph Lingens does not know Dr. Lauben personally and does not know that he is the very Dr. Lauben who recently said 'I have been wounded'. In this case Rudolph Lingens cannot know that the same thing is in question. I say, therefore, in this case: the thought which Leo Peter expresses is not the same as that which Dr. Lauben uttered.

Suppose further that Herbert Garner knows that Dr. Gustav Lauben was born on 13th September, 1875 in N.N. and this is not true of anyone else; against this, suppose that he does not know where Dr. Lauben now lives nor indeed anything about him. On the other hand, suppose Leo Peter does not know that Dr. Lauben was born on 13th September 1875, in N.N. Then as far as the proper name 'Dr. Gustav Lauben' is concerned, Herbert Garner and Leo Peter do not speak the same language, since, although they do in fact refer to the same man with this name, they do not know that they do so. Therefore Herbert Garner does not associate the same thought with the sentence 'Dr. Gustav Lauben has been wounded' as Leo Peter wants to express with it. To avoid the drawback of Herbert Garner's and Leo Peter's not speaking the same language, I am assuming that Leo Peter uses the proper name 'Dr. Lauben' and Herbert Garner, on the other hand, uses the proper name 'Gustav Lauben'. Now it is possible that Herbert Garner takes the sense of the sentence 'Dr. Lauben has been wounded' to be true while, misled by false information, taking the sense of the sentence 'Gustav Lauben has been wounded' to be false. Under the assumptions given these thoughts are therefore different.

Accordingly, with a proper name, it depends on how whatever it refers to is presented. This can happen in different ways and every such way corresponds with a particular sense of a sentence containing a proper name. The different thoughts which thus result from the same sentence correspond in their truth-value, of course; that is to say, if one is true then all are true, and if one is false then all are false. Nevertheless their distinctness must be recognized. So it must really be demanded that a single way in which whatever is referred to is presented be associated with every proper name. It is often unimportant that this demand should be fulfilled but not always.

Now everyone is presented to himself in a particular and primitive way, in which he is presented to no-one else. So, when Dr. Lauben thinks that he has been wounded, he will probably take as a basis this primitive way in which he is presented to himself. And only Dr. Lauben himself can grasp thoughts determined in this way. But now he may want to communicate with others. He cannot communicate a thought which he alone can grasp. Therefore, if he now says 'I have been wounded', he must use the 'I' in a sense which can be grasped by others, perhaps in the sense of 'he who is speaking to you at this moment', by doing which he makes the associated conditions of this utterance serve for the expression of his thought.[4]

Yet there is a doubt. Is it at all the same thought which first that man expresses and now this one?

A person who is still untouched by philosophy knows first of all things which he can see and touch, in short, perceive with the senses, such as trees, stones and houses, and he is convinced that another person equally can see touch the same tree and the same stone which he himself sees and touches. Obviously no thought belongs to these things. Now can he, nevertheless, stand in the same relation to a person as a tree?

Even an unphilosophical person soon finds it necessary to recognize an inner world distinct from the outer world, a world of sense-impression, of creations of his imagination, of sensations, of feelings and moods, a

---

[4] I am not in the happy position here of a mineralogist who shows his hearers a mountain crystal. I cannot put a thought in the hands of my readers with the request that they should minutely examine it from all sides. I have to content myself with presenting the reader with a thought, in itself immaterial, dressed in sensible linguistic form. The metaphorical aspect of language presents difficulties. The sensible always breaks in and makes expression metaphorical and so improper. So a battle with language takes place and I am compelled to occupy myself with language although it is not my proper concern here. I hope I have succeeded in making clear to my readers what I want to call a thought.

world of inclinations, wishes and decisions. For brevity I want to collect all these, with the exception of decisions, under the word 'idea'.

Now do thoughts belong to this inner world? Are they ideas? They are obviously not decisions. How are ideas distinct from the things of the outer world? First:

Ideas cannot be seen or touched, cannot be smelled, nor tasted, nor heard.

I go for a walk with a companion. I see a green field, I have a visual impression of the green as well. I have it but I do not see it.

Secondly: ideas are had. One has sensations, feelings, moods, inclinations, wishes. An idea which someone has belongs to the content of his consciousness.

The field and the frogs in it, the sun which shines on them are there no matter whether I look at them or not, but the sense-impression I have of green exists only because of me, I am its bearer. It seems absurd to us that a pain, a mood, a wish should rove about the world without a bearer, independently. An experience is impossible without an experient. The inner world presupposes the person whose inner world it is.

Thirdly: ideas need a bearer. Things of the outer world are however independent.

My companion and I are convinced that we both see the same field; but each of us has a particular sense-impression of green. I notice a strawberry among the green strawberry leaves. My companion does not notice it, he is colour-blind. The colour-impression, which he receives from the strawberry, is not noticeably different from the one he receives from the leaf. Now does my companion see the green leaf as red, or does he see the red berry as green, or does he see both as of one colour with which I am not acquainted at all? These are unanswerable, indeed really nonsensical, questions. For when the word 'red' does not state a property of things but is supposed to characterize sense-impressions belonging to my consciousness, it is only applicable within the sphere of my consciousness. For it is impossible to compare my sense-impression with that of someone else. For that it would be necessary to bring together in one consciousness a sense-impression, belonging to one consciousness, with a sense-impression belonging to another consciousness. Now even if it were possible to make an idea disappear from one consciousness and, at the same time, to make an idea appear in another consciousness, the question whether it were the same idea in both would still remain unanswerable. It is so much of the essence of each of my ideas to be the content of my consciousness, that every idea of another person is, just as such, distinct from mine. But might it not be possible that my ideas, the entire content of my consciousness, might be at the same time the content of a more embracing, perhaps divine, consciousness? Only if I were myself part of the divine consciousness. But then would they really be my ideas, would I be their bearer? This oversteps the limits of human understanding to such an extent that one must leave its possibility out of account. In any case it is impossible for us as men to compare another person's ideas with our own. I pick the strawberry, I hold it between my fingers. Now my companion sees it too, this very same strawberry; but each of us has his own idea. No other person has my idea but many people can see the same thing. No other person has my pain. Someone can have sympathy for me but still my pain always belongs to me and his sympathy to him. He does not have my pain and I do not have his sympathy.

Fourthly: every idea has only one bearer; no two men have the same idea.

For otherwise it would exist independently of this person and independently of that one. Is that lime-tree my idea? By using the expression 'that lime-tree' in this question I have really already anticipated the answer, for with this expression I want to refer to what I see and to what other people can also look at and touch. There are now two possibilities. If my intention is realized when I refer to something with the expression 'that lime-tree' then the thought expressed in the sentence 'that lime-tree is my idea' must obviously be negated. But if my intention is not realized, if I only think I see without really seeing, if on that account the designation 'that lime-tree' is empty, then I have gone astray into the sphere of fiction without knowing it or wanting to. In that case neither the content of the sentence 'that lime-tree is my idea' nor the content of the sentence 'that lime-tree is not my idea' is true, for in both cases I have a statement which lacks an object. So then one can only refuse to answer the question for the reason that the content of the sentence 'that lime-tree is my idea' is a piece of fiction. I have, naturally, got an idea then, but I am not referring to this with the words 'that lime-tree'. Now someone may really want to refer to one of his ideas with the words 'that lime-tree'. He would then be the bearer of that to which he wants to refer those words, but then he would not see that lime-tree and no-one else would see it or be its bearer.

I now return to the question: is a thought an idea? If the thought I express in the Pythagorean theorem can be recognized by others just as much as by me then it does not belong to the content of my consciousness, I am not its bearer; yet I can, nevertheless, recognize it to be true. However, if it is not the same thought at all which is taken to be the content of the Pythagorean theorem by me and by another person, one should not really say 'the Pythagorean theorem' but 'my Pythagorean theorem', 'his Pythagorean theorem' and these would be different; for the sense belongs necessarily to the sentence. Then my thought can be the content of my consciousness and his thought the content of his. Could the sense of my Pythagorean theorem be true while that of his was false? I said that the word 'red' was applicable only in the sphere of my consciousness if it did not state a property of things but was supposed to characterize one of my sense-impressions. Therefore the words 'true' and 'false', as I understand them, could also be applicable only in the sphere of my consciousness, if they were not supposed to be concerned with something of which I was not the bearer, but were somehow appointed to characterize the content of my consciousness. Then truth would be restricted to the content of my consciousness and it would remain doubtful whether anything at all comparable occurred in the consciousness of others.

If every thought requires a bearer, to the contents of whose consciousness it belongs, then it would be a thought of this bearer only and there would be no science common to many, on which many could work. But I, perhaps, have my science, namely, a whole of thought whose bearer I am and another person has his. Each of us occupies himself with the contents of his own consciousness. No contradiction between the two sciences would then be possible and it would really be idle to dispute about truth, as idle, indeed almost ludicrous, as it would be for two people to dispute whether a hundred-mark note were genuine, where each meant the one he himself had in his pocket and understood the word 'genuine' in his own particular sense. If someone takes thoughts to be ideas, what he then recognizes to be true is, on his own view, the content of his consciousness and does not properly concern other people at all. If he were to hear from me the opinion that a thought is not an idea he could not dispute it, for, indeed, it would not now concern him.

So the result seems to be: thoughts are neither things of the outer world nor ideas.

A third realm must be recognized. What belongs to this corresponds with ideas, in that it cannot be perceived by the senses, but with things, in that it needs no bearer to the contents of whose consciousness to belong. Thus the thought, for example, which we expressed in the Pythagorean theorem is timelessly true, true independently of whether anyone takes it to be true. It needs no bearer. It is not true for the first time when it is discovered, but is like a planet which, already before anyone has seen it, has been in interaction with other planets.[5]

But I think I hear an unusual objection. I have assumed several times that the same thing that I see can also be observed by other people. But

---

[5] One sees a thing, one has an idea, one apprehends or thinks a thought. When one apprehends or thinks a thought one does not create it but only comes to stand in a certain relation, which is different from seeing a thing or having an idea, to what already existed beforehand.

how could this be the case, if everything were only a dream? If I only dreamed I was walking in the company of another person, if I only dreamed that my companion saw the green field as I did, if it were all only a play performed on the stage of my consciousness, it would be doubtful whether there were things of the outer world at all. Perhaps the realm of things is empty and I see no things and no men, but have only ideas of which I myself am the bearer. An idea, being something which can as little exist independently of me as my feeling of fatigue, cannot be a man, cannot look at the same field together with me, cannot see the strawberry I am holding. It is quite incredible that I should really have only my inner world instead of the whole environment, in which I am supposed to move and to act. And yet it is an inevitable consequence of the thesis that only what is my idea can be the object of my awareness. What would follow from this thesis if it were true? Would there then be other men? It would certainly be possible but I should know nothing of it. For a man cannot be my idea, consequently, if our thesis were true, he also cannot be an object of my awareness. And so the ground would be removed from under any process of thought in which I might assume that something was an object for another person as for myself, for even if this were to happen I should know nothing of it. It would be impossible for me to distinguish that of which I was the bearer from that of which I was not. In judging something not to be my idea I would make it the object of my thinking and, therefore, my idea. On this view, is there a green field? Perhaps, but it would not be visible to me. For if a field is not my idea, it cannot, according to our thesis, be an object of my awareness. But if it is my idea it is invisible, for ideas are not visible. I can indeed have the idea of a green field, but this is not green for there are no green ideas. Does a shell weighing a hundred kilogrammes exist, according to this view? Perhaps, but I could know nothing of it. If a shell is not my idea then, according to our thesis, it cannot be an object of my awareness, of my thinking. But if a shell were my idea, it would have no weight. I can have an idea of a heavy shell. This then contains the idea of weight as a part-idea. But this part-idea is not a property of the whole idea any more than Germany is a property of Europe. So it follows:

Either the thesis that only what is my idea can be the object of my awareness is false, or all my knowledge and perception is limited to the range of my ideas, to the stage of my consciousness. In this case I should have only an inner world and I should know nothing of other people.

It is strange how, upon such reflections, the opposites collapse into each other. There is, let us suppose, a physiologist of the senses. As is proper for a scholarly scientist, he is, first of all, far from supposing the things he is convinced he sees and touches to be his ideas. On the contrary, he believes that in sense-impressions he has the surest proof of things which are wholly independent of his feeling, imagining, thinking, which have no need of his consciousness. So little does he consider nerve-fibres and ganglion-cells to be the content of his consciousness that he is, on the contrary, rather inclined to regard his consciousness as dependent on nerve-fibres and ganglion-cells. He establishes that light-rays, refracted in the eye, strike the visual nerve-endings and bring about a change, a stimulus, there. Some of it is transmitted through nerve-fibres and ganglion-cells. Further processes in the nervous system are perhaps involved, colour-impressions arise and these perhaps join themselves to what we call the idea of a tree. Physical, chemical and physiological occurrences insert themselves between the tree and my idea. These are immediately connected with my consciousness but, so it seems, are only occurrences in my nervous system and every spectator of the tree has his particular occurrence in this particular nervous system. Now the light-rays, before they enter my eye, may be reflected by a mirror and be spread further as if they came from a place behind the mirror. The effects on the visual nerves and all that follows will now take place just as they would if the light-rays had come from a tree behind the mirror and had been transmitted undisturbed to the eye. So an idea of a tree will finally occur even though such a tree does not exist at all. An idea, to which nothing at all corresponds, can also arise through the bending of light, with the mediation of the eye and the nervous system. But the stimulation of the visual nerves need not even happen through light. If lightning strikes near us we believe we see flames, even though we cannot see the lightning itself. In this case the visual nerve is perhaps stimulated by electric currents which originate in our body in consequence of the flash of lightning. If the visual nerve is stimulated by this means, just as it would be stimulated by light-rays coming from flames, then we believe we see flames. It just depends on the stimulation of the visual nerve, it is indifferent how that itself comes about.

One can go a step further still. This stimulation of the visual nerve is not actually immediately given, but is only a hypothesis. We believe that a thing, independent of us, stimulates a nerve and by this means produces a sense-impression, but, strictly speaking, we experience only the end of this process which projects into our consciousness. Could not this sense-impression, this sensation, which we attribute to a nerve-stimulation, have other cases also, as the same nerve-stimulation can arise in different ways? If we call what happens in our consciousness idea, then we really experience only ideas but not their causes. And if the scientist wants to avoid all mere hypotheses, then only ideas are left for him, everything resolves into ideas, the light-rays, nerve-fibres and ganglion-cells from which he started. So he finally undermines the foundations of his own construction. Is everything an idea? Does everything need a bearer, without which it could have no stability? I have considered myself as the bearer of my ideas, but am I not an idea myself? It seems to me as if I were lying in a deck-chair, as if I could see the toes of a pair of waxed boots, the front part of a pair of trousers, a waistcoat, buttons, part of a jacket, in particular sleeves, two hands, the hair of a beard, the blurred outline of a nose. Am I myself this entire association of visual impressions, this total idea? It also seems to me as if I see a chair over there. It is an idea. I am not actually much different from this myself, for am I not myself just an association of sense-impressions, an idea? But where then is the bearer of these ideas? How do I come to single out one of these ideas and set it up as the bearer of the rest? Why must it be the idea which I choose to call 'I'? Could I not just as well choose the one that I am tempted to call a chair? Why, after all, have a bearer for ideas at all? But this would always be something essentially different from merely borne ideas, something independent, needing no extraneous bearer. If everything is idea, then there is no bearer of ideas. And so now, once again, I experience a change into the opposite. If there is no bearer of ideas then there are also no ideas, for ideas need a bearer without which they cannot exist. If there is no ruler, there are also no subjects. The dependence, which I found myself induced to confer on the experience as opposed to the experient, is abolished if there is no more bearer. What I called ideas are then independent objects. Every reason is wanting for granting an exceptional position to that object which I call 'I'.

But is that possible? Can there be an experience without someone to experience it? What would this whole play be without an onlooker? Can there be a pain without someone who has it? Being experienced is necessarily connected with pain, and someone experiencing is necessarily connected with being experienced. But there is something which is not my idea and yet which can be the object of my awareness, of my thinking, I am myself of this nature. Or can I be part of the content of my consciousness while another part is, perhaps, an idea of the moon? Does this perhaps take place when I judge that I am looking at the moon? Then this first part would have a consciousness and part of the content of this consciousness would be I myself once more. And so on. Yet it is surely inconceivable that I should be boxed into myself in this way to infinity, for then there would not be only one I but infinitely many. I am not my own idea and if I assert something about myself, e.g. that I do not feel any pain at this moment, then my judgement concerns something which is not a content of my consciousness, is not my idea, that is me myself. Therefore that about which I state something is not necessarily my idea. But, someone perhaps objects, if I think I have no pain at the moment, does not the word 'I' nevertheless correspond with something in the content of my consciousness and is that not an idea? That may be. A certain idea in my consciousness may be associated with the idea of the word 'I'. But then it is an idea among other ideas and I am its bearer as I am the bearer of the other ideas. I have an idea of myself but I am not identical with this idea. What is a content of my consciousness, my idea, should be sharply distinguished from what is an object of my thought. Therefore the thesis that only what belongs to the content of my consciousness can be the object of my awareness, of my thought, is false.

Now the way is clear for me to recognize another person as well as to be an independent bearer of ideas. I have an idea of him but I do not confuse it with him himself. And if I state something about my brother I do not state it about the idea that I have of my brother.

The invalid who has a pain is the bearer of this pain, but the doctor in attendance who reflects on the cause of this pain is not the bearer of the pain. He does not imagine he can relieve the pain by anaesthetizing himself. An idea in the doctor's mind may very well correspond to the pain of the invalid but that is not the pain and not what the doctor is trying to remove. The doctor might consult another doctor. Then one must distinguish: first, the pain whose bearer is the invalid, second, the first doctor's idea of this pain, third, the second doctor's idea of this pain. This idea does indeed belong to the content of the second doctor's consciousness, but it is not the object of his reflection, it is rather an aid to reflection, as a drawing can be such an aid perhaps. Both doctors have the invalid's pain, which they do not bear, as their common object of thought. It can be seen from this that not only a thing but also an idea can be the common object of thought of people who do not have the idea.

So, it seems to me, the matter becomes intelligible. If man could not think and could not take something of which he was not the bearer as the object of his thought he would have an inner world but no outer world. But may this not be based on a mistake? I am convinced that the idea I associate with the words 'my brother' corresponds to something that is not my idea and about which I can say something. But may I not be making a mistake about this? Such mistakes do happen. We then, against our will, lapse into fiction. Indeed! By the step with which I secure an environment for myself I expose myself to the risk of error. And here I come up against a further distinction between my inner and outer worlds. I cannot doubt that I have a visual impression of green but it is not so certain that I see a lime-leaf. So, contrary to widespread views, we find certainty in the inner world while doubt never altogether leaves us in our excursions into the outer world. It is difficult in many cases, nevertheless, to distinguish probability from certainty here, so we can presume to judge about things in the outer world. And we must presume this risk of error if we do not want to succumb to far greater dangers. In consequence of these last considerations I lay down the following: not everything that can be the object of my understanding is an idea. I, as a bearer of ideas, am not myself an idea. Nothing now stands in the way of recognizing other people to be bearers of ideas as I am myself. And, once given the possibility, the probability is very great, so great that it is in my opinion no longer distinguishable from certainty. Would there be a science of history otherwise? Would not every precept of duty, every law otherwise come to nothing? What would be left of religion? The natural sciences too could only be assessed as fables like astrology and alchemy. Thus the reflections I have carried on, assuming that there are other people besides myself who can take the same thing as the object of their consideration, of their thinking, remain essentially unimpaired in force.

Not everything is an idea. Thus I can also recognize the thought, which other people can grasp just as much as I, as being independent of me. I can recognize a science in which many people can be engaged in research. We are not bearers of thoughts as we are bearers of our ideas We do not have a thought as we have, say, a sense-impression, but we also do not see a thought as we see, say, a star. So it is advisable to choose a special expression and the word 'apprehend' offers itself for the purpose. A particular mental capacity, the power of thought, must correspond to the apprehension[6] of thought. In thinking we do not produce thoughts but we apprehend them. For what I have called thought stands in the closest relation to truth. What I recognize as true I judge to be true quite independently of my recognition of its truth and of my thinking about it. That someone thinks it has nothing to do with the truth of a thought. 'Facts, facts, facts' cries the scientist if he wants to emphasize the necessity of a firm foundation for science. What is a fact? A fact is a thought that is true. But the scientist will surely not recognize something which depends on men's varying states of mind to be the firm foundation of science. The work of science does not consist of creation but of the discovery of true thoughts. The astronomer can apply a mathematical truth in the investigation of long past events which took place when on earth at least no one had yet recognized that truth. He can do this because the truth of a thought is timeless. Therefore that truth cannot have come into existence with its discovery.

Not everything is an idea. Otherwise psychology would contain all

---

[6] The expression 'apprehend' is as metaphorical as 'content of consciousness'. The nature of language does not permit anything else. What I hold in my hand can certainly be regarded as the content of my hand but is all the same the content of my hand in quite a different way from the bones and muscles of which it is made and their tensions, and is much more extraneous to it than they are.

the sciences within it or at least it would be the highest judge over all the sciences. Otherwise psychology would rule over logic and mathematics. But nothing would be a greater misunderstanding of mathematics than its subordination to psychology. Neither logic nor mathematics has the task of investigating minds and the contents of consciousness whose bearer is a single person. Perhaps their task could be represented rather as the investigation of the mind; of the mind not of minds.

The apprehension of a thought presupposes someone who apprehends it, who thinks. He is the bearer of the thinking but not of the thought. Although the thought does not belong to the contents of the thinker's consciousness yet something in his consciousness must be aimed at the thought. But this should not be confused with the thought itself. Similarly Algol itself is different from the idea someone has of Algol.

The thought belongs neither to my inner world as an idea nor yet to the outer world of material, perceptible things.

This consequence, however cogently it may follow from the exposition, will nevertheless not perhaps be accepted without opposition. It will, I think, seem impossible to some people to obtain information about something not belonging to the inner world except by sense-perception. Sense-perception indeed is often thought to be the most certain, even to be the sole, source of knowledge about everything that does not belong to the inner world. But with what right? For sense-impressions are necessary constituents of sense-perceptions and are a part of the inner world. In any case two men do not have the same, though they may have similar, sense-impressions. These alone do not disclose the outer world to us. Perhaps there is a being that has only sense-impressions without seeing or touching things. To have visual impressions is not to see things. How does it happen that I see the tree just there where I do see it? Obviously it depends on the visual impressions I have and on the particular type which occur because I see with two eyes. A particular image arises, physically speaking, on each of the two retinas. Another person sees the tree in the same place. He also has two retinal images but they differ from mine. We must assume that these retinal images correspond to our impressions. Consequently we have visual impressions, not only not the same, but markedly different from each other. And yet we move about in the same outer world. Having visual impressions is certainly necessary for seeing things but not sufficient. What must still be added is non-sensible. And yet this is just what opens up the outer world for us; for without this non-sensible something everyone would remain shut up in his inner world. So since the answer lies in the non-sensible, perhaps something non-sensible could also lead us out of the inner world and enable us to grasp thoughts where no sense-impressions were involved. Outside one's inner world one would have to distinguish the proper outer world of sensible, perceptible things from the realm of the non-sensibly perceptible. We should need something non-sensible for the recognition of both realms but for the sensible perception of things we should need sense-impressions as well and these belong entirely to the inner world. So that in which the distinction between the way in which a thing and a thought is given mainly consists is something which is attributable, not to both realms, but to the inner world. Thus I cannot find this distinction to be so great that on its account it would be impossible for a thought to be given that did not belong to the inner world.

The thought, admittedly, is not something which it is usual to call real. The world of the real is a world in which this acts on that, changes it and again experiences reactions itself and is changed by them. All this is a process in time. We will hardly recognize what is timeless and unchangeable as real. Now is the thought changeable or is it timeless? The thought we express by the Pythagorean theorem is surely timeless, eternal, unchangeable. But are there not thoughts which are true today but false in six months time? The thought, for example, that the tree there is covered with green leaves, will surely be false in six months time. No, for it is not the same thought at all. The words 'this tree is covered with green leaves' are not sufficient by themselves for the utterance, the time of utterance is involved as well. Without the time-indication this gives we have no complete thought, i.e. no thought at all. Only a sentence supplemented by a time-indication and complete in every respect expresses a thought. But this, if it is true, is true not only today or tomorrow but timelessly. Thus the present tense in 'is true' does not refer to the speaker's present but is, if the expression be permitted, a tense of timelessness. If we use the mere form of the indicative sentence, avoiding the word 'true', two things must be distinguished, the expression of the thought and the assertion. The time-indication that may be contained in the sentence belongs only to the expression of the thought, while the truth, whose recognition lies in the form of the indicative sentence, is timeless. Yet the same words, on account of the variability of language with time, take on another sense, express another thought; this change, however, concerns only the linguistic aspect of the matter.

And yet! What value could there be for us in the eternally unchangeable which could neither undergo effects nor have effect on us? Something entirely and in every respect inactive would be unreal and non-existent for us. Even the timeless, if it is to be anything for us, must somehow be implicated with the temporal. What would a thought be for me that was never apprehended by me? But by apprehending a thought I come into a relation to it and it to me. It is possible that the same thought that is thought by me today was not thought by me yesterday. In this way the strict timelessness is of course annulled. But one is inclined to distinguish between essential and inessential properties and to regard something as timeless if the changes it undergoes involve only its inessential properties. A property of a thought will be called inessential which consists in, or follows from the fact that, it is apprehended by a thinker.

How does a thought act? By being apprehended and taken to be true. This is a process in the inner world of a thinker which can have further consequences in this inner world and which, encroaching on the sphere of the will, can also make itself noticeable in the outer world. If, for example, I grasp the thought which we express by the theorem of Pythagoras, the consequence may be that I recognize it to be true and, further, that I apply it, making a decision which brings about the acceleration of masses. Thus our actions are usually prepared by thinking and judgement. And so thought can have an indirect influence on the motion of masses. The influence of one person on another is brought about for the most part by thoughts. One communicates a thought. How does this happen? One brings about changes in the common outside world which, perceived by another person, are supposed to induce him to apprehend a thought and take it to be true. Could the great events of world history have come about without the communication of thoughts? And yet we are inclined to regard thoughts as unreal because they appear to be without influence on events, while thinking, judging, stating, understanding and the alike are facts of human life. How much more real a hammer appears compared with a thought. How different the process of handing over a hammer is from the communication of a thought. The hammer passes from one control to another, it is gripped, it undergoes pressure and on account of this its density, the disposition of its parts, is changed in places. There is nothing of all this with a thought. It does not leave the control of the communicator by being communicated, for after all a person has no control over it. When a thought is apprehended, it at first only brings about changes in the inner world of the apprehender, yet it remains untouched in its true essence, since the changes it undergoes involve only inessential properties. There is lacking here something we observe throughout the order of nature: reciprocal action. Thoughts are by no means unreal but their reality is of quite a different kind from that of things. And their effect is brought about by an act of the thinker without which they would be ineffective, at least as far as we can see. And yet the thinker does not create them but must take them as they are. They can be true without being apprehended by a thinker and are not wholly unreal even then, at least if they could be apprehended and by this means be brought into operation.

J. M. E. Moravcsik

COMPETENCE, CREATIVITY, AND INNATENESS

Participation in rational activities requires a variety of competences. The investigation of these competences is a manifold task. It involves the discovery of norms, the analysis of concepts in terms of which a given competence can be explicated, and the empirical investigation of ways in which tasks can be and are accomplished. There is a general pattern, first developed by Plato, that is applicable to the investigation of any competence. This pattern consists of three related questions and their answers. (a) WHAT CAN BE EXPECTED OF SOMEONE WHO HAS THE COMPETENCE IN QUESTION? Answers to this question spell out the variety of things that a competent person must be able to achieve and to accomplish in order to be credited with the competence in question. For to be competent involves meeting certain standards of performance; thus answers to the first question specify what a competent agent must be able to do. For example, a competent mathematician must be able to perform certain calculations, and a competent driver must be able to do certain things with a car. Only very general and vacuous answers to this question are analytic. For our understanding of tasks to be performed and the ways in which people perform these undergoes constant change, and hopefully, development. For example, our understanding of what it is to be a competent speaker of a language is changing partly as a result of learning more about the struc-

Reprinted from *Philosophical Forum*, 1 (4), 407-37.
The first draft of this paper was read at the 1967 Summer Meeting of the American Linguistic Society in Ann Arbor, Michigan. Another draft was presented at the 1968 University of Cincinnati Colloquium on Linguistics and the Philosophy of Language. I am indebted to participants at these meetings and to friends, especially Professors W. Alston and J. Fodor, for helpful comments and criticisms.

ture of languages, and partly as a result of our increased understanding of mental operations. To say that a competent speaker of a language must be able to understand the language is perhaps vacuous enough to be counted as analytic, but the claims that a competent speaker must be able to interpret utterances that he never encountered before, and that a child competent in elementary arithmetic must be able to perform operations '0 ... 0n' are empirical claims, no matter how deeply entrenched: for the denial of neither is self-contradictory and neither will qualify as a priori synthetic.

The same considerations apply to the second question. (b) THROUGH WHAT PROCESSES CAN THE COMPETENCE BE MANIFESTED AND WHAT CONDITIONS ARE REQUIRED BY THESE PROCESSES? The dependence of (b) on (a) lies in the fact that one cannot delineate processes by which something can be accomplished without having a clear conception of what is to be accomplished. For example, one has to explicate what it is to have the competence to draw simple deductive inferences before one can investigate the nature of mental reasoning (deductive) processes, and the conditions that are required for their realization.

One might be tempted to say that answers to (b) are irrelevant to philosophy, since they contain mostly scientific information and are not in need of conceptual clarification. Let us consider, however, a competence involving some type of knowledge, e.g. arithmetic. Recognition that 'know' is an achievement word (or performative, or parenthetical) should not keep us from realizing that the ascription of knowledge to someone entails further claims that certain processes are taking place, or have taken place in the mind of the agent, and that certain conditions hold for the agent. Thus there will be certain conceptual relations between achievements and processes as well as conditions, and these call for analysis. While much of the answers to (b) will be empirical, some parts of these will not. For example, not anything that enables a person to give the right answer to a mathematical question counts as a process of calculation.

The third question is: (c) IN VIEW OF ANSWERS TO QUESTIONS (a) AND (b) WHAT MUST BE TRUE OF THE AGENT HAVING THE COMPETENCE? Underlying this question is the principle that only entities with certain properties can be agents involved in a given kind of process leading to a certain type of accomplishment. For example, only entities with certain properties can be competent mathematicians, and only entities with a certain set of properties can be competent speakers of a natural language, given certain analyses of language and understanding. Thus answers to this question give a partial characterization of the agent. The 'must' in the formulation presented is systematically ambiguous, standing for conceptual or natural necessity, depending on the nature of the investigation under consideration. As in the case of the other questions, answer to (c) yield analytic propositions only if they are so general as to be vacuous. In any case, the distinction between conceptual and empirical truths, difficult to draw in any context is especially hard to maintain when one considers answers to (c). For it is difficult to decide which characterizations, if any, of an agent with a competence are immune to revision in face of new empirical evidence.

The pattern of analysis presented can be summarized by saying that with regard to any competence we must ask: (i) What does the agent with the competence accomplish? (ii) How does he do it? and (iii) Given what he does and how he does it, what must be true of him? and we have no adequate understanding of the competence unless we have a systematic set of answers to these questions. Such a set of answers constitute a THEORY of that competence.

In recent times Noam Chomsky has provided a set of proposals and hypotheses concerning the nature of language and linguistic competence.[1] Much of what Chomsky says[2] can be reconstructed so as to fit the pattern presented above, and thus he can be interpreted as presenting a THEORY of linguistic competence in the sense of 'theory' explained above. Some of the concepts used by Chomsky are new, others seem to be ones regarded as obsolete by most contemporary philosophers. These concepts and the proposals in which they play key roles have been the object of severe criticism in recent philosophical literature.[3] The main purpose of this paper is to develop some of Chomsky's conceptual suggestions, and to clarify some of his more controversial concepts. This task calls for the explanation of new concepts and the reconsideration and reinterpretation of old ones. Though the results of this paper show that Chomsky's theory requires much further conceptual clarification, such further analysis promises to be most rewarding, and if the results of this paper are correct, the negative attitude adopted by the recent critics is unjustified since many of their criticisms miss their mark.

I

COMPETENCE. Since competences form a class of dispositions with certain properties, they — like most other dispositions — can be manifested in a

---

[1] For a general survey of Chomsky's linguistic theory and its implications for philosophy, see my "Linguistic Theory and the Philosophy of Language", *Foundations of Language* 3 (1967), 209-33.
[2] See especially *Syntactic Structures* (The Hague, 1957); *Aspects of the Theory of Syntax* (Cambridge, 1965); *Cartesian Linguistics* (New York, 1966).
[3] Cf. H. Putnam, "The Innateness Hypothesis", *Synthese* 17 (1967), 12-22; G. Harman, "Psychological Aspects of the Theory of Syntax", *Journal of Philosophy* 64 (1967), 75-87; and the review of *Cartesian Linguistics* in *Philosophical Review* 77 (1968), 229-35.

variety of ways. Since a disposition cannot be identified with its manifestations, a competence cannot be identified with its manifestations either. Thus a theory of competence is concerned with dispositions, properties, and constituents of agents, while the actual manifestations serve as evidence for or against hypotheses about these topics. This is a simple point that is applicable to all of the sciences. Actual manifestations of dispositions are never the ultimate subject of scientific or philosophical investigations. A chemist might be interested in the disposition of a substance to dissolve in water; his hypotheses cannot be restricted to deal only with the instances in which the substance actually dissolves. Likewise, the subject of investigations in linguistics is the competence to master and use a language, rather than the actual performances in which this competence is manifested. A good theory must account not only for actual but also for possible manifestations and performances; performances that could take place, but may — for all we know — never take place.

This fundamental point about dispositions in general and competences in particular provides the basis for our first distinction between COMPETENCE and PERFORMANCE. The latter is the manifestation of the former; the former is the subject of theories while the latter provides evidence for or against those theories. In terms of this distinction an initial characterization of linguistic competence is that it is a disposition with certain properties. One such property is that it requires intelligence, for some of what the competent agent is expected to accomplish requires the use of reasoning. (Space prevents us to raise the interesting, though independent, question whether the converse holds; i.e. is it necessary that an intelligent being should have linguistic competence? In any case, neither the affirmative nor the negative reply is analytic.)

Dispositions requiring intelligence can be divided into three groups: (a) those manifested in habitual behavior, (b) those involving the use of strategy, and (c) those involving the following of rules. An example of first type is the disposition to tackle difficult problems first and the easy ones later. This can be described as mere habit; i.e. it is a regularity of conduct, statistical or otherwise, that does not include correction and the having of intuitions about rule violations. Competences requiring intelligence can be found in classes (b) and (c). Competences requiring use of strategy involve corrections. For example, a debater might be regarded as competent in view of his large number of victories. His success requires the application of strategy, and this involves corrections when necessary. But the application of strategy does not involve having intuitions about rules governing the activity being violated. The recognition required in the course of using strategy is the recognition of mistakes made; this must be distinguished from the recognition of the violations of rules that determine what is and is not a legitimate part of a given activity. Thus the crucial difference between (b) and (c) is the recognition of rule violation. Both the recognition of mistakes and the recognition of rule violation can be intuitive; i.e. a belief about mistake or violation not based on previous explicit instruction regarding the relevant rule or part of strategy. The justifications given for these different types of intuitions will differ; the chess player can tell mistakes in strategy in a different way from the way in which he recognizes illegitimate moves.

Following a rule is not the only way to participate in rule-governed activity. Such participation may involve — aside from rule following — merely acting in accordance with rules. To act in accordance with a rule is to act in such a way that (i) the rule in question will fit the relevant aspects of conduct and (ii) the rule provides a reliable basis for predicting the agent's future conduct. In other words, hypotheses derived from the rule must have counterfactual force. To say that an agent *A* follows a rule *R* is to affirm (i) and (ii) and add (iii) *A* must have beliefs with regard to what does and what does not constitute a violation of *R*, and (iv) when presented with *R* he must recognize it as the rule he is following. For most typical cases we may add also (v, a) *A* must be consciously thinking of *R* at the time he applies it or immediately before application. There are, however, many types of cases, such as aspects of reasoning, calculation, chess playing, etc. that fail to meet (v, a) and yet we regard them as clear cases of rule following. In order to fit these cases we might want to substitute for (v, a) (v, b) *A* must have formulated *R* consciously some time before his application of it and this event of formulation is causally related both to the events of application and to *A*'s satisfying (iii).

Reflection on the conditions governing acting in accordance with a rule (i and ii) and the conditions holding for conscious following of rules (i-v) shows that there may be room for other types of cases. Could there not be cases that fit (i-iii) (or iv) but do not fit any version of (v) (or iv and v)? In many instances our recognition of rule violations are intuitive in the sense explained above; we do have the belief that something is illegitimate even though we have never been presented with or have consciously formulated the rule that the offending item violates. Thus there are cases in which (i-iii) are satisfied but (iv) and (v) are not. Such cases involve competences of all kinds. Consider, for example, an average third grader who is presented with an instance of violating the law of the commutability of addition. There will be many cases in which the child will recognize the illegitimacy of the formula without the law of commutability having ever been presented to him before. He has intuitions satisfying (iii) without his satisfying (v) (and possibly not even iv). Again, it may be the case that both (iii) and (iv) will be satisfied given the appropriate stimulus, but (v) will not be satisfied. Thus we need categories of rule following other than the category of conscious rule following as defined above. This need can be demonstrated even if we do not consider Chomsky's — or anyone else's — conception of linguistic competence.

The kind of competence partially characterized so far can be clarified further by considering the kinds of knowledge it requires. In recent philosophic literature it has been fashionable to distinguish between knowledge as practical skill, and knowledge as the warranted belief about the proper truth value of a given proposition. The distinction is often drawn as between KNOWING HOW to do certain things, and KNOWING THAT a certain proposition is true. In many contexts this distinction is helpful. For example, one would want to distinguish between knowing how to wiggle one's ears from knowing the muscular structure and its workings that makes ear-wiggling possible. The former is practical and the latter is theoretical knowledge; neither requires the other. There are many cases of know-how that do not require propositional knowledge, or even the characteristic of having human rationality. To know how to climb a tree is one thing, to know the laws of physics and anatomy that explain tree-climbing is another. Monkeys are better at the former and men — at least some men — much better at the latter. Thus the distinction reveals an ambiguity of 'know' that is worth keeping in mind in the course of analyzing certain skills and our understanding of these.

There are, however, types of competence that require both kinds of knowledge and the possession of which involves the causal interdependence of these. Among these types of competence is the one under consideration, i.e. the one whose instances satisfy at least conditions (i-iii) explained above. For example, let us consider the competence of a normal chess player of whom conditions (i-iii) hold. Inasmuch as he knows how to move chess figures correctly he possesses practical knowledge. Inasmuch as he can recognize illegitimate moves and forms beliefs about these he also possesses "propositional" knowledge. Furthermore, under the usual circumstances we assume that the two types of knowledge possessed by the chess player are causally interrelated. The fact that the player has intuitions about what is and what is not a legitimate move is regarded as causally related to and therefore partially explanatory of the fact that he can make the right moves and avoid illegitimate ones. We also assume under normal circumstances that the same factors that account for his know-how also account for his ability to have intuitions about well-formedness. In short, we assume that there are underlying factors that account causally both for the know-how and for the propositional knowledge under consideration. In the case of conscious rule following we describe this underlying factor as "the following of the rule". Whatever this set of mental processes may be, it is that which accounts both for the agent's ability to make the right moves and for his intuitions (or non-intuitive beliefs) concerning what counts as a violation. Thus the answer to the question: what kind of knowledge is involved in the competences under consideration, knowing how or knowing that? is: both, and they are causally related.

There is an even closer connection between these two kinds of knowledge involved in the competences under consideration. Let us consider the case of a person making a series of correct judgments with regard to the illegitimacy of certain specific moves on the chess-board. Such a person has a "know-how", i.e. he knows how to recognize illegitimate moves in chess. This know-how, of course, involves propositional knowledge (in the normal case); for the series of judgments involves assigning the correct truth value to certain propositions. The same point can be made with respect to the example of a person who knows how to calculate small sums; he knows how to calculate, but this know-how involves processes terminating in his assigning the proper truth value to certain propositions. Thus in these cases the exercise of a know-how will coincide with the manifestation of propositional knowledge.

Let us apply these considerations to linguistic competence. The fact that people correct themselves and others for reasons other than instrumental or aesthetic considerations shows that the use of language is not just habitual behavior. In order to show, however, that the proper use and understanding of language involves more than competence requiring use of strategy, one has to show that the competent user of a natural language has beliefs about specific points of violations of the rules of the language. Emphasis on this point is prominent in Chomsky's work, and once we see from the analysis presented here that these intuitive beliefs are the unique distinguishing marks of the use of language as a rule following activity, then we can appreciate Chomsky's emphasis and his claim that linguistic theory is concerned, to a large extent, with the intuitions of a competent speaker. This claim is analogous to claiming that outsiders studying human chess players and their games would have to be concerned primarily with the intuitions of chess players regarding well-formedness.

So far we have characterized linguistic competence by showing that conditions (i-iii) apply to it. Evidence available even on the level of common sense shows that neither version of (v) apply to most aspects of verbal behavior. That is to say, a competent speaker will have a wide variety of beliefs about what is or is not grammatical without having been exposed previously to the rule or rules the violation of which is responsible for the resulting ungrammaticality. Indeed, it is plausible to claim that condition (iv) fails to obtain in many cases. Thus linguistic competence falls into the "twilight zone" marked out previously. By satisfying condition (iii) we cannot classify it as involving merely strategy, or the activity as acting merely in accordance with rules. By not satisfying conditions (iv) and (v) we cannot classify a large part of linguistic competence as conscious rule following. Furthermore, given the characterization given so far, linguistic competence involves both knowing how and knowing that and the two are causally interrelated. The competent speaker knows how to produce a variety of utterances — including ones he never encountered before — and he knows that certain sequences are grammatical while others are ungrammatical. We also assume that the two kinds of knowledge are interrelated. The fact that the speaker has intuitions about what is and what is not a grammatical sequence is one of the causal factors responsible for his ability to generate the right sequences of language. Our understanding of utterances is also partly explainable by the fact that we have intuitions about what is and what is not well formed. The stronger correlation mentioned above also holds with regard to the two types of knowledge as they are involved in linguistic competence. For the exercise of knowing how to recognize ungrammatical sequences coincides in the normal cases with the manifestation of propositional knowledge that this or that sequence is ungrammatical.

In the course of giving this partial analysis of competence in general and linguistic competence in particular we were occupied with giving partial answers to questions (a) and (b) as explained in the introduction. Our analysis is incomplete at a crucial point. We have shown that linguistic competence falls in a "twilight zone" between acting in accordance with rules and conscious rule following, but we have not even outlined a proposal for dealing with linguistic competence and other competences falling in this same zone. We suggested above that the propositional knowledge and the know-how are causally interrelated, but nothing has been said so far about the nature of this relation or about the causal antecedents — if any — that might account for both types of knowledge. The know-how cannot be accounted for by supposing that we learn a few rules of language explicitly and guess the rest by inductive or deductive reasoning. This is an empirical claim, to be discussed further in the following sections. Assuming it to be true, one proposes the hypothesis that in analogy with the case of conscious rule following, in the cases under consideration too, there is a factor that is the common antecedent underlying both the propositional and the practical knowledge entailed by the use and understanding of language. Let us postulate a state of mind as this common causal antecedent. The justification for regarding this state of mind as the causal antecedent of the intuitive judgments of grammaticality is that the ability to form these judgments on the one hand cannot be a *deus ex machina*, on the other hand, one cannot suppose that our minds are equipped, innately or as a result of empirical conditioning, or explicit instruction, with an indefinitely large set of judgments concerning the grammaticality of utterances without these judgments being derived from knowledge of rules of grammaticality. As a preliminary characterization of the state of mind postulated to account for both the practical know-how of generating sequences of the language and of the intuitions of grammaticality we can describe it as a state of "having internalized rules of the language".

This is in rough outlines the argument in favor of ascribing to an agent with linguistic competence, and to any other agent with a competence meeting conditions (i-iii), the state of mind of having internalized rules. Underlying this argument is an Aristotelian principle according to which actuality is prior to potentiality; or, in other words, a disposition must be always accounted for by some structural element in the agent having the disposition. According to this principle if there are two agents and one has a disposition (competence, potentiality, etc.) that the other lacks, then it must be the case that the two agents differ also in some other respect; either one has a part that the other does not, or the parts (elements) of one are interrelated in a way in which the parts (elements) of the other are not. For every dispositional difference between two entities there must be also a difference in their constituents or in their non-dispositional properties. Therefore, neither the ability captured by condition (i) nor the one captured by (iii) can ever be the sole difference between two entities. If two agents differ with respect to either of these abilities, then they must also differ with respect to their constituents or non-dispositional properties. According to the scheme outlined here, the difference will be with respect to their states of mind.

So far all that we have said as an explanation of abilities satisfying conditions (i) and (iii) is that in the case of competences like linguistic competence they have a common causal antecedent which is either a constituent or a non-dispositional property of the agent, and which we described as the state of mind of having internalized rules. The Aristotelian principle mentioned above justifies the first half of the explanation, but we need a justification for the second half; i.e. why describe the common causal antecedent as the state of mind of having internalized rules? Part of the justification lies in the claim that knowledge of rules, rather than any other kind of knowledge seems to be required both for the ability to produce the right utterances and for having intuitions about violations of the rules of language. The support for this claim lies in a demonstration that a natural language must be viewed, if it is to be adequately understood, as a potentially indefinite set of utterances generated by a set of rules. For the purposes of this paper it will be assumed that such a demonstration has been given by so-called generative grammars. The other part of the justification lies in the analogy between what we accept as explanation for conscious rule following and what is required as explanation for the phenomena under consideration. In the case of conscious rule following we know that the internalization and application of rules account both for the ability to make the right moves and for the ability to have the right intuitions. We also know — roughly — how the internalization of rules originates. What is wanted to account for the phenomena under consideration is something similar to knowledge of rules as manifested in conscious rule following, except that there is no conscious formulation of the rule prior to the understanding of its violation under particular circumstances, and there is no explanation of the origin of internalization that would lie as close to surface phenomena as the account of the origin of conscious internalization. These considerations lead to the interpretation of the state of mind accounting for abilities in the case of competences like linguistic competence as subconscious rule following or tacit knowledge of rules, to use Chomsky's terminology.

Let us review once more the argument leading to the postulation of tacit knowledge of rules. The argument does NOT proceed merely from premisses p1. We are able to form intuitions about the grammaticality or ungrammaticality of particular utterances, and p2. These intuitions fit a pattern (or patterns) that can be captured by rule R (or rules R', R'' ...), to the conclusion c. We must have, subconsciously or otherwise, internalized rule R (or $R_,$, $R_,$ ...). In short, one cannot argue, and it is not argued here, that if a rule fits a series of performances then the performer must have internalized the rule. Apart from this being a non sequitur, given that any pattern of performances can be subsumed under an indefinite variety of rules, we would be led to the absurd conclusion that even the simplest recognition of rule violation must have underlying it tacit knowledge of an indefinite variety of rules. Our argument proceeds, rather by adding to p1 and p2 premisses p3. There must be a state of mind that accounts for the ability mentioned in p1, and p4. The state of mind postulated in p3 is analogous to the one postulated to account for conscious rule following. The conclusion is: c^*. We must have tacit or subconscious knowledge of some rule that fits our intuitions. The sense of 'fit' will be explained at least partially in the paragraphs on idealization. According to this argument we cannot assume that every rule discovered by a linguist that fits a certain class of linguistic phenomena must be known tacitly by the competent speaker of the language, but that there are some rules that both fit the phenomena and are tacitly known by the speaker and the discovery of these rules will be the result of the work of the linguist under the optimum circumstances. Competence is not the mastery of any and all sets of rules that fit the language, but it is mastery of *a* set of rules that speakers of the language use to produce and interpret utterances.

At this stage we may raise two questions about the concept of tacit knowledge of rules; first: is the concept intelligible? and second: to what extent, if any, does it have explanatory power? Answers to the first question must center on the notion of subconscious, or non-conscious, belief. For if this notion is intelligible, then there seems to be no further mystery about subconscious rule following. Tacit knowledge involving non-conscious belief arises within the framework presented on two levels. On the one hand, there is tacit knowledge about specific points regarding the grammaticality or ungrammaticality of particular utterances. One must assume that at any given time a competent speaker has tacit knowledge of an indefinitely large number of such points of grammaticality, since many of these can be demonstrated as known by the speaker even though they were never, prior to prompting, consciously formulated in his mind. In addition to this, on a higher level, we must assume tacit knowledge of some rules by the speaker if the concept of non-conscious rule following is to have any significance at all.

Our problem can be boiled down to this: should we say that it is possible for *A* to have a belief *b* at *t'* even though *A* does not have *b* consciously in mind at *t'* and never before *t'* has *A* consciously formulated *b*? It seems that the answer to this question is affirmative, even though it is difficult to produce necessary or sufficient conditions for the application of the concept. Considerations supporting this stand can be advanced even apart from any consideration of linguistic competence. For although one cannot ascribe to a person belief in all of what is entailed by his consciously formulated beliefs, neither can one restrict the totality of beliefs ascribable to a person to those that he consciously formulated. To become conscious of some of one's most fundamental beliefs and commitments is, according to Socrates and Plato, the beginning of real self-knowledge that many of us never achieve. Thus consideration of what can be reasonably regarded as one's beliefs in the realms of logic, mathematics, morality, and one's own language, shows the concept of non-conscious belief to be indispensable. The difficulties of finding defining conditions are not considerably greater with regard to non-conscious belief than they are with regard to conscious belief. The ascription of both types of belief entails claims about the presence of mental processes in the agent. These processes are only very remotely related to what is observable, and at present are only dimly understood by either scientists or philosophers. All of this suggests that though the concept of non-conscious belief is in need of much further clarification, there are no insuperable obstacles to its becoming a useful tool of analysis.

The above defends the intelligibility of the concept under consideration. It is a further step to argue for its alleged explanatory utility. The Aristotelian principle invoked previously defends the postulation of some state of mind, and the above shows that there is no conceptual obstacle to regarding this state as involving non-conscious belief; but none of this shows why it is helpful or illuminating to describe the state of mind as we have. Part of the alleged illuminating power rests on the analogy pointed out before between what would account for the phenomena under consideration and conscious rule following. Once this analogy is accepted, then the utility of the concept under consideration lies in its directing attention to the kinds of elements, linguistic and mental, that one should look for in order to arrive at an adequate understanding of the phenomena. The concept of non-conscious rule following is vague, as we dealt with it so far, and as it occurs in the contemporary literature. But it is not irreparably vague. Its vagueness is due to our lack of understanding of all but the simplest observable phenomena having to do with perceptual or mental events. As long as there is reason to suppose that these phenomena are tied — both logically and causally — to underlying unobservable entities, the vagueness in the concept under consideration can be seen as diminishable by our hopefully increasing understanding of these unobservable structures and entities.

The hypothesis that competent agents follow rules not consciously formulated can be related to the commonly acknowledged claim that the behavior of agents exercising certain competences follows laws. We must ask, however, what prevents someone from regarding all laws fitting the performances of competent agents as correlated to rules tacitly known? The answer has two parts. First, it must be pointed out that rules tacitly known can be correlated with regard to descriptive content to laws governing — under ideal conditions — the behavior of the agent. Secondly, not all laws have correlated rules attached. We saw earlier that the postulation of tacitly known rules was based partly on the existence of intuitive judgments regarding violations of rules. While such intuitions are part of our use of language, our calculating, reasoning, etc., they are not part of many other processes that are lawlike. There are no intuitions accompanying the mastery of breathing, digesting, flying, etc. Thus there is no justification for postulating rules tacitly known by agent and correlated to the laws governing the afore-mentioned activities. The satisfaction of condition (iii) differentiates following a rule from merely acting in accordance with laws.

In the previous discussions we found it necessary to say that the relation between a rule and the actual behavior that it "fits" is complex and in need of further explanation. It is time now to turn to this topic. The complexity is due to two factors; an average performance is almost always merely an approximation of what an ideal or perfect manifestation of a competence would be, and competences are at times specified for ideal rather than for actual agents. Let us consider these points in order. The first point can be made with regard to human rule following in general. Given a rule of at least fair complexity, the pattern of conduct produced by the agent following the rule will practically never duplicate but only approximate the ideal pattern, i.e. the pattern prescribed by the rules the agent tries to follow. This is the secularized version of the doctrine of original sin, with special application to the methodology of the social sciences. It is illustrated by the behavior of a third grader trying to follow the rules of arithmetic, or by an adult trying to follow a reasonable moral rule, or by a person trying to speak according to the rules of his language. The effect of this general human condition is that we must separate ideal from actual performance patterns, and that we can never derive the rule that a person is trying to follow in a given context from his performance pattern alone. (This is an additional reason for the impossibility of abstracting rules; the other, better known one, is the "indeterminacy", in short, the fact that any pattern can be viewed as the result of the prescriptions of a large number of rules.)

In spite of all of this, the actual performance must serve as one source of evidence for determining the rule that an agent follows. In order to make such determination possible it is crucial to know what factors are likely to serve as distorting conditions. In other words, we have a correct account when we can outline an allegedly ideal performance pattern and derive the actual pattern by joining to the ideal pattern certain — statistically or otherwise systematic — conditions responsible for distortions. Thus we distinguish three elements within an explanation of competence; the ideal performance pattern, the actual performance pattern, and the distorting conditions. The latter may or may not be proper objects of scientific study depending on whether they are constituted by lawlike or nonlawlike occurrences.

A theory of the ideal performance pattern would be constituted of a general characterization of the agent and a presentation of the rules the mastery of which is the competence that is manifested in the ideal pattern under consideration. These two aspects of a theory, however, are themselves subject to the dichotomy between the actual and the ideal. For a competence may be specified in terms that make it impossible for a human agent to possess it. Thus one has to distinguish between the characterization of actual agents and that of ideal agents possessing competence. For example, one might characterize linguistic competence in such a way that its possession requires infinite memory. In that case the agent whose competence we discuss is obviously an idealized agent. Again, one might characterize the ideal reasoner as someone who knows all that any of the propositions known to him entail. In both of these cases we talk not only about idealized performance patterns but also about idealized agents.

An account of the ideal, together with an account of what separates it from the actual, amounts to an account of actual agents and performances. This two-stage feature of explanation of competences has its analogue in other types of scientific explanations. In various contexts one formulates laws holding for events under certain ideal conditions, and then adds laws that account for the divergence between the predicted ideal pattern and the one found by observation. Thus idealization is not unique to accounts of competences involving following of rules.

In this account of linguistic competence we have drawn so far three distinctions that relate to the "competence-performance" terminology. First, we distinguished competence from performance as a disposition with certain properties and its actual manifestations. 'Performance' in that sense refers to a series of actual events. We proceeded to distinguish ideal performance from actual performance, and their corresponding patterns. This is a contrast between a pattern of possible events and a pattern of actual events. Finally, we contrasted the idealized agent having linguistic competence from the actual competent agent. As we complete this rough outline of the analysis of competence we have to turn to one more contrast that appears in Chomsky's writing under the "competence-performance" terminology. In connection with the discussion of the ideal and the actual we had occasion to observe that the actual performance of a competent agent is the function of and the manifestation of a variety of factors not all of which are part of linguistic competence. Thus a THEORY OF PERFORMANCE, i.e. a systematic account that explains actual performance patterns, will have to take into consideration in addition to linguistic competence other matters as well. These other matters are described by Chomsky as MATTERS OF PERFORMANCE and are contrasted with matters of competence. As Chomsky himself repeatedly emphasized,[4] matters of performance may be just as legitimate objects of conceptual and scientific study as matters of competence. Some of these matters, such as limitations on human memory, limits of attention span, ways in which it is easier for humans to interpret perceptions, etc. emerge in the consideration of factors responsible for the divergences between the ideal and the actual performance patterns. One can demonstrate that these factors are not part of linguistic competence by pointing out that an agent lacking these limitations, characteristics, etc. could still be regarded as knowing all of his language, and an investigator ignorant of these factors could still be regarded as having complete knowledge of a natural language. Someone who produces utterances that violate the so-called laws of distorting factors is not violating the rules of a language, e.g. English. He is violating some of the laws of human communication.

Apart from these factors there are other matters that fall under the matter of performance label. For there are a variety of skills and com-

---

4   Noam Chomsky, *Aspects of the Theory of Syntax*, chapters 1 and 2.

petences that are often manifested in linguistic performance and are nevertheless not part of linguistic competence. Such are, for example, various rhetorical skills involving persuasion or the meeting of aesthetic standards, and various skills required for successful daily communication involving the interpretation of the intention of other speakers. In each such case an agent could lack these skills and competences and still have full command and understanding of all of English, and making mistakes with respect to these matters does not count as violating the rules of English. As we can see in these cases the distinction between matters of performance and matters of competence is really a distinction between matters of linguistic and matters of non-linguistic competence. Performances in the first sense of 'performance' are not the subject of scientific and conceptual study, performances in the sense that is now being explicated are — as we said above — legitimate subjects of investigations. A parallel between the distinction drawn here and the philosophical analysis of the concept of action will perhaps show the importance and need of the distinction under consideration. One of the well-known difficulties of analyzing something that happened and was caused by a human agent is that there are many descriptions of it and it is the instance of a number of different properties and dispositions. A method is required to sort out the different kinds of properties and dispositions of which one event or happening is an instance. The same principle applies to linguistic performances since these are simply a sub-set of the set of events or happenings.

The examples of matters of performance given so far are unlikely to lead anyone to doubt the clarity or sharpness of the distinction we are drawing. There are, however, other examples that are likely to raise controversy. Having established the distinction by the use of some clear cases, let us consider examples that may not be universally accepted. One of these is competence in knowing how to perform what the late J. L. Austin called illocutionary acts. The claim to be considered is that knowing how to perform at least a large collection of these acts, and knowing how to interpret them is not a matter of linguistic competence. Some illocutionary acts are embedded in legal contexts; such are the 'I do' of the marriage ceremony and the taking of an oath as one takes on an office. The claim concerning these acts is that one could know all of English without knowing how to perform or how to interpret the acts mentioned, and that failure to satisfy the rules governing these acts need not be a failure to satisfy rules of English. (Although it may be, of course, that the satisfying of the rules of English is part of the set of rules governing these acts.) This claim also carries with it the implication that understanding the terms involved in these acts is not the same as understanding the acts.

Many illocutionary acts, such as promising, commanding, requesting, explaining, etc., are not wholly embedded in any legal or institutional context. Again, the claim that the performing and interpreting of these acts are matters of performance is the same as claiming that one can understand all of English without knowing how to perform or interpret these acts. Likewise, the meanings of the expressions naming these acts would have to be distinct from the acts and their significance.

A general way of supporting the claim that the performance and interpretation of these acts is a matter of performance is to point out that it is one thing to understand English, and another to understand the point of what speakers on various occasions are saying. A lack of ability to know how to command, request, etc. and how to interpret instances of these acts is a lack of communicational skill or competence; but it is not lack of linguistic competence, i.e. knowing English.

Another difficult example is referring to or identifying things in particular non-linguistic contexts by the use of language. Success in such an enterprise will depend on the extent to which speaker and hearer can join in directing their attention to some feature or element of their shared environment. Given the sense of 'refer' used here, the relation named by this expression is one between people, parts of language, and objects. In this sense, people do the referring, not words. This is not to be confused with another sense of 'refer' which is equivalent to the sense of 'denote'. To know the denotation of a term is to know what kinds of things it is true of. Thus people refer but words denote. The claim to be defended is that to know the denotation of words is part of linguistic competence but to know what speakers on various occasions mean to refer to is a matter of performance.

It is worth noting that reference in the sense considered need not be accomplished by making use of language. Gestures, even movements of the eye, can direct the attention of someone in the environment to the desired object. This by itself, however, does not show that referring by use of language is not part of linguistic competence. In order to show that we need the further premiss that there are no grammatical or semantic requirements necessary or sufficient for determining what will do in a given context as a referring expression; i.e. an expression that someone on some occasion happens to use successfully to identify something for a hearer. The ability required to produce and interpret successfully speaker-hearer relative identification is essentially the ability to know and interpret correctly other people's intentions and habits of mind. Knowledge of the language shared by speaker and hearer is helpful but not essential. In any case, one could know all of English while being completely ignorant of how to interpret or produce successfully speaker-hearer relative identifications. The ability to understand intensions is wholly independent of the ability to interpret intentions.

To support this position one should point out that it is one thing to know English and quite another to know how to talk to people and get one's point across. The former requires mastery of the rules of the language, the latter requires a variety of communicational skills.

Regardless of whether these claims presented are accepted, at least it should be clear that the matter of competence versus matter of performance dichotomy helps to reconsider what we want to classify under the heading of knowing English and what we want to regard as knowing how to communicate with people.

In concluding this rough outline of the nature of linguistic competence — and a certain class of competences in general — we should note that once the ambiguities of the "competence-performance" terminology are unravelled, we are presented with a series of useful distinctions. None of these distinctions is unintelligible and all of them play vital roles in the conceptual framework required to answer the three questions formulated in the introductory section, answers to which yield what we called a theory of competence.

II

CREATIVITY. In this section we shall consider two properties that are involved in the analysis of linguistic competence. Chomsky has called both of these properties 'creativity'.[5] One of these is the ability to interpret novel utterances, i.e. utterances that have been previously part of the language but have never been encountered on previous occasions by the speaker. The other is the property of being free from stimulus control and instrumental constraints. The first "creativity" is a property of the competent language user and is part of his linguistic competence. The second is a property of the processes underlying linguistic competence. Let us consider these in order.

In specifying creativity' the relevant sense of 'novel' needs to be defined further. This has been done elsewhere.[6] Although this is part of the linguistic competence of a competent language user, the connection between it and linguistic competence is not analytic. It could have been the case that the normal user of a natural language would have been unable to interpret utterances of his language the meanings of which have not been explained to him explicitly. The claim that this creativity is a part of the competence of a normal user of a natural language is thus an empirical claim; furthermore, it should be easy to see that the claim could be

[5] This has been explained briefly in my "Linguistic Theory and the Philosophy of Language", 222.
[6] Moravcsik, "Linguistic Theory", 216-17.

disconfirmed by direct observation. Once this hypothesis has been established, its significance is that it calls attention to an interesting aspect of linguistic competence which demands explanation. What would enable an agent to have this kind of competence? First negatively, this fact shows that the learning of language cannot be either mere explicit instruction of the structure and meaning of various utterances, and unless one supposes that each speaker comes equipped with a tacit knowledge of an indefinite number of utterances one cannot account for this type of creativity if knowing one's language is construed as merely knowing a list of sentences. In order to explain creativity' we have to assume that the use of language involves either the following of strategy or the following of rules. Thus this aspect of competence is part of the evidence that leads one to suppose that linguistic competence is more than mere intellectual habit. It is important to see, however, that creativity' by itself does not entail rule following; it could be accounted for also by the assumption of use of strategy. Once more we can see that without reference to intuitions of rule violations one cannot conclude that the use of language involves the employment of internalized rules.

The other property, creativity'', not only has a different subject, but is also further removed from direct confirmation or disconfirmation. It is ascribed to processes as yet incompletely understood that underlie linguistic competence, and this ascription partly determines the nature of explanations to be expected that will clarify the basic structure of language.

This property is complex. One part of it involves freedom from stimulus control. By 'stimulus' we mean changes in the external environment of the agent (or organism). By 'control' we mean complete determination. Thus a process is free from stimulus control if and only if changes and manifestations of the process do not stand in one-to-one correlation to changes in the environment. This does not rule out correlations that have certain stimuli followed — under certain conditions — by certain responses. Applying all of this to the use of language, it is clear that much of traditional and recent mechanical learning and teaching technique aims successfully at establishing correlations such that given under certain circumstances a stimulus of a certain type (ST) a verbal response (R) of a certain type will follow. In short, under $C' \ldots C^n$ if ST then R. The successful establishing of such correlations is quite compatible with Chomsky's claim of freedom from stimulus control for linguistic processes. For 'control' entails no R without ST. In short, control amounts to a biconditional relation between ST and R. Chomsky's hypothesis is that no such correlations hold. Although one may be taught to respond to certain questions, signals, etc. by use of a certain verbal response, that verbal response can also be employed in the absence of the questions, signals, etc.

mentioned. Thus the empirical assumption is that language use is creative inasmuch as the production of various well-formed parts of the language is not wholly determined by changes — perceptible or otherwise — in the environment. In order to see this hypothesis in proper light let us contrast it with another claim, i.e. the conceptual claim that linguistic competence does not involve the lawlike correlation of parts of language and their employment with changes in the environment. This latter claim says that knowing a natural language does not include knowing rules correlating parts of the language with changes in one's environment. There are no known languages that include among their rules a rule of the form: "Whenever you notice change C in your environment, you must produce utterance U." What makes this claim conceptual is that one would add the provision: no such rule would be regarded by us as a rule of language; if some tribe has rules of this sort, these would be a matter of performance, not of competence. The claim about freedom from stimulus control is different in many ways. It is an empirical, not a conceptual claim, and it is not about the nature of the rules of a language, but about the conditions under which language will be produced and interpreted. It is the contention of this paper that both of these claims are true. Both contribute in different ways to determining how the basic structure of language and our use of it should be characterized. It is conceivable that drastic changes in the human race could do away with freedom from stimulus control, though no such change would alter the conceptual claim made here. This shows that Chomsky's claim is about the normal human agent under natural conditions.

Apart from freedom from stimulus control, the ascription of creativity" to language use entails freedom from control by inner forces such as desires, needs, and drives, and also freedom from functional or instrumental control. These freedoms too have to be construed along the same lines as the interpretation of freedom from stimulus control presented above. The claims leave open the possibility that some speakers will produce certain utterances in the presence of certain desires, ends, etc. But the claims foreclose the possibility of certain parts of language being utterable by humans ONLY in the presence of certain desires, needs, etc. The same considerations apply to instrumental or functional constraints and freedoms from these. It may be that language is used characteristically to convey wishes, persuade others, to enable one to communicate, etc., but freedom from instrumental constraint involves the possibility (not merely logical) of language use taking place even when it is not used as an instrument for any of these purposes. Functional control would result in certain parts of language being produced and interpreted only when these have some function, such as referring, predicating, describing, etc. Again, it may be that whenever we wish to employ a part of language for some such specific function, we choose only certain ones, but creativity" involves the possibility of producing and interpreting any part of language even in the absence of such functional employment.

If one views creativity" in this manner, it appears as if it were a negative concept. It tells us what does not determine the use of language, but does not tell us what, if anything, determines this. Thus the ascription of creativity" can be considered adequately only if its consideration is coupled with the consideration of the accompanying positive claim that the use of language is determined only by the process of thinking, and that the latter is autonomous, i.e. possesses the freedoms ascribed to the use of language above. Thus the full hypothesis states that thinking is free from stimulus, need, desire, drive, and instrumental control, and that the use of language is correlated with thinking only. These empirical claims admit only of indirect verification or disconfirmation. If, as it is supposed here, they are true, they determine to a large extent the character of explaining thought and the use of language.

The claim that thinking is autonomous has been linked in the past to a number of other claims, such as the claims that thinking involves immaterial entities and that it shows determinism to be false. The connections between these claims, however, are purely historical and not logical in nature. To say that thinking is autonomous is to say that its states or stages are not completely determined by external stimuli, or desires, needs, drives, etc. This claim is logically independent of the issue of whether materialism or dualism is true, and it does not entail indeterminism. It does not say that any one stage of the thought processes is indeterminate; it says only that whatever determines any one stage cannot be analyzed exhaustively into elements that do not include previous thought stages. And if man is a perpetual *res cogitans* — as there is reason to believe he is — then there is no answer to the question: what triggers off thinking?

The implications of these claims are twofold. On the one hand, they present us with a characterization of the use of language that limits the number of plausible alternatives as answers to the question: how is language acquired? Answers of the sort: as a response to inner drives, as a result of conditioning, etc. will not do. On the other hand, the complex freedom ascribed to the use of language also determines the way in which basic processes of interpretation and thus also the basic structure of language will be explained. Given that the use of language has the property of creativity" functional explanations will not have a crucial role within the theory of linguistic competence. The use of language is conceived here as a biological phenomenon, like breathing or digesting. In the cases of breathing and digestion we can give a functional and teleological account of why these processes take place. But such accounts are in no way more fundamental, nor are they substitutes for anatomical explanations. The structure of human anatomy will not be "better understood" if we find functional explanations for its parts. Likewise, functional accounts of the parts of language and linguistic processes are no substitutes for structural accounts, and neither are functional accounts — even if available — in some sense more fundamental than structural accounts. It is a mistake to expect that basic syntactic categories or basic stages of the interpretation of language will be, or can be, given functional explanations that somehow supplement or complete the structural explanations.

Thus we see how the two properties of creativity, one ascribed to the agent, and the other to the basic processes of language use, help to answer questions (b) and (c) raised in the introductory section.

III

INNATENESS. The previous sections gave partial characterizations of linguistic competence and the processes required for the actualization of that competence. In the course of these characterizations some things were said, by implication, about the agent himself. We characterized linguistic competence as the mastery of rules that lie below the surface of the observable parts of language. This mastery was shown to entail the ability to make judgments concerning the violations of these rules. Finally, we specified as part of linguistic competence the creative use of language, i.e. the ability to interpret utterances that are 'novel' in a specified sense. The first and third characterizations are empirical hypotheses, but the connection between the first and the second is conceptual. Of course, we claimed that there is empirical evidence for the second characterization as well. Concerning the processes underlying competence, two claims were made. It was claimed that these processes must include both tacit knowledge of some rules and tacit knowledge of what counts as violation of a rule of language. It was also claimed that the use of language is creative in the sense that it is as autonomous as thinking itself; i.e. it does not depend on the nature of external stimuli or inner drives, needs, etc.

In view of these characterizations what can we say about the agent? The main claim derived from the above is that the competent agent must be in a state of mind of having internalized a set of rules for the language. It was further argued, with the help of a so-called Aristotelian principle, that this state of mind cannot be analyzed in solely dispositional terms. It is natural that our next question should concern the ways in which this state of mind is acquired. Answers to this question should give a partial characterization of the competent agent.

There is a set of statements, proposed by Chomsky and others, that became known as the innate idea hypothesis, and this set is an answer to the question of how the state of mind of having internalized rules of language is in fact acquired by human agents. The so-called hypothesis is really a conjunction of three propositions. The first is independent of the second and third, but these two entail the first, and the third again entails the second.

The three propositions are the following:

(i) Given the normal conditions of language acquisition, it must be the case that the process of acquiring a state of mind of having internalized rules of language is accounted for by a structure innate to the human mind.

(ii) This innate structure is a set of innate ideas.

(iii) This set of innate ideas corresponds to a set of non-trivial synthetic linguistic universals.[7]

The logical relations mentioned above can be explained briefly by pointing out that the claim of linguistic competence being innate does not entail that what is innate should be ideas. For example, one might claim that the ability to walk is innate and rests on an innate structure, but nobody would claim that this structure is a set of ideas. Of course, as we shall see, the fact that what is to be explained is the state of having internalized rules makes it plausible to suggest that the innate structure is one of ideas or concepts. Finally, the force of (iii) is to restrict the possibility of variations among languages which is allowed by (ii). If (iii) is true — under one interpretation of "linguistic universals" to be given below — then only languages of certain types can be learned by humans as their first language. (No restriction is implied by these propositions with regard to the possible structure of languages to be learned as second languages.)

With regard to this set of propositions a conceptual analysis should raise at least the following three questions: (a) What is meant by 'innate' and 'idea'? (b) What evidence is there for any of the three propositions? and (c) To what extent, if any, do any of the propositions have explanatory power? In short, we must raise the questions of intelligibility, evidential backing, and explanatory ability, in the order, of each of the three propositions.

In considering the meaning of 'innate' it is best to start with a few negative points. Not anything can be properly described as innate or acquired. For example, we are born with hands and feet, and nobody would describe these as innate. As a rough delineation one can say that properties, capacities, elements of the mind, and physical elements that explain or account for capacities are such that the innate or not innate dichotomy is relevant to them. From this consideration it follows immediately that 'innate' cannot mean 'what we are born with'. The example of hands and feet shows that the latter is not a sufficient condition of

---

[7] See Moravcsik, "Linguistic Theory", 224, for a development of this.

innateness and examples of competence in walking or calculating show that it is not a necessary condition either since neither of these competences are possessed at the moment of birth. As a further approximation it should be pointed out that all of the things that we regard innate are due partly to environmental factors and partly to factors within the organism. The point of calling these innate is to call attention to the different roles that environmental and organic factors play in the development of the elements in question. The difficulty with the concept of innateness is that this difference in roles is very difficult to characterize in general. One cannot say that those things that need only normal environmental conditions and are universal are necessarily innate. For according to anthropologists there is no society without religion, and thus given normal environment the property of being exposed in some way to religious teaching or practice will be universal. Yet we would not want to describe this property as given innately. Again, roughly speaking the difference in roles can be described by stating that the development of an innate element depends mostly on physical or non-physical elements of the organism and environmental factors are unimportant inasmuch as the development of the element in question will not be affected by any except extreme variations in these factors. The difficulty with this characterization lies in the task of specifying what 'mostly' and 'extreme' mean in this formulation. Perhaps such specifications depend on the nature of the item in question and our knowledge of the human mechanism. (Professor J. Fodor suggested to me that perhaps 'innate' can be given precise meaning only within some physical or psychological theory. The remarks above amount to my way of adopting this suggestion.)

Those familiar with the literature on this subject might object that we have ignored a proposal that might be interpreted as giving a more specific definition of 'innate'. In a paper dealing with the capacity for language acquisition E. Lenneberg proposed four criteria of innateness. These are: (a) no variation within the species, (b) no history within the species, (c) evidence for inherited predisposition, and (d) presumption of specific organic correlates.[8] Brief reflection should convince us that though these criteria are useful, they do not constitute a definition of innateness. Conditions (a) and (c) are not sufficient either individually or collectively. Many things may be shared universally within a species that are not innate, and (c) is so vague as to give us only evidence for ascribing with high degree of probability innateness to some element. The vagueness in (c) (how strong evidence must we have?) also prevents (a) and (c) from being jointly sufficient, though clearly both of these are necessary conditions for something being innate. (b) and (d), however, are neither necessary nor

[8] E. K. Lenneberg, "The Capacity for Language Acquisition", in *The Structure of Language*, ed. by J. Fodor and J. Katz (Englewood Cliffs, N.J., 1964), 579-603.

sufficient, individually or collectively. For (d) to be a necessary condition we would have to assume materialism; and an analysis such as ours should stay neutral with regard to such issues. As to (b) it is logically possible that something should be innate even though its development can be traced in stages through the history of a species. Thus the conditions proposed by Lenneberg are useful partly as representing some of the necessary conditions for something being innate and partly for indicating the sorts of things that count as evidence in favor of the presence of innateness.

A consideration of Lenneberg's condition leads one naturally to the treatment of the issue of evidence. Having explained — roughly — what is meant by saying that an innate structure accounts for the acquisition of language, what evidence can one adduce in favor of this hypothesis? One source of evidence is derived from Lenneberg's conditions. For the available evidence suggests that linguistic competence meets all four of these conditions. The support for meeting condition (a) lies in the fact that linguistic competence is universal and does not vary with differences in the level of intelligence in the agents or with the nature of the linguistic data available except in extreme cases. Two other considerations provide further support. One of these is the speed with which a child at an early age succeeds in internalizing rules of language, and the other is the poorness of the data available to the average child. Finally, further support would be given by the ascription of creativity" to the understanding of language if this hypothesis itself could be given conclusive evidential support. For if established, this claim would indicate that the acquisition of language cannot be explained by reference to responses to inner drives, needs, or instrumental needs arising from the social nature of man.

The point of enumerating the kind of evidence that could be given in support of the first proposition making up the so-called innateness hypothesis is not to attempt to establish in this paper that we have now conclusive empirical evidence for the claim in question. Such work is part of a scientific rather than a conceptual enterprise such as ours. The main reason for dealing with the intelligibility of the concept of innateness and the possibility of giving evidence for the ascription of innateness is to show that the concept can be given a positive account and evidence can be considered in favor of or against the ascription without bringing in other concepts of learning or acquisition. In short, the analysis above shows that at least one part of the innateness hypothesis is not purely negative; it is not a claim that says only that the known theories of acquisitions are wrong. It is not a "what else?" theory, with dubious status as a scientific hypothesis.[9]

---

[9] The contrary has been claimed by H. Putnam in "The Innateness Hypothesis".

In addition to 'innate' the other term to be clarified in our attempt to defend the innate idea hypothesis is 'concept' (or a less felicitous synonym 'idea').

As Chomsky has said repeatedly, neither in his nor in the traditional formulations of rationalist learning theories is there any implication that concepts are entities open to examination by introspection or other acts of awareness. Thus our initial negative characterization is that concepts are to be distinguished from so-called object of thought, even when one considers "intensional objects of thought". Concepts within the theory of mind propounded here are theoretical constructs rather than entities open to direct observation. This does not mean, however, that we cannot be conscious of a state or event describable as "having a concept" or "making use of a concept". According to the analysis propounded here we should regard such states and events as entities that we are sometimes aware of but which in many instances remain beneath the level of conscious awareness.

Our next move is to invoke the Aristotelian principle used previously and state that the notion of a concept or idea cannot be given a fully dispositional analysis. Having a concept and making use of concepts are dispositions to perform a variety of intellectual tasks: some of these are recognitional, others involve knowing how to verify the ascriptions of properties to things, and others may involve propositional knowledge. A concept, according to the analysis proposed, is an entity that plays a crucial role in accounting for the having of these dispositions. For according to the Aristotelian principle invoked it is impossible that there should be two people A and B, and A has a concept C that B does not have, and the two people differ only in their dispositional properties. Thus our positive characterization is that a concept is that entity that plays a crucial role in accounting for those dispositions and processes that constitute the having or making use of a concept; such dispositions being explicable in terms of recognitional, criterial and propositional abilities. Furthermore, concepts are correlated to properties inasmuch as the having of a concept is analyzed in terms of those dispositions and processes that are involved in knowing what a property is; i.e. knowing what it is for it to be true of something, knowing how to give at least a partial analysis of it, etc.

It is easily seen, of course, that this partial account of what a concept is remains very vague. According to the analysis given it is quite possible that concepts are nuts and bolts inside a human agent. To a small extent this vagueness is a virtue; for it shows that the introduction of the notion of a concept is quite neutral between materialism and Cartesian dualism. This virtue is, however, dwarfed by the relative lack of content of the analysis given so far, and the danger that the characterization given will be seen as amounting to the statement that a concept is an "I know not what" that accounts for certain intellectual dispositions. If so, our analysis would be subject to the Molière-disease; i.e. to furnishing an explanation analogous to the one given by Molière's doctor of the dormitive powers of opium. There is a tension at this stage of our account between the Aristotelian principle and the danger of Molière's disease. The danger would foreshadow fatal weakness if our analysis of 'concept' could be shown to be essentially and irreparably vague. It does not seem, however, that this is the case. The main reason for our inability to give more precise content to the meaning of 'concept' is that we know very little about the causal factors responsible for the intellectual dispositions, etc., making up the "having of a concept". There is no a priori reason to suppose that our ignorance is permanent; and, given our analysis, the notion of a concept is bound to gain more and more content as we find out more and more about the causal factors responsible for intellectual capacities and processes.

Having satisfied the intelligibility requirement let us consider the objections raised against the innate idea hypothesis by John Locke.[10] Since his attack on innate ideas has been described by some contemporary philosophers as effective, a brief review showing the weaknesses of the attack might be in order.

There seems to be some confusion in Locke with regard to the relations between innate principles and innate ideas. The beginning of chapter II sounds as if principles and notions were interchangeable.[11] In the actual discussions, however, the two are kept fairly distinct. Roughly, chapter II is an attack on innate principles and chapter IV on innate ideas. Locke claims in the latter chapter that there can be no innate principles unless their components, i.e. ideas, are also innate. He does not seem to consider the other aspect of this issue; namely, that though there can be no innate principles without innate ideas, there can be innate ideas without innate principles.

In any case, Locke's arguments against innate ideas or principles are designed to show that IN FACT there are no such things. Thus he is not challenging the intelligibility of the notions involved in the innate idea hypothesis. His claims are — with exceptions to be noted below — empirical claims, and when compared to the evidence available today, they seem weak. This is not a matter of comparing "non-scientific" with "scientific" evidence; rather, our conception of what it is that a language learner must master as well as our understanding of the early stages of language acquisition have improved.

Locke could not attack the intelligibility of the notion of an innate

---

[10] John Locke, *An Essay Concerning Human Understanding*, ed. by A. Pringle-Pattison (Oxford, 1924), Book I.
[11] Locke, *An Essay* 16.

principle in any case, since he admits the existence of such, though he describes these — the desire for happiness and the aversion to misery — as practical and not involving "impressions of truth on the understanding".[12] There is nothing in Locke to show that though one can have practical innate principles of this kind, one could not have those of the kind that involve "impressions of truth", though he tries to argue that in fact there are none.

Locke makes two points that are of conceptual interest. One of these is the sound insight that various criteria which people have invoked as necessary or sufficient conditions of innateness cannot play this role. Locke's negative views on what cannot be regarded as evidence for innateness are, however, much better than what emerges from his discussions as his view of what would count as decisive evidence for innateness.

The other conceptual point is the attack on "implicit" (or as we called it above "tacit") knowledge of principles.[13] One of the key premises of this attack is the claim that "no proposition can be said to be in the mind ... which it was never yet conscious of".[14] It is unfair to interpret this claim (as the modern editor of the *Essay* does) as the equating of thinking with conscious thinking. Locke apparently would allow for the possibility that there is a proposition in the mind at time t' even though we are not conscious of it, as long as there was some previous time t'' at which the proposition was consciously formulated. The weakness of the claim is, however, that it rules out the possibility of our having indirect evidence — such as the constant application of a principle, the seeming following of a rule, etc. — supporting the claim that an agent does have knowledge of a principle or proposition even though he has never consciously formulated it. Also, Locke does not allow for there being grounds to distinguish the mere ability to perceive the truth of a proposition if and when presented with it from the ascription of tacit knowledge. But the kind of possibilities mentioned above would justify the drawing of such a distinction.

In view of these flaws, one cannot regard Locke's attack on any parts of the innate idea hypothesis — at least as presented in this paper — as effective.

Our final task is to show what is gained by adding (ii) and (iii) to (i). The evidence in favor of adding (ii) to (i) is that the competence to be acquired involves the mastery of rules. In the case of explicit rule learning involving intellectual skills, the acquisition does involve concept-formation. It is not unreasonable to suppose that a process analogous to the one considered takes place in the case of acquiring the state of having in-

---

[12] Locke, *An Essay* 28-29.
[13] Locke, *An Essay* 18, 25.
[14] Locke, *An Essay* 18.

ternalized rules that were not introduced explicitly to the learner. It must be added, however, that until more specific content is given to the notion of a concept, the addition of (ii) to (i) represents only slight gain in explanatory power. Thesis (i) says that we have to look for an innate structure to account for language acquisition. Thesis (ii) says that this innate structure involves elements that account for certain intellectual dispositions and states involving the understanding of properties. Neither of these statements is vacuous, and neither follows from the other; but even jointly they give but scarce information about what it is that is supposed to be innate.

The addition of (iii) can be given two interpretations. On one interpretation (iii) is logically entailed by (ii). For if language acquisition is made possible by a set of concepts innate to the human mind, then the properties correlated with these concepts must be instantiated in all languages. If we define, however, "linguistic universal" as language-specific (i.e. not just some general properties that are instantiated by almost any intellectual artifice) then (iii) does not follow from (ii) and as a distinct empirical hypothesis it adds specificity to (ii).

In any case, either version of (iii) serves the important function of allowing for the possibility of disconfirming the innate idea hypothesis. For if there are no non-trivial synthetic linguistic universals, then at least (ii) must be false, and any remaining version of (i) might turn out to be at least philosophically uninteresting. Taking (iii) in the stronger sense — by making the universals unique to language — we get a very clear condition of disconfirmability. If no such universals are found, the hypothesis fails to explain language acquisition. A theory admitting such a clear condition of disconfirmability could hardly be either vacuous or irreparably vague.

If the conclusions of this paper are sound, then at least in rough outlines a theory of linguistic competence of the type advocated by Chomsky has been sketched in positive and non-vacuous terms. Thus criticisms of Chomsky that claim the conceptual hopelessness and unintelligibility of Chomsky's type of approach to linguistic competence are wide of their mark. Although this paper shows that much conceptual work remains to be done, our outline indicates that such work is most likely to be rewarding, and that allegedly disreputable concepts can be given fruitful reinterpretations. These concepts play a vital and indispensable role in the proposed theory. One of the interesting aspects of this theory is the constant interplay of conceptual and empirical investigations. Such interplay can only benefit both science and philosophy.

Stanford University.

Thomas Nagel

LINGUISTICS AND EPISTEMOLOGY

There is some reason to believe that Chomsky's views about the innate contribution to language-acquisition have a bearing on epistemological issues: on disputes over the existence of a priori knowledge, for example. Certainly if he is right, grammar provides a striking example of strong innate constraints on the form of human thought, and a natural object of philosophical fascination.

I do not propose to discuss the correctness of Chomsky's view concerning the importance and size of that innate contribution, or the adequacy of the support offered for it. The object of this paper is to investigate what epistemological consequences Chomsky's empirical hypotheses about language-learning have, if they are CORRECT. The discussion will divide into two parts. First, I shall consider how Chomsky's hypotheses are most appropriately formulated, and specifically how the concept of knowledge can enter into their formulation. Second, I shall consider the bearing of these hypotheses on the epistemological status of our knowledge of natural languages, and also what they suggest about other kinds of knowledge, particularly those sometimes thought to be a priori.

I

The following, from page 58 of *Aspects of the Theory of Syntax*, gives a clear, brief statement of Chomsky's position:

Reprinted from: *Language and Philosophy*, ed. by S. Hook (New York, N.Y.U. Press, 1969), 171-82.

It seems plain that language acquisition is based on the child's discovery of what from a formal point of view is a deep and abstract theory — a generative grammar of his language — many of the concepts and principles of which are only remotely related to experience by long and intricate chains of unconscious quasi-inferential steps. A consideration of the character of the grammar that is acquired, the degenerate quality and narrowly limited extent of the available data, the striking uniformity of the resulting grammars, and their independence of intelligence, motivation, and emotional state, over wide ranges of variation, leave little hope that much of the structure of the language can be learned by an organism initially uninformed as to its general character.

I believe Chomsky means to assert that we have here a genuine case of innate knowledge. His references to the Rationalists suggest that he does. Moreover, the alternative to an organism initially *un*informed as to the general character of the structure of natural languages would seem to be an organism initially INFORMED as to that general character. And elsewhere (p. 27) he speaks of ascribing tacit knowledge of linguistic universals to the child. However, for the purpose of this discussion, it is not necessary to settle the exegetical point. The fact is that Chomsky's contentions about language-acquisition will suggest to most students of epistemology, as they suggest to me, that we are presented here with an example of innate knowledge. It is this natural philosophical interpretation that I propose to examine, and I shall not in the remainder of this paper concern myself explicitly with Chomsky's philosophical views, but only with the philosophical implications of his linguistic views.

The first question, then, is whether the initial contribution of the organism to language-learning, alleged by Chomsky, is properly described as knowledge at all. Let us begin by considering what I take to be a natural but bad argument for a negative answer to the question. The argument has the form of a reductio.

It occurs to most philosophers to ask, at some point in their considera- tion of Chomsky's views, whether the decision to apply the concept of knowledge in this case would not also commit us to ascribing innate knowledge, perhaps even a priori knowledge, to the human digestive system (or perhaps rather to human beings in virtue of the behavior of their digestive systems). For without having to be trained, instructed, or conditioned, the individual is able to adjust the chemical environment in his stomach to break down the digestible food that is introduced, while rejecting, sometimes forcibly, what is indigestible. This formidable task of classification and variable response is carried out even by infants, so it cannot be learned entirely from experience.

Admittedly the infant is not consciously aware of the principles that govern his gastric secretions, nor is the adult, unless he has studied physiology. But this does not distinguish the case from that of language-acquisition, for neither a child, nor an adult who has not studied linguistics, is consciously aware either of the grammatical rules of his language or of the principles by which he arrives at the ability to speak the language governed by those rules, on the basis of his exposure to a subset of the sentences of that language. In light of these parallels, it might be thought that the same reasons which can be offered in support of the view that there is innate knowledge of the general character of linguistic structure would count equally well in favor of the view that there is innate knowledge of the proper chemical means of digesting various kinds of food. The consequence of this would be that either both are examples of innate knowledge, or neither is. And it would then appear that the latter possibility is the more plausible. This would allow us to say that in both cases there is an extremely important innate CAPACITY — to discriminate among and digest foods, or to acquire command of natural languages having a certain type of structure — but it would not be called innate KNOWLEDGE in either case.

The trouble with this argument is that it ignores the difference between the operations that we have in the two cases the capacity to perform. In the case of digestion, the operation is not an action at all (this is obvious even though we do not possess an analysis of action). Nor do the data on which the operation is based, i.e. the various foods introduced into the stomach, have to be brought to the awareness of the organism. In the case of language-learning, on the other hand, conscious apprehension of the data (limited as they may be) is essential; and what the individual can do as a result of his linguistic capacity is to speak and understand sentences.

Moreover, the exercise of the capacity involves BELIEFS: e.g. that a certain combination of words is, or is not, a sentence of the language. Someone who regurgitates a bad oyster, on the other hand, is not thereby said to believe that it is indigestible. Though we may not possess an adequate analysis of the distinction, it is clear that certain methods of response and discrimination warrant the attribution of beliefs and attitudes, while others do not. Only of the former category is it appropriate to consider whether they give evidence of knowledge. The phenomena of language use belong to that former category, whereas the phenomena of digestion do not.

It is clear then that such cognitive concepts are entirely appropriate to the description of linguistic capacity and performance on particular occasions. What must be settled, however, is whether the concepts of knowledge and belief can be applied at higher levels of generality and abstraction in the description of the individual's linguistic capacity, and ultimately in the description of his capacity to acquire that capacity.

We may distinguish the following two theses: (1) that the general capacity to produce a set of performances each of which provides an instance of knowledge is itself an instance of more general knowledge; (2) that the general capacity to acquire other capacities each of which is an instance of knowledge is itself an instance of still more general knowledge. The former thesis is more plausible than the latter, but both are needed to warrant the inferential ascent from cases of linguistic knowledge revealed in particular utterances to the ascription of a knowledge of linguistic universals on which language learning is alleged to depend.

It will be useful if we try to ascend step by step from the most specific and immediate case to more general capacities. It seems obvious that we can speak of linguistic knowledge whose object is not merely the grammaticality or meaning of a particular utterance, but something more general. (In fact it is doubtful that we could speak of knowledge in the particular case unless we could also speak of it on a more general level.) To take a very simple example, we can ascribe to the ordinary speaker of English, on the basis of countless particular performances and responses, the knowledge that the plural form of a noun is usually formed by adding 's', and that among the exceptions to this is the word 'man', whose plural is 'men'. Now we MIGHT verify this ascription by finding that the individual can actually state the rule; but it is important that this is not necessary. Someone can possess general knowledge of a rule of the language without being able to state it. He may never have heard the words 'plural', and 'noun', for example, and may be unable to formulate the principle in any other way. When we come to the more complicated principles to which grammatical English speech conforms, that will be the usual situation. Only professional grammarians will be able to state those rules, and sometimes even that may not be true.

Under what conditions can knowledge of a language governed by certain rules be described as knowledge of those rules? It will be instructive in this connection to consider another type of knowledge that cannot be explicitly formulated by its possessor, namely unconscious knowledge in the ordinary psychoanalytic sense. This is of course a very different phenomenon from knowledge of the rules of grammar, but it has an important feature that, as Saul Kripke has pointed out to me, may bear on the linguistic case. The psychoanalytic ascription of unconscious knowledge, or unconscious motives for that matter, does not depend simply on the possibility of organizing the subject's responses and actions in conformity with the alleged unconscious material. In addition, although he does not formulate his unconscious knowledge or attitude of his own accord, and may deny it upon being asked, it is usually possible to bring him by analytical techniques to SEE that the statement in question expresses something that he knows or feels. That is, he is able eventually to acknowledge the statement as an expression of his own belief, if it is presented to him clearly enough and in the right circumstances. Thus what was unconscious can be brought, at least partly, to consciousness. It is essential that his acknowledgment NOT be based merely on the observation of his own responses and behavior, and that he come to recognize the rightness of the attribution from the inside.

It seems to me that where recognition of this sort is possible in principle, there is good reason to speak of knowledge and belief, even in cases where the relevant principles or statements have not yet been consciously acknowledged, or even in cases where they will never be explicitly formulated. Without suggesting that knowledge of the rules of a language is in other ways like the unconscious knowledge revealed by psychoanalysis, we may observe that accurate formulations of grammatical rules often evoke the same sense of recognition from speakers who have been conforming to them for years that is evoked by the explicit formulation of repressed material that has been influencing one's behavior for years. The experience is less alarming in the former case, but nevertheless recognizably similar. It can happen if the grammatical principles are formulated in a technical vocabulary that may require a certain amount of effort to master.

So long as it would be possible with effort to bring the speaker to a genuine recognition of a grammatical rule as an expression of his understanding of the language, rather than to a mere belief, based on the observation of cases, that the rule in fact describes his competence, it is not improper I think to ascribe knowledge of that rule to the speaker. It is not improper, even though he may never be presented with a formulation of the rule and consequently may never come to recognize it consciously.

If the condition of recognizability cannot be met, however, the ascription of knowledge and belief seems to me more dubious. And this casts doubt on the possibility of carrying the ascription of knowledge to any level of generality or abstraction higher than that involved in the specification of grammatical rules for a particular natural language. Even some of those rules are highly abstract. But when we consider the alleged innate contribution to language-learning, we pass to quite another level, and there is reason to doubt that the principles of such a linguistic acquisition device, when they have been formulated, could evoke internal recognition from individuals who have operated in accordance with them.

The rules of a particular grammar deal in part with recognizable expressions, and retain some connection, in their formulation, with the speaker's conscious experience of his language. The connection in the case of linguistic universals of the kind that Chomsky suggests are innately present, is more remote. One example that he offers is the proposal that the syntactic component of a grammar must contain transformational rules. This highly abstract condition is supposed to apply to ALL languages, and to determine the way in which a child acquires knowledge of the grammar of his native language by being exposed to samples of speech. But is it supposed that he could in principle be brought some day to recognize such a principle as the proper expression of an assumption he was making at the time (once the proper principle has been formulated and its meaning conveyed to him)? This may be a possibility, but the conditions of explanatory adequacy that Chomsky accepts seem not to demand it. Explanatory adequacy is in itself of course a very strong requirement. But a hypothesis could be shown to satisfy it on the basis of observation of the language-learning feat itself. The additional test of asking the language-learner whether he can recognize the principle as one that was activating him all along seems irrelevant. It seems not to be required even that such internal recognition should EVER be available or possible, no matter how much effort is expended on it.

I may have misconstrued Chomsky on this point; but in light of it, I am uneasy about extending the concept of knowledge, and the related concepts of belief and assumption, to the description of those innate capacities that enable a child to acquire knowledge of a language — any natural language — on the basis of rather minimal data. If this is correct, then not every innate capacity to acquire knowledge need itself be an instance of knowledge — even though its structural description may be quite complex.

II

The difficulties raised so far about the ascription of innate knowledge on the basis of language-learning ability are really broader difficulties about the ascription of innate BELIEFS or ASSUMPTIONS on the basis of language-learning ability. I wish now to turn to the epistemologically more interesting question, whether there is any possibility that the other main type of condition for knowledge could be met in such cases. I refer to the justification. There has been considerable controversy over the exact nature of this condition, but I hope it will be possible to discuss the present issue without entering that maze.

The problem is this. We can imagine almost any belief to be innately present, or that there is an innate tendency to develop that belief as the result of certain minimal experiences. That is not a sufficient basis for ascribing knowledge, however. Not just any belief that one cannot help arriving at is *ipso facto* justified, even if it should be true.

Suppose that someone discovered that he was able on request to specify the square root of any integer to four decimal places, without reflection or calculation. The fact that his ability was innate would not of itself guarantee the validity of his answers. The grounding of his knowledge of square roots would be rather more complex: he and other persons could verify by calculation in case after individual case that the number which he unreflectively believed to be the square root of a given integer in fact was the square root. In virtue of this further evidence, his unreflective belief in any given case could be taken as strong evidence of its own truth. In that sense it would be self-justifying — not merely because of the innateness of the capacity, but because of its independently verifiable accuracy.

With knowledge of a language we face a very different subject matter, but certain features of the case are the same. Let us consider first an imaginary example analogous to the one just discussed — a case in which someone has an innate capacity that is not generally shared. Suppose someone discovers that he is able to extend his vocabulary merely by observing new species of plants and animals, because he finds himself able to say what they are called without being told. Again, the mere fact that he is innately disposed to call this bird a magpie does not guarantee that that is its name. But if it is discovered in case after case that his unreflective belief conforms to general usage, the belief itself will provide evidence for its own truth.

Now, the actual phenomenon of language-learning that Chomsky describes is different from this, because it reveals an innate capacity that we all share. All speakers of English, for example, reach agreement in an obedience to certain grammatical rules, and attain this naturally and without calculation after a certain amount of exposure to the language. Now, no one individual's innate propensity to arrive at these rules of itself guarantees that they are the rules of the language he is speaking. That depends on a more general conformity to those same rules by all speakers of the language, and this is guaranteed by the universality of those same innate propensities. Thus if any given individual knows that his own linguistic intuitions about sentences that he has not encountered before, and his own original linguistic productions, are in conformity with the linguistic intuitions of other speakers of his language, then he can regard his innate tendencies as providing strong evidence for their own accuracy. But that is simply because as a matter of natural fact they are in conformity with the linguistic propensities of speakers of the language in general, as determined presumably by a uniform innate contribution. I am not suggesting for a moment that we actually DO step back from our linguistic intuitions in order to validate them in this way. I am suggesting only that it is because such a justification is AVAILABLE that we can plausibly describe what our innately governed linguistic propensities provide as KNOWLEDGE of the language.

The point of all the examples is this: in each case, the fact that the

tendency to arrive at a certain belief was innate, did not by itself make it a
case of knowledge. In the special case of language, where the actual
rules are simply those by which competent speakers generally are
governed, a universal innate tendency to arrive at certain rules is enough
to guarantee their accuracy; but any one individual must still know that he
is in conformity with the universal tendency, in order to know that his
linguistic intuitions are correct. And this is a matter that is open to
empirical investigation. The crucial fact is that in any individual case
the alleged innate contribution to language-learning can itself be assessed
for its accuracy as a source of knowledge of the language. It may be that
no one ever engages in this sort of assessment, and that the innate
tendency to construct the grammar of one's language in a certain way
also includes an innate tendency to assume that other speakers will
construct it in the same way; in fact this seems likely. But that assumption
too is open to epistemological assessment by other means.

The importance of all this is that the innate factor, which Chomsky
argues must underlie our language-learning capacity, bears no resemblance to the sort of unquestionable, epistemologically unassailable
foundation on which some philosophers have sought to base human
knowledge, and which is generally referred to as a priori or innate knowledge. What has been sought under this heading is something that is not
itself open to the usual varieties of epistemological assessment and doubt,
something whose opposite is unimaginable.

But what Chomsky offers us is a system of innate propensities that
we are conveniently stuck with. It is perfectly imaginable that we should
be differently constituted, but we are not. A mere innate tendency to believe
certain things or perform in certain ways, no matter how universal, is not
a priori knowledge. Even Hume thought that we all share a natural
propensity to believe that the sun will rise again tomorrow. To point out
the natural phenomenon of human agreement, innately determined, is
simply to turn aside the epistemological demand that motivates the
search for a priori knowledge.

In fact, such a move is closely related to Wittgenstein's position[1] —
the main difference being that Wittgenstein applies it much more generally,
and not just to language-learning. He argues that if one follows any
chain of epistemological justification far enough, one comes in the end to a
phenomenon of human agreement — not conventional agreement,
but natural, innately determined agreement — on which the acceptance
of that justification depends. He supposes this to happen whether the
justification is empirical or deductive. If he is right, the procedures by
which we subject one innate contribution to epistemological assessment

---

[1]   I am aware that Chomsky does not share this view of Wittgenstein. He has been
kind enough to show me a forthcoming paper that defends another interpretation.

will themselves simply depend on another innate contribution. And if at every stage what we have reached is only a contingent feature of our constitution, then there is no unquestionable a priori foundation on which our knowledge rests. It depends on a network of innate responses and propensities; and they are simply there.

If this is so, then epistemology may be essentially impossible. Insofar as Chomsky's contentions about language suggest that similar innate contributions underlie other cognitive phenomena as well, they suggest that all knowledge is in similar straits: it lacks an unassailable foundation. Sometimes, as in the case of language, one can take further steps to justify one's confidence in the yield of one's innate mechanism. Evidence of this kind is available to any speaker who successfully uses the language to communicate with others. But the admission of such evidence may in turn depend on innate principles that, without guaranteeing their own justification, form part of one's basic constitution;[2] so the task of justification may be incompletable.

Though this is epistemologically unsettling, it has practical compensations. If we had to learn by trial and error, or by training, how to digest food, we should have a much harder time surviving. But fortunately we don't need to KNOW how to digest food, for we do it in the right way automatically. Language-learning may be similar. We do not need to KNOW how to construct the grammar of a natural language on the basis of our early childhood exposure to samples of it. We simply ARRIVE at a command of the language after a certain period of exposure, and find ourselves convinced that other speakers are following the same rules.

It may be true in many areas of human activity and experience that if we had to rely on what we could come to know, by either empirical or rational means, we should be unable to survive. But if in these areas we are fortunate enough to possess an innate endowment that suits us to deal with the world awaiting us, we do not require the knowledge that it would be so difficult, or perhaps impossible, to obtain. We can be guided by our innate ideas instead.

---

[2] I believe that this is connected with Quine's thesis of the indeterminacy of translation.

R. Schwartz

LINGUISTICS AS PSYCHOLOGY

In the past few years it has become increasingly fashionable to claim that any satisfactory account of human behavior must view this behavior as mediated by and dependent on internal representations. In this paper, I should like to examine the notion of an internal representation and raise some points about it that I feel are worth further investigation. My discussion will be primarily centered around a consideration of the psycholinguist's attribution of an internalized grammar to speakers of a given language. Though I shall spend most of my time speaking about grammars and verbal behavior, I feel the problems to be examined are merely particular instances of the more general problem of explicating the relationship between a formal specification of an activity and what a subject has learned, knows, and does. Furthermore, the issues here are closely related to the questions of understanding what it is for a given formal theory to model or be a simulation of mental processes. Thus, while I shall primarily concern myself with psycholinguistics, I feel the problems I shall raise cut across cognitive psychology in general.

Throughout my discussion I shall use Chomsky's name as an abbreviation for those linguists, psychologists, and philosophers who in general adopt a Chomskian view of verbal learning and behavior. I do not necessarily mean to attribute all of the positions under discussion to Chomsky himself. Furthermore, while it may be possible to see in which direction a linguist in particular might proceed to handle some of the problems I

This paper is a much edited version of a talk given at the University of Minnesota which in turn was based on and was an elaboration of my paper, "On Knowing a Grammar", in *Language and Philosophy*, edited by Sidney Hook. The brief ending section on innateness is taken without change from that paper.

shall raise, the issue that concerns me is to see if we can deal with these matters in a PSYCHOLOGICALLY relevant way, so that a given solution has some psychological cash value.

Broadly speaking the question I am interested in considering is what, if any, sense can be given to the claim that someone who has learned a language knows or has internally represented its grammar. Chomsky's answer is that the grammar of a language should be seen as a description of the linguistic competence of a speaker of the language. He stresses that we must be careful to distinguish between a speaker's competence and his performance, and it is the former of these that a grammar is supposed to describe. Now there would seem to be nothing particularly mysterious or peculiar to language in the distinction between competence and performance. Surely we must allow that someone can have a proficiency, skill, or competence to do something and that a description of it is to be distinguished from a description of his actual performance. For example, we might claim that any of the numerous axiom systems for addition and subtraction characterize a certain part of the mathematical competence of someone who knows or has learned simple arithmetic. This does not mean that the person can state these axioms, nor that he will ever carry out any particular addition or subtraction, nor that his performance will always satisfy these rules, for he may purposely violate them or just make a mistake. A given S's performance could be expected to satisfy the axioms describing his competence only under ideal conditions of motivation, memory, attention, etc.

There might even be some arithmetic equations generated by the axioms which, for reasons such as the size of the numbers involved and the mortality of man, we can be quite sure no one will in fact ever work out. Thus we may want to distinguish having a competence from actually BEING ABLE to do something. In this arithmetic case S may not be able to solve a particular problem due to its length but may be claimed to have the arithmetic competence to do so. We could perhaps bridge the gap between the notions of 'competence' and 'being able' by claiming that a description of competence tells us what a subject is able to do under some set of ideal conditions. To claim then that the axioms of arithmetic represent S's competence would seem merely to claim that S has the arithmetic skills to determine the correctness of an unlimited set of equations and that the various axiom systems can be used to represent or specify that set.

In a like manner it may seem reasonable to look at a grammar as a formal system for generating the grammatical sentences of a language and thus as representing S's competence in recognizing acceptable strings of that language. As the arithmetic system specifies the arithmetic strings S's competence recognizes as correct equations, so our grammar may "pick out" or generate the class of verbal strings S's linguistic competence recognizes as grammatically correct. Again, this would not imply that S can state the given grammatical rules, or that S will encounter or produce every string generated by the system, or that S's performance will always be correct. Nor is it claimed that S has a disposition or is disposed to produce any particular sentence generated by the rules. The grammar merely specifies the set of sentences that S would recognize as grammatical under some set of ideal conditions. If this then is what it means for a formal system to specify a competence I find the notion of competence-performance distinction RELATIVELY clear.[1] From this standpoint, criticisms of a grammar as a specification of competence on ground that the grammar generates an infinite number of sentences or that it generates sentences longer than anyone could be expected to produce, are not, I think, very telling.

But Chomsky does not limit his claims for a grammar to the interpretation just presented. Rather he makes the further claim that the speaker knows or has an internal representation of the rules of grammar of his language. Chomsky admits that in this instance he is not using the term 'know' in the sense of KNOWING THAT nor in the sense of KNOWING HOW, but in a third sense — that of tacit or implicit knowing. He finds the traditional 'knowing' dichotomy too restrictive. Clearly, it is admitted S does not have propositional knowledge of the rules of his language. He's not consciously aware nor need he understand or believe the rules. On the other hand, it is felt that to claim S knows how to speak a particular language while true, does not go far enough. It is just at this stage that tacit knowledge is brought in by the psychologist in an attempt to account for and to explain this know how. Chomsky's claim seems to be that in order to know how to speak a language, S must know (tacitly or implicitly) the grammar of the language.

A correct interpretation of this notion of tacit knowledge, however, is not immediately forthcoming. For, if we allow that knowledge of a grammar is neither knowing that or knowing how, what sense can be given to the claim that S has internalized the rules. I think there are several basic interpretations of this claim that in one form or another appear over and over again in the literature on language acquisition and verbal behavior, but each of these require further examination: (1) the rules describe significant regularities in S's linguistic competence, (2) S has unconscious propositional-like beliefs or knowledge of the grammar,

---

[1] Notice that while it may be claimed that anyone who has mastered a language has the competence to recognize as grammatical all the sentences of his language, the claim that he has the competence to produce them all is more problematic. For example, in what interesting sense can it be said that any speaker of English has the competence to produce of his own accord the sentences of a Shakespeare or Milton?

(3) for each sentence in his language S knows the information contained in the structural description (S.D.) the grammar assigns it (the S.D. being the complete tree structure provided in deriving the string in the system), and (4) in order for S to understand, produce, or decide on the grammaticality of a sentence, S must determine or generate its S.D.

On the first interpretation, to claim S has internalized the rules is to claim that the grammar describes significant regularities in S's linguistic competence. If this means that S knows the regularities in his language specified by the grammar, then, taken literally, this is just another way of saying that S has propositional knowledge of the rules and is admittedly false. If, however, what is meant is merely that the sentences of S's language EXHIBIT the regularities specified or specifiable in terms of the grammar, then the claim is obviously true and as far as I can see, by itself, psychologically uninteresting. Any true description of regularities of or within the set of grammatical sentences will tautologically be true of the output of S's competence. Thus the particular rule (or set of rules) that allows only transitive verbs to occur in the environment ___NP describes a regularity in S's language. But is this to say any more than that S will consider strings that violate this rule ungrammatical? Similarly, in terms of the rules, it may be possible to specify the class of sentences whose nominalizations form parts of grammatical sentences. This certainly marks a regularity in S's language, i.e. that only sentences that have a certain structure (specified BY THE LINGUIST in his grammar) will have companion nominalizations. S again might be said to "know" this regularity but only in the sense that he knows that certain strings are sentences and that he knows that certain other strings described by the linguist as containing nominalizations are also legitimate whereas other attempted nominalizations are not grammatical. These regularities though are regularities true of what S knows (namely the class of grammatical sentences) and not regularities he knows.

Analogously, consider an S who has the competence to recognize Euclidean triangles; he can distinguish triangular figures from non-triangular ones as he can distinguish grammatical sentences from ungrammatical ones. Now there are countless generalizations true of this class of figures, for example, all the geometric and trigonometric properties and relations of sides, angles, altitudes, etc. Indeed if a figure violated some one or more of these generalizations (e.g. if the sum of its angles were not 180°) it would not be a Euclidean triangle, and S wouldn't classify it as such. But are we to claim that an S who recognizes or produces triangles need know or have internally represented this and all the other truths characteristic of triangles? Rather these generalizations appear to be true of what S knows, the class of objects his competence can distinguish, and are not necessarily regularities S knows.

What is being questioned then is whether sense can be given to the claim that the grammar describes SIGNIFICANT regularities in S's competence other than the weak claim that any regularity definable on or over the set of grammatical sentences will be a regularity in the sentences recognized by S's competence. Without some independent psychological specification of what makes an exhibited regularity significant, the claim that one of two grammars that generate the same sentences is a more correct description of S's competence because it captures significant regularities would seem to lack content.

The second interpretation is that tacit knowledge be explicated in terms of unconscious propositional-like beliefs or knowledge. It is suggested that S has unconscious beliefs that the given grammar is the correct description of his competence. While S can not himself state the grammar, he can be brought to see, along say psychoanalytic lines, that the grammar really does state his underlying convictions about his language.

Now the problems with this approach are many, not the least of which is that we have no satisfactory understanding of unconscious beliefs and how to distinguish prodding from prompting the unconscious. But even if we could clarify the notion of unconscious beliefs, it is unlikely that it will be helpful in providing an account of linguistic competence. For notice, had S even more ordinary conscious knowledge of the rules — e.g. could state them — this would not be sufficient to entail that he could really speak or understand the language. To take a case from the realm of phonetics rather than syntax, S may have propositional knowledge of the phonetic rules of French yet be unable to detect faulty pronunciation or speak without an accent. If conscious KNOWING THAT is not to be equated with or sufficient for competence, why should unconscious KNOWING THAT.

Further, suppose S can be brought to see that a given grammar describes regularities in his language, there is nothing to prevent him from coming to realize that all sorts of the so-called "non-significant" ad hoc regularities are true of his language too. So the question would remain as to what special relevance his knowledge of the "significant" non ad hoc regularities have to his linguistic skills. And, of course, we must remember that this second interpretation rests on the additional unsupported and dubious premise that anyone who masters a language has these very complex and abstract underlying beliefs about rules of his language.

The next interpretation claims that not the rules but the S.D.'s the grammar assigns to sentences of the language describe what S knows or the intuitions he has about these sentences. To some extent this claim may be true. For example, in terms of the S.D.'s it is possible to specify such information as which strings are sentences, which strings are ambiguous and which strings are questions. Knowledge of this information, however, might best be seen as just a variant of knowing-that. We would expect we could get S, perhaps with a little prodding, to assert or otnerwise indicate that he knows that a particular string is a sentence or is ambiguous or is a question. Thus some interpretation can be given in these cases for the claim that the S.D.'s codify some of S's intuitions about linguistic strings. For in terms of the S.D. we can specify some of the things S knows propositionally about strings.

But the S.D. supposedly gives much more information than this. The S.D. of a sentence contains its complete derivation from a basic axiom. It provides an analysis of an underlying structure in terms of hierarchical categorizations, subcategorizations, and selectional specifications, a transformational history, and an analysis of the sentence's surface structure. Clearly, it can not be claimed that S knows or has intuitions of this information in the same sense as he knows whether a string is a sentence, is ambiguous, etc. After all, at present the linguist himself doesn't have knowledge of this sort about the S.D.'s of all sentences in the language. Thus while some of the intuitions S actually has about strings may be defined or specified BY THE LINGUIST in terms of the analysis provided in the S.D., it does not follow in any way that S has intuitions of this analysis.[2]

According to our final interpretation of the relationship between grammar and competence if S is to understand, produce or decide on the grammaticality of a sentence he must determine (generate, recover, analyze, synthesize, or whatever) its S.D. This implies that for each string he produces or perceives there would be some internal process or representation in S corresponding to a derivation of the S.D. of that string. Now although there are no a priori arguments against this claim, I find this account of verbal behavior most puzzling, it seems to run together a specification of competence with a description of the processes underlying the competence. For again, consider some of S's other cognitive competencies, his previously discussed arithmetic competence, or his competence to recognize strings as well formed formulas of the propositional calculus. While S undoubtedly employs assorted strategies and heuristics in these areas, no one, I think, feels impelled to claim that for S to

[2] Another problem with this interpretation is to determine the status of the information the S.D. provides. For example, what information are we given when we are told that a string has the category label NP or VP occurring in its deep structure? Do these labels describe some fact or make any empirical claim about the sentence? Or is it that these category labels have no status independent of a system of derivation; their significance determined solely by the role they play in the particular rules i.e. what the label is derived from and what can be derived from it? Similar questions could be raised about the status and independent empirical content of the so-called functional information, such as, subject-of or predicate-of.

judge or produce an equation or formula he must generate or recover its corresponding derivation in one of the customary formal systems.

The implausibility of this interpretation is made even more apparent when we remember that in each of these cases there are alternative formal systems and that complexity, length, etc. of derivation correspond in no regular way with psychological difficulty, processing time, etc. No one of these formal systems seems to describe or reflect anything WE DO when understanding or producing a formula.[3] Yet if our fourth interpretation of tacit knowledge were correct we would have to assume that the generation of sentences in the grammar does characterize psychological processes. But are there any grounds for believing in the case of linguistic behavior that S literally carries out a process that could be described as running through a complete derivation of the sentence? What evidence do we have that would support or be relevant to the claim that S produces derivations in one formal grammatical system rather than any other? And if such distinctions among systems is not to be drawn, is there sense to maintaining that a derivational process of this sort actually occurs? My point, of course, is not merely that this process does not go on at a conscious level but rather that nothing in the way of unconscious processing need correspond in any straightforward way to the S.D.'s provided by any generative grammar.[4]

At present then I see no compelling reason to suppose that S must generate the S.D.'s of a Chomskian grammar in order to produce or understand sentences. Nor do I find the meaning of the claim that S knows or has internalized the grammar of his language at all obvious.

In raising these difficulties I do not wish to suggest that the study of grammar and the structures of natural language is uninteresting or unprofitable. What concerns me is not so much the formal linguistics but the psycholinguistics. And here, although I have been mainly negative, I would like my remarks to be taken more as a plea for clarification. I am not claiming that no sense can be made of the notion of internalizing a grammar but that without further clarification of the relationship between a formal grammar and competence I am not at all sure what psychological data to count as support, refutation or even relevant. I do not know how the game is to be played.

Chomsky's approach to language-learning combines an attack on

---

[3] It is sometimes suggested that these formalizations be thought of as "models". However, it is unclear what aspect of psychological processing these systems are supposed to model and how such models are to aid us in understanding the related competency.

[4] Furthermore, for this account to be intelligible it would seem to require that S must have some internal language or symbol system in which to carry out these derivations. As far as I know, however, no account has been offered about what such a system would be like.

traditional learning theory with positive proposals for a language-learning device whose most notable (or notorious) feature is its possession of innate ideas. It is only this latter issue I shall discuss here and at that one particular aspect of it.

Chomsky finds it necessary to introduce his innateness hypothesis in order to explain how, on the basis of a finite, fragmentary, and frequently degenerate set of instances, an organism acquires a particular way of handling new cases. As I see it, the psychologically interesting question is whether the factors that shape the learning of language are specific to language or whether they are general features of the learning apparatus. This most certainly is an empirical matter. However, it should be noted that the child develops many skills and competences, acquires knowledge of relationships and regularities in his environment, learns games and complex patterns of social behavior, etc. in essentially the same "untaught" manner he learns language. In most of these cases, too, it is difficult to see how his behavior can be accounted for in terms of simple stimulus-response chains, stimulus generalization, reinforcement, etc. Thus Chomsky's problem would arise in all of these cases, yet it would seem implausible to claim distinct innate schemata responsible for each.

Further, as a consequence of the innateness hypothesis, it is frequently claimed that a child would encounter enormous (if not, from a practical standpoint, insurmountable) difficulty learning a language not of the predestined form. Direct evidence supporting this claim is admittedly not available. On the other hand, I believe there are good reasons for believing no INTERESTING version of this claim will prove true. For the child, before, during, and after he learns language, masters various other complex symbol systems that, as Chomsky himself points out, do not fit the natural language mold. In many of these cases, too, he does so without explicit instruction. Of course it could be claimed that any symbol system that violates the Chomskian canons is not a language and thus outside the scope of the claim, but this would only make the argument circular.

Bibliography

_ _ _ _ _ _ _ _ _ _ _ _ _ _ _

PART I

(A) Logic

Hughes, G. E. and M. J. Cresswell
  1968 *An Introduction to Modal Logic* (London, Methuen).
Mates, Benson
  1965 *Elementary Logic* (New York, Oxford U.P.).
Quine, W. V. O.
  1951 *Mathematical Logic* (Cambridge, Harvard U.P.).
  1953 *Methods of Logic* (New York, Holt Co.).
Reichenbach, Hans
  1952 *Elements of Symbolic Logic* (New York, McMillan).
Suppes, Patrick C.
  1957 *Introduction to Logic* (Princeton, Van Nostrand).
Wall, Robert
  1972 *Introduction to Mathematical Linguistics* (Englewood Cliffs, Prentice-Hall).

(B) Frege and Formal Semantics

Burks, A. W.
  1951 "A Theory of Proper Names", *Philosophical Studies* 2, 36-45.
Carnap, Rudolf
  1947 and 1956 *Meaning and Necessity* (Chicago, U. of Chicago Press).
Church, A.
  1950 "On Carnap's Analysis of Statements of Assertion and Belief", *Analysis* 10, 97-99.
Donnellan, K.
  1966 "Reference and Definite Descriptions", *Philosophical Review* 75, 281-304.
Frege, Gottlob
  1892 (1952) *Philosophical Writings*, transl. by Black and Geach (New York,

Philosophical Library).
1918 "The Thought" see under Klemke (ed.).
1923 "Compound Thoughts" see under Klemke (ed.).
Furth, Montgomery
1968 "Two Types of Denotation", *American Philosophical Quarterly, Monograph series* 2, 9-46.
Føllesdal, Dagfinn
1965 "Quantification into Causal Contexts", *Boston Studies in the Philosophy of Science* II, 263-274.
1968 "Quine on Modality", *Synthese* 19, 147-157.
Gabbay, Bernard
1973 "Representation of the Montague Semantics as a Form of the Suppes Semantics", in *Approaches to Natural Language*, Hintikka, Moravcsik, Suppes (eds.) (Dordrecht, Reidel).
Geach, P. T.
1962 *Reference and Generality* (Ithaca, Cornell University).
Hintikka, J.
1969 *Models for Modality* (Dordrecht, Reidel).
1973 (ed. and contributed with Moravcsik, Suppes), *Approaches to Natural Language* (Dordrecht, Reidel).
Kaplan, David
1968 "Quantifying In", *Synthese* 19, 178-214.
1973 "Bob and Carol and Ted and Alice", in *Approaches to Natural Language*, see Hintikka (ed.) (1973).
Klemke, E.
1968 (ed.) *Essays on Frege* (Urbana, Univ. of Illinois).
Kripke, Saul
1971 "Identity and Necessity", in *Semantics of Natural Language*, D. Davidson, G. Hartman (eds.) (Dordrecht, Reidl), 253-355.
1970 "Naming and Necessity", *Synthese* 21, 132-239.
Lewis, David
1970 "General Semantics", *Synthese* 22, 18-67.
Linsky, Leonard
1971 (ed.) *Reference and Modality* (Oxford, Oxford University).
Montague, Richard
1970 "English as a Formal Language", in *Linguaggi: Nella Societa e Nella Tecnica*, B. Visentini et al. (eds.) (Milan, Edizioni di Communita).
1973 "The Proper Treatment of Quantification in Ordinary English", in *Approaches to Natural Language*, see Hintikka (ed.) (1973).
Moravcsik, J. M.
1973 (ed. and contributed with Hintikka, Suppes) *Approaches to Natural Language* (Dordrecht, Reidel).
Partee, Barbara
1972 "Some Transformational Extensions of Montague Grammar", *Occasional Papers in Linguistics* (UCLA), 1-24.
Prior, Arthur N.
1968 *Papers on Time and Tense* (Oxford, Clarendon Press).
1971 *Objects of Thought* (Oxford, Clarendon Press).
Quine, W. V. O.
1960 *Word and Object* (Cambridge, MIT Press).
Russell, Bertrand
1956 *Logic and Knowledge*, R. Marsh (ed.) (London, Allen & Unwin).

Strawson, Peter F.
   1952   *Introduction to Logical Theory* (London, Methuen).
   1971   *Logico-Linguistic Papers* (London, Methuen).
Suppes, Patrick
   1973   (ed. and contributed with Hintikka, Moravcsik) *Approaches to Natural Language* (Dordrecht, Reidel).
Tarski, Alfred
   1956   *Logic, Semantics, Metamathematics* (Oxford, Clarendon Press).

PART II

Austin, J. L.
   1962   *How To Do Things with Words* (Cambridge, Harvard University).
Caton, Charles
   1963   (ed.) *Philosophy and Ordinary Language* (Urbana, U. of Illinois).
Cohen, L. J.
   1962   *The Diversity of Meaning* (London, Methuen).
Davidson, Donald
   1967   "Truth and Meaning", *Synthese* 17, 304-23.
Grice, H. P.
   1957   "Meaning", *Philosophical Review* 66, 377-88.
Hall, Roland
   1959   "Excluders" in Caton (1963).
Ryle, Gilbert
   1957   "The Theory of Meaning" in Caton (1963).
Searle, John R.
   1969   *Speech Acts* (Cambridge, Cambridge University Press).
Strawson, Peter F.
   1950   "On Referring", *Mind* 59, 320-44; also in Caton (1963).
Urmson, J. O.
   1952   "Parenthetical Verbs", *Mind* 61, 480-96; also in Caton (1963).
Ziff, Paul
   1960   *Semantic Analysis* (Ithaca, Cornell University).

PART III

Scott, Dana
   1970   "Semantic Archeology: A Parable", *Synthese* 21, 399-407.
Vendler, Zeno
   1967   *Linguistics in Philosophy* (Ithaca, Cornell U. Press).
Wittgenstein, Ludwig
   1958   *The Blue and Brown Books* (Oxford, Blackwell).

PART IV

Chomsky, Noam
   1969   "Linguistics and Philosophy. Comments on Harman's Reply", in *Language and Philosophy*, in Hook (1969), 51-94, 152-59.

Fodor, J.
1968 "An Appeal to Tacit Knowledge in Psychological Explanation", *Journal of Philosophy* 65, 627-40.
Goodman, Nelson
1967 "The Epistemological Argument", *Synthese* 17, 23-28.
Harman, Gilbert
1969 "Linguistic Competence and Empiricism" in *Language and Philosophy*, in Hook (1969), 143-51.
Hook, Sidney
1969 (ed.) *Language and Philosophy* (New York, New York U.P.).
Putnam, Hilary
1967 "The Innateness Hypothesis", *Synthese* 17, 12-22.
Quine, W. V. O.
1953 "The Problem of Meaning in Linguistics", in *From a Logical Point of View* (Cambridge, Harvard U.P.).